THE DAWN OF
CARRIER STRIKE

Lieutenant William Paulet Lucy DSO Royal Navy

THE DAWN OF CARRIER STRIKE

And the World of Lieutenant W P Lucy DSO RN

David Hobbs

First published in Great Britain in 2019 by
Seaforth Publishing,
A division of Pen & Sword Books Ltd,
47 Church Street,
Barnsley S70 2AS

www.seaforthpublishing.com

British Library Cataloguing in Publication Data
A catalogue record for this book is available from the British Library

ISBN 978 1 4738 7992 8 (HARDBACK)
ISBN 978 1 4738 7993 5 (KINDLE)
ISBN 978 1 4738 7994 2 (EPUB)

Pen & Sword Books Limited incorporates the imprints of Atlas, Archaeology, Aviation, Discovery, Family History, Fiction, History, Maritime, Military, Military Classics, Politics, Select, Transport, True Crime, Air World, Frontline Publishing, Leo Cooper, Remember When, Seaforth Publishing, The Praetorian Press, Wharncliffe Local History, Wharncliffe Transport, Wharncliffe True Crime and White Owl.

Set in 10.75/13.2pt Minion Pro

Typeset and designed by JCS Publishing Services Ltd,
www.jcs-publishing.co.uk
Printed and bound in Great Britain by TJ International Ltd, Padstow

Lieutenant W P Lucy DSO RN, Lieutenant M C E Hanson DSC RN and their contemporaries deserve to be remembered for their considerable achievements against high odds in carrier-borne operations over the Norwegian littoral in April and May 1940. These were the first of their kind, and the gallant actions of these men marked the 'dawn' of the era of carrier strike operations. This book is dedicated to them.

Contents

Foreword

NAVAL AVIATION SURVIVED AS an important discipline within the Royal Navy after the armistice that ended the Great War in November 1918 because it had already demonstrated its importance. HMS *Argus*, the world's first aircraft carrier, was in commission and a number of aircraft were embarked in other warship types from battleships to seaplane carriers. There was, thus, an institutional structure for specifically naval aviation that had to be carried forward as part of the peacetime fleet even though politicians insisted that the Air Ministry should have administrative control of training and procurement to balance against the Admiralty's operational control at sea. The British Army, on the other hand, maintained no large formations at division, corps or army level like those that had fought on the Western Front. Unlike the Navy, therefore, it had no tactical air arm under its own orders.

This distinction is important because it helps to explain the basis of the argument that enabled the Admiralty, ultimately, to regain full control of its embarked air arm after nearly two decades of dual control and considerable political opposition. The era of dual control was undoubtedly a complex failure and in this book I shall examine why this proved to be the case in two ways. First by explaining the complex arguments and giving a sense of proportion to them, and then by making reference to the career of one man who distinguished himself during the period in question, Lieutenant William Paulet Lucy DSO RN. Known to friends and family as Bill, he joined the RN on 15 January 1924 to become a seaman officer and specialised as a pilot, flying fighters and reconnaissance aircraft from both aircraft carriers and cruisers in UK waters, the Mediterranean and on the China Station. In 1939 he was serving as a watch-keeping officer in the cruiser *Manchester* but was soon appointed to command 803 Naval Air Squadron (NAS), which had recently been re-equipped with the RN's first monoplane, the Blackburn Skua dive-bomber/fighter. On the day after the German invasion of Norway, after some weeks defending the Home Fleet in Scapa Flow and Allied convoys to and from Norway, he led the first air strike operation in history that sank a major warship, the German cruiser *Königsberg* alongside the Skoltegrund Mole in Bergen. Bill Lucy was awarded the DSO for this operation, carried out at the aircraft's extreme radius of action in company with 800 NAS from the RN air station at Hatston near Kirkwall on the Orkney mainland. During 803 NAS's subsequent brilliant embarked operations in the aircraft carriers *Glorious* and *Ark Royal* off the Norwegian coast, Bill Lucy carried out hazardous strike operations and flew fleet air defence missions, during which he became the first pilot in any Commonwealth or Allied air arm to shoot down five enemy aircraft, a total that would have led to him being described as a fighter 'ace' in the United States Navy.

Before the war the Admiralty had expressed concern that the Fleet Air Arm lacked sufficient reserves to cope with heavy casualties but their recruitment in various forms was always opposed by the Air Ministry, and politicians failed to accept the Admiralty view. Events in 1940 were to show the justification of the Admiralty's concern and by the end of the short Norwegian campaign the RN had lost about one third of its front-line aircrew. They could not be replaced in the short term and among those lost were Lieutenant Bill Lucy and his observer Lieutenant Michael Hanson, who were shot down and killed on 14 May 1940.

For a variety of reasons that will be described below, the aircraft operated by the RN in 1940 were not the best of their type, but the quality and determination of their aircrew made a distinct difference and allowed the squadrons that fought in the Norwegian littoral to take on an enemy air force that should have been overwhelmingly powerful. That they achieved so much against such high odds is to the everlasting glory of the Royal Navy's air arm. Bill Lucy was such a striking example of what an outstanding individual could achieve within that air arm between 1924 and the first months of the Second World War up to May 1940 that even brief references to his career give insight into the development of naval aviation.

Alongside the human story, I have described how the aircraft carriers and aircraft developed after 1919, how progress in the RN differed from that in the USN and how the RN eventually regained full control of its air arm with the Inskip Award of July 1937. There are lessons from this period that apply directly to defence matters two decades into the twenty-first century and I hope that this book will stimulate interest and discussion in a wide cross-section of readers.

David Hobbs MBE
Commander Royal Navy (Retired)
Alnwick
July 2018

Acknowledgements

As always, my writing efforts have been encouraged and helped by my wife Jandy together with my son Andrew and his wife Lucyelle. The material for the bulk of this text was gathered in research carried out over many years in the Naval Historical Branch at its locations in Empress State Building and New Scotland Yard in London and, to a limited extent, at its present location in Portsmouth Naval Base. I also carried out research at the MOD Archive when it was located at Hayes. I am indebted to David Brown, Christopher Page and Stephen Prince, Heads of the Naval Historical Branch at various times for their enthusiasm and support for my work and to Jenny Wraight, the Admiralty Librarian. My thanks also go to Barbara Gilbert of the National Museum of the Royal Navy for her help.

Although the bulk of the material came from my extended research into the development of naval aviation, the concept of using Bill Lucy as the exemplar to illustrate the career of an RN pilot in the era of dual control and as the outstanding British pilot during the Norwegian campaign came from a chance meeting with John de Lucy, Bill's nephew, in 2015. He made me aware of the collection of photographs in Bill's albums and took the trouble to scan them and make them available; without his input this book would not have been possible in the format in which it has evolved, and for this I am very grateful.

As in other projects, it proved possible to illustrate much of the text from my own photographic archive, a collection I have built up over decades of experience and research. Apart from John de Lucy's images, I am also grateful to Philip Jarrett who made some of his own extensive photographic collection available. This publication contains Public Sector information licensed under the Open Government Licence v 1.0 in the UK. My thanks also go to Anthony Cowland who painted the cover illustration, Peter Wilkinson who drew the map, together with Steven and Jessica Williamson who edited and page-set the book.

Over the years I have been fortunate enough to have discussions on the development of naval aviation with many friends at historical symposia and other events in the UK, Australia and the USA. These have stimulated my own thought processes and encouraged me to look at events from differing angles. Norman Friedman in the USA, David Stevens in Australia and both Eric Grove and Andrew Lambert in the UK are among those who have set me thinking. That said, of course, any errors or omissions in the text are entirely my own.

Rob Gardiner deserves particular thanks and I am grateful to him for his continuing support; this book is the eighth in our successful publishing partnership and another is already in the pipeline.

David Hobbs

Glossary

1SL	First Sea Lord
2SL	Second Sea Lord
3SL	Third Sea Lord
5SL	Fifth Sea Lord
AA	Anti-Aircraft
AAA	Anti-Aircraft Artillery
A & AEE	Aeroplane & Armament Experimental Establishment
ACNS	Assistant Chief of the Naval Staff
AED	Air Engineering Department
AFO	Admiralty Fleet Order
AMSO	Air Member for Supply and Organisation
AOC	Ait Officer Commanding (RAF)
AOC-in-C	Air Officer Commanding-in-Chief (RAF)
AS	Anti-Submarine
Asdic	RN term for sonar before and during the Second World War
Avgas	Aviation Gasoline
BRNC	Britannia Royal Naval College (Dartmouth)
CAFO	Confidential Admiralty Fleet Order
CAP	Combat Air Patrol
CAS	Chief of the Air Staff (Air Ministry)
CB	Confidential Book
C-in-C	Commander-in-Chief
CID	Committee of Imperial Defence
CIGS	Chief of the Imperial General Staff (Army)
CO	Commanding Officer
CPO	Chief Petty Officer
CS	Cruiser Squadron
CV	USN designation for a fleet aircraft carrier
DAD	Director of the Air Department (Admiralty)
DAM	Director of Air Material (Admiralty)
DBR	Dive-Bomber Reconnaissance (aircraft)
DCNS	Deputy Chief of the Naval Staff
DF	Destroyer Flotilla
DLCO	Deck Landing Control Officer
GP	General Purpose (bomb)
FO	Flag Officer
FFO	Furnace Fuel Oil
HE	High Effect (bomb)

HF	Home Fleet
HMS	His Majesty's Ship
HOD	Head of Department
hp	horsepower
IFF	Identification Friend or Foe
IJN	Imperial Japanese Navy
LA	Leading Airman
lb	pound
MAC	Merchant Aircraft Carriers
MAEE	Marine Aircraft Experimental Establishment
MAP	Ministry of Aircraft Production
MC	Medium Capacity (bomb)
MPA	Maritime Patrol Aircraft
NA	Naval Airman
*NAS	Naval Air Squadron
nm	nautical mile
PO	Petty Officer
RAAC	Rear Admiral Aircraft Carriers
RAE	Royal Aircraft Establishment
RAF	Royal Air Force
RAFR	Royal Air Force Reserve
RAFVR	Royal Air Force Volunteer Reserve
RANAS	Rear Admiral Naval Air Stations
RCNVR	Royal Canadian Naval Volunteer Reserve
RFA	Royal Fleet Auxiliary
RFC	Royal Flying Corps
RM	Royal Marines
*RN	Royal Navy
*RNAS	Royal Naval Air Station (or, prior to April 1918, Royal Naval Air Service)
RNC	Royal Naval College
*RNR	Royal Naval Reserve
*RNVR	Royal Naval Volunteer Reserve
ROP	Report of Proceedings
R/T	Radio Telephone
SAP	Semi-Armour Piercing (bomb)
SBD	Spotter/Bomber/Dive-bomber (USN)
SHP	Shaft Horsepower
SR	Spotter Reconnaissance (aircraft)
ss	Steam Ship
TAG	Telegraphist Air Gunner
TBR	Torpedo Bomber Reconnaissance (aircraft)

TNT	Tri-Nitro Toluene (explosive)
TSR	Torpedo Spotter Reconnaissance (aircraft)
UK	United Kingdom
US	United States
USMC	United States Marine Corps
USN	United States Navy
USS	United States Ship
VA	Vice Admiral
VAA	Vice Admiral Aircraft
VF	USN designation for a fighter squadron
VT	USN designation for a torpedo-bomber squadron
W/T	Wireless Telegraphy

Chapter 1

RAF Contingents in His Majesty's Ships

On 31 March 1918 Admiralty records listed 55,000 men serving with the RNAS, a statistic that included pilots, observers, gunlayers, specialist air engineers, artificers and mechanics. However, it did not include officers of the RN, RNR and RNVR who provided the bulk of the supporting staff in ships, squadrons and at naval air stations throughout the world, many of whom were still employed on flying duties as observers or telegraphists. Among these were the commanding and administrative officers, paymasters, surgeons, dentists, instructor officers and chaplains who now found themselves on loan to the new service. Non-technical branches such as writers, cooks, stewards, artisans, carpenters and sailmakers also found themselves awkwardly placed until the RAF was able to organise its own infrastructure. The majority of officers and men serving in the RNAS had joined after the outbreak of war and only 397 officers, 217 men and 604 boys, a total of 1,218, were permanent members of the RN who had the right to opt to return to their parent service after being lent to the nascent RAF. Many of the remaining 53,782 might well have been content to be demobilised and seek civilian employment when hostilities ended, but officers who wished to continue a service career found themselves in a difficult position. First, they were specialists in naval aviation but from 1 April 1918 this was the responsibility of the RAF and it was no longer possible to be a pilot in the RN. Those short-service officers who wished to continue a flying career had, therefore, no choice but to remain part of the RAF. Those who wanted to stay part of the RN would have to resign from the RAF and seek to rejoin the RN and re-specialise in roles such as submarines, gunnery, torpedoes or navigation, competing for promotion with long-serving naval officers who had already specialised. Senior RN officers who had been part of the naval aviation community such as Admiral Phillimore and Captain Dumaresq were now forced out of it because the RAF did not recognise their knowledge and skill as part of its future plan and, in any case, felt that its own people had all the expert understanding that might be required. Ratings, too, had no choice but to remain with the RAF or be demobilised since there was no longer an air technical branch in the RN. Many historians have noted that the great majority of RNAS personnel elected to stay with the RAF after April 1918 but few have understood, completely, the underlying reasons why they did so. In practice, only the small number of regular personnel had any choice because of the way in which the British government had implemented a controversial change without public scrutiny or even, apparently, caring about the consequences. In the US Navy there was also a drive for a unified air service but through open debate and logical assessment it was not taken forward. The USN's more successful experience, and the reasons for it, will be described in a later chapter.

Naval air warfare survived into 1919 as a distinct entity, however, because the RN had the aircraft carrier *Argus* in commission together with a number of other air-capable warships, including *Furious*, battleships and cruisers that had been fitted with take-off platforms. Some of the wartime seaplane carriers, including *Ark Royal* and *Pegasus*, were retained as aircraft ferries and for experiments with seaplanes. Aviation had been proved central to modern fleet operations and since powerful Atlantic/Home and Mediterranean Fleets remained in being, the post-war RAF had little choice but to accede to government policy and provide the necessary aircraft and the men to fly and maintain them. The demobilised British Army after 1919 was not so fortunate since it did not retain operational all-arms formations of divisional or even brigade size. It quickly returned to peace-keeping duties around Great Britain's global empire and the need for an integrated air component within large-scale military operations was not, therefore, immediately obvious to the RAF, which was set on pursuing its own policies or – as it should have been – to the British government.

Of the many wartime naval air stations only a few were retained by the RAF for use by the aircraft that continued to work with the fleet. In the UK these included Gosport and Leuchars, which operated a variety of aircraft with wheeled undercarriages. Seaplanes were based at Calshot and Lee-on-Solent. In Malta, the Mediterranean Fleet's base, Hal Far was used by wheeled aircraft and Calafrana by seaplanes while their ships were in harbour. Large numbers of aircraft were disposed of from 1919 as surplus to immediate requirements but small numbers of Sopwith 2F.1 fighters, T1 Cuckoo torpedo strike aircraft and One-and-a-Half 'Ship' Strutters were retained to which a few new Parnall Panther reconnaissance aircraft were added.[1] The aircraft embarked in carriers began to establish distinct unit identities from February 1920 when 210 Squadron was formed at Gosport as an airborne torpedo training unit to assume the tasks formerly undertaken by 185 Squadron and 201 Torpedo Training Unit at East Fortune. The new number was a logical choice as it followed the practice of renumbering RNAS units in the 200 series when they were subsumed into the RAF, 1 (Naval) for instance, becoming 201 Squadron RAF. In March 1920 a second unit, 203 Squadron, formed at Leuchars as a fleet fighter squadron equipped with 2F.1 Camels and in April 1920, also at Leuchars, 205 was formed as a fleet reconnaissance squadron equipped with Panthers. This could at least be described as an attempt to provide a historical link connecting the new force with the RNAS but, perhaps for that very reason, the next unit to be formed, in October 1921, was identified as 3 Squadron. It was tasked with naval air co-operation and equipped with the new Westland Walrus, a three-seat spotter version of the de Havilland DH 9A light bomber. The new unit's equipment demonstrated the air staff's belief that any aircraft could, if necessary, operate from a carrier and that the required number could be provided

Argus at anchor in 1919. (Author's collection)

by squadrons allocated to the metropolitan air force and their pilots. It was not made clear whether 3 or 203 Squadron was intended to trace its ancestry back to the RNAS and an unnumbered naval co-operation unit operated a small number of Short 184 seaplanes split between Calshot and Lee-on-Solent until 1921 when they were replaced by Fairey IIIDs.

Argus was taken into dockyard hands in December 1918 to have the prototype system of retaining wires removed and an improved system fitted.[2] She emerged in March 1919 and began a series of flying trials intended to improve deck operating techniques. After ferrying aircraft to the British Expeditionary Force operating against the Bolsheviks at Archangel in June 1919 she embarked an air group of eight Sopwith 'Ship' Strutters, four Sopwith 2F.1 Camels, two de Havilland DH 9As and two Fairey IIID seaplanes for the Atlantic Fleet Spring Cruise to Gibraltar and the Western Mediterranean. Further improvements to the retaining gear were made in the light of this experience and then most of 1921 was spent in training new pilots in deck landing techniques. Since the RAF saw no need for a specialised group of carrier pilots, the need to train a large number of ab initio pilots as they were cycled through the carrier squadrons was found to be necessary. Most did not stay for long and their move to other areas of the RAF meant that such expertise as they had gained was lost to the fleet and further training had to be carried out to replace them.

Important trials were, however, carried out on the incomplete new aircraft carrier *Eagle* which had been launched on 8 June 1918. The need to evaluate deck operating techniques and further refine the concept of the starboard-side island structure after the trial of a wood and canvas mock-up in *Argus* resulted in Admiralty Board approval being given in November 1919 for *Eagle* to be completed as quickly as possible to the minimum standard needed for aircraft to be operated from her deck. Only one of her two funnels was fitted and only a proportion of her machinery was operable but she raised steam for the first time on 3 March 1920 in Armstrong's Walker Naval Yard on the Tyne and sailed for Portsmouth on 23 April. She began trials in the English Channel on 28 May 1920 with a special *Eagle* Flight embarked. When not on *Eagle* the flight was shore-based at Gosport.[3] To gain the widest possible experience, the flight was equipped with a number of different aircraft types including the Sopwith 2F.1 Camel, Parnall Panther, Bristol Fighter, Sopwith T.1 Cuckoo and de Havilland DH 9A. First to land on was a 2F.1 Camel on 1 June 1920. As the trial progressed the ship moved further north to the Pentland Firth between the Orkney Islands and the mainland, looking for bad weather to evaluate its effect on flying operations. A total of 143 deck landings were carried out with only twelve minor incidents and no casualties, a remarkable achievement for the time. The trial was formally completed on 27 October 1920 but its early success had already prompted the Admiralty to accept that the island arrangement was the best way forward and instructions had been given for the ship to be completed in Portsmouth Dockyard. She was the most advanced ship of her kind and the Admiralty agreed to make *Eagle*'s plans available to the US and French navies to inform their own aircraft carrier development projects.

Among other things, the *Eagle* trial explored the best way of ranging and launching carrier aircraft. None of the aircraft that operated from her were fitted with wheel-brakes and the best way of ranging and preparing them for start-up

Aircraft on the flight deck of the semi-complete *Eagle* for flying trials in May 1920.

and launch was found to be aligning them fore and aft on the flight deck centreline with their wheels chocked. Catapult launches were not deemed to be necessary from a carrier deck and all aircraft types carried out rolling take-offs. Space had, therefore, to be available for the aircraft that was at the front of the range to take off and the last aircraft in the range had to be chocked and lashed forward of the after round down. This left sufficient space on *Eagle*'s deck for six aircraft to be arranged nose to tail with space between them for mechanics, handlers and chock-men to carry out their tasks when necessary. The majority of contemporary aircraft had rotary engines which over-heated quickly if there was no significant airflow through them and it was also found that six was the ideal number to start up and launch before over-heating became a problem. The Admiralty decided, therefore, that six would be the ideal size for the units that would be embarked in carriers since it appeared to be the largest number that could take off together and form a cohesive tactical unit once airborne. *Eagle* was not completed for the trial with retaining wires and her aircraft all relied on friction and the handling party to stop them once they landed. The procedure was for pilots to fly individually judged approaches, with no form of guidance, to the deck. Once the aircraft had come to a standstill and the handling party had control of it, the pilot would switch off its engine and it would be man-handled onto the cruciform-shaped forward lift with its wings still spread. It was then struck down into the hangar where the wings were folded as quickly as possible, parked close to other aircraft and lashed down. Once the lift was back at flight-deck level the next aircraft could land on the clear deck after an interval of between two and four minutes. Once the handlers were worked up and practised, the drill reached the quicker end of the spectrum but constant practice was essential to keep it there. On her full completion in 1923 *Eagle* was fitted with retaining wires but they were seldom used as, by then, aircraft had become significantly heavier and there was less risk of their being blown over the side after landing. The wires were removed completely in 1926 and from then until arrester wires were fitted in 1936 aircraft landed on a bare deck.

Aware of the important role aircraft were expected to play in future naval warfare, the Admiralty planned a modest expansion from 1923 to provide aircraft for *Eagle*, *Hermes* and the reconstructed *Furious* as well as *Argus* and new six-aircraft flights began to replace the earlier squadrons. At the end of 1920 the Admiralty had calculated that it needed a total of forty-five spotter aircraft, twenty-two reconnaissance aircraft, twelve torpedo aircraft and 'as many fighters as can be embarked'.[4] The ratio demonstrated contemporary naval staff thinking – lacking the input that would formerly have been made by RNAS officers – in which the priority was to find the enemy fleet and for big-ship guns to bring it to action with their fire spotted and corrected by aircraft. Torpedo aircraft were expected to slow or hamper the enemy's movements and the fighters were to prevent enemy aircraft from providing similar functions for their own fleet. The promise of torpedo attack had been demonstrated against the Atlantic Fleet at anchor in 1919 at Portland[5] but the RAF lacked the imagination to promote the concept. Worse, the Air Ministry generally opposed making progress in naval air warfare because it preferred to further its own concept of bombing as a method of waging all future wars. It feared that if the Admiralty did manage to regain full control of its own air arm, the ensuing loss of squadrons and manpower might jeopardise the very existence of the RAF. Thus the early 1920s saw the Admiralty forced into an awkward position over air matters. An advisory organisation that would not advise on matters that it saw as contrary to its own interests had been imposed on it and air-minded senior naval officers were cut off from frank discussion with embarked pilots by an artificial and politically inspired division. Even former RNAS officers such as Wing Commander Kilner, who had taken part in the Cuxhaven raid in 1914 and had now become the senior RAF officer in *Eagle*, found themselves in an especially difficult position. If they took the line on air operations that senior RN officers asked for, their chance of promotion within a different service could be significantly reduced when they returned to RAF duty ashore. On the other hand, if they tried to impose RAF dogma on the carrier in which they were serving, their relationship with the captain and other heads of department could be compromised. Most managed to walk a fine line that achieved successful operations but failed to introduce dynamic new capabilities like those being achieved by men of vision such as Commodore Reeves in the USN. Given the unfortunate circumstances, however, it is difficult to see how Kilner and his contemporaries could have done any better.

An eponymously named Blackburn Blackburn, S1153, of 450 Flight taking off from *Argus* in 1929. The large space under the pilot's open cockpit was a cabin for the observer and TAG which provided protection for their equipment. (Author's collection)

The four early carrier squadrons had been numbered within the RAF system but the new ship's flights were allocated numbers in a new 400 series that applied only to aircraft embarked in ships of the RN. These unit identities were sub-divided to indicate the flight's role with fleet fighter flights numbered from 401 upwards; fleet spotter flights numbered from 420 upwards; fleet reconnaissance flights numbered from 440 upwards and fleet torpedo bomber flights numbered from 460 upwards. The first, 401 Flight, was formed at Leuchars on 1 April 1923 for service in *Argus* with Nieuport Nightjars inherited from 203 Squadron. Within a year the Nightjars were replaced by Fairey Flycatchers, a new and successful single-seat fighter that was to remain in service for a further decade. 402 Flight formed with Flycatchers at Leuchars on the same date for service in *Eagle*,[6] and further fighter flights formed sequentially at Leuchars until 406 Flight in 1924; the latter intended for service on the China Station in *Hermes* after trial launches were made from the battlecruiser *Renown* and the battleships *Revenge* and *Royal Sovereign* to prove that Flycatchers could take off from the turret platforms that had been fitted during the war. The trials proved successful.

420 Flight formed with six Westland Walrus spotter aircraft taken over from 3 Squadron on 1 April 1923 and embarked in the newly reconstructed *Furious* in May. Further flights in this series formed at Gosport during the year. 440 Flight formed at Lee-on-Solent on 1 May with pilots from 205 Squadron but it was equipped with the new Supermarine Seagull II amphibian for service in *Eagle*. Further flights in this series formed at Leuchars with Parnall Panthers at first, then Fairey IIIDs and, from 1927 the Fairey IIIF which was to be the mainstay of fleet spotter/reconnaissance flying operations for many years. Other reconnaissance aircraft used during this period included the Avro Bison and the eponymous Blackburn Blackburn. 460 Flight formed with the new Blackburn Dart torpedo-attack aircraft at Gosport on 1 April 1923 and embarked in *Eagle* from March 1924 in the Mediterranean Fleet. Further torpedo aircraft flights continued to be formed at Gosport at intervals up to 466 Flight in April 1931, by which time the Blackburn Ripon had replaced the Dart.

No matter what their background – RNAS, RFC or post-war direct RAF entry – all the pilots in these embarked flights were RAF officers and after some early misgivings carrier captains generally conceded that once the flights had been embarked for some time and had grown used to carrier operations their performance was creditable. The major problem, as the Admiralty discovered, was that RAF pilots spent too little time at sea to acquire the deep specialist skills needed to advance naval air tactics. Too much sea time was spent giving initial deck training to new pilots who then returned to shore-based RAF duties when they were approaching their peak performance at sea. There was another major shortcoming which had become immediately obvious in the units with multi-seat crews: the lack of trained observers. The Air Ministry view was that these officers should be skilled first in the science of air warfare and could easily be taught such

A Fairey IIID fitted with floats for operation from cruisers and aircraft carriers at anchor. (Author's collection)

naval matters, such as ship recognition, that they needed to know once they were embarked. The RAF was, at the time, convinced that specialisation was a bad idea and that all pilots should be generalised experts capable of flying any type of aircraft, anywhere, with suitable ancillary skills in navigation, reconnaissance and spotting.[7] The reverse quickly proved to be the case and failures such as the mistaken identification of a group of fishing smacks as battleships during a fleet exercise brought matters to a head. After some argument with the Air Ministry, the Admiralty unilaterally insisted on the reintroduction of an observer branch for naval officers in 1921, stating that navigation over the featureless sea, controlling ships' gunfire and warship recognition were primary tasks that required a naval specialist with a high order of training and knowledge.[8] At the suggestion of Hugh Trenchard, Chief of the Air Staff, a trial was arranged for which the Air Staff selected an RAF officer with considerable experience gained while he had served with the RFC, of spotting Army gunfire and making corrections. After the trial this officer insisted that specialised naval observers were necessary and the branch came into existence in 1921.

RN observer courses began on 11 April 1921 with the first comprising six students.[9] It was divided into two phases, the first involving some weeks at the RN Signal School in Portsmouth during which they had to learn the complete theory of wireless transmission in a few short lessons and how to 'read' Morse Code at up to twenty-two words per minute in a classroom in order to be able to 'read' fifteen words per minute whilst flying.[10] Different people displayed different aptitudes for the required skill and those who did not make the grade at the first test ran the risk of being removed from the course. This phase ended with two weeks at the RN Gunnery School, HMS *Excellent*, at Whale Island, Portsmouth, where they were greeted enthusiastically as potentially valuable members of a fire control team that was expected to achieve the best results for the big guns in a surface action. The second phase began at Lee-on-Solent on 18 July 1921 and lasted until 15 December, during which time the students spent half their working day in the classroom covering theoretical subjects and, when the weather was suitable, the other half airborne in Fairey IIID seaplanes.

On completion of their training, observers had no flying badge[11] and were appointed to ships capable of embarking aircraft and not to the flights themselves. Thus, they remained with the ship when flights disembarked to airfields ashore for continuation flying and were given a range of ship's duties to perform, including watch keeping, like any other specialist officer. Whilst this introduced a sense of 'air-mindedness' into the ship, it was undoubtedly a bad idea and limited the extent to which multi-seat aircraft crews could work up together to a high standard. In 1922, when the first observers joined their ships, there were no RN pilots[12] and

A Parnall Panther two-seater spotter-reconnaissance aircraft landing into the retaining wires on *Argus*' flight deck in 1919. (Author's collection)

A Fairey IIIF spotter-reconnaissance aircraft of 445 Flight from *Courageous* photographed over Dundee in October 1931. (Author's collection)

as their numbers and experience increased in the late 1920s there were more observers available to fill the growing number of senior positions than pilots. This imbalance was to have a significant effect on the Fleet Air Arm as it evolved in the decade ahead in that potentially disproportionate value was placed on the need for naval aircraft to have observers as well as pilots, even in fighters. The renewal of pilot training for naval officers will be covered in the next chapter.

Lighter-than-Air Craft after 1918

The Admiralty and Air Ministry had agreed in early 1918 that airships would not be treated in the same way as heavier-than-air aircraft on the formation of the RAF. Consequently, on 1 April 1918 airship personnel were transferred to the new service and had to adopt military ranks but the Admiralty retained ownership of the airships themselves and remained in sole charge of their operational command and deployment. The majority of personnel continued to wear RNAS uniform until the airship service was fully adopted by the RAF in October 1919. A number of airship stations remained in commission immediately after the war, including East Fortune, Howden and Pulham, but by the early 1920s these were handed over to nominal civilian use as Trenchard's RAF had 'neither experience of airships nor any enthusiasm for them'.[13] On 11 November 1918 there were 107 British airships in service, of which six were rigids. During the next six months, a further six non-rigids and the rigid airships R32, R33 and R34 were completed and delivered to the Admiralty. Another, R38, was sold to the US Navy on completion. Many of the wartime airships were deflated soon after the Armistice and never flew again but some were maintained in airworthy condition to train USN crews waiting to take over R38. When the RAF finally assumed full control of the airship service in 1919, over sixty airships were sold for scrap. Tragically R38 broke up in midair on 23 August 1921, killing forty-four of the forty-nine American and British airmen on board.[14] Among the dead was the former RNAS airship expert, now head of the British Airship Service, Air Commodore Edward Maitland RAF. The Airship Service ceased to exist as a separate entity soon afterwards and the RAF took no further interest in lighter-than-air aviation. The last two British rigid airships, R100 and R101, were both built from the outset as civilian aircraft.

There was, however, one notable achievement by a British rigid in the immediate post-war period. R34 was completed by Beardmore at Inchinnan on 14 March 1919 and was accepted into service by the RN at East Fortune in May. It proved its long-range capability by flying a six-hour sortie around the Firth of Forth in company with R29 during June and a fifty-six-hour armed flight around the Baltic coast of Germany as part of a series of measures intended to demonstrate to the German government that its only option was to sign a peace treaty at the Versailles negotiations. R34 then earned a place in history by carrying out the first double crossing of the Atlantic, taking off from East Fortune on 2 July 1919.[15] It landed at Mineola, Long Island, in the USA after a flight of 108 hours 12 minutes, a world endurance record for an airship,[16] against headwinds that had caused concern about fuel usage in the last hours, but all turned out well and the crew were given a tumultuous welcome. The return flight took advantage of the westerly wind and was completed in only 75 hours and 3 minutes. The flight actually ended at Pulham after an adverse weather forecast for East Fortune caused it to be diverted. R34 had achieved the first east–west crossing of the Atlantic by air, the first double crossing and the first direct flight between the United Kingdom and the United States. The first non-stop transatlantic flight from west to east had been carried out on 14/15 June 1919 by former RNAS pilot Captain A W Alcock with Lieutenant A W Brown in a Vickers Vimy bomber. Unfortunately R34 was destroyed at its mooring at Howden in 1921, after which military airship flying in the UK virtually ceased.

Chapter 2

Politics and the Trenchard/Keyes Agreement

In December 1918 the Secretary of State for Air, Lord Weir, forwarded a memorandum containing his vision for the future of the newly formed RAF to his Cabinet colleagues.[1] In it he proposed the creation an Imperial Air Staff, within the Air Ministry, which would be responsible for all air matters. Operationally the RAF was to consist of a long-range bomber force, fighters for the defence of the UK and, in due course, specialised units to be trained for operations with sea and land forces. These were, however, to remain very much part of the RAF. Sir Oswyn Murray, Permanent Secretary of the Admiralty, minuted that the whole tenor of Weir's paper could be summed up as 'centralisation of air work and personnel' but Admiral Sir Rosslyn Wemyss, the First Sea Lord, felt in general terms that 'the policy advocated appears to be sound, in the best interests of British aviation and calculated to assist the Empire to jump to a similar position as regards commercial air routes to that occupied in the commercial sea routes'. However, he also gave it as his opinion that the RAF should be permeated 'with naval and military sentiment' and that to achieve this, officers and men should be seconded to the new service for periods of about two years, after which they should return to their own service for at least a year before, perhaps, carrying out a second flying tour. This gives the impression that he thought of the RAF as being structured like the original Royal Flying Corps with Naval and Military Wings to which RN and Army officers could be attached to gain flying experience while a small cadre of professional airmen maintained standards and promoted new ideas from within a Central Flying School. This was not at all the way the RAF saw its own future, however, and Wemyss' proposal consequently pleased no one. From a naval perspective, two flying tours were unlikely to give officers the deep specialist knowledge that would eventually enable them to command naval air operations at the highest level and from an RAF perspective the new service was desperate to develop its own doctrine and sentiment and not to be permeated with those of the other services from which its advocates felt that it had now broken free.

By 1919 flag officers at sea were already complaining about the RAF's inability to meet their aviation needs in the way that the RNAS had done and they were beginning to put pressure on the Admiralty Board to request that 'all personnel for naval air purposes afloat' should be naval officers and ratings although it was reluctantly accepted that they would have to receive their aviation training in RAF schools.[2] The Air Ministry reacted to this criticism with predictable hostility since it regarded such comments as thinly disguised attempts to restore the RNAS, a step that it believed would undermine the very existence of the RAF during the difficult period of demobilisation that followed the end of hostilities. However, a growing body within the Admiralty and the majority of the flag officers at sea now opposed the centralisation of all air matters within the RAF and wanted to fight for a return of an air arm under full naval control. An inter-service meeting was, therefore, held in May to discuss RN concerns about the inadequate provision of aircraft for the fleet at which Trenchard proposed that all RAF units serving with the RN should be formed into a single command,[3] the air officer commanding (AOC) of which would become the technical advisor to the Admiralty on air matters although Trenchard himself would remain the chief advisor on all aerial questions, with the last word on any discussion of policy or tactics. He was forced to accept, however, that in practical terms the Admiralty would have operational control over RAF groups working with the fleet, a concession that was received favourably by Wemyss' Admiralty Board.

Trenchard's proposal was put into effect with the formation of RAF Coastal Area Command which included both carrier-borne aircraft and others that were based ashore but intended for operations over the sea. The AOC of the three groups that initially formed the new command was Air Vice Marshall A V Vyvyan. Air Ministry Weekly Order 1663[4] announced the establishment of the new force and stated that Vyvyan was 'to act as adviser to the Admiralty and to naval Commanders-in-Chief on all questions of naval aerial policy' but he was to be responsible only to the Air Ministry for the supply and maintenance of his command's aircraft and other equipment. Although the statement in print that he was to act as advisor seemed to be unequivocal, it soon caused some embarrassment to the Air Staff when it realised the degree of intimacy that this might foster between Coastal Area Command and the RN. The question of seconding naval officers to the RAF as pilots for a fixed period was not resolved at the May meeting and remained a point of contention, as did the length of time that RAF officers should be appointed to flights embarked in ships. The Air Ministry view was that RN officers should be seconded to the RAF for flying duties for at least three years. Anything less than this, they felt, would allow officers to move freely between naval general service and flying duties and 'would be tantamount to the re-establishment of the RNAS, which, being contrary to the declared intentions of the Cabinet, the Air Ministry was not at liberty to discuss'.[5] Wemyss was concerned that the Admiralty view now opened him to a charge of inconsistency since he had, himself, suggested lending RN officers to the RAF and he took the view that since the RAF now existed it seemed reasonable to accept its proposals on pilot training. However, he failed to convince his Board colleagues and on 24 October 1919 he gave up on the issue and minuted that he would 'not have any further dealings with it', leaving the matter for his successor.

On 1 November 1919 David Beatty replaced Wemyss as 1SL and, since he had spoken so strongly in favour of a unified air service when he commanded the Grand

A Fairey IIID disembarked from *Hermes* at RAF Kai Tak in 1927. (Author's collection)

Fleet in 1917, he now found himself in a most difficult position. From his first day in office he was made aware that a considerable body of naval opinion believed that too much emphasis was being given to the independent functions of the RAF and not enough to the vitally important need for sea power, including the use of naval aircraft as an integral component of the various deployed fleets. There was also a concern that officers seconded to the RAF on flying duties for lengthy periods, perhaps in excess of three years, might be minded to transfer permanently to the new service and thus become lost to the RN. On 17 November 1919 Trenchard wrote personally to his fellow chiefs of staff to explain that the post-war demobilisation of the RAF would inevitably lead to a reduction in operational capability and to ask for their forbearance until a regular peacetime force could be established. On the same day the Air Ministry wrote officially to the other service departments promising a satisfactory final result in return for short-term acceptance of any shortfall in operational capability. On 22 November 1919, Trenchard sent a further personal letter to Beatty that was to become the focus of a long-running debate.[6] It contained his vision for the future RAF that was to include two elements which would be 'trained for and work with' the Navy and Army as 'an arm of those services' but the main part of the RAF was to remain an independent force. Once more he asked for a period of tranquillity and freedom from criticism in order to make this happen but he ended with the statement: 'it may be in two or three years' time, then, and not till then, will be the time to consider a modification by which the older services will each pay for its own portion of the air service without the danger of its breaking up the Air Force'. The Admiralty took considerable encouragement from this statement since it believed that government departments that paid for something must inevitably exercise considerable control over it.

In *Naval Policy Between the Wars*, Stephen Roskill wrote that Trenchard's biographer, Andrew Boyle, had stated in *Trenchard: Man of Vision* that Trenchard had called on Beatty in December 1919 to ask in person for twelve months' grace to allow him 'to get [the RAF] started'.[7] Sir Henry Wilson the CIGS was also present at the meeting. Boyle also stated, unfortunately without quoting documentary proof, that Beatty had agreed to this proposal on the condition that the RAF met the Navy's air requirements during that period. Both Boyle and Roskill seem to have accepted that this meeting took place and that Beatty's acceptance was a fact. This would certainly explain why the Admiralty made no reply to several Air Ministry letters about the subject at this time. It is, however, difficult to comprehend why Beatty made such a condition when Trenchard had told him in writing only days before that the RAF could not meet it. It is equally difficult to understand why Trenchard agreed so readily to a condition that he knew he could not possibly meet since he had asked in writing on 22 November and verbally at this meeting for twelve months' grace before operational requirements could be met. The only rational conclusion is that he said whatever he had to say at the meeting to preserve the RAF intact through the demobilisation process and would reflect on what capability it could or could not deliver at some later date if forced to do so.

Much of the early post-war inter-service argument had already became academic, however, following Prime Minister David Lloyd George's announcement of the 'Ten Year Rule' on 15 August 1919 which instructed the Admiralty, War Office and Air Ministry to formulate their future plans on the basis that there would be no major war for ten years. The drive for government economies now forced considerable reappraisal and Lord Weir's plan, still only months old, was clearly no longer tenable. By early 1920 the number of RAF units intended to work with the fleet had reached its lowest level with only four squadrons active and was totally incapable of meeting Beatty's condition. On 11 December 1919 Winston Churchill, who was now the Secretary of State for both the War Office and the Air Ministry, presented a revised plan for the peacetime organisation of the RAF to Parliament.[8] The result of some months' work by both Churchill and Trenchard, the new plan, like its predecessors, maintained the line that the bomber force was central to the future development of the RAF but it also stated that there was to be 'a small part especially trained for work with the Navy' and a similar component trained for work with the Army and that both these elements would 'probably become, in the future, an arm of the older services'. Boyle claimed that Trenchard subsequently stated that these phrases were only inserted 'as a sop to the jealousy' of the Admiralty and War Office and were a 'fatal lapse of judgement'[9] on his part. Roskill, however, notes that in the voluminous correspondence between the departments during this period there is nothing to suggest that either of them put any pressure on the Air

Ministry to make such a statement and, moreover, Trenchard had made a very similar prediction in his personal letter to Beatty on 17 November 1919. It has, therefore, to be seen as a concept that he was happy enough to promote when it suited him but which he subsequently regretted when the time came to implement it with those departments that had trusted his word.

The period between 1919 and 1924 saw an increasingly acrimonious exchange of correspondence between the Admiralty and the Air Ministry over the state of naval aviation and its potential development, which had the effect of hardening the resolve of senior naval officers to fight the matter to a finish. However, Sir Oswyn Murray, head of the Admiralty Secretariat, warned his Board colleagues that impasse could only lead to the question being placed before the Cabinet. Having recently decided that all air matters should be the responsibility of the Air Ministry, he felt it unlikely that the Cabinet would change its mind and agree, so soon, to the re-creation of a separate naval air service. His advice was to gather evidence and wait for the occasion, which would undoubtedly come, when Cabinet opinion could be swayed towards the more realistic view now being championed by flag officers. In 1920 the ACNS, Admiral Chatfield,[10] re-formed a Naval Air Section with Commander Bell Davies as its head within the Admiralty, effectively replacing the Naval Air Division which had stood down after the RNAS was subsumed into the RAF. It became a division once more in 1928[11] when Bell Davies was promoted to Captain after appointments at sea and could, thus, become a Director. The Air Ministry objected to the formation of the Air Section and refused to appoint a liaison officer to it on the grounds that the AOC Coastal Area Command was 'the official source of advice on air matters'.[12] However, when the Admiralty did actually seek this AOC's advice in early 1921 about the potential development of a large flying boat for naval patrol duties, the Air Ministry wrote at once to the Admiralty, stating in the strongest terms that it objected 'to questions of future policy being referred for the opinion of officers of Coastal Area with whom the Air Staff might disagree'.[13] The Admiralty responded, of course, by drawing the Air Ministry's attention to its own terms of reference for this particular AOC to act as the Admiralty's 'adviser on all questions appertaining to naval aerial policy' and asking why, therefore, a rebuke had been considered appropriate when he had actually been consulted. Although the incident may seem trivial it does show how charged the atmosphere between the two services had become at ministry level. The Air Ministry's new attitude made it clear that until the Navy could expand its own cadre of aviation experts it was virtually cut off from all levels of advice outside the Air Ministry itself. It also meant that such experts on the speciality of naval aviation as there were within the higher echelons of the RAF were now cut off from the day-to-day contact with RN officers that would have allowed them to keep pace with contemporary thinking on naval warfare and its challenges.

In March 1921 Trenchard forwarded a paper to the Committee of Imperial Defence (CID) in which he outlined his revised concept of the future role of the

RAF[14] now that it appeared to have survived demobilisation. Defence of the British Isles against invasion was given as its principal role, to be achieved not by fighters but by a counter-offensive against the aggressor by the independent bomber force. Next, the tasks carried out by the other services throughout the Empire such as imperial policing, coast defence and the protection of shipping were to be carried out 'more economically' by aircraft than by troops on the ground or patrolling warships. Third, the paper recommended the independent use of aircraft in the way originally recommended by the Smuts Report of 1917[15] rather than their use as what were referred to as auxiliaries to operations being carried out by the Army and Navy. The paper showed little evidence that Great War experience, rather than theory, had been taken into account and, predictably, it aroused considerable opposition within the Admiralty and War Office. In consequence the matter was referred to the full CID in May 1921, where Trenchard argued that naval and military units should be placed under RAF command in future, in the same way that RAF units in aircraft carriers were placed under naval command. The CID was unable to resolve the question and decided that the Standing Defence Sub-Committee, chaired by A J Balfour, a former First Lord of the Admiralty, should investigate and report in due course. After a short study, his report was forwarded to the CID on 26 July 1921.[16] Surprisingly, in view of his own opposition to the creation of an independent air force when he was First Lord in 1917, Balfour recommended that the RAF must continue to be 'autonomous in administration' and that in the defence of the UK against air attack the Navy and Army must play a secondary role. However, Trenchard's more extreme ideas were rejected and Balfour recommended that 'in military operations by land or naval operations by sea the RAF must operate in strict subordination to the General or Admiral in command.' With regard to coastal defence, the protection of shipping and attacks on enemy harbours, he recommended that co-operation rather than subordination were necessary. In concluding a report that had come nowhere near settling the fundamental issue, he noted that the relationship between the RAF and the other services had no precedent and would continue to require tact and good judgement from all concerned.

Only a few days after the Standing Defence Sub-Committee's report was announced, Admiral Sir John de Robeck, C-in-C Mediterranean, wrote again to the Admiralty expressing his dissatisfaction at the failure of the RAF to meet the aviation requirements of his fleet. Bell Davies described it as 'a magnificent letter, clear and incisive, depicting the situation in the Mediterranean as he then saw it.'[17] Increasingly, de Robeck felt, the defence of vital sea communications was becoming dependent upon a combination of British surface and air strength but there was no air strength to support his fleet. He finished the letter with a heartfelt appeal to the Admiralty Board, regretting that his own time on the Active List of officers was nearing its end. He observed with 'even more regret' that members of the Board were in a similar position. Were they, the generation of flag officers

A flight of Fairey Flycatchers over *Furious*. (Author's collection)

who had served throughout the war of 1914–18 and could speak with authority, 'to pass onto the Retired List leaving to their successors a state of affairs which they knew to be unsatisfactory'? Every flag officer was known to agree with de Robeck's sentiment and the heads and directors of the Admiralty's staff divisions unanimously minuted their support for his view, leaving the Board no choice but to put its case before the government.

Notwithstanding the soundness of de Robeck's argument and the unanimous support for it that was evident within the RN, Beatty was, at first, hesitant. No doubt this was because he now regretted his ill-considered and enthusiastic support for an independent air force in 1917 but the equally ill-considered verbal truce he had agreed with Trenchard soon after becoming 1SL must also have been a factor. If he was to maintain the trust of his Board colleagues and flag officers, however, he had to act. After some weeks' consideration he decided to make a determined attempt to persuade the government to return naval aviation to the full control of the Admiralty. Unfortunately there was a complication since Sir Henry Wilson, CIGS, had already spoken out strongly against the independent air force and demanded an examination of RAF finances, which he felt sure would offer proof that the independent air force was more expensive to maintain than reverting to the RNAS and RFC. Beatty decided to link the naval case with this argument[18] rather than put forward the operational case which had been explained by de Robeck and fully supported by the naval staff. Trenchard's astute reaction was to accept the implicit challenge to the future of the RAF on the single condition that the scrutiny of expenditure must embrace all three services. In consequence the question was passed to the government's Committee on National Expenditure under Sir Eric Geddes, another former First Lord, who had been tasked in August 1921 with making recommendations to the Chancellor of the Exchequer, Sir Robert Horne, for making 'all possible reductions in national expenditure on supply services.'[19] Wilson's demand could be described as an indirect attack on the future of the RAF but the consequences of this approach and Beatty's support for it proved to be unfortunate. Bell Davies wrote subsequently[20] that, had the Admiralty made its case on the principle of operational effectiveness, the staff 'would have been on firm ground and much of the subsequent friction might have been avoided'. The resulting close questioning by Geddes and his committee led the staff deep into the minutiae of financial argument. To defend the status quo the Air Ministry claimed that it could operate aircraft at sea more cheaply than the RN. The Admiralty had to prove that costs would be reduced if it took over but found that RN artificers were paid more than RAF technical sergeants and the argument descended into farcical wrangles over saving the cost of a single skilled man if both services had coppersmiths embarked in the same aircraft carrier. If vice-benches were installed for both RN and RAF mechanics there were arguments about how the cost of a single vice-bench could be saved if one or the other service was in control. On his way to Washington for the conference on naval limitations in October 1921, Chatfield wrote to Admiral Keyes – who was about to become DCNS – to say, 'we have at last started to officially attack the Air Ministry but only indirectly at present through the Geddes Committee'.[21]

It soon became clear, however, that Beatty had made a major tactical error in supporting the War Office line, since the Geddes Committee refused to accept the premise that breaking up the RAF to re-establish separate Navy and Army air arms would result in economies. On the contrary, it expressed the belief that without a separate and independent air force the development of air power, which might revolutionise methods of attack and defence and so perhaps affect future government expenditure, would not be advanced. As in the Smuts recommendations of 1917,[22] it is immediately obvious that the words 'might' and 'perhaps' had been used when describing the potential future of air operations. This was the sort of statement that the Admiralty should, immediately, have attacked since de Robeck and the other flag officers had provided documentary evidence that independent air power was not working and that the resultant lack of operational efficiency was detrimental to the global interests of the British Empire. The Geddes Committee's own expression of belief had lacked such substance and this should have been obvious to the government but, for whatever reason, the

Geddes Committee accepted that the air needs of the fleet were best served by an independent air force that stood aloof from the day-to-day business of naval operations, which were regarded as out-dated and unnecessary by the Air Ministry. It went even further in its final report to claim that overlapping between the three services had caused considerable and unnecessary expenditure. In consequence it recommended draconian cuts to all three services' annual estimates and the Cabinet now found itself embroiled in a complex argument with all three service ministries over Geddes' recommendations. Faced with this opposition, the Cabinet formed another committee, this time under the chairmanship of Winston Churchill, with terms of reference which required it to review Geddes' findings.

In January 1922 the Admiralty forwarded its views on naval aviation to the new Churchill Committee,[23] stressing that since aircraft carriers and their personnel formed a key element of the fleet at sea, 'the demand for a separate naval air service is logical and reasonable'. The Admiralty also refuted Geddes' views on development and held that a naval air arm would actually be more likely to develop air weapons capable of replacing older equipment at sea. Admiral Keyes, DCNS, also took issue with Geddes' proposal that the number of air squadrons serving with the Navy should be cut from four to two. 'Such a number of machines', Churchill was told emphatically, 'would be quite useless to the Navy since they would be insufficient to ensure that any of the duties for which aircraft are required would be carried out'. Beatty forwarded a summary of the Admiralty Board's opinion to the Cabinet, underlining all the naval arguments with the observation that the Admiralty had 'in the past been responsible not only for advising as to the whole of the requirements necessary for carrying out the naval policy of the Government, but also for seeing that the expenditure approved for this purpose is allocated to the best possible advantage'. Moreover, 'the advent of the air weapon, which has become an integral part of our fleets, has provided the sole exception to this wise rule'. Much of the discussion with Churchill was handled by Beatty himself,[24] and the resulting recommendations showed some sympathy for the naval case. For instance, he pointed out that Geddes had made no allowance for the reduction in the value of the pound since 1914, thus making his comparison of costs fallacious. Whilst savings could be made, and he recommended a number in all three services, Churchill felt that larger inroads could not be made without gravely injuring Britain's naval power. He added that he was conscious of how easy it was to propose economies when one did not bear the responsibility for carrying them out or seeing that the nation's safety was maintained. With regard to naval aviation, however, Churchill unfortunately recommended a continuation of the status quo.

None of these committees had come close to resolving the basic question, however, and on 16 March 1922 the Cabinet asked Churchill to bring 1SL and CAS together for informal talks with the aim of resolving the question. A day later he sent both officers a note containing a series of compromise proposals.[25] It read thus:

NOTES ON ADMIRALTY-AIR MINISTRY RELATIONS

1. The culmination of all naval operations is the supreme sea battle. The study and direction of this battle belongs in its integrity to the Admiralty.
2. It follows that the role of aircraft in the sea battle must be prescribed by the Admiralty, who for this purpose should avail themselves of the highest developments of the science of aviation.
3. It follows also that the Admiralty should define the role and prescribe the quantity of aircraft employed and also the proportion [that] naval expenditure on aircraft for battle purposes should bear to other elements in the naval battle.
4. It follows further that the Admiralty should ask Parliament for the money to pay for the aircraft they require, and should also have full and unfettered control over the said aircraft while employed for naval purposes.
5. The Air Ministry on the other hand is the repository of the sciences of aviation in all its branches and aspects, and the supreme professional authority on aerial war as a whole.
6. The relations of the Air Ministry to the Admiralty in respect of purely naval services should partake largely of the nature of a laboratory and a shop for material and a school and staff college for personnel.
7. It is important that the general unity of the air service should be preserved even in regard to airmen of naval origin serving under the Admiralty for naval purposes. For this purpose there should be a certain interchange of personnel between the RN and RAF and every effort should be made in the system to prevent crystallisation into opposite and rival schools.
8. In the event of a war against a power which had no navy but a very large air force the air squadrons attached to the Navy should be capable of rapidly rejoining the main air force. Similarly in the event of a war against a power which had no air force but a powerful fleet equipped with aircraft it should be possible for the naval air squadrons to be reinforced to the fullest extent either by additions to the existing seaplane and aeroplane carriers or by air squadrons operating in conjunction with the fleets from land.
9. The RAF should be regarded as the parent service for all airmen in their capacity as airmen.

It is suggested that if agreement could be reached on the above general principles between the high personnel of the Admiralty and Air Ministry, there should be no insuperable difficulty in working out details. This task could be remitted to small technical committees of subordinates referring points of differences as they arose to their superiors.

WSC

Vice Admiral Keyes, later Admiral of the Fleet Lord Keyes of Zeebrugge and Dover GCB KCVO CMG DSO. (Author's collection)

Air Chief Marshal Trenchard, later Marshal of the Royal Air Force Viscount Trenchard of Wolfeton Bt GCB OM GCVO DSO. (Author's collection)

Far from setting out a formula that might end the argument, the obvious contradictions in Churchill's notes actually made the situation worse. If, as he stated, the supreme sea battle was to be the culmination of all naval operations and the integrity[26] of its study and direction lay with the Admiralty, logic would surely dictate that that body alone must, therefore, define the role and both prescribe and fund the number of aircraft deemed to be necessary in proportion to other weapons systems, including the battle fleet, flotillas, submarines and mine warfare vessels. To take the view that a separate and independent ministry would be required to contribute one element of a three-dimensional battle at sea made no sense at all and was a recipe for bureaucratic muddle rather than sharp planning. Churchill stated in his opening notes that this would be a sea battle and so, given the advances in technology pioneered by the Royal Navy between 1914 and 1918, elements of the battle would be fought concurrently on, under and above the sea surface. The Royal Navy's air service had pioneered virtually every aspect of combat aviation, including fleet air defence, long-range reconnaissance over the sea, anti-surface vessel strike and both day and night bombing sorties. Why, therefore, should the RAF have to be 'regarded as the parent service for all airmen in their capacity as airmen'? Even if their aviation knowledge was deemed to be worthy of consideration, it must surely take a subordinate place in the overall planning carried out by the Admiralty in defence of the British Empire. If the culminating sea battle was to be won it was surely necessary for airmen to study and fully comprehend every aspect of the battle in which they would fight. In practical terms this meant that, logically, they would be naval officers, not independent specialists arguing that the nature of combat must, somehow, be altered to connect with their own untested theories.

Tellingly, Churchill's note number 5 seemed to indicate that he now fully accepted the bomber lobby's theory that any future war would be fought out in the air between rival fleets of long-range bombers attempting to destroy the protagonists' major cities with air raids. If he really did believe this to be the case, he might have been concerned that over time admirals would understand less about strategic bombing and such unproven knowledge as there was would lie with the air marshals. Given his background and driving enthusiasm from 1911 to expand the naval air arm, it is surprising that Churchill could not see the inconsistencies in this approach but, like most other politicians during this period, he failed to give any consideration to the possibility that a future enemy might use aircraft tactically rather than strategically to enhance the otherwise conventional capabilities of its naval and military forces. If this were to happen it would leave the British Empire's navies and armies at the mercy of tactical aircraft used in a type of warfare about which the air marshals could contribute little expertise because of their concentration on strategic bombing. Looking ahead, this was almost exactly what was to happen in April and May 1940 when the British policy of concentration on bomber operations left both the Home Fleet and British Expeditionary Forces fatally exposed to Germany's tactical use of aircraft in methods that Trenchard and the Air Ministry had not predicted or planned against. The confused opinions expressed by Churchill in his notes could, therefore, only lead to further argument – and they did. Brigadier P R C Groves wrote a series of articles in *The Times* on the subject later in March, and in July Lord Lee sent a memorandum to the CID in which he supported the Admiralty argument that aircraft should constitute an arm of the fighting fleet and 'act with other such units in battle'.[27]

Churchill's attempt at mediation having failed; there was a lull in the exchange of arguments that autumn during the political crisis that followed the fall of Lloyd George's coalition government and its replacement by a Conservative government under Andrew Bonar Law. The new government had no immediate enthusiasm to continue the debate but the dispute over how best aircraft could be operated by Britain's deployed fleets across the world would not go away and in March 1923 the Prime Minister set up a sub-committee of the CID under Lord Salisbury, the Lord President of the Council, to inquire into co-operation between the armed forces generally and more specifically 'to deal with the relations of the Navy and Air

Force as regards fleet air work'.[28] Subsequently known as the Salisbury Committee, the group also included Stanley Baldwin the Chancellor of the Exchequer, Lord Curzon the Foreign Secretary, Lord Derby the Secretary of State for War, Lord Peel the Secretary of State for India, Sir Samuel Hoare the Air Secretary, Leo Amery the First Lord and Lord Weir. Sir Maurice Hankey, secretary of the CID, prepared papers for the new sub-committee which summarised the long and complicated debate which had preceded its formation. At its first meeting, Lord Salisbury delegated the relationship between the Navy and Air Force for fleet air work to a further sub-committee comprising Lords Balfour, Peel and Weir, subsequently known as the Balfour Sub-Committee, which took a great deal of written and oral evidence before rendering its report on 21 July 1923. In it they expressed the view that some changes were obviously necessary but that they did not consider it advisable to separate a naval air arm from the remainder of the air force. In their view, 'a course somewhere between these two extremes' represented the ideal.[29] They made thirteen recommendations, the most important of which was that the Air Ministry 'shall provide all the material which the Admiralty demand' and that if this was not done for any reason 'there shall be an appeal by either party to the CID'. The question of funding the cost of what was now referred to as the Fleet Air Arm from the Navy Estimates was also accepted and the details were to be worked out between the Admiralty, Air Ministry and Treasury. The vexed question of the command and control of embarked RAF personnel was to some extent hedged by the sub-committee's statement that there was 'some obscurity

A Fairey Flycatcher over *Eagle*. (Author's collection)

A running range of Hawker Ospreys about to launch from *Eagle*. They are photographed from the flying control position where signal flags that controlled deck operations can be seen in position. (Author's collection)

hanging over the subject', but it was agreed that the position of RAF officers did not 'differ in law and should not differ in practice from the position of the Royal Marines'. Importantly, the Balfour Sub-Committee agreed that the 'personnel, material and reserves of the Fleet Air Arm should not be withdrawn without either the consent of the Admiralty or the decision of the Cabinet'. The report went on to propose that officers should be exchanged between the naval and air staffs and that at least 30 per cent of the pilots in a carrier should be provided by the RAF with the remainder being provided by the RN. The final recommendation was that all fleet reconnaissance and spotting for naval gunfire should be 'entrusted to naval officers, whether seconded or otherwise'.

Balfour was 74 when he became chairman of the sub-committee that bore his name. Unfortunately, ill-health prevented him from attending every meeting but the final written report shows evidence of his renowned dialectical skill. In the first volume of *Naval Policy Between the Wars* Roskill stated his belief that there is evidence to show that Balfour, who had argued against the subjugation of the RNAS into a unified, independent air force when he was First Lord, was not averse to the Fleet Air Arm returning completely to Admiralty control but was overborne by Lord Weir who had been one of the greatest advocates of a single air service. Nearly a century later it is difficult to measure the relative influence of the three sub-committee members. Peel had little previous experience of air matters but Weir's hostility to the Admiralty when he served on Lord Cowdray's Air Board in 1917 and as Secretary of State for Air in 1918 leaves little doubt that he was utterly opposed to the concept of a naval air arm that was not part of the RAF. Significantly, Admiral Keyes, who was a member of the Board of Admiralty at that time, subsequently referred to Weir in the House of Commons as the 'evil genius' of the Balfour sub-committee.[30] Thus Weir might well have been the major influence within the sub-committee but it should not be forgotten that Balfour was content to set his name to the report and could not, therefore, have been altogether against the recommendations, which sought to find a compromise that could end the argument. Amery, the First Lord, tried again, after reading the report, to argue the case for a 'clean cut' of the Fleet Air Arm from Air Ministry back to Admiralty control but in Balfour's absence due to illness, Peel and Weir claimed to have gone fully into the question and expressed surprise that it should be raised again.

Interpretation of the report led to a continuing exchange of correspondence between the Admiralty, Air Ministry and CID, putting forward arguments over interpretation which had still not been resolved on 23 January 1924 when Ramsay MacDonald became Prime Minister of the first UK Labour government. In this new administration Lord Chelmsford replaced Amery as First Lord and Lord Thomson replaced Sir Samuel Hoare in charge of the Air Ministry. The change made little apparent difference to the continuing disagreement, however, and an argument over whether RAF Coastal Area Command was part of the Fleet Air Arm or not was soon added to the correspondence between Departments on how best to implement the Balfour Report. This led Lord Thomson to observe that since

Pre-1939 Royal Navy pilots' 'wings' badge of the type Bill Lucy would have worn on his left uniform sleeve during his first flying appointments. (Author's collection)

there appeared to be little hope of settling the issue in this way, he recommended that the matter should be referred to an impartial authority for judgement.[31] The First Lord agreed and on 12 March 1924 the Cabinet appointed Lord Haldane, the Lord Chancellor who was deputy chairman of the CID, to inquire into the issues under dispute. He began his task a few days later by holding preliminary discussions with Trenchard and Keyes. The former immediately objected on the grounds that Haldane's questions had appeared to give the impression that he agreed with the Admiralty's interpretation of the Balfour Report. As if that was not enough, to complicate matters, Lord Thomson protested that Keyes was not the Chief of the Naval Staff but the deputy and, thus, might not be able to speak as Trenchard's equal. At the time Beatty was out of the country and had delegated full powers to Keyes; it was, therefore, entirely reasonable that he should represent the Admiralty, and Lord Haldane certainly entertained no difficulties on that score. He wrote to Thomson on 7 April 1924[32] explaining that he fully accepted Keyes' authority to act and added,

> it is best so … Trenchard and Keyes are settling a draft concordat. This they will do best by themselves and I am a little nervous about spoiling things if an uninformed mind comes in *ab extra*. Let us leave well alone if possible. Hankey tells me today that private enquiry has made him think that the relations of the two services never promised so well before.

The reason for this optimism was that the two senior officers were related by marriage. In 1906 Keyes had married Eva Bowlby, daughter of E S Bowlby; thirteen years later Trenchard had married her younger sister Katherine, the widow of Captain the Honourable James Boyle. Faced with the potential displeasure of their wives, therefore, the two officers proceeded to make their way line by line through the Balfour Report and hammer out an agreement. That family ties did indeed make a difference is underscored by the fact that they addressed each other by their Christian names throughout the lengthy correspondence that continued throughout their discussions, a method of address that would otherwise have been considered remarkable between senior officers at the time. The resulting document known as the Trenchard/Keyes Agreement contained thirteen subject heads and was both large and complicated to read.[33] In his covering letter Haldane referred to it as an excellent piece of work and 'an example of what skill combined with forbearance can effect'. The Cabinet accepted the Agreement with some relief in July 1924 and directed that it should be incorporated into the records of the CID. It was from this time that the organisation that operated aircraft from HM ships at sea became known, formally, as the Fleet Air Arm although the Agreement was inevitably seen by the Admiralty as a compromise in which Trenchard had managed to maintain the principle that the Fleet Air Arm should remain part of the RAF. In every other aspect, however, the Agreement went some way towards

Carrier flying was a dangerous occupation. The 'plane-guard' destroyer moves quickly towards a ditched aircraft to rescue the aircrew. To make Fleet Air Arm operations as safe as possible, constant practice was required to maintain skill levels and improve technique. (Author's collection)

meeting Admiralty requirements; it was to state the number and performance of the aircraft that it required although the Air Ministry would then draft specifications for circulation to industry. The RN would specify the type of training to be carried out by disembarked units and naval ratings were gradually to replace airmen on board aircraft carriers to carry out a wide range of duties and trades. Up to 70 per cent of pilots in the Fleet Air Arm could be provided by the RN and RM and whilst on flying duties they were to be 'attached' not 'seconded' to the RAF for specific periods, during which they were to be granted dual RAF rank which might well not be the same as their RN rank but would reflect their flying experience and aptitude. Naval 'wings' worn by pilots over the left cuff rank lace were reintroduced at this time. All observers were to be naval officers who would not be attached to the RAF but would remain in their ships when flights disembarked. They wore no flying badge until 1942 when it was finally accepted that observers should be appointed to naval air squadrons rather than ships.

Volunteers to train as pilots in the Fleet Air Arm were called for in a series of Admiralty Fleet Orders, starting with AFO 1058/24, which were also re-published as Air Ministry Weekly Orders. Officers accepted for such training were informed that they would initially be attached to the RAF for four years, after which they would return to naval general service for two years. Those who wished could then volunteer for further periods of flying duty to enable them to fill senior flight and staff appointments. The Agreement also confirmed the Balfour Report's recommendation that the cost of the Fleet Air Arm should be covered by a Grant-in-Aid of Air Votes for which a lump sum was to be provided out of the Navy Estimates. A figure of £1.75 million was agreed and incorporated into the 1925/26 financial year. The Trenchard/Keyes Agreement was ratified just in time to allow the training of the modest expansion in the number of aircraft and pilots needed to equip the newly modified aircraft carriers *Glorious* and *Courageous* and the extra flight of torpedo bombers being demanded by Admiral Sir Henry Oliver, the C-in-C Atlantic Fleet. The fact that aviation was seen to be so important in 1924 underlines the Admiralty's enthusiasm and understanding of the evolving technology, but the lengthy negotiations needed to make such progress as there had been certainly underline the Admiralty's concerns about relying on another department for the production of weapons that were regarded as an essential element of the fleet. One important question that was not resolved, however, was the need for a significant number of reserves. The Admiralty took the view that any future war against a major power was likely to be prolonged and that reserves would be needed that could both augment the front line and quickly replace the inevitable casualties. The Air Ministry took the contrary view that it expected the new aerial form of warfare to be of short duration and any replacements in embarked squadrons that might be required could easily be provided from the independent air force and its own reserve. How very wide of the mark the Air Ministry view actually was became apparent in 1940, by which time it was too late to train the pilots, observers and telegraphist air gunners (TAGs) needed to replace operational casualties in the short term and the Fleet Air Arm suffered badly as a consequence. Overall, however, the Trenchard/Keyes Agreement brought to a temporary end the six years of bitter dispute that had followed the subsumation of the RNAS into the RAF in 1918, but there can be little doubt that naval opinion still believed that the existing arrangements inhibited technical progress in the Fleet Air Arm and that only full control, the re-establishment of a naval air service, would ever solve the problem.

Chapter 3

Joining the Royal Navy as an Officer and Training to be a Pilot

William Paulet Lucy was born on 13 May 1910 and began his naval career at the Britannia Royal Naval College, Dartmouth, on 15 January 1924, aged 13.[1] His progress was typical of the individuals who saw the enormous potential of aviation in future naval operations and I have used his career to illustrate the human aspects of the development of carrier strike warfare. Like his colleagues in this era, he had to cope with dual control and the other politically inspired problems that beset the Fleet Air Arm but his early progress followed the normal pattern, with an appointment to the battleship *Marlborough* on 1 September 1927 after passing out of the Britannia Royal Naval College at Dartmouth. On 1 May 1928 Bill Lucy was promoted to Midshipman, remaining in *Marlborough*, which formed part of the 3rd Battle Squadron in the Atlantic Fleet. On 4 September 1928 he transferred to the cruiser *Emerald* which was serving on the East Indies Station and, after successful completion of his Midshipmen's Fleet Board, he was promoted to Acting Sub Lieutenant and appointed to the Royal Naval College Greenwich for courses in every naval subject, eventually achieving first-class passes in Seamanship and Torpedoes with second-class passes in Navigation, Gunnery and the final Greenwich exam. Passes in these subjects allowed young officers to be confirmed in the rank of Sub Lieutenant and the grade of pass determined the seniority achieved and thus the date at which they would be promoted to Lieutenant, higher grades earning the earliest promotion. Eventual promotion to Lieutenant Commander was automatic after eight years' service as a Lieutenant.

On 30 December 1931 Sub Lieutenant Lucy was appointed to the new heavy cruiser *Exeter* which was serving with the Atlantic Fleet. He was promoted to Lieutenant on 1 August 1932 and would have kept watches on the bridge at sea and on the quarterdeck in harbour, working towards the award of his Bridge Watch Keeping Certificate and Ocean Navigation Certificate, the latter qualifying him to navigate one of HM Ships out of sight of land. As a member of the Executive Department he would also have been the officer responsible for a division of twelve or more sailors, ensuring that their service certificates were kept up to date; that they were put forward for courses to help with their advancement; that they were efficient members of the ship's company at action stations and for general matters of discipline and welfare. The captain would have taken an interest in Lucy's own career and no doubt given advice on what step to take next.

Bill Lucy, photographed with officers and other midshipmen in the cruiser *Emerald* during 1928. He is in the front row, fourth from the right, holding his cap in his right hand. (John de Lucy collection)

Hermes operating aircraft in the South China Sea. With the low natural wind evidenced by the glassy sea surface, she had to steam at high speed to recover the Fairey IIIF that has just landed on. (John de Lucy collection)

Gunnery was still regarded as the primary means of engaging and destroying an enemy fleet and specialisation as a Gunnery Officer was seen as a good path to promotion. Alternatively, Navigation gave a good grounding in ship handling that would be a useful stepping stone for those who went on to command their own ships. The Torpedo Branch was also responsible for ships' electrical systems and attracted officers with interests in technical matters. The Submarine Branch offered early command for those who passed the Submarine Command Course, known throughout the service as the 'Perisher', but was still seen as a somewhat ungentlemanly occupation colloquially known as 'the Trade' because officers were required to be proficient in a variety of tasks, such as signalling, that were more usually performed by their men in big ships.

There is a myth that some commanding officers tried to dissuade young officers from becoming pilots because of a general aversion to aviation in the RN. This could not be further from the truth and, while some may not have actually recommended aviation as a career path, it should be understood that the majority of senior officers did see a significant future for naval aviation but were unhappy about its dual control arrangements and the general lack of RAF interest in naval warfare. Some captains certainly advised their young officers to think very carefully about the impact flying would have on their subsequent naval careers before volunteering for training as a pilot but this was because of the need to have a dual, invariably lower, RAF rank imposed on them by politicians who gave no thought to its practical implications. Take, for example, two lieutenants, both of the same seniority, one of which chose to specialise in Gunnery, the other as a pilot. The former would have become Gunnery Officer of a cruiser or destroyer flotilla on qualification, advising the captain on the best use of one of his primary weapon systems in action. His reports would reflect this, marking him out from less qualified lieutenants in the Navy List who were competing with him for promotion. The lieutenant who chose to become a pilot, on the other hand, would have dual rank inflicted upon him during every flying appointment and – whatever his seniority as an RN lieutenant – he would join his first squadron as a Flying Officer RAF, the equivalent of a sub lieutenant, and be reported on as such by the RAF authorities that administered it as part of the RAF. To reach high rank like his contemporaries, a naval pilot would need to have had ship command, and time spent in a squadron disembarked at an airfield ashore would not have given the same amount of sea experience that his contemporaries in other specialisations were achieving. This was why observers were appointed to carriers for executive duties and only flew when required to do so whilst squadrons were embarked. They did not form part of squadrons, or disembark with them on a regular basis, until the Admiralty regained full control of the Fleet Air Arm in May 1939. Despite these rather depressing warnings, the Fleet Air Arm offered the chance of early command as a Lieutenant and the excitement of a new form of naval warfare that was beginning to show its potential notwithstanding the element of danger associated with it. Those pilots who did

Float-fitted Hawker Osprey S1696 of 803 NAS over *Hermes* on the China Station in 1935. The ship is at anchor, note the jack right forward, and her aircraft have been converted to operate as floatplanes. Wheeled undercarriages would be refitted when she got under way again for any length of time. (John de Lucy collection)

well had the chance to stand out in their chosen specialisation, overcome the drawbacks and, ultimately, to achieve high rank.

Warnings against choosing to specialise in aviation probably did not apply to Lucy in *Exeter*, however, because his captain, Captain I W Gibson OBE MVO RN[2] had been the director of the Admiralty Air Department from December 1928 to April 1930 and was, therefore, fully aware of the need to encourage men like him to specialise as pilots. Whether he already intended to become a pilot when he joined *Exeter* or whether Captain Gibson persuaded him we shall never know for certain, but the balance of probability is that he had already made up his mind to specialise in aviation because he volunteered for pilot training at the earliest opportunity. As soon as he had been promoted to Lieutenant and been awarded his Bridge Watch Keeping and Navigation Certificates, the basic requirements needed before any executive officer could volunteer for a specialist course, his request for pilot training was accepted and he left *Exeter* on 25 August 1932.

Bill Lucy was appointed to Number 24 Naval Pilots' Course at RAF Leuchars in Fife which began on 18 September 1932, the second of two courses carried out at this airfield during that year[3] with Number 1 Flying Training School, which was

Hawker Ospreys of 803 NAS on *Hermes* photographed by Bill Lucy from the after lift which was just below flight deck level. (John de Lucy collection)

used exclusively to train RN and RM pilots for service in the Fleet Air Arm. This course included five other officers, Lieutenant A R Burch RM, Lieutenant J C H Price RN and Sub Lieutenants E G Clutton, N McI Kemp and G W R Nicholl RN. It lasted seven months and took students from *ab initio* flying on the Avro 504N, through advanced training and onto operational types including the Hawker Nimrod and Osprey. The nearby Tentsmuir range was used to teach air-to-ground bombing and strafing, and banner targets towed by aircraft were used to teach air-to-air gunnery over the sea. On successful completion of this course, pilots were graded by the RAF as Flying Officers and appeared as such in the Air Force List in addition to their substantive RN rank in the Navy List. They were then appointed to operational units for what were referred to as full flying duties, annotated as 'FFD' in their service records. Bill Lucy completed the course on 22 April 1933 and was awarded the naval 'wings' which were worn over the left sleeve lace like the eagle badge once worn by pilots in the RNAS. He was appointed to 802 Squadron and joined it at an interesting time. A new squadron numbering system devised in

1933 by Rear Admiral Henderson, Rear Admiral Aircraft Carriers, had just come into effect, bringing with it larger fleet squadrons numbered in the 800 series to replace many of the earlier flights, numbered in the 400 series. The new squadrons were equipped with up to twelve aircraft, which reflected better aircraft operating techniques on carriers made possible by new aircraft technologies. These included brakes, which allowed them to be taxied out of larger ranges aft to line up for a free take-off, and more reliable engines which made it possible for aircraft to start up in larger ranges without the risk of overheating before their turn came to take off. There were obvious tactical advantages for the larger squadrons in action.

802 Squadron was formed on 3 April 1933 by the amalgamation of 408 and 409 Fleet Fighter Flights which were embarked on the aircraft carrier *Glorious* serving in the Mediterranean Fleet. Its first commanding officer was Lieutenant Commander E M C Abel-Smith RN (dual-ranked as a Squadron Leader RAF) who had commanded 408 Flight since 1930. The new squadron was equipped with nine Hawker Nimrod single-seat fighters and three two-seater Hawker Osprey fighters which could also be used for reconnaissance duties. Abel-Smith was relieved by Squadron Leader W E Swann RAF on 10 June 1933 and Bill Lucy joined in September 1933, having taken a sea passage to Alexandria in Egypt where *Glorious* had arrived on 5 September. While the ship was in harbour, 802 Squadron disembarked to the RAF airfield at Aboukir, where pilots could maintain flying currency and practise their individual and formation tactical and gunnery skills.[4] When the ship returned to Malta and was moored in Grand Harbour in October 1933 and January 1934, 802

Hermes at anchor on the China Station in that station's white-and-buff paint scheme. Note the Fairey IIIFs on floats with the seaplane crane attached to the one on the left and the awnings rigged to provide shade. (John de Lucy collection)

803 NAS photographed while disembarked. Bill Lucy is seated fifth from the right but the photograph was, unfortunately, not dated and the others in it named, but Dick Partridge could be the Royal Marines officer on his left. Note the mix of RN and RAF personnel typical of the dual-control era. (John de Lucy collection)

and the rest of the air group disembarked to Hal Far. After a successful commission in the Mediterranean, *Glorious* returned to the UK to pay off for a refit in May 1934 but 802 followed the normal pattern for a disembarked fighter squadron with spells at Netheravon and Upavon for continuation flying and an armament training camp at Sutton Bridge in August 1934 to prepare for further embarked operations, this time in *Courageous*.

The squadron's new carrier was serving with the Home Fleet and was carrying out the customary series of low-key visits to UK ports intended to show the public what the Royal Navy looked like. 802 embarked on 7 September 1934 while the ship was off the Humber Estuary and a visit to Scarborough followed, after which the ship operated for short periods in the Firth of Forth, Moray Firth, Cromarty Firth and then back in the Firth of Forth again in October. In that month Bill Lucy was appointed to 803 Squadron which was serving in *Eagle* on the China Station. He was one of a number of men intended to re-commission the squadron on station in the Far East and he was instructed to proceed first to RAF Upavon where the administrative details of his passage were worked out, after which he sailed for Singapore, where the squadron was disembarked to RAF Seletar while *Eagle* underwent a maintenance period. The squadron's commanding officer changed at this time with Lieutenant Commander C W Byas RN replacing Lieutenant Commander R R Graham RN. Both appeared in the Air Force List under their dual rank of Squadron Leader and Byas was to show how misplaced the theory that specialisation as a pilot could damage an officer's career prospects by being promoted to Commander on 31 December 1936 while still in command of the squadron. On 27 December 1934, 803 Squadron re-commissioned at Seletar for service in *Hermes* with a nominal strength of six Hawker Ospreys. On 1 January 1935 the ship sailed for Hong Kong with 803 embarked, arriving on 6 January when three more Ospreys were added from storage at Kai Tak airfield to bring the total up to nine. From then on *Hermes* operated with the cruisers of the China Station on the sort of exercises and visits that were normal peacetime events. Between May and July, in the heat of the summer, the fleet moved its base from Hong Kong to the British Concession Territory on the island of Wei-Hei-Wei, after which visits were made to Chingwangtao and to Chemulpo in Manchuria to show the flag and emphasise the British presence in the region. Apart from a brief visit to Port Swettenham in Malaya in early December 1935, *Hermes* spent several months from the end of September in Singapore with 803 Squadron disembarked at RAF Seletar.

By then Bill Lucy was a very experienced fighter pilot with a number of flying hours in Hawker Nimrods and Ospreys. Contemporary Admiralty policy required all the aircraft procured for operation from warships to be adaptable with alternative wheeled undercarriages or floats. Thus float-fitted seaplanes, including

On 11 March 1934 storm force waves smashed through the forward doors into *Glorious*' upper hangar, destroying the six aircraft seen here and causing other damage. At the time Bill Lucy was serving in her with 802 NAS. (John de Lucy collection)

Hawker Ospreys of 803 NAS from *Hermes* during the period that Bill Lucy was serving with it disembarked to RAF Kai Tak in the Crown Colony of Hong Kong. (Philip Jarrett collection)

fighters, could be operated from the water while carriers were in harbour, lowered onto and off the water by large cranes. The policy also meant that any carrier aircraft fitted with floats could be embarked in a catapult-equipped cruiser, being recovered by crane after landing alongside at the end of a sortie. Some 400-series flights had been retained after 1933 to provide aircraft for cruiser squadrons and on 15 January 1936 Bill Lucy was re-appointed to 403 Flight which provided Hawker Osprey fighter-reconnaissance aircraft for the 5th Cruiser Squadron[5] on the China Station. The squadron comprised the County-class heavy cruisers *Berwick*, *Cornwall*, *Cumberland*, *Kent* and *Suffolk* and each ship was fitted with a Type SIIL catapult. When not embarked, the flight's aircraft operated from RAF Kai Tak in Hong Kong. Ospreys had gradually replaced Fairey Flycatcher single-seat fighters in 1934/35 and Bill Lucy was appointed to *Cornwall* as its flight commander with 403 Flight on 15 January 1936. His appointment would have appeared logical to the Naval Secretary's Department in the Admiralty since he was already current on the Osprey and required no conversion course; he was already in the Far East and would not, therefore, require a long passage from the UK. As a seaman officer with cruiser experience, he would also be able to keep watches whilst at sea in *Cornwall* and accrue some of the sea time necessary for ultimate promotion to higher rank. His new appointment could be said to offer him the best of both worlds.

The five Hawker Ospreys of 403 Flight were fitted with floats but were still fairly agile and capable of operating as fighters against anything they were likely to encounter at sea. This gave the advantage that when they were used on

This Fairey IIIF, S1823, had an accident similar to Bill Lucy's while operating disembarked at RAF Hal Far in Malta during 1935, although in its case it hit the wall while practising night take-offs and landings. (Author's collection)

Captioned by Bill Lucy as 'Jacko left, self and Carmichael on a lunch visit to Stone Cutters' (Hong Kong). The child was not named but the image gives some idea of officers' recreational activities on the China Station, and the moored Hawker Osprey in the background gives a rough idea of date. It is K3645 which carried the side number 591 while serving with 715 Flight for the 5th Cruiser Squadron from July 1936. It was embarked in *Berwick* at Hong Kong in August 1936 and struck off charge in May 1937. (John de Lucy collection)

Bill Lucy's deck landing accident on 17 January 1935 while he was serving with 803 NAS in *Hermes*. The accident report stated that K2790 'swung on landing, hit island' and that Bill was slightly injured. The aircraft was subsequently repaired and flew again. (John de Lucy collection)

reconnaissance missions they could, if necessary, fight for their information. It was an anomaly of the time that the five pilots stayed with the flight when it disembarked but the five observers were appointed to the ships themselves and would only fly when embarked unless there was a particular reason for them to move ashore and do so. This gave the RN more control of their activities but was hardly likely to produce the best results. The aircraft were allocated side numbers in the range from 590 to 594 and individual aircraft were painted with their cruiser's badge on their tail fins. The 5th Cruiser Squadron was intended to operate as a cohesive unit in battle or as individual ships on open ocean searches for raiders or pirates. Thus the pilots of 403 Flight practised both working together and on individual surface searches with their ships' observers. From time to time the observers' skill with the Lewis machine gun fitted in the rear cockpit was honed by throwing a brightly painted barrel into the sea from the parent cruiser so that it could be shot at. As a weapon system, it was identical to that of an RNAS Short 184 during the Great War but it offered some flexibility of response and a feeling of security for the aircrew. The pilot had a single forward-firing Vickers Mark III machine gun fitted on the port side of the fuselage firing through the propeller arc with an interrupter mechanism to prevent rounds hitting the propeller blades. Practice shoots were carried out against banners towed by other aircraft when disembarked and against targets set up on ranges for strafing. During Bill Lucy's time with 403 Flight *Cornwall* operated between Singapore and Hong Kong.

On 20 April 1936 Bill Lucy returned to 803 Squadron which was disembarked to Kai Tak from *Hermes*. Much of the remainder of 1936 was spent embarked in *Hermes*, which visited Kobe, Kagoshima and Nagasaki in Japan. The ship then returned to Wei-Hei-Wei for two months before beginning an autumnal series of visits to Port Arthur, Tsingtao, Shanghai and Amoy, after which it returned to Hong Kong. In the spring of 1937 *Hermes* visited the Philippine Islands and the Dutch East Indies before proceeding to Penang and Colombo on her way back to Devonport, where she was to be paid off into reserve. 803 Squadron disembarked to Colombo on 1 April 1937 and was disbanded. Bill Lucy took passage back to the UK to be was appointed to the administrative shore establishment HMS *Victory*, additional, for service at RAF Gosport, where he spent a few months on general flying duties from 15 July 1937. On 13 September he was appointed back to the cruiser *Cornwall* which had returned from the Far East and been refitted in Chatham Dockyard with, among other things, improved aviation arrangements including a hangar capable of containing two Supermarine Walrus amphibians and an athwartships Type DIH catapult fitted amidships. On re-commissioning she joined the 2nd Cruiser Squadron in the Home Fleet. The flying unit that provided aircraft for this cruiser squadron was 712 Squadron, which had formed on 15 July 1936 with six Hawker Ospreys. This was a time of significant expansion for the Fleet Air Arm and this new squadron had four different commanding officers

Hawker Ospreys of the 5th Cruiser Squadron practising formation flying over Hong Kong. (John de Lucy collection)

The heavy cruiser *Cornwall* at anchor. Note the large shed-like hangar and aircraft cranes amidships. (Author's collection)

in the first ten months of its existence. When Bill Lucy joined on 13 September 1937, Lieutenant Commander E H Shattock RN, dual ranked as a Squadron Leader RAF, was in command and the unit was shore-based at RAF Mount Batten near Plymouth. By then he had converted onto the Supermarine Walrus which was replacing the different types of seaplane that were embarked in battleships and cruisers, and Bill Lucy was designated as Flight Commander of the detachment of two Walrus intended for *Cornwall* after she re-commissioned in November 1937. 712 Squadron establishment expanded to twelve Walrus after the last Ospreys were retired in June 1937.

January 1938 was spent carrying out sea trials with new equipment, including the catapult, and in early February she took part in the annual Home Fleet cruise to carry out exercises with the Mediterranean Fleet based in Gibraltar. Visits were made to French ports in order show the flag and she returned to the UK in March to carry out the usual series of visits to British ports. Bill Lucy left both 712 Squadron and *Cornwall* on 20 July 1938. His time in this appointment would have been exciting because in July 1937 Sir Thomas Inskip, the Minister for Defence Co-operation had ruled that full control of naval aviation, the squadrons that embarked in carriers and other warships together with the training units ashore that prepared people for them, should be handed back to the Admiralty no later than by July 1939. The failed experiment of dual control was about to end and the largest recruiting campaign carried out in peacetime was underway to replace

RAF personnel in squadrons. RN training and administrative organisations were being prepared amid a major programme of re-armament that had begun in 1936 because of fears that wars with Germany, Italy and Japan were becoming a distinct possibility.

With his seniority and experience, Bill Lucy could look forward to playing an important role in the Fleet Air Arm as it became a fully integrated part of the RN, but for the moment he had completed the four years as a Lieutenant considered normal for a first spell of flying duties and for the good of his career he had to be appointed to a warship for watch keeping and executive duties. On 29 July 1938, therefore, he was given another appointment to the administrative shore establishment HMS *Victory*, this time to stand by the new cruiser *Manchester* which was being built at Hawthorn Leslie's yard on the River Tyne and to form part of her first ship's company when she commissioned. She was completed on 4 August 1938 and commissioned for service with the 4th Cruiser Squadron on the East Indies Station. His duties on board were centred on the Executive Department and seamanship but he would have taken a professional interest in the embarked flight

Cornwall's wardroom in 1938 during the ship's spring cruise to the Mediterranean. Bill Lucy is seated towards the right on the club fender between the two Royal Marines officers and his caption for this picture read, 'Freeth, Phillimore, Parker, Scott-Moncrieff, Enlleouc, Clarke and self on right'. (John de Lucy collection)

Dorsetshire's Hawker Osprey taking off from Hong Kong harbour in formation with other 5th Cruiser Squadron aircraft. Until seeing this image I had not appreciated that cruiser flights regularly practised together like this. (John de Lucy collection)

of three Walrus[6] from 714 Squadron. After trials with her new Type DIH catapult and the general setting-to-work of her weapons and systems, *Manchester* sailed for the Indian Ocean on 26 September 1938 and passed through the Suez Canal on 8 October. She then carried out an extensive series of visits to ports in India, Ceylon and Burma to show the inhabitants that the RN retained powerful warships in the region and was prepared to take action in their defence if necessary. In April 1939 she arrived in Colombo for a two-month maintenance period and Bill Lucy, aware from Admiralty Fleet Orders that control of the FAA would be handed back, fully, to the Admiralty in a few weeks' time, was keen to return to flying duties.

Flying in the 1930s was still a dangerous occupation and in Ray Sturtivant's collected data on the Fleet Air Arm of the period, he lists three occasions in which Lucy was involved in accidents. Interestingly, two of them took place while he was operating from airfields ashore and only one of them while deck landing on a carrier. The first happened just a month after he joined 802 Squadron while it was disembarked to RAF Hal Far in Malta. On 13 October 1933 Lucy, then dual ranked as a Flying Officer RAF, was flying with an un-named passenger in Fairey IIIF

S1457, an aircraft allocated to the air station's Miscellaneous Flight. On approaching to land he descended below the ideal glide path, undershot the landing area and wiped off his aircraft's fixed undercarriage on one of the many stone walls that surround the airfield.[7] Both occupants survived the subsequent belly-landing but the aircraft was written off and saw no further use. The incident was, no doubt, put down to pilot error.

Bill Lucy's only recorded deck landing accident happened on 17 January 1935 after he had joined 803 Squadron. His Hawker Osprey, K2790, swung to starboard after landing on *Hermes* and hit the island, injuring him slightly. He appears to have been flying the aircraft solo without an observer and the cause of the swing was not recorded; it may have been due to a fault in the ship's newly fitted arrester wire retardation system. The aircraft continued in service and was with the RN Fighter School at RNAS Eastleigh in 1940. He had a second Osprey accident on 17 August 1937 while he was flying from Gosport. S1682 bounced on landing and the starboard undercarriage collapsed; it finally came to rest on its nose and port lower wing tip. Again he was flying without an observer but this time he was unhurt. The aircraft was repaired for further service.

In the complicated era of dual control, RN pilots had to be reported on by both RN and RAF authorities and recommended, or not, for promotion. Annotations

Bill Lucy captioned this photograph 'Crossing the Line Ceremony in *Hermes*, 1937'. (John de Lucy collection)

on his service history show that senior RAF officers strongly recommended Lucy for promotion to Flight Lieutenant RAF in both 1936 and 1937. Both were endorsed by Captain Fraser RN. Other annotations mark his qualifications in both day and night deck landing and, interestingly, a parachute course successfully completed in 1937 together with a conversion course in which he learnt to fly the Walrus after his long experience on Ospreys.

Following the Munich Crisis in 1938 and the German invasion of Czechoslovakia in March 1939 Bill Lucy and his contemporaries must have realised that war with Germany, and possibly Italy and Japan as well, was becoming more and more likely. He knew that he needed sea time in *Manchester* to prepare himself for the promotion to Lieutenant Commander that he was due by seniority on 1 August 1940 but he would have been less than human if he did not want to get back to flying, where he could make the most use of his experience for the coming war effort. In May 1939 the Admiralty regained full control of the Fleet Air Arm and Bill Lucy wanted to show what naval aviation could achieve now that the 'dead hand' of RAF bureaucracy was removed from progress. The Admiralty had been carrying out a recruiting drive for pilots which had attracted volunteers including former airline pilots and RAF officers who had served at sea with the Fleet Air Arm. To boost numbers still further, the Admiralty had also started a short-service commission scheme for direct-entry pilots and training for ratings – who were referred to by authority rather quaintly as 'aircraft coxswains' for a while but, mercifully, the title did not stick and they were known simply as rating pilots. The Admiralty would have been as keen to get Bill Lucy back to flying duties as he was to do so. Consequently, as soon as he had achieved the minimum time at sea to 'brush up' his seamanship, he left *Manchester* and was re-examined for his fitness for flying duties after his eight months away and found to be fit. The word 'FIT' was hand-written in capitals on his documents lest there be any doubt about the matter. He was appointed administratively to HMS *Daedalus,* the Royal Naval Air Station (RNAS) Lee-on-Solent, which was now the headquarters of the RN Fleet Air Arm, for a refresher flying course on the Hawker Osprey. On successful completion of this, he was appointed to 758 Naval Air Squadron (NAS) on 1 July 1939, the day that this unit was commissioned from a nucleus within 759 NAS under Lieutenant Commander W H G Saunt RN. The squadron also operated Blackburn Sharks and its role was training TAGs, a task that entailed giving them air experience while they operated their W/T sets and fired their rear guns at towed targets. It would have seemed mundane to Bill and he evidently pressed the Naval Secretary's Department for a more demanding, operational appointment. His service history notes that on 17 November 1939 he applied for what was termed 'special services' in Confidential Admiralty Fleet Order 2983/39. There was, however, a certain amount of 'sorting out' to be done after the Admiralty regained full control of what it now termed the Air Branch of the Royal Navy on 26 May 1939. Some new squadrons were formed only to be renumbered after a few weeks; 758 NAS had been one of them. Fortunately for Bill, however, RNAS Eastleigh, HMS *Raven*, became the RN Fleet Fighter School on 1 November with 759 NAS re-formed to act as its flying element, equipped with nine Blackburn Skuas, five Blackburn Rocs and four Gloster Sea Gladiators. On 14 January 1940 Lucy was selected to take command of 803 NAS, a fighter squadron that had converted from Ospreys to Skuas in December 1938. He carried out a conversion onto the Skua at Eastleigh and would have been given an introduction into the latest fighter tactics. A monoplane with a retractable undercarriage, four front guns rather than the Osprey's one and only a few months in operational service, the Skua represented a considerable advance over the Osprey, and Lucy would have thoroughly enjoyed finding out all he could about this new type before he joined 803 NAS. On 8 February 1940, Lieutenant W P Lucy RN took over command of 803 NAS from Lieutenant Commander D R F Cambell RN.[8] His time in command will be described in later chapters.

Chapter 4

Technology: Ships, Aircraft, Weapons and Tactics

Training Appointments

For much of the twentieth century the RN maintained designated units to run as training ships. They had reduced ships' companies and relied on the trainees to provide manpower for labour-intensive tasks. Those under training included officer cadets and boys who had joined the service straight from school but were not yet old enough to sign on as men. The cadets would have been given a variety of tasks throughout the ships' various departments to give them an understanding of what was required from their men in their future careers and some knowledge of life at sea. The ships were ideally placed to carry out visits to both UK and foreign ports to show the flag and to broaden the experience of the trainees. Not considered fully operational, the ships' systems were maintained in a serviceable condition and they could have been brought up to operational standard quickly with manpower from the home port drafting authorities and the Royal Fleet Reserve.

Marlborough in 1919; note the Sopwith 2F.1 Camels on 'B' and 'Q' turret ramps. (Author's collection)

HMS *Marlborough*

Used as a cadet training ship in 1927, *Marlborough* was the second ship of the *Iron Duke* class, completed in June 1914. She served as the flagship of the 2nd Battle Squadron of the Grand Fleet and fought at Jutland, where she was hit by a single torpedo but managed to remain in action for several hours. Repairs were completed by 29 July 1916. After the Great War, she transferred to the Mediterranean Fleet in 1919 until 1924 when she became a training ship in the Atlantic Fleet. After paying off in 1931 she was used for experiments in which internal explosions were used to evaluate bulkhead strength and as a target for aircraft bombs. She was scrapped in 1932.[1]

Length:	622 feet 9 inches overall
Beam:	90 feet 1 inch
Draught:	32 feet 9 inches at deep load
Displacement:	31,400 tons at deep load
Machinery:	4 shafts; 29,000SHP; 21 knots 18 Yarrow boilers
Fuel:	3,250 tons coal; 1,050 tons furnace fuel oil
Range:	8,100nm at 12 knots. Coal consumption at this speed was 135 tons per day but was over 500 tons at full power.
Complement:	1,180 in 1918
Armour:	Main belt 12 inches tapering to 8 inches. Bulkheads 6 inches to 4 inches
Armament:	10 x 13.5-inch Mark V guns with 100 rounds per gun; 12 x 6-inch Mark VII with 130 rounds per gun; various smaller.

HMS *Emerald*

This was an operational cruiser in which Bill Lucy served as a Midshipman. Officers below the rank of Lieutenant were accommodated in the gunroom, rather than the wardroom and midshipmen would have had an officer designated to supervise their training. This period marked the transition from the basic instruction in the training ship to the wider understudying of officers of all specialisations as they carried out their duties. Midshipmen were usually placed in charge of one of the ship's larger boats while the ship was in harbour, working with the experienced rating coxswain to run an often busy routine regulated by the officer of the watch. Time running a boat helped to teach both ship handling and man management skills that would be important later in their careers.

Emerald can be regarded as the ultimate expression of the wartime British light cruiser,[2] laid down in the last weeks of the Great War but not completed until

Emerald in China Station paint scheme with a white hull and buff funnels. (Author's collection)

January 1926. The main feature of the design was a requirement to achieve 32 knots in service, a figure she actually exceeded. By the time she was completed, however, her armament was already somewhat behind the latest technical developments with single, hand-loaded, 6-inch guns which fired a 110lb shell, considered to be the heaviest that could be loaded by hand. Her sister-ship *Enterprise* had the prototype twin 6-inch turret fitted forward, and a third ship, *Euphrates*, was cancelled and broken up on the slip at the end of the war. Later cruiser designs such as the *Leander* class evolved from her hull design. especially the pronounced 'knuckle' forward which deflected spray and increased bow lift in rough weather.[3] As completed she had a rotating aircraft platform amidships which could be turned into the relative wind to launch a lightweight, wheeled fighter such as a Fairey Flycatcher rather than a floatplane. There was no hangar and aircraft were not always embarked. When Bill Lucy served in her she was on the East Indies Station and was painted with the scheme used on that station, white hull and buff masts and funnels.[4]

Length:	570 feet
Beam:	54 feet 6 inches
Draught:	18 feet 6 inches
Displacement:	7,550 tons at deep load
Machinery:	4 shafts; 80,000SHP; 33 knots 8 Yarrow boilers

A typical Avro 504 training aircraft. Variants served with the RNAS, RFC and RAF for two decades in a number of roles. (Author's collection)

Fuel:	1,746 tons furnace fuel oil.
Range:	3,850nm at 20 knots
Complement:	572
Armour:	Full-length side belt, 2 inches tapering to 1 inch; 1 inch decks.
Armament:	7 x 6-inch with 250 rounds for forward facing guns, 215 rounds for others; 3 x 4-inch high angle with 200 rounds per gun; 4 x triple 21-inch torpedo tubes.

Avro 504N

The Avro 504 was a remarkable aircraft that remained in production from 1913 to 1932, by which time over 10,000 had been built. It was used by the RNAS for one of the earliest long-range strike operations in history against the Zeppelin factory at Friedrichshafen in November 1914 and for numerous other actions as both a bomber and as a fighter.[5] By 1918 the RNAS used the Avro 504K variant as a trainer and the type went on to become the standard RAF trainer until 1933. The Avro 504N was redesigned for the RAF with a more powerful engine replacing the original 80hp Gnome rotary; 598 examples of this version were produced. It was a safe and reliable aircraft on which to learn the basics of flying and every pilot of Bill Lucy's generation would have flown it at some stage of their training.

Length:	29 feet 5 inches
Wingspan:	36 feet
Height:	10 feet 5 inches
Maximum weight:	1,574lb
Engine:	1 x Armstrong Siddeley Lynx; 160hp
Fuel:	25.5 gallons avgas
Performance:	maximum speed 72 knots at sea level; service ceiling 13,000 feet
Endurance:	3 hours
Armament:	None fitted

Operational Appointments

HMS *Exeter*

Cruisers fulfilled a variety of functions in the Royal Navy during this period and the Admiralty consistently argued that seventy was the minimum number required to defend the sea lanes that held the British Empire together. They were expected to be capable of long-range independent operations, or cruising, in any of the world's oceans. The machinery that enabled them to do so had to be backed up by extensive workshops that allowed regular maintenance by their own ships' companies during long deployments away from a main base or dockyard. They had to be capable of destroying any smaller warship and outpacing a capital ship with

Exeter with a Fairey IIIF floatplane on the starboard catapult. (Author's collection)

its superior firepower. They had also to be capable of operating with a fleet and were used both to locate the enemy and to protect the battle fleet against attacks by torpedo craft and light cruisers. Cruisers spread on a screen ahead of the battle squadrons were known as the A–K line after the individual stations the ships were tasked to fill. In the 1920s carrier-borne aircraft began to augment the A–K line and in the 1930s to replace it.

The Washington Treaty imposed qualitative limits on cruisers, and the Admiralty anticipated, correctly, that the other signatories would build 'treaty cruisers' up to the full limit of 10,000 tons and 8-inch guns. The resulting British treaty cruisers were the seventeen ships of the County class, two of which were built for the RAN, designated as heavy cruisers to differentiate them from light cruisers armed with 6-inch guns. They proved to be expensive ships both to build and to operate and an attempt was made to produce more affordable, scaled-down versions which evolved into the *York* and *Exeter*, both of which had three rather than four 8-inch twin turrets. *Exeter* was built in Devonport Dockyard and completed in July 1931; she was, therefore, a new ship when Bill Lucy joined her and she was fitted with two EIIH catapults fixed at 45 degrees to port and starboard of the bow. Both would have had a Fairey IIIF secured on it with a large crane installed on the starboard side by the after funnel to recover aircraft from the water after landing and return them to the catapult. The same crane would have been used to lower the larger boats into the water and recover them. Hawker Ospreys replaced the IIIFs in 1933.

A seaman officer's duties on a cruiser would have included acting as the divisional officer for a number of men, taking charge of the armament at action stations either as captain of a turret or co-ordinating the anti-aircraft lookouts. On the bridge the officer of the watch would have been primarily concerned with the ship's navigation and station-keeping within the fleet or A–K line. Station-keeping was carried out visually using the Pelorus to take bearings of other ships and a Stewart & Lloyd distance meter to measure distance accurately. In action ships would be stationed at high speed as little as 1 cable, 200 yards, apart so that their gunfire could be co-ordinated onto an enemy. Both on the bridge at sea and on the quarterdeck in harbour the officer of the watch was the captain's representative responsible for running the ship's routine minute by minute. In harbour he would run the boat routine and look out for senior officers afloat in their barges and other warships, both of which must be saluted or have their salute returned promptly.

Exeter was to earn fame in December 1939 in the Battle of the River Plate when, together with the light cruisers *Ajax* and *Achilles*, she engaged the German 'pocket battleship' *Graf Spee* and forced her to seek shelter in Montevideo. She was sunk by the Japanese cruisers *Nachi* and *Haguro* together with the destroyer *Ikazuchi* during the Battle of the Java Sea on 1 March 1942.[6]

Length:	575 feet
Beam:	58 feet
Draught:	17 feet
Displacement:	10,500 tons at deep load
Machinery:	4 shafts; 80,000SHP; 32 knots 8 Admiralty 3-drum boilers
Fuel:	1,900 tons furnace fuel oil
Range:	10,000nm at 14 knots
Complement:	620
Armour:	3-inch main belt with 1-inch bulkheads; 1-inch deck.
Armament:	6 x 8-inch guns in 3 twin turrets; 4 x 4-inch high angle single mountings; 2 x triple 21-inch torpedo tubes.
Aircraft:	2 Fairey IIIF.

Hawker Nimrod – 802 Squadron

The Hawker Nimrod was a single-seat biplane fighter initially designed as a private venture by Hawker but the Air Ministry eventually wrote Air Ministry Specification 16/30 around it to clear the way for production.[7] The first prototype flew in 1930 and the first production example, S1578, in October 1931. Fifty-four Nimrod Mark Is were built. Like all aircraft intended for use with the Fleet Air Arm in this era, the Nimrod could be fitted with either a wheeled undercarriage or floats; the latter configuration reduced maximum speed by about 40 knots and the extra weight made it a more sluggish performer, not a good thing for an air-superiority fighter. Superficially they looked like the RAFs Hawker Fury single-seat fighter but the Nimrod was larger, had naval radios and sealed compartments in the wings and fuselage to give sufficient buoyancy for the pilot to get out if the aircraft ditched. The Nimrod was, thus, somewhat heavier than the Fury and had a slightly lower top speed. Nimrods were intended to engage enemy bombers as they attacked the fleet but were expected to remain within visual range of surface ships as there were concerns about the ability of the pilot to navigate back to his carrier without a homing beacon or observer to assist him.

Endurance, at just over an hour and a half, was modest for a carrier-borne aircraft and would have forced the parent carrier to turn into wind to launch and recover fighters at intervals of little more than an hour during intensive flying periods. The contemporary USN Grumman F2F-1 biplane fighter had an endurance of over four hours with the same armament, making it a much better carrier-borne aircraft. Unlike the RN, however, the USN could specify the aircraft it wanted and did not have to argue with Air Ministry officials over what could and could not be procured. The Nimrod's armament of two fixed Vickers machine guns firing through the propeller arc by means of an interrupter mechanism was no better

A Hawker Nimrod of 408 Flight embarked in *Glorious* during 1931. This aircraft was lost in 1932 when it went over the side after landing. The pilot, Lieutenant J P G Bryant RN was rescued unhurt. (Author's collection)

than the Sopwith F.1 Camel of 1918 and another conservative aspect of the design, insisted upon by the Air Ministry, was that both guns had to be mounted at the fuselage sides where the pilot could reach the breeches in order to re-cock them if they jammed. Overall, the Nimrod was slightly better aerodynamically shaped and faster than Great War fighters but hardly reflected the sort of dynamic progress that politicians expected from the independent air force which was still seen as the font of all aviation knowledge and the expert body to which all questions of air warfare had to be addressed.

The Nimrod Mark I had no arrester hook and relied on friction and the aircraft brakes to stop it after landing on deck. The technique used in *Glorious* when Lucy joined 802 Squadron in September 1933 involved the deck being cleared for every landing. Once the affirmative signal was given, pilots left their orbiting position around the ship one at a time and carried out an approach with no form of control or advice from the ship. Individual pilots evolved their own techniques and sought to land at the after part of the deck, from where they had space to stop the aircraft just aft of the forward lift. Once it had slowed to a walking pace, handlers would run in from the island and catwalks to grab the aircraft and hold it on deck. Once under control it was pushed onto the forward lift and struck down into the hangar to clear the deck for the next landing; both lifts were cruciform in shape so that aircraft could go down with their wings spread to save time. They were then folded

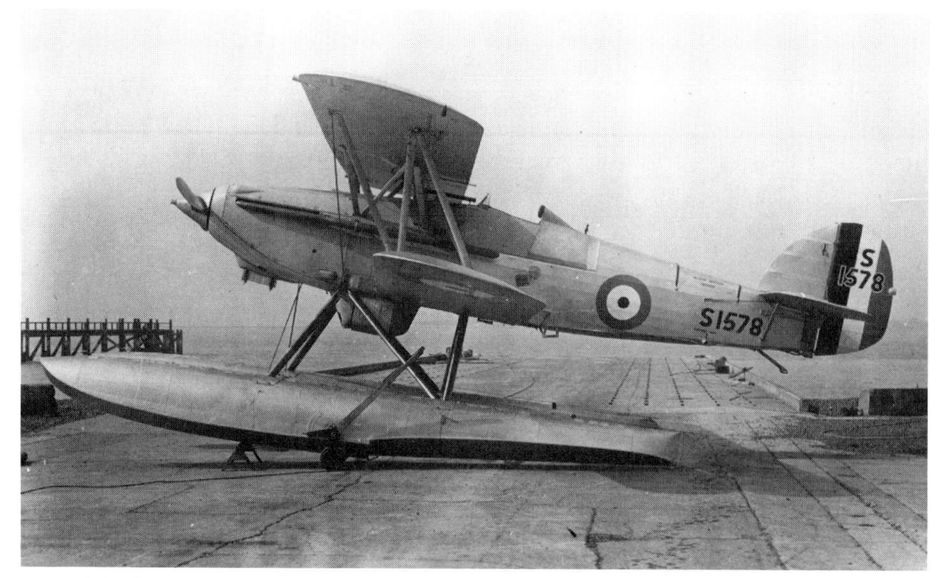

One of the first production batch of eleven Hawker Nimrods seen fitted with floats for trials at the MAEE Felixstowe in 1932. (Author's collection)

as the aircraft was wheeled aft into its parking slot in the hangar and the lift raised to flight-deck level. Only when it was up and locked in place could the next aircraft land on, thus there was a gap of up to four minutes between landings, which limited the number of aircraft that could be landed on in one group. The handling parties comprised RAF mechanics and seamen allocated to the air department for handling duties. The latter clearly improved with practice and it was obviously better to keep those who did well working with the flight-deck party rather than allocate seamen on a day-to-day basis. These men were the origin of today's RN Aircraft Handler Branch. The Nimrod did not have folding wings because it fitted the lifts in *Glorious* and *Courageous* and the hangars were sufficiently large to stow it with relative ease.

Mark 1 Nimrods replaced Fairey Flycatchers in 402, 408 and 409 Flights during 1932 and during Bill Lucy's time in 802 Squadron would have been considered as new, high-performance fighters. There is no surviving record of the number of hours he flew on Nimrods and Ospreys during his time in the squadron but it would have been typical of the period to fly both types frequently. His accident at Hal Far in a Fairey IIIF shows how pilots were expected to be able to handle a variety of aircraft types concurrently. Some pilots found it difficult to fly with a second crew member, especially an observer who would frequently tell them what to do, but Bill Lucy's subsequent specialisation on the Osprey may indicate that he was found to be a considerate pilot who got on well with observers and worked with them to achieve the aircraft's full potential.

The Nimrod Mark II was introduced in 1935 and had an arrester hook to take advantage of the wires being fitted in all contemporary carriers. Mark IIs were also fitted with a more powerful version of the Rolls-Royce Kestrel engine which gave a modest increase in performance. Nimrod Mark IIs remained in front-line service with 802 Squadron until May 1939, when the Admiralty resumed control of naval aviation. A few remained in service with 759 NAS at the Fleet Fighter School at RNAS Eastleigh after the outbreak of war.

Length:	27 feet 11.75 inches
Wingspan:	33 feet 6.25 inches
Height:	9 feet 9 inches
Maximum weight:	4,258lb
Engine:	1 x 525hp Rolls-Royce Kestrel IIs
Fuel:	64 gallons
Performance:	Maximum speed 160 knots at 13,000 feet; service ceiling 26,000 feet
Endurance:	1 hour 40 minutes at 10,000 feet

Hawker Osprey – 802, 803 and 712 Squadrons

The Osprey evolved from a Hawker private venture intended to meet a 1926 Admiralty request for a high-performance fleet spotter and reconnaissance aircraft that would also be capable of acting as an interceptor fighter. The Air Ministry wrote Specification 19/30 around the design and a prototype was built which was embarked in *Eagle* for the British Empire Trade Exhibition in Buenos Aires during 1931. Production Ospreys began to join the Fleet Air Arm in 1932, replacing Flycatchers; 802 Squadron in *Glorious* included three Ospreys that had been issued to 409 Flight early in 1933, shortly before it joined with 408 Flight to form the new unit. The Osprey was, therefore, a new aircraft when Bill Lucy joined 802 in September 1933 and the squadron would still have been evaluating its full capabilities. It was effectively the first in a series of fast, two-seater fighter designs that were unique to the RN; later designs included the Fairey Fulmar and Fairey Firefly, the latter remaining in service until the mid-1950s.

Like all contemporary naval aircraft, the Osprey could be fitted with floats as an alternative to the wheeled undercarriages used on aircraft carriers and at airfields ashore. With floats fitted, the maximum speed of the Osprey Mark I was reduced by about 20 knots. Mark I and II Ospreys differed in the type of float that could be fitted and a Mark III variant was produced from late 1933 which differed in having a survival dinghy stowed in the starboard upper wing, an engine-driven generator

A Hawker Osprey landing on *Eagle*. Note the pilot's good view of the deck in the landing attitude. This photograph was taken before the ship was fitted with arrester wires and the aircraft has no hook. (Philip Jarrett collection)

and a Fairey-Reed fixed-pitch, two-bladed metal airscrew.[8] A Mark IV variant was produced from 1935 which featured an up-rated Kestrel engine which gave slightly improved performance.

The Osprey was built in relatively modest numbers and total production amounted to forty-three Mark I/IIs, sixty-eight Mark IIIs and twenty-six Mark IVs. Six of the Mark IIIs had stainless steel rather than aluminium fuselage structures to evaluate the former's more corrosion-resistant properties in the salt-laden sea atmosphere in which naval aircraft had to operate.[9] During Bill Lucy's time in 802 Squadron it operated a mix of Mark Is and IIIs which were coded 548, 549 and 560. 803 Squadron Ospreys were side coded 285, 286, 287, 289, 290, 291, 293, 294 and 295. Ospreys began to be withdrawn from front-line service in 1938 but continued in use with training squadrons ashore until 1940 when the type was declared obsolete.

Length:	29 feet 4 inches; 31 feet 10 inches as a seaplane.
Wingspan:	37 feet; 15 feet 7.25 inches folded.
Height:	10 feet 5 inches; 12 feet 5 inches as a seaplane.
Maximum weight:	4,950lb; 5,570lb as a seaplane.
Engine:	1 x 630hp Rolls-Royce Kestrel II MS
Fuel:	90 gallons avgas
Performance:	Maximum speed 147 knots; 128 knots as a seaplane. Maximum height 23,500 feet; 20,700 feet as a seaplane.

Endurance: 2.25 hours
Armament: 1 x fixed forward-firing Vickers 0.303 machine gun; 1 x Lewis 0.303 machine gun of rear cockpit mounting with 6 x 97-round drum magazines in rear cockpit; 8 x 20lb or 2 x 112lb bombs could be carried on underwing racks for light strike operations.

HMS *Glorious*

Glorious was originally completed as a large light cruiser armed with two twin 15-inch gun turrets. The Admiralty took the decision in 1920 to convert her into a flush-deck aircraft carrier together with her sister-ship *Courageous*. She was stripped down to the upper deck in Rosyth Dockyard and then towed to Devonport Dockyard to be reconstructed to a design by J H Narbeth.[10] She had a starboard side island and funnel arrangement which proved more efficient than the flush-deck arrangement in *Argus* and *Furious* and a double hangar arrangement intended to allow the maximum number of aircraft to be stowed in what was a relatively small hull. She had the same cruciform lifts as *Eagle* and *Hermes*, intended to allow aircraft to be struck down into the hangar after landing with their wings still spread. Both ships had a small flying off deck over the forecastle with doors

Glorious photographed at anchor outside the breakwater in Plymouth Sound during 1935. Note the conning deck extended across the flight deck to give the captain and navigating officer a view over the ship's port side in pilotage waters. The hangar door at the after end of the short flying-off deck which led into the upper hangar is open. (Author's collection)

opening onto it from the forward end of the upper hangar so that fighters could be launched quickly, even if the main flight deck was blocked by a range of aircraft that could not be launched quickly.

Doors opened onto the quarterdeck from the after end of the lower hangar through which seaplanes could be moved to be lowered into the water by cranes which stowed flush with the hangar bulkhead when not in use. The gun armament was intended mainly for anti-aircraft use in barrage fire with four directors, two on each beam below flight-deck level. The workshop arrangements were the most comprehensive yet fitted in a British carrier and the air group of forty-eight aircraft was a significant advance over earlier ships. In January 1932 she took part in exercises as part of a multiple carrier group directed by Admiral Henderson, Rear Admiral Aircraft Carriers, whose thinking was, in some ways, ahead of that in the US Navy at this time.

When Bill Lucy joined 802 Squadron in *Glorious* in 1933 she would have been painted in the Mediterranean Fleet light grey and her aircraft had just been reorganised into squadrons from the earlier flights and now comprised 802 with Hawker Nimrods and Ospreys; 812 with Blackburn Ripon torpedo strike aircraft and both 823 and 825 with Fairey IIIF spotter/reconnaissance aircraft with twelve aircraft in each squadron. Aircraft could be launched using the two hydraulic catapults fitted at the forward edge of the flight deck but free take-off was the normal method. With no arrester wires, all landings were made onto a clear deck. On 11 March 1934, shortly before Lucy left *Glorious*, storm force waves smashed through the door from the lower flight deck into the upper hangar and destroyed six aircraft. The ship returned to the UK from the Mediterranean and began a refit in Devonport Dockyard in May. During this refit, arrester wires were fitted on the flight deck, the upper hangar doors were welded shut and the flight deck round-down was extended aft, supported by a unique 'W'-shaped support structure.

Length:	786 feet 6 inches
Beam:	110 feet
Draught:	28 feet
Displacement:	27,560 tons at deep load
Machinery:	4 shaft; 90,670SHP; 30 knots 18 Yarrow boilers; Parsons geared turbines
Fuel:	3,685 tons furnace fuel oil
Range:	2,920nm at 24 knots
Complement:	1,260
Armour:	3-inch side belts; 3-inch forward and 2-inch aft bulkheads; 1.75 inches over machinery and steering gear.
Armament:	12 x single 4.7-inch QF Mark VIII HA.

Courageous anchored inside the breakwater in Plymouth Sound. The Fairey Flycatcher was the last fighter able to use the short flying-off deck and the doors onto it from the upper hangar were eventually welded shut. (Author's collection)

HMS *Courageous*

When Bill Lucy joined *Courageous* with 802 Squadron the biggest difference he would have found from her sister-ship was the prototype arrester gear which had been fitted during her 1930/31 refit. By May 1934 new deck landing techniques would have been established by her senior air officers that would have used the arrester wires to best advantage although the lack of a barrier forward of the wires would have precluded the use of a deck park and the deck still had to be clear for every landing. While Bill served in *Courageous* she would have been painted in Home Fleet dark grey.[11] Data for *Courageous* would have been similar to that of *Glorious* listed above except that she had sixteen rather than twelve 4.7-inch guns. The aircraft operating data below[12] applied to both ships after *Glorious* had been fitted with arrester wires.

Flight deck:	530 feet x 91 feet 6 inches
Hangars:	Upper 550 feet long, 50 feet wide, 16 feet high
	Lower 550 feet long, 50 feet wide, 16 feet high
Catapults:	2 hydraulic capable of launching a 10,000lb aircraft at 52 knots end speed relative to the deck
Arrester wires:	4 capable of arresting aircraft up to 11,000lb at 53 knots relative to the deck

Lifts:	Forward 46 feet by 47 feet cruciform Aft 46 feet by 47 feet cruciform
Aircraft:	48 – all could be stowed in the hangars
Aircraft fuel:	35,700 gallons avgas
Air weapons:	18-inch torpedoes; 500lb bombs; 250lb bombs; 100lb bombs; 20lb bombs; 0.303-inch machine gun ammunition; flares and pyrotechnics.

Supermarine Walrus

Designed by R J Mitchell who later achieved fame as the creator of the Spitfire, the Walrus was another aircraft type that began as a private venture. It was first ordered by the Australian government for operation by RAAF Flights embarked in RAN cruisers and given the name Seagull V. Test flying, including an embarkation in the battleship *Nelson*, was carried out in the UK and the trials officer, Lieutenant Caspar John RN, spoke highly of the aircraft's capability. Admiralty interest, therefore, led to an order for twelve being placed in 1935 and a further 204 during the re-armament programme which began in 1936 The name Walrus was given to aircraft operated by the RN but the Australians retained the name Seagull. Further orders followed and after 287 had been built, production was transferred to Saunders-Roe ('Saro') so that Supermarine could concentrate on Spitfire production. Saro-built Walrus differed in being made of wood rather than aluminium.

The Pegasus engine was mounted between the wings as a pusher with the propeller aft. This allowed the TAG or observer to climb up onto the upper wing to attach a sling so that the aircraft could be hoisted inboard from the sea without the fear of having to pass close to the propeller; just one ingenious feature of what was a very practical design. With its long endurance, enclosed crew space and boat hull, the Walrus was well-liked by its crews who nicknamed it the 'Shagbat'. It replaced Ospreys in battleships and cruisers fitted with heavy catapults (cruisers with light catapults operated the smaller Fairey Seafox). The Walrus had several idiosyncrasies, one of the most notable being the pilot's control column. It was designed to be flown by a single pilot whose seat was to the left of the cockpit, the observer and TAG sat behind him inside the fuselage. There was no dual control trainer but a canvas seat could be lowered for a second pilot to the right of the normal pilot's seat; control could be handed over by turning the pilot's column through 90 degrees to the left and lifting it out of its slot. It could then be passed to the right-hand seat occupant, who slotted into his own position, turned it 90 degrees to the right and assumed control of the aircraft. Many stories, most probably apocryphal, tell of accidents while passing the column back and forth between pilots.

The normal method of launch at sea was by catapult and Bill Lucy would have undergone catapult training ashore before embarking with his Walrus flight.

Birmingham's Supermarine Walrus, L2212, taxiing under the ship's crane jib for recovery in 1938. Note the TAG sitting on the upper wing ready to hook the aircraft on; access for aircrew to get onto the wing safely was the reason for placing the airscrew aft of the wing in the aircraft's clever design. (Author's collection)

Alternatively, the aircraft could be lowered onto the water for take-off but this option would be limited by the sea state, especially in windy or choppy conditions. Landings had to be made onto the water and the rugged Walrus could set down in waves of up to 6 feet if necessary but there were procedures for the recovery ship to provide a relatively calm patch of water for the landing (these were described in detail in my earlier book, *A Century of Carrier Aviation*).[13] The Walrus also had a retractable, wheeled undercarriage which made it possible for them to land on aircraft carriers and at airfields ashore although the lack of an arrester hook meant that they relied on brakes to come to a standstill on the former and, thus, required a big area of deck to be free of parked aircraft.

With its robust construction and an endurance of five hours, the Walrus proved to be an ideal spotter reconnaissance aircraft for operation from battleships and cruisers, some of which had as many as four embarked. In the desperate early years of the Second World War it was to be used with success in a number of roles that Mitchell would never have considered likely, ranging from VIP transport and maritime patrol aircraft to dive-bombing and strafing enemy ground forces when no other British aircraft were available. By 1940, all catapult flights were centralised into 700 NAS which then had forty-two Walrus on its strength, a number that increased as more ships were completed.

Length:	37 feet 3 inches
Wingspan:	45 feet 10 inches; 17 feet 11 inches folded.
Height:	15 feet 3 inches
Maximum weight:	7,200lb
Engine:	1 x 775hp Bristol Pegasus II
Fuel:	150 gallons avgas
Performance:	Maximum speed 118 knots; ceiling 18,500 feet.
Endurance:	5 hours at cruising speed
Armament:	2 x Lewis or Vickers K machine guns; 2 x 250lb bombs or 2 x Mark VII depth charges on underwing racks.[14]

HMS *Cornwall*

Cornwall was built in Devonport Dockyard as one of the Royal Navy's first group of five treaty cruisers which together with the two RAN ships could be distinguished from later units of the County class by their prominent external bulges.[15] Prior

Cornwall photographed with the starboard hangar roller door partially open and both aircraft crane jibs raised. (Author's collection)

to her 1936/37 refit she operated a Hawker Osprey while serving with the 5th Cruiser Squadron on the China Station. After the refit she had improved aviation arrangements, including a hangar and a more powerful athwartships catapult that enabled her to operate the more capable Supermarine Walrus. Other work carried out in her refit included the fitting of a 5-inch armoured belt inboard of the bulges and improved close-range anti-aircraft weapons. After the outbreak of war she served in the South Atlantic and East Indies Stations and was sunk by Japanese naval aircraft south-west of Ceylon in April 1942.

The class's high freeboard allowed the Counties to have unusually high deck heads at 8 feet but gave them a rather stiff roll. They sacrificed armour for speed and although they looked impressive on foreign stations, it had to be accepted that building up to the full treaty limits had resulted in ships that were too big and expensive, hence the reversion to light cruisers armed with 6-inch guns in the 1930s. However, with accommodation that was considered spacious at the time, excellent steaming qualities and general seaworthiness, they proved to be popular ships.

Length:	630 feet overall
Beam:	68 feet 3 inches
Draught:	16 feet 3 inches
Displacement:	13,450 tons at deep load
Machinery:	4 shaft; 80,000SHP; 31.5 knots 8 x Admiralty 3-drum boilers
Fuel:	3,400 tons furnace fuel oil
Range:	13,300nm at 12 knots
Complement:	700
Armour:	5-inch belt; 1-inch deck over machinery; 1-inch bulkheads; further armour around magazines and steering gear.
Armament:	8 x 8-inch in twin turrets; 8 x 4-inch in twin mountings (originally 4 singles prior to 1936); 2 quadruple 2pdr pom-pom; 8 x 21-inch torpedo tubes – removed in 1936.
Aircraft:	Originally 1; up to 3 after 1937.

Chapter 5

Doctrine, Operations and Exercises

In the years that immediately followed the Armistice in 1918 it would be fair to say that aircraft carrier operations were largely experimental; until 1922 *Argus* was the only aircraft carrier in the world and learning the best way to operate aircraft from her took time. Deluded politicians, especially Lord Weir, assumed that the RAF would not only co-operate with the RN but would provide advice about all air matters; this proved not to be the case. Senior ex-naval RAF officers were not even permitted to speak directly to their RN opposite numbers to discuss issues of co-operation. How then could they hope to keep abreast of naval developments in an era of considerable technological change as the lessons of the Great War were absorbed? The Air Ministry could never admit that the RAF's primary role was the provision of air support to the Navy and Army because if it did so it could not justify its separate existence. Instead, it chose to concentrate on strategic bombing based on the speculative theory that all future wars would be fought by independent air operations. It also claimed that effective air defence against the bombers would be impossible.[1] It must also be understood that the effective development of naval aviation by the RNAS during the Great War had included both shore- and ship-based aircraft working together as part of a single sea service. The air arms of the US Navy and Imperial Japanese Navy (IJN) continued to be so to their great advantage as they developed the technology and tactics they would use to fight the next world war. The UK was unique in having such maritime patrol aircraft as it possessed allocated to the independent RAF with its separate command and communications structure.

The Evolution of Doctrine

In the 1920s and 1930s the RN concentrated on the problem of fighting a fleet action against a near-peer opponent. For most of the period Japan was seen as the most likely enemy although by the late 1930s both Italy and Germany had begun to pose a threat and re-armament from 1936 had to take into account the worst-case possibility of having to fight all three together. The RN fully understood that carrier-borne aircraft operating with the battle fleet gave it two important advantages:[2] reconnaissance aircraft could locate the enemy fleet before it came into contact with any surface ship and then shadow it, releasing the cruisers of the A–K line for other attack and defensive priorities. Once the enemy fleet's position

800 NAS Hawker Nimrods from *Courageous* in 1937; K2826, side number 106, is nearest the camera. Both the fuselage band and the diamond patterns on the upper wing were blue, the former indicating the parent carrier. (Author's collection)

was fixed, strike aircraft could attack it considerably beyond gun range and the RN believed that its aircraft provided the only means of slowing the enemy or of preventing its escape from the superior gunnery of the British battle fleet. The phrase 'Find, fix and strike', came into use in the mid-1920s to describe the Fleet Air Arm's role and the key to success was accurate navigation over the featureless sea. The annual RN report on tactical progress was pleased to note in 1930 that air reconnaissance had been carried out as far as 164nm from the parent carrier. In 1929 the furthest achieved had been 135nm. Because the fleet commander had no control over shore-based RAF aircraft, both conventional aircraft and flying boats, he had to rely on his own carrier-borne aircraft for all reconnaissance missions but this was not the case in the American and Japanese Navies, however, both of which operated a wider range of aircraft under naval control. The USN used very long-range flying boats for open ocean reconnaissance[3] but the IJN used specialised reconnaissance floatplanes which were embarked in considerable numbers in cruisers for the purpose. Both the American and Japanese navies, therefore, used

Blackburn Dart torpedo-bombers of 810 NAS embarked in *Courageous* during 1933. The aircraft in the left foreground is N9541, side number 07, and that on the right is N9622, side number 09. Their fuselage bands were coloured blue to indicate their parent carrier. (Author's collection)

non-carrier aircraft to find and fix the enemy which then sent a constant stream of data to other naval assets including both carrier-borne and shore-based aircraft to enable them to launch the largest possible strike. The RN differed in having no control over shore-based aircraft; it could use its own cruiser-borne aircraft but these were only available in small numbers. British carriers were smaller than their contemporaries and in consequence they had smaller air groups. Even then the Admiralty had to fight the Air Ministry for every aircraft embarked and the Air Ministry refused to agree to the allocation of aircraft for deck parks to expand the size of the air groups in the newly converted *Courageous* and *Glorious*. The result of all this was that British carrier air groups had to provide aircraft to search for the enemy fleet and to shadow it when it was located, limiting the number of aircraft available for a strike. That is why the multi-role torpedo-strike-reconnaissance (TSR) Fairey Swordfish was so important from 1936 onwards since it displaced single-role reconnaissance aircraft such as the Fairey IIIF from the air group and made every aircraft a potential strike aircraft.

Because numbers were so limited, searches had to be flown by single aircraft and if they could not locate their parent carrier at the end of a four-hour sortie the air group would lose a valuable aircraft and an even more valuable crew. For this reason the Admiralty placed great emphasis on the development of the Type 72 aircraft homing beacon in the 1930s. Its use ran counter to the long-held view that fleets should operate without making any transmissions to avoid detection by enemy radio-location devices. It was decided, however, that if aircraft really could find, fix and strike, the risk was worth it. As a measure of the standards required from the carrier's air reconnaissance in 1930, observers were required to fix an enemy force's position accurately to within 6nm after one hour on patrol. This required the observer to find accurate winds frequently and to plot his position, course and speed made good through the air with unprecedented accuracy, something no RAF navigator was required to do. To their very great credit, RN observers proved able to do so and even single-seat pilots became adept at studying the surface of the sea and maintaining a mental plot of their position.

The pernicious impact of Air Ministry policy had another effect on reconnaissance and strike against surface ships. The Admiralty wanted long-range fighters both to escort strike aircraft and to remain over the British fleet in action to prevent enemy reconnaissance and strike aircraft from reaching it. However, the Air Ministry had convinced politicians that it needed to concentrate on its bomber force because air defences against it would not be practical; it could hardly, therefore, agree with the Admiralty that carrier-borne fighters would provide a good defence against enemy bombers attacking the fleet. For this reason, British fighter designs concentrated on what the RAF thought necessary and anyone else's ideas were rejected as unnecessary. Designers concentrated on pedestrian RAF fighter specifications until the mid-1930s, when, in frustration, they produced private ventures such as the Supermarine Spitfire. The tragedy of this blinkered British approach was that long-ranging escort fighters such as the North American P-51 Mustang which had a major impact on the war had to be designed in the USA.

The Air Ministry's dominant approach had another negative impact on naval aviation since it became accepted British government doctrine from 1924 that carrier-borne aircraft would not strike at enemy targets on land. Thus British carrier-borne aircraft, unlike their American and Japanese contemporaries, were specifically not required to engage land-based enemy fighters because Air Ministry experts said they would never need to and politicians believed them, despite the absence of any supporting logic or evidence. Exercises in the 1930s seemed to show that carrier-borne aircraft of even modest performance could achieve success in attacking ships in the open sea if they were caught unawares by an approach using cloud cover. The Air Ministry view on the procurement of new aircraft was that since they were unlikely to encounter high-performance, shore-based enemy aircraft, maximum performance was less important than other characteristics such as a low take-off and landing speed on a carrier. Put simply, this was the wrong approach and was at variance with American and Japanese thinking; both of these navies realised that they would have to fight whatever aircraft they came up against when necessary. Given Air Ministry specifications for naval aircraft that emphasised low-speed handling over maximum performance, these were what the designers produced and the Admiralty should have argued against the basic premise that RN aircraft would never have to fight over or near the land. This policy was to have a significant effect on British operations in 1940, especially during the Norwegian campaign.

Eagle photographed with the eastern shore of Gibraltar in the background. Both her lifts are down; note the cruciform shape of the forward lift which allowed aircraft to be struck down into the hangar quickly with their wings still spread, expediting recovery in the pre-arrester wire/barrier era. The photograph was taken before 1936, when the ship was fitted with arrester wires. (Author's collection)

The government and Air Ministry's failure to appreciate the importance of naval aviation made things difficult for the aircraft industry and we can look back now and see that, had greater importance been given to the design of aircraft for the RN, aircraft designers would have been afforded greater scope and incentive. This would have had the effect of accelerating general progress instead of locking fighters into the short-range interceptor template favoured by the RAF. Between the wars the British carrier force never had more than sixty fighters embarked in five ships at any one time and it is hardly surprising that any new requirement was unattractive to manufacturers since the design cost could not have been amortised over a relatively large production run.[4] What could be done by a nation that laid greater emphasis on naval power was demonstrated by Japan, which built very long-range land-based strike aircraft such as the G3M to work with the fleet and the superb Mitsubishi Zero-Sen carrier-borne fighter which proved to be more than a match for any Allied fighter in 1941/42.

The RAF's Coastal Command suffered similar doctrinal limitations because its flying boats practised that service's own concept of anti-surface vessel operations and paid insufficient attention to long-endurance scouting in support of task forces at sea. The Air Ministry's paranoia about losing control of its assets led to unfortunate communications delays as flag officers sought to gather situational awareness about fast-moving naval operations. An RAF flying boat that sighted what it believed to be an enemy force at sea had to encode its report and then transmit it to its own Group Headquarters. If that Group thought the message important it would pass it to the Admiralty by land line and the message, by then potentially some hours old, would be passed to the commander of the fleet at sea. These dogmatic concepts paid little regard to practicality or the way in which other navies, especially the USN, did things. The Admiralty should have done more to challenge them but always faced the difficulty of having to fight the entrenched opinions of politicians such as Weir who, despite the evidence, still considered the RAF to be expert in all matters to do with aviation.

In 1931 the Admiralty appointed Rear Admiral Reginald Henderson as the first Rear Admiral Aircraft Carriers. The Air Ministry objected to the appointment, disingenuously stating that senior RAF officers could provide any necessary input although it had actually banned its senior officers from communicating directly with the Navy. Henderson was a forceful personality who was not qualified as a pilot but had commanded the aircraft carrier *Furious* and believed strongly that the RN needed a powerful Fleet Air Arm. He became Third Sea Lord and Controller in 1934 and was to be responsible for driving forward the armoured carrier design in the shortest time frame but died of over-work whilst still 3SL in 1939. Henderson organised a series of exercises intended to evaluate multi-carrier operations and find the best way of carrying out reconnaissance, denying enemy reconnaissance, shadowing and the conduct of air operations during a major battle between fleets. These were the 'known unknowns', but even with Henderson's forceful imagination there were 'unknown unknowns' that could not, easily, be resolved even if they had been revealed in exercises. Prominent among the latter was the fatal lack of provision of air cover for a British expeditionary force deployed onto a hostile shore from the sea. As we saw above, the RN was not allowed to carry out air operations over land and political oversight failed to detect the fact that the Air Ministry had failed to make any but the most vague preparations for such an eventuality. The Norwegian campaign in 1940 was to reveal the unreality of British defence planning.

One key factor that did emerge from Henderson's evaluations was the need for adequate reserves to replace front-line aircrew who became early losses. At the time the RN was struggling to find the numbers it needed to train in order to provide 70 per cent of the pilots in front-line squadrons and could not provide casualty replacements. The Air Ministry rejected a number of initiatives, especially the training of rating pilots, and claimed that if necessary it could provide pilots from its own reserves but failed to explain how they could fit quickly into a naval environment. Eventually the Admiralty did manage to increase numbers with a short-service commission scheme, the training of some RNVR (Air) officers and a rating pilot scheme that achieved only limited success. The numbers achieved were still completely inadequate in 1940.

Some of the 'unknown unknowns' that were not appreciated by Henderson's evaluations were a consequence of what Norman Friedman referred to as 'mirror imaging',[5] in other words assuming that a potential enemy would think or act in the way that the RN would. In 1938 the Admiralty intelligence publication CB 1815 which listed world naval vessels and naval aircraft listed the IJN G3M 'Nell' as a coastal reconnaissance bomber with a range of 723nm and stated that it would be used for 'defence against sea-borne attack … and to locate and destroy enemy carriers that may have escaped her main fleet'. In fact the G3M was a torpedo bomber with a maximum range of 2,365nm and was intended to strike at, and reduce the size of, an approaching enemy fleet before it had been brought to action. The later G4M 'Betty' had an even greater range of 3,256nm with the same torpedo armament. The Japanese concept for these aircraft was to compensate for the limited number of capital ships they were allowed under the Washington Treaty and, in the event of war between America and Japan, to wear down the US battle fleet as it made its way across the Pacific. Such a plan was completely alien to the Air Ministry and its supporters in the British government and caused shock when these Japanese naval aircraft sank the *Prince of Wales* and *Repulse* off Malaya on 10 December 1941.

The Admiralty policy that all naval aircraft should be operable from battleship and cruiser catapults as well as aircraft carriers with either wheeled or float-fitted undercarriages set limits on aircraft weight and both launch and recovery speeds. These were relatively undemanding in the early 1920s but by 1935 they made a considerable difference as monoplanes with high wing-loadings and powerful engines were introduced. In 1932 a fleet exercise proved that a single carrier could not provide sufficient numbers from the two flights of spotter/reconnaissance (SR) aircraft embarked as standard. More were needed but the Air Ministry would not accede to greater numbers of aircraft for the Fleet Air Arm to be embarked as a deck park. This was one of the drivers for procuring the Fairey Swordfish TSR, able to swing between the three roles at short notice or even in the same sortie. The requirement for low landing and take-off speeds, however, meant that the aircraft had to be a biplane to meet a specification in which high performance was given no very great priority. Although more powerful engines and advanced monoplane aircraft began to appear in the late 1930s the limitations placed on naval aircraft made it impossible for the RN to benefit from them until the restrictions were rescinded and carrier operating methods changed after the outbreak of war. Here it should be pointed out that the Air Ministry did not set out to fob off the Admiralty with second-rate aircraft. Surviving records show beyond doubt that air technical departments were always willing to review proposed naval aircraft specifications. The problem was that they had no knowledge of naval warfare or the part that particular aircraft were expected to play in it. Thus they could not comment on the

Three running Fairey Flycatchers ranged on the centreline of their carrier about to be launched. The men on the wing tips were there to help the pilot keep straight before he rolled forward to take off. Note the complete mixture of RN and RAF personnel typical of the period. (Author's collection)

larger consequences of proposed specifications. What was required was a direct loop between the operators, the procurement agency and the manufacturer; this happened in the USA and Japan but not in the UK.

Fleet doctrine sometimes had a significant impact on flying operations, and radio silence was a good example. During the First World War the RN had made extensive use of radio location and signals intelligence to find out where the German fleet was and what it was doing. Fears that a potential enemy might use similar techniques led the RN to practise stringent radio silence at sea. This made navigation over the sea difficult as aircrew were unable, routinely, to ask for a homing bearing to their carrier and, as we have already seen, led to the Type 72 homing beacon only being considered usable in extreme situations to save a valuable aircraft. A consequence of the need for accurate navigation over the sea was the RN preference for multi-seat aircraft with a specialist observer in addition to the pilot. In 1930 the Fleet Air Arm operated a mixture of long-endurance SR, single-seat torpedo bombers (TBs) and short-endurance single-seat fighters. The TBs were single-seat because contemporary engines lacked the power to lift a half-ton torpedo, fuel for a reasonable strike radius and a second crew member. They were expected to be led to their target by SR aircraft which lacked performance because of their heavy fuel load and three-man crew of pilot, observer and TAG.

By the 1930s the USN had demonstrated conclusively that the best way to hit a fast, manoeuvring warship was by dive-bombing, effectively pointing straight at the target in a steep or even vertical dive. An additional benefit of this form of attack was that the rapid change of height made the dive-bomber an extremely difficult target for guns to engage and not an easy one for fighters once it was established in the dive. The RN 'discovered' the technique in 1931 when Lieutenant Commander St J Prentice RN visited the United States and immediately saw its value.[6] The Admiralty agreed and sought to add value to this method of attack by procuring specialised weapons, a dive-bombing sight and by combining dive-bombing with a torpedo attack to distract the enemy's attention. This was a method that worked to the USN dive-bombers' advantage during the Battle of Midway in 1942 although, it has to be admitted, not to that of the torpedo aircraft. The specialised weapon was the 'B' bomb, effectively a 500lb bomb in a buoyant casing intended to be dropped into the sea short of the target ship but with sufficient forward momentum to detonate close under its keel and break its back. Its successful use would require the attacking aircraft to use a specialised sight to get the aiming point short of the ship just right but the Air Ministry came up with every excuse it could think of to avoid designing it: its design staff were too busy, it was technically not feasible and the Ministry's opinion that dive-bombing was of little or no value. This last statement was staggeringly wide of the truth but, as with all matters aeronautical, no one in government seemed to notice or care. The effectiveness of Luftwaffe Ju 87 dive-bombers in defeating the British Expeditionary Force in France in 1940 needs no further comment.

A Fairey IIIF landing on *Furious*. Note that the after hull is painted black to hide staining from the aft-vented funnel gases. The streamer on the photographer's aircraft indicates that it is flown by the unit CO or a flight commander. (Author's collection)

A realistic series of bombing trials were begun against the radio-controlled target battleship *Centurion* in 1933 and these found that if the ship steered a steady course, roughly 15 per cent of bombs dropped were likely to hit. However, if the ship was manoeuvring, that figure fell and it was calculated from trial observations that it would take eleven bombs dropped by dive-bombers or thirty dropped by high-level bombers to obtain a single hit on a cruiser-sized target. On the other hand, a torpedo bomber was very likely to score a hit if a well-trained pilot could get within 1,250 yards of a target without being too fine on the bow and he could estimate the speed accurately – something torpedo pilots were trained to do. This tactical superiority explains the priority given to the Fairey Swordfish in carrier air groups from 1939.

Exercises in 1933 had demonstrated that fighters could be held on deck to make the best use of the limited numbers available and the ship's modest avgas supply until enemy bombers were sighted visually by lookouts. Fighters would then be ordered into the air and controlled onto the bombers by a specified directing officer. On average lookouts in the task force were able to give the carrier fifteen minutes' warning of the approach of enemy aircraft; just enough time for a deck-launched interception to be carried out. As bomber speeds increased, deck-launched interception ceased to be practical as there was insufficient warning time before the advent of radar to get fighters into an attacking position before the enemy released his weapons. The possibility of keeping fighters airborne on combat air patrols (CAPs) was ruled out by the lack of fighter numbers and the limited quantity of avgas available. The RN elected to build armoured carriers with heavy defensive gun batteries and largely ruled out the possibility of using high-performance fighters to break up bomber formations before they could attack. Enemy carriers were to be located at long-range and attacked before they could mount a strike of their own. Such fighters as the RN was able to embark in carrier air groups, therefore, had to double up as dive-bombers or strike escorts, hence the Blackburn Skua in the former role and, from 1940, the Fairey Fulmar in the latter.

What emerges from this look at doctrinal development is that the RN was just as enthusiastic about aviation as the USN and IJN but was unlucky in its timing and unfortunate in that everything it tried to do was opposed by another government department that was given equal status by ministers. It had been obliged by the political limitations placed on it after 1918 to adopt a unique set of operating methods that differed from other first-rate navies. Even then, this did not detract in any major way from capability until the beginning of the radical improvements made possible by high-powered aircraft engines and all-metal, monoplane aircraft. The financial crash prevented investment just when the RN needed it most to compete with its rivals and when re-armament did begin in 1936 the orientation towards Germany as the most likely enemy meant that the RAF was given priority for aircraft production and the Admiralty's vital requirements were not given the priority they deserved.

Thomas Hone, Norman Friedman and Mark Mandeles make the interesting observation[7] that, from a USN perspective, the RN had been 'painted into a corner' by 1931 since forces outside Admiralty control had limited both the performance and the number of embarked aircraft. From its own perspective the RN staff was well aware that the number of aircraft in USN carriers was 'proportionally much higher than in the RN, largely due to the practice of storing some aircraft permanently on deck'. It believed that the USN had about 273 aircraft in front-line units, including those in battleship and cruiser flights, compared with 153 in the RN. What the British naval staff did not seem to have fully appreciated was that the USN had a large number of aircraft in reserve to replace action losses quickly and a statistically large pilot reserve. The USN was, therefore, considerably better placed than the RN to replace battle casualties but there was little the staff could do in the short term to redress that situation.

It is enormously to the Admiralty's credit that it continued to fight for an air arm that was capable of playing a full and effective part in contemporary naval operations. Had it not had such an intense interest it could never have fought for so long and, ultimately, successfully to regain control of the Fleet Air Arm. A myth was even spread by those who should have known better that admirals were not 'air-minded' and were somehow averse to the new technology. The truth of the matter was the RAF was not 'sea-minded' and was encouraged by the Air Ministry to focus on strategic bombing and to regard all other forms of warfare as obsolescent. There was a fatal flaw in this policy which was to undermine the potential for Britain to fight a war against a major industrialised nation: what would happen if Britain's enemies did not invest in a strategic bomber force and, instead, invested heavily in tactical aircraft to support their armies and navies wherever they were deployed? This is effectively what happened in the first three years of the Second World War with Bomber Command making feeble and inaccurate attempts to bomb Germany while British expeditionary forces in Norway, France and Belgium had to fight German armies ably supported by dive-bombers, fighters and medium bombers used in a tactical role to interdict operations on the ground.

Squadron Numbering Systems

During the period when Fleet Air Arm aircraft were divided into flights numbered in the 400 series, individual aircraft were identified by a one-, two- or three- digit side number painted prominently on the fuselage sides and the top wing centre section. Flight commanders usually had prominent markings applied so that they could be recognised by other aircraft in flight and flights often had a unit badge painted on the tailplane. Aircraft from specific carriers could be identified by coloured bands painted round the after fuselage which often had the side number superimposed on top of it. Band colours were green for *Argus*; red for *Furious*;

black for *Eagle;* white for *Hermes;* pale blue for *Courageous* and yellow for *Glorious.* After *Argus* was paid off into reserve, green was adopted by *Hermes.* The last carrier to have its aircraft thus marked was *Ark Royal*, which had dark blue and red stripes but after the Munich and Czechoslovak crises aircraft began to be camouflaged and the system fell into abeyance. From May 1939, when the Admiralty resumed full control, the system ceased officially and the parent carrier was indicated by a letter painted on the tailplane or as part of the side code.

Technical progress by 1931 meant that many more than six aircraft could be launched from a single range. Aircraft brakes meant that they could be ranged in 'herring-bone' fashion on the after part of the deck, taxiing out of the range onto the centreline controlled by a flight deck officer and his handling party before running up to full power for a rolling take-off. Aircraft engines had improved to the extent that longer periods in a running range were acceptable so up to three times as many aircraft could be flown off in a single range. Until the introduction of barriers and landing signal officers, or batsmen, in the late 1930s, recoveries still took time but it was clear to Admiral Henderson that six-aircraft flights no longer represented the optimum unit size for embarked operations. Torpedo aircraft worked best when attacking in large numbers that had trained together and the ideal way to achieve this was with squadrons of twelve aircraft sub-divided into flights of three for the attack. Administratively, the number of flights had grown to twenty-seven by this time but there were few opportunities for more senior RN pilots. The appropriate rank for a flight commander was Lieutenant but there were few openings for Lieutenant Commanders, with the result that some good men had to return to general service when they might have had important flying appointments before them in a better organised force. For all these reasons, Henderson devised a new system of squadrons with a nominal strength of twelve aircraft, the exact number depending on the size of the carrier. These could be commanded by lieutenant commanders with more junior lieutenant commanders as their second-in-command, giving far more aviation openings for experienced naval pilots.

The new system was introduced in April 1933 and continues in use with the Fleet Air Arms of the UK and Australia into the twenty-first century. The new squadrons were given numbers in the 800 series so that they could be distinguished from the core RAF units, giving them considerable scope for expansion. From 1936 catapult flights were reorganised as squadrons in the 700 series and when the Admiralty resumed control second-line and training squadrons that normally operated ashore were added to the 700 series. As in the flights, the new squadron numbers were initially allocated in type blocks: fighter squadrons were allocated numbers beginning with 800; torpedo squadrons beginning with 810 and spotter squadrons 820 onwards. After 1939 further blocks were allocated in the range up to 899 and more squadrons added in the 1700 and 1800 series.

Plans for the Decisive Battle

Put simply, the Admiralty based its war fighting doctrine during the inter-war period on the assumption that hostilities would begin with a blockade that would, ultimately, force the enemy to use its main fleet to seek battle in an attempt to lift it. The destruction of the enemy fleet would guarantee for Great Britain and its allies the absolute control of the sea, allowing the movement of expeditionary forces and their air components as necessary. It needs to be added that the submarine menace was deemed to have been eradicated by a combination of treaty limitations and the invention of sonar detection systems fitted in destroyers and escort vessels known within the RN as Asdic. This term remained in use until after the Second World War and will, therefore, be used throughout this book.

Admiralty doctrine between the wars anticipated the deployment of an enemy fleet to be detected by signals intelligence, allowing the British battle fleet to steam towards an intercept position while maintaining strict radio silence to avoid revealing its own position. From 1920 Japan was seen as the most likely enemy, after the Abyssinian crisis Italy was seen as more likely and from 1936 onwards Germany represented the most immediate threat. The worst-case scenario against which re-armament had to be directed, was the possibility of simultaneous war against all three acting in concert. The 1924 battle plan[8] envisaged a fleet of about twelve battleships, preceded by cruisers on the A–K line with destroyer and fast submarine flotillas acting as part of the fleet.[9] There were to be four small carriers, two of which would be just astern of the cruiser line, with air groups of reconnaissance and torpedo aircraft used to search an area up to 135nm ahead of the fleet and up to 100nm on either flank. As soon as the enemy was located, the torpedo aircraft would be launched to attack it and weaken or slow its big-gun ships. Two further carriers with air groups of spotters and fighters would use their aircraft to prevent enemy reconnaissance aircraft from locating and reporting the fleet and to escort strikes and spotter aircraft. The spotters would be launched when contact with the enemy was made and would be used to enable RN battleships to pour accurately corrected, concentrated fire onto the enemy battle line at extreme range. Gunnery technology in 1924 meant that ranges beyond the battleship's own visual horizon were possible so air spotting was essential for such indirect fire; so too was the fighter defence of the spotting aircraft. It was agreed throughout the RN that aircraft provided it with both strategic and tactical initiatives and that a fleet without them would be impotent against a better-equipped enemy. That is why the Admiralty tried so hard for so long to get the aircraft, weapons and personnel it wanted.

As technology improved through the 1930s, the idea of a decisive naval battle remained constant but the means of winning it changed, with aircraft assuming even greater importance. It had been realised by then that numbers counted and a smaller number of larger carriers with big air groups would be more efficient than four small ones. A commander-in-chief could use the aircraft to gain tactical

A Fairey IIIF taking off from RAF Hal Far, Malta, with a towed sleeve target for live firing practice during the Abyssinian crisis. The aircraft's dark appearance shows that it has been camouflaged, as many were at this time. (Author's collection)

objectives in the same way as any other element of the fleet, such as the destroyer flotillas. In the combined Home and Mediterranean Fleet exercises in March 1938 it was planned to see if carrier aircraft could reduce the effectiveness of an enemy battle line in the critical minutes before it was engaged. To achieve this *Glorious* and *Courageous* flew off a combined force of seventy-eight torpedo aircraft and dive-bombers to attack the battle line. *Glorious*' aircraft made a 'not very successful attack' on the van of the enemy fleet while *Courageous*' aircraft attacked the 'enemy' battle line.[10] The battleships were deployed in two divisions in line ahead with *Warspite* leading *Nelson, Malaya* and *Rodney*, followed by *Royal Oak* leading *Ramillies* and *Revenge*. The twelve Swordfish of 821 Squadron flew parallel to the 'enemy' line and then dived to attack *Warspite*, scoring four hits. *Nelson,* the next astern, was hit twice as the aircraft carried out text-book attacks. Dive-bombers hit ships of the second division thirty seconds before Swordfish of 820 and 810 Squadrons dived to attack in formation, scoring five hits on *Royal Oak* and three on *Revenge.* As the attack commenced, the battleships had turned hard out of formation and lost the cohesiveness they needed to fight a gun action and were not well placed to face the 'enemy' battle line. Of course there was no defensive anti-aircraft fire but even if there had been hits were still likely and some of the ships would, at the very least have been stopped in the water as the Italian cruiser *Pola* was at the Battle of Matapan in 1941. For real, *Warspite, Royal Oak* and *Revenge*

A running range of Fairey IIIFs on *Furious*' flight deck photographed from another that has just taken off. (Author's collection)

might well have been sunk. Even if all the torpedoes had all missed, the battle line had lost its cohesion and was not at all well placed to fight a surface action. No ship of the first division was within 1,500 yards of another. As we now know, the big battle envisaged by the Admiralty did not happen but thoughts that it might be imminent in April 1940 had a significant impact on events as they unfolded, and the Fleet Air Arm that fought as part of the Home Fleet in 1940 had been trained against the requirements of the 'big battle' concept.

Operations between 1919 and 1939

The so-called years of peace after 1919 involved RN aircraft carriers in a series of operations that bore little resemblance to the concept of operations for which they had been created. For those who had eyes to see, however, they began to demonstrate the versatility of aircraft as an element of sea power and its continuing importance to the British Empire.

The War of Intervention in Russia

When the Tsarist regime was brought to an end in Russia by the revolution of March 1917, the new provisional government announced that it would remain with the Allied cause in the war against Germany. As a result, huge quantities of war material continued to be shipped to the ports of Archangel and Vladivostok. After the seizure of power by the Bolsheviks in the October Revolution, the Allies landed troops at these two ports and at Murmansk to prevent the arms falling into their hands.[11] By the time the Treaty of Brest-Litovsk in March 1918 ended the war between Russia and Germany, Britain and France had become heavily involved in north and south Russia, Siberia and the shores of the Caspian and Black Seas. The Foreign Secretary, Balfour, announced that 'recent events had created obligations which last beyond the occasion which gave them birth'. He identified the anti-Bolshevik movement in many parts of Russia and the 'nascent nationalities' in the Baltic provinces which had appealed to Britain for aid. The ensuing operations on land which lasted until 1920 are beyond the scope of this book but aircraft and seaplane carriers did play a small part in British strategy.[12]

The seaplane carrier *Pegasus* was sent to Archangel in May 1919 with a small number of Fairey IIIC seaplanes which were disembarked with their air and ground crews and a logistic support package to operate from a shore base in support of British forces. For a few months the ship gave workshop support, effectively acting as a floating second-tier maintenance base. Without her, the aircraft would have been more difficult both to deploy and to sustain and there were lessons to be learnt about the deployment of expeditionary forces. She returned to the UK in September. Meanwhile in June 1919, *Argus* ferried a number of Fairey IIID seaplanes to Archangel where they joined the aircraft from *Pegasus*. It was her first operational task after completing trials with the retaining wires fitted in Rosyth Dockyard and, having delivered her aircraft, she returned to the UK to carry out the first embarked air operations with the Atlantic Fleet in 1920. The seaplane carrier *Nairana* was deployed with *Pegasus* and disembarked four Fairey Campanias and three Sopwith 2F.1 Camels to Archangel, where they operated ashore with maintenance support from the ship. These were ferry rather than carrier strike operations but they did show that carriers contributed more than just a launch and recovery capability; they delivered a floating workshop, stores warehouse and weapons magazine that formed an essential element of expeditionary air operations. Aircraft were ready to commence flying operations as soon as they arrived.

For a time in 1919 both *Furious* and *Vindictive* were used to ferry aircraft to the Baltic where they were landed to operate ashore in support of British units in the Baltic republics against the Bolsheviks. By 1919 *Furious* was back in Rosyth Dockyard, where she was reduced to reserve prior to being rebuilt as a flush-deck aircraft carrier. *Vindictive* was used to ferry a variety of aircraft to the Baltic in July 1919, including 2F.1 Camels, Short 184s, Sopwith One-and-a-Half Strutters

Fairey IIIF spotter-reconnaissance aircraft in the recovery pattern over *Furious*. The 'plane-guard' on the carrier's starboard quarter is a 'V and W' class destroyer. (Author's collection)

and Grain Griffins. She grounded for a while off Reval (later Tallin) and remained stuck fast for eight days before being refloated. The aircraft she had deployed into theatre relied on the ship to provide technical and logistics support but operated with reasonable success ashore. At one stage they carried out a bombing attack on Kronstadt. *Vindictive* also supported a flotilla of eight motor torpedo boats which operated with success. She returned to Portsmouth in December 1919 where she was reduced to reserve.

The Chanak Crisis

During the latter part of the First World War, the British Prime Minister, Lloyd George, entered into a number of secret agreements with Italy and Greece which became the cause of acute embarrassment after the end of hostilities against Turkey. Of interest, the armistice between the Allied Powers and the Turkish Empire was signed on a British battleship at Mudros in October 1918 but the United States was not party to the agreement because hostilities had never been declared between Turkey and the USA. This was to produce a number of anomalies and friction between the former Allies. The Greek enclave of Smyrna on the west coast of Anatolia, effectively modern Turkey, soon became a centre of friction and the Italian government sent troops to the south-western corner of Asia Minor at Adalia. It should have been predictable that violent resentment would be caused in Turkey by Greek occupation of Smyrna. It led to the rise of a new form of Turkish nationalism under the inspired leadership of Mustapha Kemal, who had earned his reputation at Gallipoli in 1915.[13] In September 1922 Turkish forces attacked Smyrna, fire broke out and within hours the city was burning from end to end. The panic-stricken population gathered at the waterfront where harrowing scenes ensued and the Commander-in-Chief Mediterranean, Admiral Sir Osmond Brock, ordered all boats from the British fleet anchored off the port to be sent inshore to rescue refugees regardless of their nationality.

Lloyd George took the view that control of the narrow waters separating Europe from Asia was a 'cardinal British interest' and that any attempt to cross them by Turkish nationalist forces was to be resisted by force. Small detachments of British troops held so-called neutral zones at Chanak on the eastern shore of the Dardanelles and on the Ismid shore of the Bosporus and for a while it looked as if they might be overwhelmed by superior Turkish forces. A division was sent to reinforce them and the Mediterranean Fleet was reinforced by three battleships, two aircraft-carrying ships, a destroyer flotilla and a battalion of Royal Marines from the Atlantic Fleet. The evolution of this crisis is also beyond the scope of this book but it brought down Lloyd George's coalition government in the UK and revealed a distinct unwillingness on the part of the Dominions, Australia and Canada, to become involved.

The two aircraft-carrying ships were *Argus* and *Pegasus* which were used to ferry RAF aircraft to the theatre in 1922. *Argus* carried twelve RAF Bristol F.2B fighters to the Dardanelles in September; they were landed with their air and ground crews together with a logistic support package to operate in support of troops on the ground. She did not operate them from her deck and, having delivered the aircraft she returned to duty with the Atlantic Fleet. *Pegasus* ferried the Fairey IIID seaplanes of 'L' Flight 267 Squadron RAF to the Dardanelles at the same time and, having put these aircraft ashore she remained with the Mediterranean Fleet for use as an aircraft ferry.

Patrols and Exercises

In 1925 *Vindictive* had her flight decks removed but retained the forward hangar for use as a seaplane carrier[14] and in January 1926 she deployed to the China Station with six Fairey IIIDs embarked which were used for anti-piracy patrols off the coast of China as well as exercises with the fleet, returning to the UK in 1928.

With a growing number of aircraft carriers in commission, the RN was able to evaluate their use in a series of fleet exercises that simulated likely wartime scenarios. At this time the potential enemy was Japan, and Exercise MU2 in the spring of 1928 saw ships of both the Home and Mediterranean Fleets taking part in an investigation of the problem of passing a fleet through the Malacca Strait against well-established opposition. It lasted two months and involved eighty-two warships with both fleets having a single aircraft carrier. Alboran Island off the coast of Algeria represented Singapore and Gibraltar represented Hong Kong for the purposes of the exercise, with the Mediterranean Fleet acting as the Japanese. The task of the Home Fleet was to relieve 'Hong Kong' and defeat the enemy fleet before it could capture 'Singapore'. In the 1929 combined exercises, three aircraft carriers took part, *Furious*, *Courageous* and *Eagle*, and began to demonstrate the value of multi-carrier task forces. Aircraft operations were refined and the essential role of the Fleet Air Arm to find, fix and strike the enemy was fine-tuned. Arguably the RN was ahead of the USN in its thinking on using several carriers together although individual carrier operating techniques were not as well honed.

In 1929 *Courageous* was still serving with the Mediterranean Fleet with 404 and 407 (Fairey Flycatcher), 445 and 446 (Fairey IIIF) and 463 and 464 (Blackburn Dart) Flights embarked when inter-racial violence between the Arab and Jewish communities broke out in Palestine. She embarked the 2nd Battalion South Staffordshire Regiment with its equipment and landed it at Jaffa, where it was used to restore peace. Some of her air group were disembarked to Gaza to support troops ashore and *Courageous* was able to operate her aircraft from the sea if necessary to provide further support.

Admiral Henderson directed a number of multi-carrier exercises in the early 1930s that demonstrated that aircraft carriers were now potentially decisive weapons systems in their own right. On 19 January 1932 the air groups of *Courageous* and *Glorious* combined to launch a strike with practice torpedoes against the Mediterranean Fleet at anchor in a southern Greek harbour. The result was a conspicuous success which showed that fleets now had nowhere to hide from or seek safety from a fleet that included aircraft carriers. After the original Grand Fleet strike plan of 1918, this was the logical next step on the road that was to lead to the historic Fleet Air Arm attack on the Italian fleet at Taranto in November 1940.

Continuing Activity on the China Station

For much of the inter-war period an aircraft carrier was maintained on the China Station which helped to suppress the activities of pirates. In 1931 *Hermes* was deployed 600 miles up the Yangtse River to the port of Hangkow where there were considerable British business interests. Even this far in land the river was still over

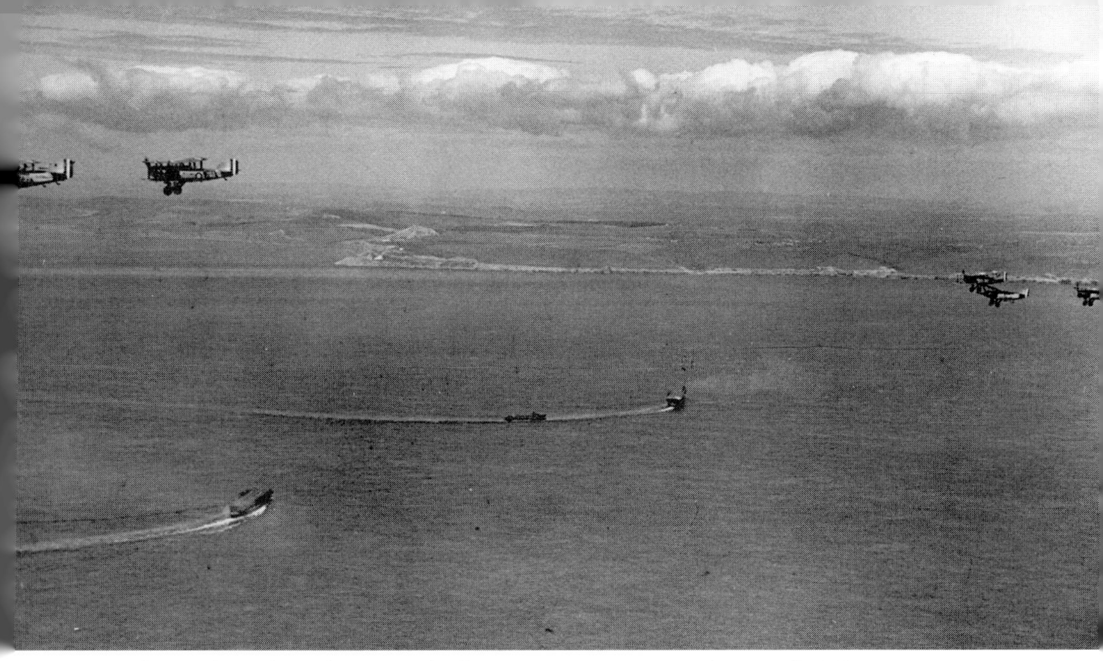

One of a number of Royal Navy multiple carrier exercises carried out in the Western Mediterranean during the early 1930s. (Author's collection)

a mile wide and the carrier had been sent for two reasons: first she was to put down mutinies among the Chinese crew members in several British-owned merchant vessels, and secondly she was to assist with flood relief operations. In the latter role her aircraft were fitted with floats and flown on detailed flood surveys at the request of the Chinese government. The aircraft were marked for these flights with Chinese characters which could be read from the ground.[15]

Shortly after Bill Lucy joined *Hermes*, on 29 January 1935, the China Steam Navigation Company's ship *Tungchow* sailed from Shanghai with passengers that included seventy British and American children returning to a mission school at Chefoo. The ship was British owned and had British officers and White Russian security guards. Pirates seized the ship that evening, killing an officer and a security guard, and took the ship to their base at Bias Bay near Hong Kong. When she was reported missing the RN sailed a number of ships, including *Hermes*, to look for her. By 1 February with the passengers held in the saloon under armed guard, the pirates started to unload the ship's cargo into a junk which was secured alongside. They had only just begun when one of three Fairey Seals flown off *Hermes* located the ship, radioed its position and proceeded to make a number of low passes which frightened the pirates into making off ashore. Ship, schoolchildren and cargo were rescued and taken to Hong Kong. This is just one small, though interesting, example of the continual campaign waged by the RN against pirates throughout this period. In 1933 *Eagle* had carried out a series of air strikes against pirates and their junks on the Chinese coast when requested to do so by the Chinese authorities.

Abyssinian Crisis

In the early 1930s the Italian dictator Benito Mussolini had ambitions to seize part of Abyssinia, and a border incident intended to start the process was fabricated at Walsall on 5 December 1934. Abyssinia sought arbitration through the League of Nations but border incidents continued. An Italian invasion followed on 3 October and the Council of the League of Nations condemned the act and brought sanctions into effect. The only force capable of implementing sanctions was the British Mediterranean Fleet, which moved to Alexandria and was heavily reinforced from other stations. While the crisis was at its height, it seemed that war with Italy might come at any moment.[16] In the event there was no war but the concentration of force in the Eastern Mediterranean did teach lessons about the logistic support of an aircraft carrier task force operating a considerable distance from a main base that were to be of value in the Second World War. *Glorious*' air group was able to formulate a plan and practise the necessary techniques for a night attack on the Italian fleet at its main base at Taranto. This, too, was to be of value in the war to come.

Training

Training the expanding RN with its new array of weapons during the period of re-armament became increasingly important. In 1937 combined Home and Mediterranean Fleet exercises took place in the Atlantic with over 100 warships, including aircraft carriers. *Glorious*' air group concentrated on the skills of night flying and torpedo attack and by 1939 they were arguably the most capable naval strike force in existence.

The Spanish Civil War

Sudden and heavy demands for the presence of British warships on non-intervention patrols off Spain were made soon after the conclusion of the Abyssinian crisis. By July 1936 there were fifteen British warships off the Spanish coast. The broad dispositions were that the Home Fleet covered the northern sector, keeping one or two capital ships and half a destroyer flotilla off the coast while the Mediterranean Fleet, based on Gibraltar, covered the southern sector. Both fleets deployed aircraft carriers from time to time which used their aircraft to carry out low-intensity searches to maintain situational awareness of surface shipping activity. While showing another aspect to carrier capability, these operations cannot be said to have added greatly to the advancement of carrier strike operations.

Chapter 6

Observers

Lieutenant Lucy's naval career has been followed through a study of his service history in the MOD Archive, the surviving records which describe the accidents and incidents in which he was involved and the histories of the ships and squadrons in which he served. In later chapters I will use his combat reports to describe his wartime career in greater detail but in this chapter I shall concentrate on the training and role of observers in the period between the wars. Fortunately, I have been able to draw on the autobiography of 'Hank' Rotherham,[1] one of Bill Lucy's contemporaries, to provide both detail and human interest.

As a young officer serving in destroyers, Rotherham had become convinced that aircraft were the weapons of the future and he volunteered for the Observers' Course. To him this was an entirely logical step because it did not involve the complication of dual rank and a prolonged period at an RAF training establishment but would put him right at the heart of carrier-borne flying. He was appointed to Number 22 Course which began at the RN Signal School in Portsmouth on 31 October 1932, a month after Bill Lucy had started his pilot training with the RAF at Leuchars. The other members of 22 Course were Lieutenants E H C Chapman, G C W Fowler, J G Hunt, T G C Jameson, K A Short and W Thomson RN, and its first phase consisted of learning what seemed to be 'the complete theory of wireless transmission in the space of a few lessons' whilst, at the same time, working up their ability to read Morse Code transmissions at up to twenty-two words per minute so that they would be able to read fifteen words per minute with ease whilst flying. It was harder work for some than others and failure to make the grade would almost certainly have led to removal from training. The second phase of the course was at the Gunnery School, HMS *Excellent*, at Whale Island to the north of Portsmouth Dockyard. Here the student observers 'were delighted to be received as disciples of the art rather than as mere course-fodder'. Spotting the fall of shot was, by then, a well-established tactic which enabled gunners to hit their targets at long range, and observers were seen as valuable members of the team. Finally, on 17 March 1933, the student observers moved to Lee-on-Solent near Gosport which was at that time an RAF seaplane base and the home of the School of Naval Co-operation. Even the name of the school shows how detached the RAF was since it implied that aircraft were co-operating with the fleet as a separate entity rather than forming an integral and essential part of it.

Rotherham described Lee-on-Solent in 1933 as a hybrid affair with a complete mixture of RN and RAF personnel. It was commanded by a Group Captain RAF, all

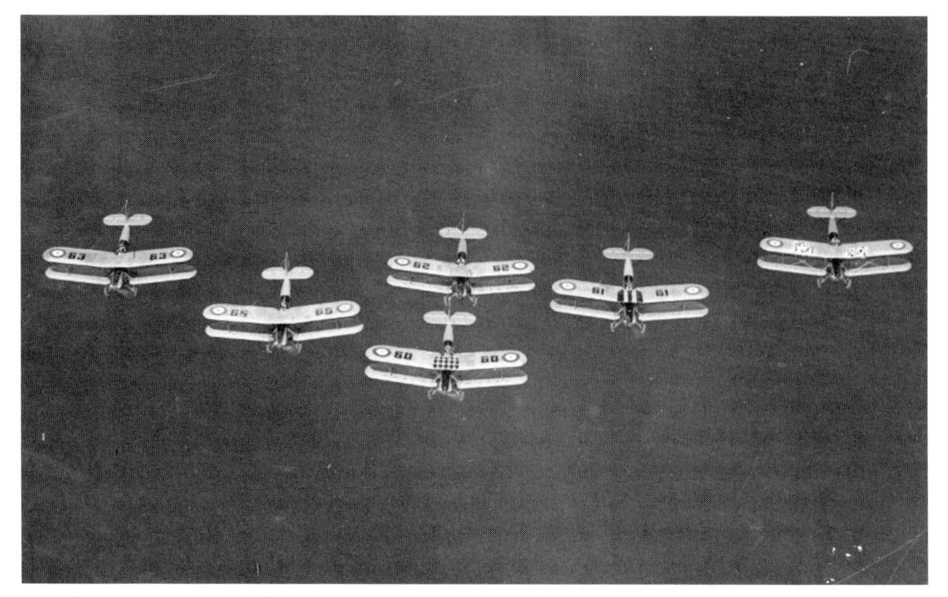

A tight formation of Blackburn Ripons from *Glorious* evaluating level bombing techniques in the early 1930s. (Author's collection)

the pilots were air force officers but the small cadre of observer training staff were all RN, including both observers and telegraphist air gunners who were expert in radio operation and Morse work. Generally, the pilots 'seemed to think that Lee-on-Solent was some sort of punishment posting' although on an individual basis Hank found them to be decent people who did their best to help. They just lacked any incentive to do well in the world in which they found themselves. Half the working days were spent in the classroom on theoretical work and the other half airborne in Fairey IIIF seaplanes flying over both land and sea. This element of the course ended on 23 June 1933 with the students' qualification as observers, after which they were to be appointed to aircraft carriers as members of the ships' company. This arrangement had worked in the 1920s but with the new structure of larger squadrons created by Admiral Henderson observers found themselves spending more and more time with squadrons. In 1933 there was no observer's flying badge as the Admiralty regarded them as executive officers who were carrying out a specialist appointment like submariners, gunnery and torpedo officers. There was no equivalent specialisation in the RAF and thus there was no question of dual rank. Observers remained within the naval reporting system and this was one of the reasons why there were more volunteers to become observers than pilots in the early 1930s. Since observers were considered to be ships' officers rather than members of an RAF squadron, they did not always disembark with the aircraft when carriers were in harbour unless there were particular reasons for them to do so. This was divisive but by the late 1930s as the Admiralty began to resume control of the air arm after the Inskip Award the advantages of having complete crews trained and worked up together became paramount and observers began to be appointed to squadrons in the way that pilots were. An observers' flying badge was belatedly introduced by the Admiralty in September 1942; it was worn over the left sleeve lace like pilots' wings and immediately overcame the embarrassment felt by many observers that they were not recognisable as aircrew when working with the RAF or USN.

In the autumn of 1933 Hank joined *Glorious* at about the same time as Bill Lucy and the two would certainly have known each other well. In his autobiography Hank reflected that the captains of aircraft carriers often had little previous knowledge of the practical aspects of aviation and the Wing Commander RAF in charge of the embarked aircraft often had no prior experience of deck landing or of Fleet Air Arm methods and tactics. He found the situation to be 'strangely reminiscent' of the situation described by E Keble Chatterton in his *English Seamen and the Colonization of America*,[2] in which he wrote about Elizabethan warships where Landsmen, ignorant of nautical matters, were often found in overall command but Ship Masters, who had spent considerable time at sea, were in charge of the vessel and its safe navigation. He found that author's words to be particularly apt when he wrote that 'where the Captain was able to unite in his person the ability of shipmaster and pilot, then he was a genuine superman whose authority was unique'. In its way, this was a fair description of the fundamentally flawed system of dual control. Fortunately, Rotherham found that at the everyday level of flying, people were sufficiently adaptable to make things work but, unlike in the USN and Japan, there was no incentive for improvement. The higher echelons of the RAF had no particular interest in whether the Fleet Air Arm was efficient or not; in their scheme of things it was of little importance and flying at sea was just something members of the RAF had to put up with until they got what they considered to be a better posting.

RAF officers knew that they were only likely to spend one tour at sea with the Navy and most had no inclination to develop new concepts or improve the way in which aircraft could work as part of the fleet. The Air Ministry was naturally inclined to channel new design work, using the limited funds it had available, towards RAF rather than naval requirements, however well the latter might have been thought out. The failure to develop a dive-bombing sight despite repeated Admiralty requests is a good example of this failing. Hank also mentions that as late as 1938 Fleet Air Arm aircraft were still using TF-T21C radios which had been introduced two decades earlier and actually used in the First World War; despite the need for good communications at sea the Air Ministry had failed to give their development the level of importance they deserved.

Flying was still a risky business and, inevitably, there was an element of black humour that surrounded accidents. If you did something silly you were said to have joined a club. There was the 'Seven League Boot Club'[3] for those who plotted the speed wrong; the 'Where it Listeth Club' for those who got the wind wrong and were blown off course, and many others. The 'Rat Club' was reserved for those who, realising that their aircraft was going over the side, jumped out to avoid a swim. There was one remarkable member of this club, an observer named Edwards, who decided that his aircraft was not going to make its landing on *Hermes* in the days before arrester wires or brakes and jumped out of the aircraft onto the deck. His pilot came to the same conclusion and opened the throttle in the hope of getting airborne again, a possibility that Edwards had thought impossible, and staggered off, flew another circuit and landed on successfully, to find his observer stood on the flight deck waiting for him. Since he had been unaware of Edwards' impromptu departure he was somewhat shaken.[4] There was an even more exclusive club for observers who were left alone in an aircraft destined to go over the side when its pilot jumped out of it. This was known as the 'Trapped Rat Club'. Aircrew who 'joined' more than one club were known as 'Men About Town'. The clubs may be considered silly now but the idea kept aircrew from dwelling on the dangers of carrier operation. *Glorious* was, at this time, a happy ship in which Rotherham was delighted to serve and he found the RAF pilots, who made up about half the total, willing to work with their observers as well as their RN counterparts. The difference between them was that the RN pilots would make use of their experience by returning to carrier flying in more senior positions but RAF pilots would be lost to other RAF commands, unlikely ever to return. Rotherham became proficient in the 'tools of the observer's trade', reconnaissance, navigation and spotting for the guns, and he had also become expert in taking aerial photographs of destroyer flotilla and strike aircraft torpedo attacks so that the exact behaviour of the 'tin fish' could be seen and analysed. By the end of his time in *Glorious*, Hank Rotherham was deemed to be 'in the first flight of back-seat men'; he would have had a certificate of competence in role in his flying log book, signed by both the Captain and the Wing Commander Flying.

He would also have been one of the selected few observers that the Admiral's staff would wait to hear from in order to resolve any conflicts in the reports of enemy position and movement given by other aircraft. Each observer was assigned his own letter as part of his aircraft's callsign to enable the fleet to know who was doing the reporting. The callsigns comprised three letters, the first identified the carrier, the second the individual observer and the third the duty being carried out.

Hank moved to *Furious* in 1934 and, whilst waiting for her after *Glorious* left Malta he spent some time at Hal Far and took part in high-level bombing trials against the radio-controlled target battleship *Centurion* which was, after an initial straight run, allowed to take full avoiding action. Observers were gradually moving from a ship-centric environment towards a fuller involvement with squadrons

Both aircrew appear to have joined the appropriate 'club' as they have leapt clear of their aircraft before it went over the side of their carrier. (John de Lucy collection)

and this was helped by the fact that 822 Squadron had an RN pilot in command, Lieutenant Commander A P Colthurst RN,[5] who had been in Number 2 Naval Pilots' Course and was now on his second tour of flying duty. Under his leadership there was considerable enthusiasm for innovation within the squadron and Hank became its senior observer, invariably flying with the commanding officer. High-level bombing was completely neglected by the RAF at this time because it had been found easier to bomb accurately from lower altitudes and the results looked better on paper without needing to give detailed explanations. However, for a bomb to have the speed on impact to penetrate the armoured deck of a warship it had to be dropped by a bomber flying straight and level from at least 10,000 feet. Even dive-bombing could not achieve the necessary speed, thus if level bombing was to be of any value for naval aviation, it had to be done from high-level and accurate methods had to be developed to do so. Accuracy required solutions to be found to two problems: first the actual wind over the target had to be found so that aim could be adjusted to compensate for it and secondly bombs had to be dropped in a close pattern by a number of aircraft in order to give the best chance of ensuring a hit.

The wind-finding technique method taught by the RAF was naive, of little practical value and, when employed in a real attack against a ship that was shooting at the attacking aircraft, excessively dangerous. Bombers were expected to make

A Fairey IIIF over *Eagle* on the China Station; note the carrier's white-and-buff paint scheme. (Author's collection)

three runs over their target from different directions, dropping practice bombs on the first two and making a rough estimate of the wind direction as they did so by observing where they fell. The likelihood of achieving success with this method with a close formation of aircraft under fire was not explained. The method evolved by 822 Squadron was to send one aircraft ahead of the remainder about 15nm short of the target to drop a sea marker and fire a smoke puff for the remainder to fly through. A bearing and distance of the sea marker while flying through the smoke allowed an accurate assessment of wind speed and direction to be made with just sufficient time for it to be set on bombsights. Aircraft flew the attack profile in a formation intended to produce a pattern of bombs 450 feet square, individually spaced 90 feet apart. Rotherham calculated that a battleship with a length of 700 feet and a beam of 100 feet would sustain five or six hits from such a pattern and virtually any large target was likely to be hit. The first attack on *Centurion* achieved six hits while she steered a steady course. After she was allowed to take full evasive action the squadron still achieved six hits. Vertical cameras were used to ensure that there could be no arguments over the hits scored.

The attacks were carried out with the whole squadron flying in two flights of six aircraft each in flat 'V' formations. Good formation was essential and pilots had to follow minute course and speed variations in order to maintain station on the leader. Bomb dropping had to be co-ordinated down to fractions of a second since even at 90 knots the aircraft were covering 150 feet on the ground every second. The back-seat crews spent time practising in the hangar in order to hone the mixture of hand and radio signals used and reduce the reaction time between brain and hands. As the squadron made the run towards *Centurion*, Rotherham lay on his stomach in the after cockpit looking down through the bombsight which was fitted in an open space in the floor. As the sight came on he signalled his TAG by hand to release his Morse key and the other aircrews would all release their bombs at the same instant or as close to it as possible.

There can be no doubt that 822 Squadron proved this method to be effective and the IJN used a very similar technique successfully against the *Prince of Wales* and *Repulse* in December 1941. Unfortunately for the RN the knowledge went no further than the squadron. Despite a commendation from the Commander-in-Chief Mediterranean Fleet, the RAF, under whose administrative command the squadron nominally operated, did not consider the results worth following up and the Mediterranean Fleet had no air organisation of its own to formulate air warfare doctrine. The technique essentially 'fell down a crack' between the two control authorities, adding further evidence, if it were needed, of the system's basic failure.

Of interest 822 Squadron was equipped at this time with twelve Fairey IIIFs, which are generally thought of as spotter reconnaissance aircraft. They did, however, have a significant weapons capability with hardpoints under the wings capable of carrying up to 500lb of bombs. The most likely strike load would be two 250lb semi-armour-piercing bombs, one under each wing, but it was possible to carry a single, asymmetrical 500lb bomb under one wing. The IIIF also had a fixed, forward firing Vickers machine gun in the nose firing through the propeller arc by means of an interrupter mechanism, and a single Lewis gun in the after cockpit on a Fairey high-speed mounting. Both were of First World War vintage and so too, in all probability, was the ammunition they fired. The IIIF had an endurance of up to four hours at 90 knots with full fuel and to achieve the best radius of action from a carrier with a bomb load the TAG could be left behind, saving about 250lb from the aircraft's maximum weight, to allow the maximum fuel load to be carried. The IIIF has some claim to be considered an early form multi-role aircraft and 379 were procured, paid for out of the Navy Vote, for service with the Fleet Air Arm. A further 243 were procured by the Air Ministry for RAF service at airfields around the world. A few IIIFs remained in use with second-line units after the outbreak of war but the type was finally declared obsolete in 1940.

A letter from the C-in-C, Mediterranean, Admiral W W Fisher, seeking to congratulate Rotherham on the *Centurion* bombing trial, is an interesting illustration of the complex command arrangements at the time. It was dated 26

July 1934 and addressed to the Air Officer Commanding Mediterranean, an RAF air marshal who probably had no idea what had been going on. By then *Furious* had arrived on the station and Hank had joined her, but the ship's captain was only a copy addressee. The message finally reached Hank through the RAF General Office, Fleet Air Arm, HMS *Furious*. He observed that 'only through the goodwill of the working ranks could such an organization operate' and added that 'further examples of this chaotic system, which we were convinced could have been designed only by someone with a warped sense of humour' were abundant. All naval pilots had dual naval and RAF ranks which were not necessarily equivalent and had the suffix (P) after the naval rank to indicate that they were qualified pilots. Observers had the suffix (O) but had no dual rank since there was no equivalent RAF 'trade', hence the lack of a flying badge. Pilots' RAF rank took precedence when they were working within a squadron or ashore at an RAF airfield despite the fact that they continued to wear RN uniform. However, when carrying out ships' duties on board, their naval rank applied. One Commander RN was only a Flying Officer RAF; he could command a warship but not lead a flight of aircraft.

Air reconnaissance had been refined by the Fleet Air Arm into a fine art by 1934. Once an 'enemy' ship was located, the co-operation between pilot and observer was critically important. Accurate navigation could, temporarily, be dispensed with since the position where the ship was found would be calculated as accurately as possible and transmitted together with her course and speed. By keeping it plotted the observer could take departure relative to it when the time came. This coincided with the primary task of keeping the fleet informed of the 'enemy'

Preparations to launch a running range of Fairey IIIFs have been completed as their carrier, followed by the 'plane-guard' destroyer, turns into wind. Conditions, including the clear sky and flat calm sea, seem ideal. (Author's collection)

Hawker Osprey K2777, side number 207, becomes airborne after being catapulted from the cruiser *Neptune* in 1934. Note the cumbersome trolley which was used to launch the aircraft in a flying attitude. The attachment points for it on the airframe contributed to the high drag factor which limited the float-fitted Osprey's performance. (Author's collection)

movements by shadowing it after it was located. The location of any consorts was also important and as the pilot worked round the 'enemy' using whatever cloud cover was available, the observer was kept busy reporting her position and mean line of advance to the carrier. The identity and position of consorts could usually be estimated from the type of 'enemy' found and, being ships' officers, observers had a good understanding of the likely 'enemy' force composition and reaction to discovery, helping to provide information that would be vital for their own fleet to make contact. Needless to say, the requirement to steer, accurately, the courses ordered by the observer was of critical importance. Naval pilots knew instinctively that this was essential but some RAF pilots resented being told what to do by a back-seater, especially one that had no RAF equivalent. It had to be drummed into them that any error could be fatal if it meant that the carrier could not be found at the end of a long reconnaissance sortie. It was frustrating that by the time they had accepted this fact of life, many of them moved on to other commands, never to return to carrier flying. Discussions in the wardroom after sorties sometimes contemplated when it would be worth taking extreme risks, even to the extent of

The observer is holding the slings ready for attachment to the ship's crane as *Leander*'s Hawker Osprey K2775, side number 201, taxies up to the ship in 1935. (Author's collection)

shadowing a contact to the last drop of fuel and hoping to be rescued after the ensuing battle. There were to be occasions during the Second World War when this actually happened in both the RN and USN.

In Rotherham's opinion, the RAF regarded pilots as 'gods' and observers counted for nothing. The absurdity of this situation was illustrated by a Fleet Air Arm squadron that disembarked to an RAF station at Manston in Kent. Every day the senior officer present was expected to take command of a morning parade but one day the senior officer was an RN observer from a disembarked Fleet Air Arm squadron who had no dual RAF rank. Having a 'back-seater' in naval uniform take charge of his parade was more than the group captain could stomach, however, and from that day forward observers were instructed never to attend the parade, in order to prevent a recurrence. Rotherham found time spent at RAF stations to be alarming from a professional viewpoint as well; during a visit to the Catfoss air bombing range in Yorkshire he made the interesting discovery that RAF bomber crews were not trained to use any method of finding the actual wind over a static target on land. Instead they relied implicitly on the forecast winds given to them by the meteorologist at their parent air station before take-off. During the same time at Catfoss he complained to a visiting air marshal about the standard-issue RAF bombsight, 'a lamentable device' in which the magnetic compass needle spun endlessly because of aircraft vibration. The air marshal said that this was the first complaint he had ever heard on the subject and Rotherham put this down to the fact that in RAF bombers the device was operated by 'other ranks' whose opinions were not given much consideration; only pilots were expected to have opinions.

Like Bill Lucy, Hank Rotherham was appointed to a cruiser flight with Hawker Osprey seaplanes after serving in aircraft carriers. In January 1936 he joined the light cruiser *Apollo*[6] which had two aircraft of 718 Squadron, side numbers 790 and 791, embarked when she was commissioned for service on the America and West Indies Station. Before deployment there was a trial with the ship's fixed, athwartship catapult to see if aircraft could be launched with a 30 knot cross-wind. A test pilot flew the aircraft but, as the flight's senior aviator, Hank occupied the rear seat since a second crew member was needed to hook the aircraft onto the retrieval crane when it returned and taxied up to the ship's side after alighting on the water. On the day of the trial the 30 knot wind was achieved with the ship stopped in the water. When catapulted, it just reached an end speed of 55 knots, slightly less than the minimum flying speed. The wind had shifted and was slightly from behind the aircraft; as a result it did a succession of bounces from wave-top to wave-top before the Rolls-Royce Kestrel engine dragged it into the air. Nevertheless, it was decided that the Osprey could be catapulted no matter what the ship was doing and which way the wind was blowing.

An observer's-eye view of the receding *Eagle* as the first aircraft climbs away after launching from the densely packed range. The ship is moving at over 20 knots to generate sufficient wind over the deck for the short take-off run in front of the range. Note the seaplane crane trained out to starboard. (Author's collection)

Hawker Ospreys of 801 NAS in formation. (Philip Jarrett collection)

The Ospreys' primary missions were reconnaissance and gunnery spotting, for which it was still well-suited, providing there was no realistic air opposition. They were also used for a variety of other tasks ranging from surveying, showing the flag and even, on one occasion, riot control working with the Jamaican police authorities. The cruisers on station often joined company to carry out shoots against a battle practice target towed at a considerable distance behind a tug. *Apollo*'s shooting was invariably good, which made the observer's task easy; *Exeter*'s shooting was invariably poor. On one occasion *Exeter* followed *Apollo* and Rotherham tuned in to her frequency and moved over to watch her shoot. He could not hear her aircraft on the radio so he asked if she would like him to spot for her. The reply was affirmative but on this day her fire was worse than usual. The first salvo fell so far short that he had to give a correction of 1,500 yards, a distance that he considered to be too great to estimate with complete accuracy. By good chance, however, he was exactly right and the second salvo hit the target. The Commodore America and West Indies at this time was Commodore Henry Harwood RN, later to achieve fame leading *Exeter*, *Ajax* and *Achilles* against the *Graf Spee* at the Battle of the River Plate in December 1939. Rotherham wrote to congratulate him on his victory and he was kind enough to reply, 'I wish I could have called you over to spot as I did in 1937' – a kind thought, and one that illustrates what a good observer could achieve. It is also worth noting what a unit with RN pilots and observers could achieve when operating at a distance from RAF bureaucracy.

In 1937 *Apollo*'s gunnery officer, Lieutenant Commander R Hinds RN, asked if Rotherham could devise a method of spotting for anti-aircraft fire against a sleeve target towed by an aircraft.[7] From the firing ship it was easy to see the line of fire but nearly impossible to determine whether the range was accurate and whether the shells were bursting ahead of or behind the target. He decided that if he flew under the towing aircraft so as to be well clear of the wire pulling the target, the bursts could be observed and their positions recorded relative to the target using the 'clock code'. When the time came to try this technique, he discovered that the rate of fire was too rapid for him to both spot and write the results so Lieutenant Wally Blackwell RN, his pilot, had to fly with one hand while writing furiously on a knee pad with the other, trying to keep pace with the speed at which the results were shouted down the Gosport tube by Hank. Unfortunately, while they were thus employed, *Exeter* kept sending Morse radio signals to the aircraft. Hank could read them whilst otherwise occupied but in order to reply he had to drop everything and use the Morse key.[8] In exasperation he signalled *Exeter* and asked her not to send any more signals. This seemed a bit too impertinent a thing for a lieutenant to say to a commodore and the rather strait-laced Harwood was about to dictate a very blunt signal in response when his Chief Yeoman of Signals stepped in to the observer's defence. 'You know, sir,' he said, 'he's pretty busy doing your job, my job, the telegraphist's job and the Gunnery Officer's job.' This was a fair description of the observer's work and it saved the situation and Hank was able to continue spotting the effect of the anti-aircraft shoot without interruption. It illustrates the point that it was, and is, as necessary for those in the ship to know what is going on in the aircraft as it is for those in the aircraft to understand what is happening in the ship.

Whilst serving in *Apollo*, Hank applied for the Staff Course at Greenwich and was duly appointed to it. There was some time before he joined what was to be the last pre-war course, starting in the autumn of 1938, and to fill it he was appointed to *Courageous*. This was after the Inskip Award and the Admiralty was making rapid preparations before it regained full control of the Fleet Air Arm but there were also other remarkable changes since he had started flying only five years earlier. During the Munich crisis *Courageous* joined other ships of the Home Fleet at Invergordon. While she was there, Hank was told to take a flight of aircraft from the ship back over the land and thence, via any route of his choosing, lead them back out to sea to make a dummy bombing attack on the cruiser *Sheffield* which was approximately 15nm off the coast. After completing the exercise and returning to the carrier he went to file his report and expected to be asked where he had taken the flight. To his amazement, he was told in exact detail the course it had taken and the time of each turning point. At the time he had no idea how this had been achieved but later he realised that they had been tracked by the first sea-borne radar, which had been fitted in *Sheffield* earlier in 1938.

Chapter 7

Progress in the United States Navy

By 1918 the development of aviation at sea by the Royal Navy's Air Service had been so successful that Captain G W Steele USN, sent to study aviation in the Grand Fleet and report his findings to the General Board,[1] wrote that so many ideas had been gained from the British that any discussion of the subject must consider their methods. The Board had already become aware how far it lagged behind the latest developments when the USA entered the war on the side of the Allies in 1917 and Royal Navy Constructor Stanley Goodall[2] had been lent to the Bureau of Construction and Repair. He took with him a number of warship plans, including those of the projected aircraft carriers which evolved into *Eagle* and *Hermes* together with instructions to summarise the impact of the latest operational doctrine on warship design. He was able to brief the General Board that 'air fighting had become a feature of naval operations' and that 'the tactical movements of a fleet before an engagement opens will, most probably, be governed by information obtained from air scouts', by which he meant reconnaissance aircraft. This search for tactical information and its denial to the enemy meant that in all probability 'a series of fights between opposing aircraft will most likely be a preliminary to a fleet action'. Any fleet should, therefore, include both fighters and reconnaissance aircraft in its composition. The Board accepted this philosophy and, boosted by the evidence of the large number of aircraft carriers being built for the RN, it pressed for the construction of its own carriers.

The Early Development of Carrier Aviation in the USN

After the Armistice, however, Congress refused to allocate the necessary funds for a new construction programme but did sanction the conversion of a collier into an experimental aircraft carrier. The ship chosen was the USS *Jupiter*, which had originally been completed in 1912 and which was to be renamed *Langley*, CV-1, after conversion. Design work was completed in July 1919 and she entered Norfolk Navy Yard in March 1920; emerging in March 1922. By then it was four years since *Argus* had been completed for the RN and *Eagle* had already run her initial flight deck trials with a starboard side island in place. *Langley* was an austere conversion with a parallel-sided wooden flight deck built onto a lattice-work structure over the former upper deck. The original bridge, now under the flight deck, was retained with little modification, as was the original aft superstructure which provided accommodation and a large sick bay. She had six holds, the foremost of which was modified for use as an avgas storage tank and the fourth contained machinery that worked the single lift in the upper half with an air weapons magazine in the bottom half. The remaining holds, two forward and two aft of the lift were used to stow dismantled aircraft.[3] The boilers were modified to burn fuel oil rather than coal and funnel smoke was originally discharged through a short, single funnel on the port quarter which was folded aft during flying operations; it was close to where the original fixed smoke-stack had been sited. This arrangement proved unsuccessful, however, and she was refitted with two funnels which hinged outboard to port in about the same position which worked much better. *Langley* had a turbo-electric drive which gave her a maximum speed of 15 knots but more usually 14 knots some months out of dock in average sea conditions. The direction of drive of her two electric motors could be reversed, in theory giving her the same speed astern as ahead which meant that aircraft could land over the bow as well as the stern but, like her British contemporaries, she was fitted with fore and aft retaining wires on the after part of the flight deck which meant that they were not ideally placed for aft-facing landings and few were ever carried out. Of interest, a pigeon loft was sighted right aft on the working deck; the RNAS had carried pigeons in both long-range flying boats and the seaplanes operated by seaplane carriers. The latter were fitted with pigeon lofts to keep the birds in good shape while they were not 'flying' and the practice was obviously adopted by the USN. Two masts to support W/T aerials and yards for flag signals to aircraft were fitted on the port side of the flight deck where they could be lowered to the horizontal during flying operations. Two conventional cranes were fitted, intended to lift seaplanes – when they were carried – from the working deck onto the water and back. Originally two catapults, each 94 feet long and capable of launching a 6,000lb aircraft at an end speed of 55 knots relative to the deck, were fitted forward but they were found to have little practical value and they were removed in 1928.

At first she had retaining wires identical to those fitted in British carriers and the first deck landings were carried out with these in place during October 1922. The USN was never happy with them and arrester wires were soon fitted athwartships to stop aircraft fitted with arrester hooks. The criss-crossed wires must have been very difficult to walk or manoeuvre aircraft across. *Langley* had no hangar and the former upper deck was largely open at the sides except for the steel structure that supported the flight deck, which had the appearance of a cover over the ship, hence her nickname the 'covered wagon'. The former upper deck was now used as a working deck on which aircraft could be prepared for flight. Since the sides were open they could even have their engines run up to full power so that they could be fully tested and warmed through. Rails were fitted centrally under the flight deck on which two 3-ton travelling cranes could run, one forward and one aft of the lift. Each had a swivelling section to allow aircraft suspended from them to be lowered onto the lift when it was in the down position and to lift aircraft that were not

USS *Langley*, CV-1, photographed off Pearl Harbor on 28 May 1928 with thirty-four aircraft ranged on deck. All of them could have been launched in a continuous stream if the ship was under way but it is anchored with the smoke stacks in the raised, non-flying, position. (Author's collection)

parked centrally under the crane on the working deck or in the holds. Dismantled aircraft and their components were stored in holds two, three, five and six. They were raised to the working deck, assembled and prepared for flight. When ready they were hoisted onto the single lift, which was just forward of the centre of the flight deck, raised and then man-handled into position right aft, where they were chocked and lashed prior to take-off.

The unusual aircraft stowage arrangements undoubtedly affected the way they were operated in *Langley*, and space on the flight deck was obviously at a premium. At first she was used for trials which advanced at a leisurely pace. One complication was that the lift could not descend to a position level with the working deck, it stopped about 6 feet above it. Thus aircraft could only be loaded onto it by crane, a process that took about twelve minutes. In British carriers the lifts were flush with the hangar deck when down and aircraft could be pushed onto and off them in a matter of seconds. Worse for the USN, once an aircraft was on the lift it took a further two minutes for it to be raised to flight-deck level, pushed aft and secured.

For this reason only eight aircraft were embarked at first and they took off singly. One reason why the catapults were seldom used is that it took even longer to fit an aircraft onto one of them than it did to range it onto the after flight deck for a free take-off. On recovery, aircraft would fly back to *Langley* and orbit overhead until the 'affirmative' flag was broken out on the horizontal mast to port. They then flew left-hand circuits to land on a completely clear flight deck after a long, flat approach at a height just above flight-deck level. This too replicated RN practice in the initial 1918 trials on *Argus*. Once the aircraft had landed and the handling party had charge of it, it was pushed onto the lift, folded and struck down, having to reverse the ranging process with a crane needed to lift it off the platform and move it to a clear space on the working deck. The next aircraft could not land on until the lift was back at flight-deck level. This slow procedure dramatically limited not only the number of aircraft that could be airborne at once but also their radius of action since they would have to return with a considerable proportion of their fuel left in order to wait for the aircraft ahead to be struck down and the lift to come back up. Until something could be done to speed up this procedure, CV-1 could not be considered as an operational, or even particularly useful, aircraft carrier but nevertheless she joined the Battle Fleet in November 1924 at the nominal end of her trial period. In February 1925 she embarked VF-2 Squadron, the first USN squadron trained to operate from a carrier and in March she was the first carrier to take part in a USN fleet exercise[4] but by then politics had begun to influence the way in which US naval aviation was to develop.

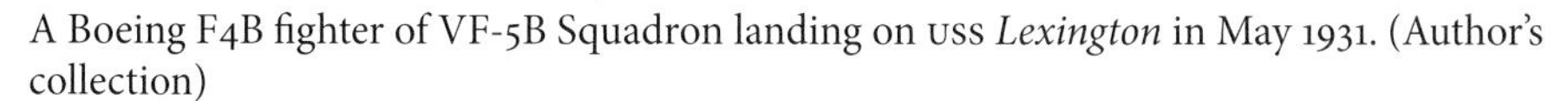
A Boeing F4B fighter of VF-5B Squadron landing on USS *Lexington* in May 1931. (Author's collection)

The Morrow Board

Paradoxically, the RAF had been created in the UK before technology had delivered the developments needed to carry out operations that could be fully independent of established naval and military forces.[5] In the harsh financial climate after 1918 it might not have endured if its leaders had merely planned to do what the RNAS and RFC had done and, in order for it to survive, the air marshals had to argue a case for strategic substitution warfare in which bombers took the place of battle fleets and armies. Similar arguments were put forward by Brigadier General 'Billy' Mitchell, US Army, who had commanded the US Army Air Corps element in France in 1918. A bizarre confrontation followed in which proponents of US air power actually opposed the use of tactical aircraft by the USN and demanded the creation of a unified air service like that in Great Britain. Both the Navy and Army Boards saw this as going much too far, being detrimental to the operational efficiency of their services and not the best approach to the aviation problems of the nation. However, the controversy did have the effect of formalising the status of aviation within the US Navy and, as we have seen, funds were allocated for the conversion of the collier *Jupiter* into the prototype aircraft carrier *Langley*, CV-1. As important, the Bureau of Aeronautics (BuAir) under Rear Admiral William Moffett was authorised in 1921, charged with 'all that relates to designing, building, fitting out and repairing Navy and Marine Corps aircraft'. This was the key structural element that had been missing from the RN since 1918. Throughout the next decade Admiral Moffett fought and won a series of political battles to keep aviation within the Navy, to provide funds for new carriers and their aircraft and to work with the fleet and the Naval War College to develop the roles and capabilities of naval aircraft. Unlike the RN, which had to rely on an ad hoc arrangement with a separate armed service, therefore, the USN had the benefit of complete organisational, institutional and operational foundations for naval aviation that have endured without change to this day.

In September 1925 General Mitchell reacted to the crash of the Navy airship *Shenandoah* by expressing his opinion that this and other accidents were the result of 'incompetency, criminal negligence and almost treasonable administration of the national defence by the Navy and War Departments'. For this he was court-martialled and after this ill-considered outburst he effectively ceased to be a factor in the debate about aviation. He had made headlines, however, and President Coolidge sought to end that debate by setting up what was known officially as the President's Aircraft Committee chaired by a prominent lawyer, Dwight D Morrow. It has subsequently become known as the Morrow Board. He took extensive evidence and rejected calls for a unified air service, producing his final report before the work of another committee, the House Military and Naval Affairs Committee, usually known as the Lampert Committee after its chairman Florian Lampert. This had started in 1924 and taken evidence from Mitchell at greater length and over a wider variety of topics than any other witness. Many felt it had lost its momentum and been outmanoeuvred by the Morrow Board which had worked directly under the authority of the President of the United States. He avoided mention of Mitchell by name but rejected the radical claims and allegations that he had made concerning the state of America's military aviation and soundly rejected the ideas of having a Department of Aeronautics and a separate air force. The latter would, Morrow believed, 'only multiply problems of command and deprive the Army and Navy of direct control of the aviation assets essential for their success in time of war'.[6] Viewed from an RN perspective he was exactly right. Unlike the 1917 Smuts Report that had led to the creation of the RAF in the UK, Morrow had weighed evidence publicly and come to his conclusions after rational debate rather than accepting claims made without evidence behind closed doors by those who had private agendas. The Morrow Board was a milestone in the history of American military aviation that led to significant changes although both reports had to be debated at length in Congress before actions were agreed and taken.

The last USN biplane fighter type in front-line service was the Grumman F3F- 3. This example from VF-5 Squadron was photographed landing on USS *Yorktown*, CV-5, in 1938. (Author's collection)

In the naval case, Morrow's recommendations were included in the Naval Expansion Act of 1926 which was signed into law in June. An Assistant Secretary of the Navy for Aviation to handle air matters was created and authorisation was given for a five-year building programme to provide the Navy with an operational force of 1,000 aircraft by 1931, half of them flying boats, patrol types and bombers based ashore. New rules were agreed for aircraft procurement and important improvements were made in the status of naval aviators including new rules on flying pay. Command of aircraft carriers and seaplane tenders was restricted to either naval aviators or naval aviation observers. The latter designation was created in order to allow senior officers to qualify for important sea-going ship and aviation commands. One further point is of interest: although expansion of the number of aircraft in Army and Navy service had been authorised, there was little extra money. Funding had to be found from efficiency savings or the replacement of other, less important projects. Broadly speaking, this period of open argument and legislation produced a naval air arm within the USN that was considerably better placed than the RN's Fleet Air Arm to fight a major war against sophisticated opposition after 1939.

Making USS Langley *Work*

The recommendation that only naval aviation specialists could command aircraft carriers had a dramatic impact because none of the Navy's early fliers was senior enough to command a carrier, even a small one like *Langley*; it would still be some years before Commander John H Towers USN, naval pilot number 3, for instance, would be promoted to Captain. This encouraged many senior officers, some of them in their late forties or even early fifties, to become pilots or naval aviation observers – among them the future Admiral 'Bull' Halsey who was later to earn fame in the Pacific. One of the most outstanding figures in the early development of naval aviation came out of the group trained as naval aviation observers in 1925. He was Captain Joseph M Reeves USN, who was 53 when he joined the course at NAS Pensacola in Florida. He had been selected by Admiral Edward W Eberle, the Chief of Naval Operations, to become the Commander Aircraft Squadrons Battle Fleet, a post that carried with it the command of *Langley*. Previously specialising in gunnery, his forceful leadership had produced record-breaking achievements in a number of ships and had brought his name to the fore. He had also been the head of the Tactics Department at the Naval War College and had a reputation as an innovative thinker who was always keen to evaluate new ideas. To round off his credentials, *Jupiter* had been his first sea command and he had carried out a detailed evaluation of her then-novel turbo-electric drive.

Reeves completed the naval aviation observer's course on 3 September 1925 and was pronounced 'ready for duty involving actual flying in aircraft, including

Captain Reeves, Commander Towers and Admiral Moffett watch flying operations from the starboard after catwalk in the USS *Langley*, CV-1, during 1927. (Author's collection)

airships, balloons and airplanes'.[7] He was promoted to Commodore and assumed command of *Langley* and the Battle Fleet's aircraft squadrons at San Diego in California at the height of the national debate about the future of military aviation. Admiral Moffett could put forward lucid arguments about the theoretical utility of aircraft within a modern navy but it was clearly up to practical sailors to prove their case in the air over the sea. Reeves was the ideal man to do so and he fully understood that to be effective, aircraft must be embarked in significant numbers. He was surprised, therefore, on joining *Langley* to find that she had never operated more than eight aircraft. If he was to provide air superiority over the Battle Fleet he needed to do much better, but for the first few weeks of his command he watched flying operations and noted techniques. Then in November 1925 he called the officers under his command to a meeting in the auditorium at NAS North Island and laid down the principles on which he believed naval aviation should be developed. His audience, some of whom had, by then, accumulated considerable flying experience, was shocked when he told them bluntly that they had demonstrated 'no conception of either the capabilities or limitations of the naval air force' and followed that forthright appraisal with a series of sharp questions. What were the most efficient methods of launching aircraft? How best to recover them and to handle them on deck? What were the ideal tactics to be employed by the various types of aircraft employed on scouting, fighting, bombing and torpedo attack, and how would they affect flight deck operations? What was the best that an air group embarked in *Langley* could deliver as part of the Battle Fleet?

A Douglas TBD-1 Devastator torpedo-bomber of VT-6 squadron from USS *Enterprise*, CV-6. (Author's collection)

USS *Lexington*, CV-2, at anchor with aircraft parked densely in Fly 1. The photograph shows the extent to which the USN always sought to put the largest possible flight decks onto its aircraft carrier hulls. (Author's collection)

In adopting this approach Reeves broke new ground and after voicing his list of questions he told his officers frankly that he did not yet know the answers. To discover them, *Langley* and the fleet squadrons would have to become a 'school' that would learn its lessons on the flight deck and in the air. His staff produced a booklet entitled 'A Thousand and One Questions' listing all Reeves' questions and others that occurred to them after his address. Not all of Reeves' officers agreed with him and there were some who believed that his ideas were actually dangerous, but as results were achieved they began to realise that they were writing what would become the manual of carrier warfare and literally inventing the tactics that the whole US Navy would use in a future war. There could not be a greater contrast with the RN, which had to suffer the 'dead hand' of the Air Ministry as its supposedly equal partner, an organisation which had little belief in the future role of the entire Navy let alone its carrier arm in a major conflict. Moffett and Reeves were actively encouraged by the USN General Board to demonstrate not just what aircraft could be flown off carriers but that the whole spectrum of naval aviation could be absorbed into the fleet's tactics to stimulate a revolution in naval warfare.

It was an exciting period and when Reeves wrote the orders for the aviation aspects of the fleet exercises planned for January 1926 he increased the size of *Langley*'s air group from eight aircraft to fourteen. Some of his pilots protested that his proposals would be both dangerous and unworkable but Reeves proved them wrong. On the first day at sea with the enlarged air group *Langley* turned into wind and launched six fighters of VF-2 from a single range led by the unit's commanding officer, Lieutenant 'Spig' Wead USN, tasked to intercept a theoretical bombing attack. Minutes later a second range of six fighters was launched to prove that the ship could get tactically significant numbers of aircraft into the air quickly and Reeves continued to drive his men hard. They did more and better every day and now he did more than just watch them. He frequently took charge of the flight deck himself with a stopwatch in one hand, standing on the ladder that connected the bridge to the flight deck. He oversaw the ranging of aircraft onto the flight deck into a tightly packed group, the forward edge of which was dictated by the foremost aircraft's minimum requirement for a take-off run. He calculated the ship's heading and speed required to give the best wind over the deck for launch and recovery, made sure that the watch-keeping officers understood his method and did their best to achieve it. The ship's air officer was placed in front of the range and, at a signal from Reeves, he ordered the aircraft to start engines and then to have their chocks and lashings removed. On a further signal he commenced the launch with subsequent aircraft, sailors holding tightly onto their wing tips to assist movement because they had no brakes, taxiing onto the centreline and rolling forward as soon as the aircraft ahead lifted clear of the deck. The operation of aircraft from a carrier is a function of space and time, often said to resemble a game of three-dimensional chess. Reeves was the first man to realise that making the maximum use of both would improve the operation of the whole package as a weapons system. Ten years earlier, Goodall had stated the British view that fleets should be 'attended' by aircraft-carrying ships. Reeves showed that aircraft were not an attendant force but an essential component, an integral part of a wartime fleet without which no navy could expect to operate effectively. His views were accepted by the US General Board and were to be proved exactly right by events in 1940.

By April 1926 *Langley* was regularly operating twenty aircraft from her flight deck, an achievement made possible by the changes Reeves had driven in equipment, concepts and technique. First to go were the cumbersome retaining wires which he believed to be over-cautious and unnecessary as the weight of aircraft had increased. Apart from making movement difficult, they had continually damaged aircraft that entered them with any sideways drift and their removal actually led to a reduction in the number of deck landing accidents. On the other hand, athwartship arresting wires, rejected by the RN in 1917, were found to be extremely effective. Once stopped, the aircraft was held steady until handlers took charge of it.[8] The wire pull-out was constant for a given weight of aircraft with the retarding force being provided in the first instance by friction drums. With the help of *Langley*'s executive officer, Commander John H Towers USN, Reeves reduced the tasks required of sailors on the flight deck into a number of specific functions. Groups of men were then trained to perform them as quickly and efficiently as possible in response to hand signals since the noise on deck was too loud for verbal instructions to be understood. These tasks included the engineers who worked the wires; mechanics who maintained the aircraft; the hook-men who pulled arrester wires clear of the hooks after an aircraft had landed and the handlers who pushed aircraft quickly and accurately into their allotted positions on deck. In charge of them all were the marshallers who wore yellow shirts so that they could be seen easily by pilots and the command team. Coloured shirts were also introduced for other groups so that their work on deck could be comprehended at a glance. These included blue for aircraft handlers, purple for the fuelling party, white for engineers, brown for aircraft mechanics and green for the hook-men. They persist in every carrier navy to this day. To improve efficiency still further the handlers were divided into numbered teams with the number painted conspicuously on their shirts so that the same men always worked together under the same petty officer. Handlers were absorbed into a specialised Aviation Branch which gave their work stability and formalised training. The Number 1 yellow shirt was the flight control officer, who had total charge of the deck under the captain's authority. As aircraft were brought quickly onto the centreline from the range aft, these officers controlled the launch, pilots saluted them to indicate that they were ready and were then signalled to take off by the launch control officer lowering a chequered flag briskly to the deck.

The most radical of Reeves' innovations was the barrier. Good drill had reduced the time taken to strike aircraft down onto the working deck and get the lift back to flight-deck level but it was still not good enough. Reeves believed that because of the cumbersome arrangements on the working deck, the best place for aircraft

The first aircraft to take off from a deck-load strike ranged on *Lexington*, CV-2's flight deck can be seen just clear of the bow. (Author's collection)

that were not flying was on the flight deck from where they could be launched quickly when necessary. He wanted a safe deck park and achieved this by having a barrier constructed of steel wire rope supported on either side by collapsible metal stanchions. When raised this would prevent aircraft that missed all the arrester wires from rolling forward into the aircraft in the new deck park. In use it was manned by an operator positioned at a control console in the port catwalk; as soon as he saw that the next aircraft to land on had caught a wire he would lower the barrier to allow it to taxi forwards quickly over the barrier into the tightly parked area on the forward part of the deck – referred to by handlers as Fly 1. As soon as the aircraft had passed safely over the barrier, it was raised to allow the next aircraft to land on. The new landing technique made possible by the barrier immediately reduced the interval between aircraft landings from an average of three and a half minutes to ninety seconds, but this was still too slow for Reeves who wanted that time halved. The improved launch and recovery times meant that *Langley* could now increase the number and diversity of the missions flown by her aircraft and transformed her into an aircraft carrier that could genuinely be declared operational.

Douglas SBD-3 Dauntless dive-bombers. Unlike the RN Skua, these could carry 1,000lb bombs and the yoke that threw them clear of the propeller disc can be seen in the retracted position on the centreline just aft of the lower engine cowling on the aircraft nearest the camera. (Author's collection)

Langley sailed for a fleet concentration off Puget Sound, Washington, in August 1926 with thirty-four aircraft embarked.[9] The exact composition of the air group is believed to have been twelve fighters, twelve spotters, four torpedo bombers and six seaplanes kept in the holds for potential use when the ship was at anchor. Commander Towers described her as a 'perfect mass of men and aeroplanes' but everything worked and Reeves was idolised by his growing team; there were no more complaints that things could not be done. Flying operations began on 7 August with launch intervals averaging fifteen seconds but recovery intervals were still an unacceptable ninety seconds. On 9 August *Langley* set a record of 127 sorties in a single day, an achievement that meant most aircraft flying four sorties and some of them more. No British aircraft carrier came near this record until well into the Second World War, even though most ships were bigger and better designed than *Langley*. By 1929 improved American aircraft design, driven by the close relationship between industry and BuAir, was also making a contribution to improved deck operations.

The aircraft embarked in *Langley* during 1926 had no brakes and tail skids rather than tail wheels. The skid had to be lifted into a steerable wheeled box that enable the aircraft to be pushed around and spotted on deck. The lack of brakes meant not only that aircraft had to be held, chocked or lashed down at all times when on deck but also that they had a slow acceleration out of the range when a pilot opened his throttle to take off because the engine had to run all the way up from idle to full power. The provision of brakes and a tail wheel that could be unlocked by the pilot to help him turn out of a herring-bone range onto the centreline made an enormous improvement and also gave the ability to pack aircraft more closely in Fly 1 under the control of a marshaller after landing. Brakes also meant that an aircraft could be run up to full power before starting the take-off roll, decreasing the length of deck required to become airborne and, in turn, increasing the size of the range that could be launched from behind the minimum deck run. The only negative aspect of this was that bigger ranges of aircraft with their engines running made the task of chock-men and lashing numbers more dangerous but here too training and good leadership made a difference. As the ship turned into wind lashings were removed and chock-men lay on the deck, one man to each wheel, holding chocks in place both in front of and behind the tyres. When the officer in charge of the deck gave the signal to remove chocks they had to run clear in the shortest possible time, dragging their two chocks by their lanyards while carefully avoiding other aircraft and their spinning propellers. Even the slightest error could have been fatal but their slick reactions were another factor in reducing the time taken to launch aircraft. Similarly chocking and lashing aircraft in Fly 1 after they had been parked but before engine shut-down was a dangerous operation that required knowledge and skill but the professional status of the aircraft handlers within the Aviation Branch made sure it was available.

Another of Reeves' innovations in the late 1920s was the deck landing control officer or 'batsman'. To start with, every pilot had judged his own approach to land on *Langley*, as the Fleet Air Arm would do on its own carriers for another decade, flying a standardised left-hand circuit to line up in the 'straight away' a few hundred feet aft of the deck, then closing the throttle over the deck to drop into the arrester wires. This resulted in a spread of touch-down points that was larger than strictly necessary because individual techniques varied and this lengthened the time taken by the hook-men to run to the aircraft from the catwalk and free the aircraft from the wire so that it could taxi forward over the barrier. Making every aircraft touch down as close as possible to the same point would shave seconds off the recovery interval and, potentially, reduce the number of arrester wires required. A target touch-down point in the centre of the arrester wire spread would also have the effect of reducing the number of aircraft that missed all the wires and went into the barrier after a badly judged approach. The new batsmen were pilots from the embarked squadrons that were given specialised training and made aware of the aim; they wore brightly coloured overalls that made them obvious as pilots turned finals and held brightly coloured bats at arm's length.[10] They soon became icons of naval aviation and qualification as a batsman was something for squadron pilots to aspire to. Unlike the similar system adopted by the RN a decade later, however, their signals were advisory not mandatory. Raised bats like a 'V' indicated that the approaching aircraft was too high and an inverted 'V' indicated that it was too low. Arms level indicated that it was on the ideal approach path. The responsibility to do something about the signal remained with the pilot of the approaching aircraft and it was a matter of pride as well as discipline to catch the designated target wire. Since they watched every recovery, batsmen were able to debrief pilots after particularly good or bad landings.

Reeves was promoted to Rear Admiral and eventually commanded the US Fleet, the first air admiral to do so. Although he had been criticised by some of the early pilots as a latecomer because of his lack of actual flying time, Reeves achieved more than any other individual of his era in the development of flight deck operating technique and one cannot but wonder what the RN could have achieved had it not lost the RNAS in 1918 and then suffered the Air Ministry's lack of interest in naval aviation. Reeves was fully aware of the capability he had created and demonstrated so effectively; in a letter to Admiral Moffett dated 4 October 1928 he admitted that he had hidden *Langley*'s operational capability during a visit by the RN's Vice Admiral Fuller. 'Of course I did not tell Fuller that we operated not 20 but 36 aircraft and could operate 42 and, possibly, 48 airplanes.' Sadly, Fuller would have been pre-conditioned by the contemporary RAF view that only a handful of aircraft were needed in carriers, that their operation posed difficulties that were difficult to resolve and that, in any case, aircraft designed for carrier operation must always be inferior to those designed for operation from land bases by the RAF. He would not, therefore, have thought to question Reeves' misinformation.

Dwight D Morrow, photographed outside the White House. (Author's collection)

After *Langley* came the big conversions *Lexington* and *Saratoga* whose hulls had become available when the Washington Treaty terminated their construction as battlecruisers. Both had large, distinctive funnels and starboard-side islands that had more in common with British carrier design than *Langley* but they were built on an altogether larger scale. At the time some in the USN thought them to be too big. They were not completed until 1928 and thus benefited from all the experience gained to date including arrester wires and barriers. They used Reeves' techniques from the outset and were capable of both embarking and operating in excess of 100 aircraft. Their completion had been delayed slightly after Reeves' insistence that aircraft were to be refuelled and re-armed on the flight deck from a number of points and not in the hangar. The first big test of these new ships was Fleet Problem IX in January 1929 which took place in the sea areas off Panama, during which Reeves commanded the Fleet's Air Squadron flying his flag in *Saratoga*. He detached from the main fleet to launch a seventy-aircraft strike against the Panama Canal from a range of 140nm. The attacking force caught the defenders completely unawares and many of them used the new and effective dive-bombing technique against the locks. Obviously no live weapons were used but we have no reason to think that the attacks would not have been effective and Reeves' pilots would have wanted to do their best to show what naval aviation could achieve. They certainly showed that carriers had the potential to act as the centrepieces of powerful mobile forces.[11] Captain E E Wilson, Reeves' Chief of Staff, described the task force as 'America's first strategic air force'. Admiral Pratt, who commanded the US Fleet, was less enthusiastic because he felt that the attack had not been sufficiently realistic to definitely prove carriers' strike capability but he did believe that it had boosted the aviators' morale and shown aircraft carriers to be credible operational, as opposed to attendant, warships. Such an exercise would not have been possible for the RN because the Air Ministry had insisted that only the RAF bomber force could carry out attacks of this nature and successive governments had accepted this as their defining policy in any future war. Aircraft carriers' only weakness lay in the huge quantities of avgas and ammunition they carried in their lightly armoured hulls. USN war games involving carriers continued to be carried out at the Naval War College, and the class of 1930 noted that aircraft carriers 'combine great power with extreme vulnerability'. Simulations highlighted this dichotomy into the 1930s and showed time after time that the fleet with a carrier force that struck first invariably emerged the winner. This confirmed the view that aircraft were needed in large numbers to find and annihilate the enemy carrier task force before it could launch its own strike and this thinking was to form part of USN tactical planning in the Pacific War that was to come.

In the UK the Admiralty had arrived at similar conclusions but the means to improve carrier operations to an acceptable level were held back by the continued political demand for joint control with the Air Ministry despite the accumulated evidence that it was not working. As re-armament got under way in 1936, the obvious disparity between what could be achieved as shown by the USN and what the RN was able to achieve under the policy of dual control convinced the First Sea Lord, Admiral Sir Ernle Chatfield, that 'now if ever was the time to put things right'.[12]

Chapter 8

The Inskip Award

In January 1933 Admiral Sir Ernle Chatfield GCB[1] became First Sea Lord and on taking up his new post he found himself faced with only one 'battle' which gave him any real anxiety, that for full organisational control of the Fleet Air Arm.[2]

The Admiralty Perspective

Chatfield had absolutely no doubt, after years spent at the Admiralty and long periods of senior command at sea, that progress in realising the RN's full potential in modern warfare was impossible as long as the Fleet Air Arm remained under the organisational control of the Air Ministry. The Admiralty's early attempts to regain control have already been described but despite the Trenchard/Keyes Agreement of 1924 the problem had never gone away and successive problems had resulted in increasingly bitter exchanges of correspondence. Apart from the Balfour Committee which had preceded the 1924 agreement, the existing arrangement had been confirmed by the Salisbury Committee in 1929 but in Chatfield's opinion the failure of the system of dual control 'was patent to the Fleet and, indeed, to many airmen'. Lord Salisbury had given it as his opinion that to develop naval aviation to its fullest scope during the years of peace it had to be part of the RAF, adding that the RAF must be the 'teachers' and the Navy the 'taught' so that 'the air experience and skill of the RAF would drive forward progress in air fighting under sea conditions'. The fact that the RAF had, at the time, nothing new to add to the achievements of the wartime RNAS seems to have eluded Lord Salisbury but he did admit in his report that 'ultimately the Fleet Air Arm may be cut loose from the remainder of the air [force] and become in all respects a special branch of the Fleet like any other'.

The Naval Staff under Chatfield's leadership now believed that the situation had changed since the Balfour and Salisbury Reports had been submitted. The RAF had expanded considerably and was continuing to do so, centred around the activities of Bomber and Fighter Commands. There was thus no longer a danger that removing naval air activities would leave the RAF in too weak a state to survive; on the contrary, the Air Ministry was now taxed to the limit to administer its own growing, independent air operations and had little to spare for the advancement of naval aviation. However, so deep was the entrenched political view that the RAF should be responsible for all British military aviation, regardless of the evidence that dual control was not working, that Chatfield's first battle was to get the question of administrative control of the Fleet Air Arm reopened at all. A lesser man would have quailed but he believed deeply that the transfer back to the RN of full control of its own air arm was a task he had been set by fate to accomplish and he could not give up his office as 1SL unless it had been accomplished. 'The Navy expected the Admiralty to do it, it was unhappy and uneasy, unable to understand why that which it considered a wrong principle, hampering naval efficiency, could not even be enquired into again.' To reopen the question Chatfield had to approach the Cabinet through the political head of the RN, the First Lord, and his task was made more difficult by the fact that during this last period of intense struggle he had three First Lords, one of whom had previously been Secretary of State for Air for a number of years. He proved himself to be loyal to the Navy but it must have been a struggle to convince him that the system of control he had, himself, been partly instrumental in imposing needed to be changed.

The Admiralty campaign to regain full administrative control of both the Fleet Air Arm and Coastal Command, that part of the RAF that operated aircraft over the sea on naval tasks from shore bases, began on 10 May 1935. On that day the

Admiral Chatfield, later Admiral of the Fleet Lord Chatfield GCB OM KCMG CVO PC. While serving as First Sea Lord he succeeded in arguing the case for Great Britain to retain seventy cruisers for the protection of Empire trade routes rather than the lower number recommended by the London Naval Conference; he claimed that battleships still had an important role to play in naval warfare and that full control of its air element should be restored to the Royal Navy. He was one of the greatest and most resourceful holders of the appointment. (Author's collection)

The Admiralty establishment in London was spread across several buildings; this is Admiralty Arch, completed in 1910. The First Sea Lord's official residence was in the right-hand block seen here from the Trafalgar Square side and Admiral Chatfield would have spent many hours at his desk in it working on how best to carry forward his arguments for the restoration of full Admiralty control of naval aviation. Note that the right-hand block has three floors and the left, originally designed as offices, has four. Unfortunately, Admiralty Arch no longer has any formal links with the Royal Navy but White Ensigns are still flown from it on state occasions as seen here. (Andrew Hobbs collection)

First Lord, Sir Bolton Eyres-Monsell, sent a memorandum to the Prime Minister, Ramsay MacDonald, which explained the Admiralty's causes for dissatisfaction and suggested that there should be an inquiry by ministers into the unsatisfactory state of affairs caused by dual control and which were impeding the development of naval aviation. A particular grievance was the refusal of the Air Ministry to train ratings as pilots to make up the numbers required in front-line squadrons and, in the longer term, to help provide a sufficient reserve to replace aircrew lost in action in a major conflict. In his reply the Prime Minister promised to consider ways of solving the problems at issue without having to bring the matter before the Cabinet, but before he could do so he resigned the premiership and became Lord President of the Council. The new Prime Minister, Stanley Baldwin, was briefed on the matter but gave it as his considered opinion that representatives of the Admiralty and the Air Ministry should meet and attempt to reconcile their differences without reopening the general question of control. Why he imagined such a course would succeed in 1935 having failed since 1918 was not made clear. Unsatisfactory as this was to the Admiralty, meetings between the First Lord, Secretary of State for Air and their various advisors took place in October and November 1935 but little was achieved and the questions of naval rating pilots and the need for reserves were not even discussed.

In January 1936 the Admiralty tried to find a way out of the impasse by suggesting an inquiry by an impartial person into the general working of the Trenchard/Keyes Agreement but there was no satisfactory response from the Air Ministry. Chatfield was beginning to feel that there was no way around the impasse but in March 1936 Sir Thomas Inskip CBE PC KC was appointed as the Minister for the Co-ordination of Defence.[3] Both the new ministry and the fine legal mind of its first head appeared to open up a new line of approach and the First Lord took an early opportunity to explain the matter to Inskip and asked him to carry out an inquiry into the whole problem. He replied that he would do his best to find solutions but that an examination of fundamental issues would require Cabinet approval. In June 1936 Sir Bolton Eyres-Monsell left office and was succeeded as First Lord by Sir Samuel Hoare who had previously served as Secretary of State for Air. Chatfield briefed him on the situation with some trepidation but was relieved when the new

Sir Thomas Inskip. (Author's collection)

First Lord declared himself sympathetic and anxious to help. However, in view of his background he felt that he could not take an active part in negotiations and this placed an even greater burden on 1SL and his uniformed Admiralty Board colleagues as they would have to face considerable political opposition alone. Meanwhile Inskip was as good as his word and held a series of meetings to discuss the provision of air personnel, periods of service and reserves with extensive input from both departments.

It soon became clear to Inskip that a limited investigation of this sort into a deep-rooted problem could not lead to a satisfactory result and he made this clear in a written report to the Prime Minister in November 1936.

Despite Inskip's good intentions, Chatfield felt that the report offered no real solution. On 16 November 1936 he told the First Lord emphatically that now, if ever, was the time to put things right if they were unsatisfactory as naval aviation clearly was. The vital point that politicians must grasp was that nothing less than the future efficiency of the RN was at stake and that fact alone ought to justify the Admiralty in pressing for a full investigation of the matter at this moment. Chatfield fully appreciated that Inskip had gone as far in his report as had been made possible by his limited terms of reference but his investigation had barely touched the fringes of many points at issue; it had been confined to the consideration of specific details, leaving the Minister unable to consider evidence bearing on the fundamental defects of the system from which these details had originated. Chatfield wrote that the principle of a single unified air service that had so appealed to the Balfour Committee when it framed its recommendations in 1923 no longer applied. He noted that the Fleet Air Arm was now embarked in a number of aircraft carriers as part of the fleet, not the tiny shore-based force that embarked occasionally for exercises that had existed in 1923. Furthermore, the Fleet Air Arm was no longer considered to be part of the metropolitan air force operating from the UK but was its own entity trained and specialising in naval warfare. The interchangeability of flying personnel in the Fleet Air Arm, the vast majority of which were now RN, and the metropolitan air force was no longer considered practicable by the Air Ministry itself because the operation of aircraft as part of the fleet was so highly specialised in almost every particular. Every new development emphasised the differences in training, equipment and technique required for air work over the sea. That the system of dual control was seriously defective was not, Chatfield wrote, his own personal opinion and nor was it an Admiralty opinion; 'it was a deep conviction of the Naval Service as a whole'. Throughout the Navy there was a feeling that it had been badly let down by political attitudes that were difficult to comprehend and that efficiency had suffered as a result. Growing awareness of what the USN had achieved over the same time frame served to accentuate this feeling and it would be fair to say that there was unease about the latent capability of the Japanese carrier strike fleet even though intelligence sources had failed to comprehend its full potential.

It was essential, if the RN was to be able to re-arm and stand ready to fight a potentially global conflict, that the disastrous experiment of dual control must be ended; no matter what politicians thought the RAF ought to contribute to three-dimensional naval warfare it was demonstrably not doing so.[4] Chatfield emphasised to the First Lord that the operation of aircraft as part of the fleet was as important to it as efficient gunnery and torpedo disciplines; all were vital facets of the same requirement for skill-sets, and failure of any one would spell disaster for the British Empire. Divided responsibility was the root cause of inefficiency, Chatfield wrote, stressing that it was incompatible with quick decisions, rapid development, flexibility of organisation and operational mobility, all of which were essential features of the fleet he was determined to create. It is worth mentioning here that in 1936 the RN had begun the largest aircraft carrier construction programme in the world with the first two of the six *Illustrious* class armoured carriers ordered, a clear indication of the importance placed on naval aviation by the Board of Admiralty. Superimposed on the failure of dual control was the dual set of allegiances placed on officers of the Fleet Air Arm and the lack of a well-defined chain of command. So long as each service regarded the embarked squadrons and flights as being part of its own organisation there must be confusion, contention and an unwillingness to seek improvements. Chatfield had no doubt that the system that followed the Trenchard/Keyes Agreement had resulted in a grave shortage of air personnel at the very time when expansion was required to man the new squadrons that would embark in the new carriers and create a flexible, operational reserve of aircrew. The road ahead seemed to be one of increasing difficulty and deficiency which could not be remedied without rapid and radical changes in manning arrangements which would be impossible under dual control and dual administration.

Astutely, Chatfield minuted at this time that in asking for undivided control of its air arm, the RN was not seeking to revert to the system of individual supply of aircraft and air material practised by the RNAS prior to 1917. He did so to allay fears that there would be a competition for aircraft and engines with which industry would be unable to cope during a period when the RAF was expanding exponentially. This was not to say that he was satisfied that the present system had given the RN the aircraft or, indeed, the air material it required but he did not want to be accused of hampering the RAF's own plans. If ever the fleet's air units failed under the test of war, he summarised, the fleet itself might fail and responsibility for it doing so would be laid not upon the RAF but on the Navy itself. The RN ought not to be asked to shoulder this vital responsibility without being granted the full and undivided powers in regard to all the forces which were required for its constituent elements. Events in the Norwegian campaign from April 1940 onwards were to prove him exactly right. Chatfield submitted his carefully considered judgement that only a complete and immediate change in the organisation, administration and control of the Navy's air services would suffice to set matters right. The earliest possible consideration must be given to this most urgent matter of the transfer to full Admiralty control of the Fleet Air Arm. The First Lord communicated these views to the Prime Minister and also discussed them with the Secretary of State for Air; the latter, however, was not prepared to go further than the limited recommendations already made by Sir Thomas Inskip in late 1936.

In February 1937, therefore, Chatfield felt it necessary to reiterate to the First Lord the seriousness of the situation into which he believed the RN was drifting and to lay stress upon the difficulty of his own position. If the situation was not to be addressed and remedied immediately, he considered that he had no choice but to resign his position as 1SL. The First Lord was 'exceedingly sympathetic' to this line and suggested that Chatfield should ask leave to brief the Prime Minister personally. Stanley Baldwin granted him an interview in February 1937 and Chatfield gave him what he described in his autobiography as 'a full and frank account of the feelings of the Navy' and told him that 'a feeling existed not only of anxiety but of injustice'. The particular examples of which he had previously been made aware 'were only examples of an unworkable administrative system' and he asked the Prime Minister for an immediate and impartial inquiry by a ministerial committee. Baldwin agreed to this and in the following weeks terms of reference for the committee were settled and a statement of the Admiralty's case was submitted in which it sought to regain full control not only of the Fleet Air Arm but also of the shore-based units that formed Coastal Command of the RAF. Despite these positive steps, however, political opposition to the Admiralty's case was still a major factor and the Cabinet decided that there must be a preliminary investigation by the Chiefs of Staff under Sir Thomas Inskip. This was announced in the House of Commons in March 1937 and the investigation was completed, as far as the Chiefs of Staff were concerned, on 18 May 1937. Despite pressure from the First Lord, however, Inskip's covering report for the ministerial committee was not ready by 28 May, when Neville Chamberlain replaced Baldwin and carried out a Cabinet reshuffle. Sir Samuel Hoare was re-appointed as Home Secretary and his place as First Lord was taken by Duff Cooper. Chatfield had come to respect Hoare and was deeply saddened by the need to brief a third First Lord on the problem of the Fleet Air Arm and to convince him that the Admiralty case was exactly right. However, Duff Cooper rapidly grasped the fundamentals of the problem and minuted his belief in the Board's arguments.

Another complication was the looming Parliamentary recess and so, on 28 June 1937, Chatfield laid before the new First Lord a full statement of the current position with an account of the discussions to date and his own conviction that if the inquiry was not completed before the House rose for the summer recess it would not be justifiable for him to remain as 1SL. The First Lord discussed the matter with the new Prime Minister, Inskip and the Secretary of State for Air and, as a result, Sir Thomas Inskip undertook to make an immediate report to the Cabinet on his own responsibility. Chatfield accepted this on the understanding that it would be done immediately but as the weeks slipped by he felt increasingly agitated; if the report was not submitted in time for Parliament to act on it before the recess he would have no recourse but to resign. On 20 July he felt it necessary to impress upon the First Lord the urgency with which he viewed the situation but, to his relief, Inskip submitted his report a day later, on 21 July 1937. In it he recommended that all ship-borne aircraft should be placed under the administrative control of the Admiralty but that Coastal Command should remain a part of the RAF. The report was approved by the Cabinet before the end of July and it was left to the Admiralty and the Air Ministry to work out the precise details of the Fleet Air Arm's transfer, with Inskip's assistance where necessary. It must be said that once this decision was taken, the Air Ministry proved helpful and co-operative in the steps needed to make it happen; perhaps, secretly, there was actually a degree of relief that it could now concentrate on the problems of its own rapid expansion and preparation for the war which was to come.

The failure to obtain control of shore-based aircraft working for the Navy reduced Chatfield's satisfaction with what was to become known as the 'Inskip Award' but he was delighted that the logical case he had put forward for regaining control of the Fleet Air Arm had, at long last, proved to be successful. It had been a supreme effort and, had it not been for Chatfield's drive and personal initiative, the process would probably have faltered as many previous attempts had done. If the Admiralty had refused to accept Inskip's decision because of the Coastal Command issue the whole matter would have been put back 'into the melting pot' and might never have been resolved at all. Time was of the essence and the Navy could not wait since the task of assuming full control of the Fleet Air Arm was an immense one. Airfields had to be taken over from the Air Ministry, if it would release them, and both technical manpower and aircrew had to be found in large numbers to replace the RAF officers and men in squadrons, aircraft carriers and the airfields ashore to which aircraft would disembark while their ships were in harbour. Chatfield predicted that if war broke out, the operational control of Coastal Command would inevitably pass to the Admiralty. This proved to be the case but only after the inadequacy of the minimal resources allocated to its 'Cinderella' coastal arm by the RAF had become plain and its inability to provide the level of support for convoy escort operations had been realised by the government.

In his autobiography Chatfield explained that the struggle even to get an inquiry into the Navy's air grievances, let alone resolve them, had been the most important aspect of his time as 1SL. From instigating what he described as his 'great endeavour' on 10 May 1935 it took him two years and two months to reach the final adjudication by Inskip and its acceptance by the Cabinet. It was period of 'sustained effort and extreme anxiety while other immense problems including the fight for money, the Naval Conference, the Abyssinian and Spanish crises and many other great matters were running concurrently'. There was also the threat from Japanese expansionist policies in the Far East. To all this must be added what

Chatfield described as the 'almost impenetrable opposition' in Whitehall, the theory that such awkward questions would be best left alone until some nebulous future date when all might be resolved. He felt at times that the fight was like punching cushions which sprang back into their former shape after every blow. It is greatly to his credit that throughout this time he did not resort to underhand methods such as leaks to the press and managed to keep the wider naval opinion firmly behind his Board and its initiatives. That said, Chatfield was grateful to those sections of the press and those Members of Parliament who did their best to apply political pressure without which the Sea Lords might not have achieved what they did. He gave credit to Rear Admiral J D Cunningham, his Assistant Chief of the Naval Staff (ACNS),[5] who had borne with him 'the brunt of the fighting' in Whitehall and placed on record the Navy's gratitude for his determined efforts.

Chatfield ended his account of this last, successful, bid to regain control of the Navy's air arm by noting that on two occasions he was on the point of resigning. He wanted to emphasise, however, that he had not considered such a step lightly; there was little point in doing so unless the move was based on grounds of judgement that the nation would understand and support and there would always be the fear that a new incumbent might not be able to fight the battle as well. However, in this instance he saw resignation as a duty and its threat actually had the effect of bringing matters to a head; it proved to be the only check to the delaying tactics of the Admiralty's opponents. Chatfield regarded his threat as a proper indication of the serious view he took of the British Empire's naval security and he used it in that spirit. The RN should always hold him in the highest regard for having done so.

Sir Thomas Inskip's Report

Sir Thomas Inskip's typewritten report[6] dated 21 July 1937 ran to twenty-two pages and was addressed to the Prime Minister. It began by stating that it was the result of a request by the then Prime Minister, Stanley Baldwin, to examine the factors involved in the question of the Fleet Air Arm and shore-based aircraft for work in co-operation with the RN and, as one might expect from an eminent King's Council, it is a lucid document that demonstrates its author's ability to concentrate on the central point of the argument. The first few paragraphs described, briefly, the background to the situation as he found it in 1937 and defined the Fleet Air Arm and its administration:

> The Fleet Air Arm is part of the Royal Air Force. The Air Ministry provide the aircraft and equipment (except torpedoes) in accordance with the needs of the Admiralty who specify the numbers and types they require. The Admiralty provide the ships together with their equipment, including all special apparatus required for the aircraft. The crew of each machine consists of a pilot and observer or air gunner

> or both. The observers and air gunners are drawn from the Navy and do not hold Air Force rank. The pilots on the other hand all hold Air Force rank, either as Air Force officers or sergeants, or as Naval officers who have been given temporary Air Force commissions in addition to their Naval rank on being attached or seconded to the Air Service. The carriers have a staff of Air Force officers and a maintenance personnel of Air Force tradesmen. Otherwise the personnel of the carriers is naval. The personnel of the Fleet Air Arm comes under Naval discipline afloat and Air Force discipline ashore.[7]

As a brief description of the organisation, this would suffice to show how incredibly complicated it was and it is difficult to understand how any rational human being could have expected it to be efficient.

With regard to Coastal Command, Inskip wrote that 'the Air Ministry are responsible for providing all shore-based aircraft. They settle the numbers and types. Likewise the personnel in connection with shore-based aircraft are drawn from the Air Force'. In fact, he observed, 'these aircraft and their personnel are an ordinary part of the Air Force, though, as circumstances require, a certain number of them may be employed on such duties over the sea or in coastal areas as reconnaissance, anti-submarine work or attacks on enemy sea-borne forces'.[8] After summarising previous attempts by the Admiralty to regain full control of its air arm, Inskip made a telling point in paragraph 17 of his report, noting that the proportion of 30 per cent reserved for RAF officers within the Fleet Air Arm by the Trenchard/Keyes Agreement might have been intended originally as minimum and not as a fixed proportion. He went on to say, 'however that may be, the policy adopted by the Admiralty, in exercise of the discretion given to them by the Balfour Report, of making the Fleet Air Arm predominantly naval in its pilot personnel, cuts across the theory that the Fleet Air Arm is concerned with the air and therefore belongs to the Air Ministry'. In paragraph 17 he mentioned a further Admiralty claim before moving on to discuss 'the principles upon which the two Departments respectively base their present contentions'. This was the question of training naval ratings as pilots, a measure the Admiralty had requested in 1928 and 1934 and which had been refused on both occasions. It had been one of the matters referred to Inskip by Baldwin in 1936 and he had recommended that twelve to fifteen naval ratings should be trained 'by way of experiment with a view to the permanent incorporation of rating pilots in the Fleet Air Arm'. The Secretary of State for Air undertook to make the experiment, 'but my report on this point was stillborn; the Admiralty thought my suggestion came too late and in any case was too small to merit a trial. The efficiency and indeed the existence of the Fleet Air Arm were said to be in jeopardy and the Admiralty raised the whole question of its control'.

Inskip found:

> the conflict between the two Services on this question of naval rating pilots is an example of the causes which have kept alive the present controversy. The only way of making the system with its cross-allegiances, and complex organisation work is by maintaining complete accord and co-operation both as to the objects to be attained and the methods to be used.

In 1932 the Air Ministry had, by agreement, secured the right to train a limited number of RAF sergeants as pilots for the Fleet Air Arm but no agreement could be reached concerning the corresponding use of naval ratings. Moreover, the Admiralty which was, in the words of the Balfour Report (paragraph 4), 'responsible for the safety and success of our Battle Fleets' and which provided the officers and other personnel required by the aircraft carriers were not adjudged by the Air Ministry to be able to settle a matter of this sort by themselves. The Air Ministry's case was largely based on the contention that 'the petty officer in the Navy is not so suitable for flying training as the sergeant in the Air Force'. Whichever view was right, it is plain that the friction resulting from such differences was not likely to promote smooth working.

This is the point where Inskip reached the focal point of his report and to avoid any misunderstanding of his recommendations I shall quote paragraphs 17 to 23 in full[9]:-

> 17. I now pass to consider the case presented by the Admiralty and the arguments on principle by which it is supported. It divides what are called by the Admiralty 'Naval Air Units' into two classes, (i) those employed on a mobile basis, (ii) those employed in specific areas. The first class consists of the ship-borne aircraft, or, in other words the Fleet Air Arm. They come under the general operational control of the seagoing fleet but, as already stated, they are provided and maintained by the Air Ministry and organically and administratively are part of the Royal Air Force. The second class takes in all units whether flying boats or seaplanes or ordinary aircraft, which are employed in tactical co-operation with the Navy upon such duties as trade defence, coastal or sea reconnaissance, anti-submarine work and other local patrols, and attacks on enemy sea-borne forces. The Admiralty take as a text or title for their general argument the phrase 'naval air work'. As used by the Admiralty it connotes the assistance which the Navy must have in the air in order to enable it to carry out the task of Imperial Defence in all its aspects. The Air Ministry do not recognise any distinction between naval air work and other air work: to the Air Ministry it is all air work, and flying over the sea is in its essential features no different from flying over the land. The Admiralty dispute this in limine: they say that a number of naval functions are now performed in suitable circumstances by an improved method, that it is to say by aircraft instead of by seagoing ships. The functions, however, remain naval and to carry them out efficiently it is

necessary to specialise in the training of the personnel and in the design of the aircraft. The use of aircraft with the Fleet, they say, is a natural part of a complex naval operation. The Naval Commander, therefore, it is said, must have the operational control of the aircraft working in this close tactical co-operation, and operational control carries with it responsibility for organising, manning, training and equipping the air units concerned. It is to be observed that there is no difference of opinion between the Departments as to operational control.

18. The above argument as set forth in the Admiralty memoranda is represented, at any rate sometimes, as applicable to the whole of the air units both ship-borne and shore-based which are considered by the Admiralty to be engaged on naval air work. Close examination of the Admiralty memoranda seems to show that it is intended to apply only to ship-borne aircraft. But however this may be I have to make up my mind as to whether the argument is sound first with regard to the Fleet Air Arm and secondly with regard to the shore-based aircraft. Before stating my conclusion on these two questions, I must summarise the Air Ministry answer to the Admiralty. Their thesis is that it is impossible to define the several roles of the Services so as to draw a hard line between what belongs to one Service and to another. A modern war carried out in three elements requires a full measure of co-operation and flexibility in the use of all the armed forces. No one Service can be made independent and self-contained. The system under which the Army and the Air Force co-operate with each other is taken as an illustration. There is a permanent allocation of 'a few specially trained and equipped squadrons' for employment with the Field Force, provided and maintained by the Air Force but under the complete operational control of a Military Commander. For the rest the Army relies on the temporary allocation as and when required and in accordance with the needs of the situation as a whole, of Air Force fighter and bomber squadrons.[10] The Air Ministry argument is enforced by reference to the fact that our resources in finance, material and personnel are limited while at the same time demands on the total air striking power of the country are very heavy. Specialisation is not conducive to economy in the use of our resources.

19. I find this line of argument very convincing though its application to any particular proposal remains always to be considered. There is no room for doubt as to the interdependence of the three Services. Illustrations could be multiplied. Whether the interdependence extends only to the strategic sphere or to tactical operations also, seems to me largely a question of words and their meaning. Any major operation is almost certain to involve the support of one Service by another, and the day-to-day duties of each Service are complementary to the duties of the others. The proper answer to a demand for naval forces to assist the Army both strategically and tactically is not to create in the War Office a Naval department. Similarly on general principles the right solution of the probable use of air power in aid of the Navy is not to make the

Navy self-contained in point of its air requirement but to call on the Air Force to meet them.

20. These, however, are general principles and they do not necessarily provide the right solution of a particular problem. As far as possible, if I am right in accepting them, they should be observed, but the facts cannot be forced into the framework of a system which they do not fit merely because the system is in theory an ideal one. Both the Admiralty and the Air Ministry have attempted to crystallise the controversy between them in the form of a single question. The Air Ministry propose the following question:–

    Can the fighting resources of this country be utilised better under a system of self-sufficiency of the Services or under that of the maximum of flexibility in co-operation between them?

    The Admiralty define the issue as a contest between specialisation which implies the close identification of the naval air units with the Royal Navy on the one hand, and on the other hand the unification of all the country's air forces. I find neither of these statements wholly satisfactory. The maximum of flexibility may be very undesirable if pressed too far. Self-sufficiency on the other hand is not the Admiralty's goal. It is plainly unattainable in practice and, moreover, in my opinion wrong in theory. The Admiralty's definition of the critical question on the other hand errs in assuming that specialisation is obnoxious to the Air Ministry. I agree with the Admiralty as to the importance of specialisation. No all-purpose machine or training could possibly be satisfactory. Specialisation, however, is not inconsistent with the unification of all the country's air forces under the Air Ministry. The question as it presents itself to me is whether or not unification ought to be rigidly maintained and if not, how far the exceptions should go. In answering this question it is necessary to consider separately first the Fleet Air Arm and secondly shore-based aircraft.

21. First as to the Fleet Air Arm, the employment of these aircraft is the responsibility of the Admiralty. It is not in dispute that they are assigned permanently to the Admiralty, subject to cabinet decision to the contrary. It makes no difference to their strategic use whether administratively they come under the Admiralty or the Air Ministry provided they are to be treated operationally as a fixed part of the Naval Forces. The Admiralty say that they are responsible for the security of the Empire against sea-borne attack. That proposition as a broad statement descriptive of the Admiralty's position seems to me true, though it is subject to the important rider that the Admiralty cannot discharge the responsibility without the aid of the Air Force working in close co-operation. The question, however, goes further than that. The Fleet Air Arm, as the phrase suggests, not only co-operates with the Fleet: it is an integral part of the Fleet. If it was possible to draw a line between the ship and its personnel and the aircraft and its personnel and to treat the latter as part of an external entity finding accommodation in the ship but not being in any way concerned with

the life of the ship, I should take the view that the aircraft in question should be administered by the Air Ministry. But the air unit in a carrier or in a capital ship is a great deal more than a passenger in a convenient vehicle. It forms part of the organisation of the ship, and as such is a factor in the efficiency of the ship, its whole raison d'être being the employment of air power in naval operations. The Naval Officers primarily concerned with the working of the ship are not only responsible in some degree for the success of the work of the aircraft but they have to accept a large measure of responsibility for the safety of the crews of the aircraft. I find it impossible to resist the inference that when so much that concerns the air units depends on the naval element in the ship and in the Fleet, the Admiralty should be responsible for selecting and training the personnel, and generally for the organisation of the Fleet Air Arm. Again the work of the Fleet Air Arm with its inevitable naval environment and having regard to the high degree of specialisation in equipment is in my opinion more likely to be efficient if the Admiralty are now responsible. This if accepted will mean that a pilot in the Fleet Air Arm will no longer be an Air Force Officer. I am informed that there is a serious shortage of pilots. As already pointed out, it is possible this could have been avoided by diminishing the proportion of naval officers in the ranks of the pilots. But even if the accepted proportion of naval officers were reduced so as to produce all the pilots required, I should still not regard the system as satisfactory today. I do not for a moment throw doubt upon the wisdom of the decision taken by the Balfour Committee and repeatedly affirmed. The proportion of the Fleet Air Arm to the Air Force was considerably smaller at the time of that enquiry and there was reason to believe that the separation of the Fleet Air Arm in those circumstances would be likely to cause duplication and waste. Undoubtedly another consideration of great importance was the desirability of fostering a spirit of co-operation between the two Services instead of merely considering the problem from the point of view of the interest of a single fighting Service. These and other considerations led both the Balfour Committee and the Government to decide adversely to the contentions of the Admiralty in 1923, but the recommendations were not at the time and in my opinion ought not now to be regarded as a final judgement. Today co-operation between the Services is axiomatic and is exhibited in practice so much that it is safe to assume it will not be jeopardised by the transfer of the Fleet Air Arm. Reconsideration of the whole question and of the arguments involved has led me to the conclusion already stated.

22. I have not considered the detailed measures which will be necessary on the footing of my recommendation. The organisation of a wholly Naval Fleet Air Arm is bound to take a long time, and it is likely that it will be necessary to do the work in stages. Responsibility for supply and design is not a primary demand on the part of the Admiralty. They recognise the advantages of a unified organisation of supply, at any rate up to the stage of delivery of the manufactured

material. The working out of the details of the supply organisation can only be done by the two Departments concerned; that there are possible objections cannot be disputed, but I have no doubt at all that such an organisation can be made to work satisfactorily and that the two Departments will take care that nothing is wanting in a determination to make it work. The Admiralty ask to have closer contact and a more decisive voice in setting the type of machine suitable for use in the Fleet Air Arm. I think this is reasonable.

23. Similarly plans for the provision of training of personnel now to be undertaken by the Admiralty must be devised by the Admiralty in consultation with the Air Ministry. The experience of the Air Ministry will be indispensable to the Admiralty in the formation of these plans. In so far as the Admiralty are not able to provide personnel in sufficient numbers new methods will have to be considered. So far as numbers are concerned, these will be restricted by the capacity of the carriers and capital ships. I assume that the number of carriers will be regulated by Cabinet decisions.

At last, after nineteen years of struggle, the Admiralty had achieved its object of regaining full administrative control of the Fleet Air Arm. Having made this judgement, Inskip now turned his attention to the question of shore-based aircraft administration. It will be remembered that the RNAS had operated aircraft from shore bases as well as ships and the former included flying boats, seaplanes, conventional aircraft and both rigid and non-rigid airships. Since 1919 the airships had gone but small numbers of flying boats, seaplanes and other aircraft remained within what was now known as Coastal Command of the RAF and on overseas stations that coincided with, but were not part of, RN fleets and stations. They were manned entirely by RAF and both commanded and controlled by an RAF Group structure. It was up to the Group Commander whether he wished to share his information with the relevant naval commander-in-chief or to act independently. Even if he did choose to share it, the delays caused by de-coding messages, passing them up the RAF chain of command, across and then down to the naval commander on the spot often invalidated time-sensitive information. With the knowledge of what was to go wrong in 1940 it is difficult to imagine a more cumbersome system, and Coastal Command was eventually placed under the operational control of the Admiralty but none of this could, of course, have been known to Inskip in 1937.

In paragraph 24 Inskip noted that 'the Admiralty claim is for the specific allocation of a certain irreducible minimum of shore-based aircraft' for the duties that had been mentioned in paragraph 17. On the face of it, this must have seemed to Chatfield and Cunningham to be a reasonable request intended to ensure that a sufficient number of what would now be known as maritime patrol aircraft (MPA) would be available to form part of convoy defences in the Atlantic, Mediterranean and elsewhere. Again with the wisdom of hindsight we know what a struggle it was to stop every long-range aircraft from being drawn into Bomber Command to

The Inskip family had other connections with the Royal Navy after the 1937 Award. The aircraft carrier *Victorious* was launched by Lady Augusta Inskip on 14 September 1939 at Vickers Armstrong's Walker Naval Yard on the Tyne. This photograph was taken a few minutes before the ceremony took place. (Author's collection)

replace its enormous losses but Inskip's analytical mind took note of the fact that no number had been specified in the Admiralty memorandum. Any allocation in peace or war would, he felt, be necessarily subject to revision and he did not feel that such an allocation would be 'a maximum of the Navy's demands upon the Air Force'. It was the wording of the Admiralty memorandum that was the underlying problem and Inskip inferred that the term 'a certain irreducible minimum' showed that the Navy was likely to have requirements above this suggested allocation. The circumstances of the moment would dictate these requirements which could only be provided by the RAF. In other words, the RAF would 'be expected to provide aircraft to carry out the duties of reconnaissance, convoy, anti-submarine operations and similar duties in co-operation with naval forces whenever the "irreducible minimum" number of aircraft operated by the Navy were considered inadequate'. The Admiralty further contemplated, he wrote, that 'the specific allocation for which they ask shall be made effective by transferring to them as in the case of the Fleet Air Arm both operational control and responsibility for equipment, organisation, manning, training and operations in peace'. The basis of this request was the Admiralty's belief that 'operational control in war over units required at all times to operate in close tactical co-operation with ships on purely naval duties is valueless without the above-mentioned responsibility'.

Inskip considered this claim in the light of the 'very careful and elaborate' examination by the Chiefs of Staff Sub Committee into the problem of protecting sea-borne trade in the event of war with Germany. The role to be played by aircraft had, he felt, been adequately covered by that Sub Committee in its report[11] and it had been agreed that large numbers would be required, even after allowing for the reconnaissance facilities of sea-going forces, including ship-borne aircraft. Inskip observed that the limitations on the nation's overall resources mentioned earlier in his report 'make it impossible to keep continuous observation over the whole of

In 1937 the Fleet Air Arm faced many challenges, including the transition from biplane to monoplane aircraft types. Hawker Nimrods, the penultimate biplane naval fighter type, can be seen here landing on. Note how closely the second aircraft is backing up the first which is about to engage a wire. Inskip accepted that the development of the techniques required to advance carrier-borne flying were very much the responsibility of the Admiralty. (Author's collection)

the North Sea'.[12] He commented on the difference between an ideal system of trade defence as far as aircraft were concerned and what would be practical: 'to lock up aircraft in order to keep every area simultaneously under continuous observation' would be, he felt, 'unjustifiable'. The only practical alternative was 'to distribute the available air forces so as to provide the necessary services at the right time'. This would entail the closest co-operation between the two commands, which could not, easily, be maintained, and he described as 'an excess of optimism' any thought that the Navy would always have the number of shore-based aircraft it wanted for trade defence. He therefore saw no alternative to the distribution of available air forces 'at the right time'. He obviously had some sympathy with the Admiralty case but at a time when

> the strain on the national resources imposed by the plans for the Air Defence of Great Britain is tremendous. The proper balance between the air forces used in trade defence and those used in the defence of Great Britain as well as those required for co-operation with the land forces can only be preserved by a continual process of adjustment in consultation between the three Services.

A measure of specialisation was obviously necessary but this could, in the case of shore-based aircraft, 'be attained by a good understanding and a close liaison between the Admiralty and the Air Ministry'. Inskip came to the conclusion, therefore, that the Admiralty's claim with regard to shore-based aircraft ought not to be admitted.

Summary

We saw above that Chatfield decided not to contest the Inskip Award because continued argument over the control of shore-based MPAs might have led to the whole question dragging on for more years, time the Admiralty Board knew it did not have if the fleet being created by the re-armament programme was to be effective. It may be, of course, that Inskip deliberately chose not to recommend the transfer of Coastal Command because he thought that this step would cause the Air Ministry to contest his whole report and lead to an unresolved impasse. Both recommendations can, therefore, be seen in a positive light from that perspective. The RN achieved its primary aim and the Air Ministry accepted the fact. In fact, relations between the two departments improved rapidly now that the Fleet Air Arm was no longer a bone of contention and the Air Ministry did all it could to help expedite the transfer. Ministers allowed two years for the transfer to be completed by July 1939. In fact all was ready by May 1939 and the transfer officially took effect from that date.

Chapter 9

The Air Branch of the Royal Navy in 1939

The Admiralty's *Naval Staff History: The Development of British Naval Aviation, 1919–1945, Volume 1*[1] began its summary of inter-war development with the statement that 'the air equipment of the Fleet had not, by September 1939, reached that stage of development which world progress in naval aviation justified'. Its author added, 'in 1939 the development of naval aircraft and of much of the equipment in the ships from which they were operated was behind the equivalent development in the United States Navy and, possibly, also that of Japan'.[2] These points were certainly true but the fact that the RN had an air arm at all and that it was under its own control in September 1939 and forming an integral part of the operational fleet was greatly to the Admiralty's credit. The period of transition began immediately after the Inskip Award was announced in Parliament by the Prime Minister, Neville Chamberlain, in July 1937, and to put the successes of naval air squadrons after the outbreak of war into perspective, the scale of Admiralty achievement in that short period must be explained.

Personnel in General

In July 1937 the RN had very few senior officers with flying qualifications and most of these were observers. Hugh Popham noted in *Into Wind*, his perceptive history of naval aviation[3] that thirty commanders qualified as pilots were required for Admiralty and liaison appointments but in the spring of 1939 only eighteen were available. Nominally 70 per cent of the pilots in operational squadrons were RN officers but in practice this percentage had not always been reached and the balance was made up by RAF pilots seconded to the Fleet Air Arm for periods as short as a year and many of these were on short-service commissions. All observers and TAGs were RN officers and ratings but there were not enough of them either. There were no RN air engineer officers and no naval maintenance ratings of any kind. Not only did the Admiralty have to replace the RAF personnel in the organisation it took over but its re-armament plans required the air arm to be doubled in size. At the beginning of the transition period the Admiralty had to identify and train a number of air engineering specialist officers and about 4,000 technical ratings ranging from highly -trained and qualified artificers to basic mechanics. At the time the Fleet Air Arm had slightly over 200 front-line aircraft but by 1942 the government had authorised an expansion of that figure to 450, which would

Hawker Ospreys of 800 NAS in 1939. Nearest the camera is K5742, side number 108, with the coloured tailplane which indicated that it was the CO's aircraft. The fuselage band comprised red and blue stripes to indicate the squadron's parent carrier, *Ark Royal*. (Author's collection)

require at least 8,000 RN maintenance ratings, all of which had to be trained in the space of four years, many of them from scratch.

At the end of the previous chapter I wrote that the Air Ministry had accepted Inskip's Report without objection but the Secretary of State for Air and the Chief of the Air Staff did, initially, comment that they felt the report had been hastily concluded without giving them a chance to state their own case fully. Reading through the files, however, the impression is gained that they did so more for the sake of form after years of debate than for any wish to complicate their own expansion plans by demanding yet another look at this long-running problem. The overall reaction of the Air Ministry was to be as helpful as possible and one gains the impression of a sense of relief that the arguments were over. Arrangements were made for the initial loan of about 150 technical officers and several thousand aircraft maintenance and stores personnel until the RN could train its own men. A relatively small number of RAF officers and men with Fleet Air Arm experience volunteered to transfer permanently to the RN and these proved to be an invaluable core of expertise around which the new branch structure could coalesce. Thus it was that on the outbreak of war the Navy was not only deficient in the number of aircraft it could deploy and in their technical development but it also had difficulty in finding personnel with any experience capable of manning, maintaining and controlling its aviation activities. Little margin remained for the immediate expansion demanded by war, for taking full advantage of the new circumstances for developing and improving naval aviation or for building up the reserves that would be needed to replace losses in action.

The Admiralty was reluctant to retain the name Fleet Air Arm which was associated with the RAF by many of the public. It was decided, therefore, to adopt a new title, the Air Branch of the Royal Navy, from 1938. In my opinion this was a good title that exactly described what the Admiralty wanted the RN's new air arm to be; it was unambiguous and could hardly be mistaken for part of another service. The older title remained in familiar use, however, and both were used throughout the war[4]

Flag Officers and Naval Air Stations

One senior aviation appointment had already existed since 1931 when Rear Admiral Sir Reginald Henderson was appointed the first Rear Admiral Aircraft Carriers (RAAC). He held the post until 1934, as noted above and, while not himself a pilot, he had commanded the aircraft carrier *Furious* and was a staunch advocate of naval aviation. By 1939 the incumbent was Vice Admiral Sir Lionel Wells KCB DSO, the higher rank indicating the greater emphasis placed on naval aviation by then. The expansion of the carrier strike fleet led to an increasing number of flag officers commanding task forces built round aircraft carriers as the war progressed. Another senior post that had existed since the establishment of a Naval Air Division in the 1920s was that of Assistant Chief of the Naval Staff (Air), ACNS (Air), whose task was to advice the Board on matters of air doctrine and policy. At first his work centred on liaison with the Air Ministry on what the Navy wanted its aircraft to achieve but after the Inskip Award he gained a technical responsibility and became responsible both for policy and the statement of staff requirements for new material to meet it.

A link with the RNAS was established in 1938, however, when the newly promoted Rear Admiral Richard Bell Davies VC CB DSO AFC took up the new appointment of Rear Admiral Naval Air Stations (RANAS). Between 1935 and 1937 he had served as Commodore of Devonport Barracks, one of the RN's three drafting depots,[5] and it is likely that he was given that appointment to learn how to run a large-scale drafting organisation effectively. Put simply, his immediate task was to create a Fleet Air Arm barracks from scratch and to administer the drafting of air ratings from it to ships and squadrons as well as building up reserves in every trade. His brief covered a variety of disciplines, the first of which was to establish naval air stations ashore which could be used to parent what were now naval air squadrons when they disembarked from their carriers, capital ships and cruisers. They were also to become the focus of dedicated naval air schools that would cover everything from advanced and operational flying training to technical training and the wider application of naval air subjects to officers and men from throughout the fleet. This was a huge remit which took some years to implement fully. In July 1937 there were no naval air stations since the Fleet Air Arm had used whatever RAF airfields were deemed suitable. Generously, the Air Ministry agreed to hand over four airfields as soon as their RAF lodger units could be moved to other locations. Lee-on-Solent was the first. It had been a naval air station in the First World War and operated as an RAF seaplane station since 1918. By 1938 it had expanded with a grass airstrip laid out on adjacent fields which were soon to be replaced by hardened runways with nearby dispersal pans near extensive hangarage. At the time it was the headquarters of RAF Coastal Command under Air Marshal Sir Frederick Bowhill GBE KCB CMG DSO*, a former RN officer who had served in the RNAS and commanded HMS *Empress*, 8 (Naval) Squadron and RNAS Felixstowe prior to 1918.[6] He offered to evacuate the RAF squadrons based there by

Ark Royal alongside in Portsmouth during 1939. Note the conspicuous de-gaussing coil fitted around the upper hull. The structures on either side of the forward flight deck round-down are the forward extremities of the two BH-3 hydraulic catapults, each capable of launching an aircraft of up to 12,000lb all up weight at an end speed of 56 knots relative to the deck. (Author's collection)

the spring of 1939 and, as important, he undertook to vacate his own headquarters at Wickham Hall, inside the airfield boundary, at the same time and this became RANAS's headquarters. Until it was ready, Bell Davies operated from an office in the Admiralty with Captain Lachlan Mackintosh RN as his Chief of Staff and Commander Eric George RN as his secretary.[7] Lee-on-Solent was commissioned on 24 May 1939 as HMS *Daedalus* to combine the functions of airfield and drafting barracks for the Air Branch. The RN Observer School was already established there and, for a time remained but soon moved out as accommodation was at a premium.

The other airfields handed over to the Admiralty included Donibristle on the north shore of the Firth of Forth, which had been the Grand Fleet air park in 1917/18; it was commissioned on 24 May 1939 as HMS *Merlin* and used as a repair base and storage for reserve aircraft. The other two airfields commissioned on the same date were Worthy Down, HMS *Kestrel*, and Ford, HMS *Peregrine*. Both were used by disembarked squadrons and new air schools, such as the School of Air Photography, as they were established. The Admiralty also obtained permission to use part of the airfield at Eastleigh, near Southampton, which commissioned as HMS *Raven* on 1 July 1939. It was home to the RN Fighter School until 1940. This handful of air stations was inadequate to meet the Navy's rapidly expanding needs but the RAF, in the midst of an unprecedented period of expansion, felt unable to offer more and so the Admiralty set out to build a number of new, permanent air stations to its own standardised design. Some used sites that had been used as airfields before and typical of these was RNAS Hatston, just outside Kirkwall in the Orkney Islands, which was commissioned on 2 October 1939 as HMS *Sparrowhawk*. It was the first military airfield in the UK to be completed with paved runways, a task made easier by laying the main east/west runway along the line of the old Kirkwall to Stromness road. A new road had to be built by the council around the airfield perimeter. Other new-builds included RNAS Arbroath, HMS *Condor*, commissioned on 19 June 1940; RNAS Yeovilton, HMS *Heron*, commissioned on 18 June 1940; RNAS St Merryn, HMS *Vulture*, commissioned 10 August 1940 and RNAS Crail, HMS *Jackdaw*, commissioned on 1 October 1940. Commissioning, equipping and manning so many air stations while carrying out the world's largest programme of aircraft carrier construction in 1940 at the same time as fighting a war that did not develop at all as expected was a magnificent achievement by the Admiralty which has not been given the recognition it deserved.

Pilots

Although the majority of the pilots in the active Fleet Air Arm were already naval officers, many more would be needed to meet the expansion programme already authorised and to provide a war reserve. The inter-departmental agreement reached after the Inskip Report made the RAF responsible for all elementary and basic flying training up to the standard required for the award of the flying badge or 'wings'. The Admiralty was to set up its own schools at naval air stations as they became available to teach specialised advanced and operational flying for naval pilots. With the exception of the Observer School, the RAF had previously refused to allow the Navy to set up schools at its airfields because of its policy of non-specialisation. Consequently aircraft carriers had to be used for every stage of training, not just the final qualification in deck landing technique, and this had limited the amount of time they could spend on operational development with the fleet. However, it was now up to the Admiralty to select the students it wanted to put up for flying training. Until 1937 all RN pilots had been regular officers who volunteered to sub-specialise in flying duties, but with every other branch of the service implementing its expansion plans there could not be enough of these to meet the required numbers, even if a high proportion of young officers volunteered. We saw above how Admiralty attempts to train ratings as pilots had foundered because of Air Ministry opposition but now the Admiralty was able to proceed with such a scheme.

The first course of twenty ratings arrived at Number 1 Flying Training School at RAF Leuchars on 9 May 1938 to begin Number 41 Naval Pilots' Course,[8] the last in the sequence of courses that had begun in 1924.[9] Five of these did not qualify but, contrary to the fears expressed by Air Ministry experts, the remainder did well overall and the first of them achieved his deck landing qualification on HMS *Courageous* early in 1939. Subsequent courses began a new series starting with Number 1 on 27 June 1938. These were all made up of both officers and ratings and were carried out at Elementary and Reserve Flying Training Schools at Sywell, Rochester, Yatesbury, Netheravon, Gravesend, Peterborough, Desford, Shawbury, Castle Bromwich, Elmdon and Sydenham. The big increase in the number of schools gives a clear idea of how the overall British flying training organisation was expanding at the time. Some of the sites made use of civilian flying schools with their instructors inducted into the Royal Air Force Volunteer Reserve (RAFVR). As an example, Number 2 Pilots' Course which began on 2 January 1939 concurrently at Sywell, Yatesbury, Rochester and Netheravon comprised thirty-nine officers and nineteen ratings. Looking through the list of names, there are many who went on to earn distinction in the Second World War.

The Admiralty had to find still more methods of increasing numbers, however, and it did so in several ways, the first of which was to introduce a short-service commission scheme for officers from February 1938. Prior to that the Admiralty had insisted that extensive sea experience was required for naval pilots to be sufficiently knowledgeable to take tactical decisions in the air but this requirement had to be waived if the numbers needed to man the front-line squadrons were to be achieved. New entries underwent a minimum of naval training and had to be aged between 17½ and 22 years on entry and were expected to serve for a minimum of seven years, which could be extended. The Admiralty was also at

Blackburn Shark torpedo-bombers over a battle fleet which includes both *Nelson* and *Rodney*. (Author's collection)

pains to point out that those who wished to seek suitable sea-going qualifications would be considered for permanent commissions on the active list. Once qualified as pilots they were commissioned as Midshipmen or Sub Lieutenants depending on age and wore the straight gold sleeve lace of the regular Navy but with a letter 'A' embroidered inside the executive curl on the upper row of lace indicating that they were Air Branch officers who could not command ships or hold certain other executive appointments and their rank as shown in the Navy List marked with the suffix (A). This actually became a source of pride in their new branch and they referred to themselves as 'Branch Types'. They were expected, first and foremost, to fly and since many of them became involved in the early fighting from the Norwegian campaign onwards they learnt quickly and became expert in the application of naval air warfare – more so in fact than many senior RN executive officers. By the middle war years many commanded naval air squadrons and some went on to become admirals in the post-war Navy. Overall the RN was pleased with its new Branch Types, they were immensely enthusiastic and because they were intended to fly without other distractions, they found themselves doing precisely

A revised RN pilot's 'wings' badge, modified by the addition of a crown over the foul anchor but still worn proudly over the left sleeve rank lace on blue uniforms, was introduced in 1939. (Author's collection)

what they had volunteered to do. At the same time as the new Air Branch was announced, a new form of pilot's badge or 'wings' was introduced; still worn over the left sleeve lace the new badge superimposed a crown above the foul anchor which was surrounded by a laurel wreath with albatross wings to either side as in the earlier badge.

Regular and short-service officers made up the majority of elementary pilot courses during 1938/39 but the Admiralty was determined to gather as many pilots as it could who had already qualified and had some experience of the Fleet Air Arm. Typical of those who entered the new Air Branch in this way were John Wellham and Eugene Esmonde, both of whom were to distinguish themselves flying Swordfish. Wellham was serving on a four-year short-service commission with the RAF in 1938 when he saw an Air Ministry Order 'stating that suitably qualified pilots of the RAF were invited to apply for commissions in the new Air Branch of the Royal Navy and that those accepted would be given every opportunity to qualify for executive status'.[10] He duly applied and 'soon received a letter from the Admiralty accompanied by a long list of uniforms and pages of rules and regulations about the Air Branch'. The letter informed him that he had been granted a commission in the RN in the rank of Sub Lieutenant (A) with the seniority of his present RAF rank. This pleased him because a Sub Lieutenant equated to a Flying Officer RAF and at the time he was only a Pilot Officer, one rank lower. This gave him sufficient seniority to be promoted to Lieutenant (A) at the age of 20 and by 23 he was an acting Lieutenant Commander (A) in command of a naval air squadron. He was one of the pilots that attacked the Italian Fleet at Taranto on 11 November 1940. Eugene Esmonde had also served on a short-service commission with the RAF during which he had flown with 463 Flight embarked in HMS *Courageous*. He failed to be considered for a permanent commission and transferred to the Royal Air Force Reserve (RAFR) in December 1933 after which he joined Imperial Airways. The Admiralty wrote to him in 1938 asking if he would be prepared to join the Air Branch and he accepted. He joined Lee-on-Solent as a Lieutenant Commander (A) in April 1939 for a short conversion course onto the Supermarine Walrus and was appointed in command of 754 NAS, part of the Observer School at Lee on 24 May 1939. The squadron gave him the chance to get used to the RN in general and the Air Branch in particular and on 31 May 1940 he was appointed to command 825 NAS. He was to earn the DSO for leading the squadron's strike from *Victorious* against the *Bismarck* in May 1941 and a posthumous VC for leading six of the squadron's Swordfish against German warships during the 'Channel Dash' action on 12 February 1942.

Despite the success of these schemes, the Admiralty appreciated that if war broke out the Air Branch would need pilots in unprecedented numbers and few of them could have the level of experience considered usual before the war. An Air Branch of the RNVR was established in 1938 and Number 1 RNVR (A) Pilots' Course began at Desford in May 1939 with twenty-five students. They wore the wavy gold lace of the RNVR with the letter 'A' woven into the curl and when war broke out this group was at Hyeres in the south of France, from where they carried out deck landing training in HMS *Argus* in the relatively safe and calm waters of the Mediterranean. Once qualified they were appointed to front- and second-line squadrons in line with all the other pilots out of the training pipeline. Of interest the majority of men fed into the Air Branch training scheme during the war were RNVR (A) and by 1945 they comprised the largest portion of the total number qualified. Even then the Admiralty could not have reached its expansion targets without volunteers from the Commonwealth, particularly New Zealand.[11] By 1945 roughly half the pilots and observers in front-line naval air squadrons came from Australia, New Zealand, Canada and South Africa. Some of these joined

A Blackburn Skua in flight painted in one of the camouflage schemes adopted on some aircraft in 1939. (Author's collection)

the RNVR Air Branch directly, some served with their own naval reserves. The Royal Canadian Naval Volunteer Reserve (RCNVR) was unique in having no Air Branch of its own, although its members flew with the RN; thus they had no 'A' in the curl of their sleeve lace. From 1941 most elementary flying training was carried out in the Empire Air Training Scheme in Canada or under the Towers Scheme with the US Navy. In September 1939 there were 406 fully trained pilots in the Air Branch available for front-line duties with a further 352 under training. By July 1945 those numbers had increased to 3,243 fully trained pilots with a further 1,295 under training.

Observers

In 1938 RN observers still had no flying badge – that would not appear until 1942 when resentment at what was by then considered a lack of recognition in comparison with the RAF forced the Admiralty to act. In the RAF pilots were always considered to be of paramount importance but in the Fleet Air Arm observers frequently took tactical command of aircraft and worked closely with the fleet on reconnaissance missions and spotting for the long-range fire of capital ships and cruisers. By 1939 the Observer School had moved to RNAS Ford but it was attacked by enemy aircraft in August 1940 and was deemed untenable as a training base. Observer training therefore moved to two new schools, one at RNAS Arbroath in Scotland and the second at RNAS Piarco in Trinidad, which was close to the sea, had a good weather factor and was, at the time, well clear of any likelihood of enemy attack.[12]

Like pilots, regular officer observers were augmented by ratings from 1938, known rather quaintly at first as Observers' Mates. Short-service commissions

Blackburn Skuas of 803 NAS from *Ark Royal* flying over *Nelson*. The lead aircraft's blue-and-white striped tailplane indicate that it is a flight commander's aircraft and the blue and red fuselage stripes indicate the parent carrier. (Author's collection)

were also open to observers under the same terms as pilots with some joining as direct entries and others joining their numbers who had failed pilot training but shown some aviation initiative. By 1939 a number had joined the RNVR (A) scheme and like pilots they joined a shore establishment, HMS *St Vincent*, at Gosport as naval airmen and were not commissioned until they completed their course successfully. The course consisted of both theoretical work in such subjects as navigation, communications, ship recognition, photography and flying. Many sorties comprised navigation over the sea 'taking departure' from an imaginary aircraft carrier, calculating the actual wind and then 'intercepting' its projected position after a specified time in the air. The ability to do so even under the most adverse conditions would be something that the lives of the observers' crews would depend on when they reached a front-line squadron, and the technique had to be drummed in until it was second nature. Air-to-air firing was carried out against a sleeve target towed by another of the training squadron's aircraft; the weapon was a 0.303-inch Vickers Type K machine gun, a marginal improvement over the First World War Lewis gun. Ammunition, like the Lewis, was in pre-loaded drums or 'trays' which had to be changed in flight and if the gun jammed observers and TAGs were expected to strip it, fix the problem and carry on firing while the aircraft manoeuvred hard under attack.

Operations officers who planned carriers' flying activities were all qualified and experienced observers and as the war progressed many of the early 'old hands' found themselves filling this role. In September 1939 there were only 260 fully trained observers and by July 1945 that number had risen to 1,843.

Telegraphist Air Gunners

Like observers, TAGs had formed a specific group within the Fleet Air Arm since 1924. By 1938 most front-line aircraft including the new Skua and Roc fighters and the Swordfish TSR had two or more seats and required a TAG. From 1939 TAG training was carried out at RNAS Worthy Down but a Naval Air Gunnery School was established in Canada at the RCAF base at Yarmouth in Nova Scotia. Some volunteers for TAG training came from the fleet, with telegraphists who wanted more excitement than their usual routine as obvious candidates; others were direct entries trained at HMS *Royal Arthur* at Skegness[13] at first and then *St Vincent* before commencing flying training. Their required skills to 'speak' rapidly in Morse code using a Morse key and to use a machine gun on a flexible mounting in what might well be the last-ditch defence of their aircraft had to be learnt quickly and had to be relied upon by their crew-mates in action. They formed a tight-knit group that was never large.[14] There were 350 trained TAGs available for front-line duties in September 1939 and only 1,248 in January 1945.

Air Engineer Officers

In 1937 the RN's engineer officers were annotated (E) in the Navy List and after their rank, thus an engineer Lieutenant appeared as a Lieutenant (E). There were no air engineering specialists in 1937 and the Admiralty took urgent steps to provide the necessary numbers. Some transferred directly from the RAF, some cross-trained from other sub-specialisations such as mechanical engineering and some were recruited directly from civilian life, attracted by short-service commissions and cash incentives. Electrical matters were the responsibility of the RN Torpedo Branch at that time and similar measures applied although the requirement for air electrical sub-specialists was not as great at first.

By 1939 there were just sufficient to provide air engineering officers for front-line squadrons and the larger second-line ones, usually a Lieutenant (E). Every carrier and naval air station had an air engineering department (AED), which was to back up the squadron personnel by carrying out deep maintenance, battle-damage repairs and important aircraft modification programmes that had been authorised by the Admiralty, which now had responsibility for the safe operation of its aircraft. Unlike the RAF, the Air Branch had to operate its aircraft from moving bases which might be thousands of miles away from the nearest aircraft repair yard and air engineers had, therefore, to have access to the largest range

Swordfish of 825 NAS over *Glorious*. This squadron was the first to re-equip with the type in July 1936. (Author's collection)

of spares that could be accommodated on board and to make use of the cramped workshops to the best of their ability. A number of stores items such as nuts, rivets, plugs and the like were listed as general air stores but many were type-specific. The latter included spare wings, undercarriage legs and propellers: large items that had to be stowed in every available space not just the store rooms low-down in the hull. The deep beams between the girders that supported the flight deck and hangar bulkheads were particularly suitable for securing large objects. Like every type of ship, carriers would pitch and roll in any but the calmest of seas and every aircraft, spare part and tool box had to be securely lashed down when not being moved or used. The maintenance carrier *Unicorn* was specifically designed at this time to support fleet carrier operations and had exceptionally comprehensive workshop facilities, a double hangar structure for reserve aircraft and a vast stores complex capable of holding the entire stores range for British-built naval aircraft. Although designed at the insistence of Admiral Henderson, 3SL, she was unfortunately not completed until 1943 but was to play a key role in operations in the Indian and Pacific Oceans and, later, the Korean War. From the outset, the RN established bases known as RN air yards ashore, Donibristle being the first, to carry out deep maintenance, store aircraft and carry out a range of survey and repair tasks. These were all partially manned by civilians but also needed air engineering officers, artificers and mechanics in increasing numbers as the war progressed.

Other branches were also involved intimately with aviation in carriers and had been for a decade or more. Catapults – known in carriers at first as 'aircraft accelerators' to differentiate them from the cordite-powered catapults in battleships and cruisers – and arrester wires were the responsibility of Commander (E) and his Marine Engineering Department and flight deck lighting was the responsibility of the Electrical Department.

Aircraft Artificers and Mechanics

In 1937 the Admiralty calculated that roughly 4,000 air technical ratings must be recruited to take over the task of aircraft maintenance from the RAF by 1939. The new Air Engineering Branch followed the established pattern of the Marine Engineering Branch with artificers as the most highly skilled ratings, capable of carrying out any task within their specialised areas. The first three-year course for engine and airframe artificer apprentices began at RAF Halton in August 1938,[15] and courses for air electrical artificer apprentices and ordnance artificer apprentices began at Rosyth Dockyard in January and August 1939 respectively, the latter at RAF Cosford. In August 1939 the RAF decided to dilute the quality of its own artificer training and reduced the course to only two years but the Admiralty was not prepared to do the same thing for two reasons: it wanted air artificers to be of a comparable standard to engine room and all other types of RN artificer and it needed men capable of carrying out any task a long way from the nearest air yard. In consequence the Admiralty set up its own Air Artificer School at an outstation to Lee-on-Solent's school for air mechanics at RAF Lympne on the south coast. Initially this RN air facility was commissioned as HMS *Buzzard* but it was soon renamed HMS *Daedalus II* as it operated as a tender to Lee-on-Solent for pay and administration. The school subsequently moved to Newcastle-under-Lyme in Staffordshire but by then all RN artificers did one year of common training at Rosyth before sub-specialising for the remainder of their course.[16] Artificer apprentices wore the Class III uniform of men not dressed as seamen and on completion of their training they were rated as Petty Officers and, when qualified by time, Chief Petty Officers (CPOs). They wore no badges on their jacket other than their rate. The pinnacle of the 'artificer tree' was the Chief Aircraft Artificer; usually every squadron would have one, and several would cover differing disciplines within an AED or air yard.

This proved to be the most difficult area to take over from the RAF since new entries took three years to train and only about 300 were recruited annually. Once war broke out the only suitable civilians tended to be in reserved occupations so it was hard to recruit suitably qualified engineers. Some gaps were filled by cross-training other artificers but the majority of the gaps were filled by RAF artificers. Some of these volunteered to transfer to the RN but others opted to serve with the Navy but remain members of the RAF. In May 1939 the Air Ministry generously agreed to leave 1,460 men on extended loan to the RN until they could be replaced. Many of these had previous experience of the Fleet Air Arm and gave valuable service. Some were still serving with the Navy in late 1944. More than any other branch of the RN, air artificers struggled to provide the numbers required as the Air Branch expanded ten-fold before 1945.

Next in line beneath the artificers in both skill and knowledge were air fitters, who wore the same Class III 'fore and aft' rig as artificers but had a badge comprising a four-bladed propeller on their right arm. Initially they sub-specialised in either airframes or engines with 'A' or 'E' under the badge but as aircraft became more complex the sub-specialisations of air electrical and air ordnance were added with the letters 'L' or 'O' under the badge. Over 12,000 had been trained by 1943. Their training lasted twenty-five weeks with less theory than artificers but a great deal of bench work and practical application. Volunteers usually had some engineering background and they could expect to be promoted to at least Leading Air Fitter within six months of qualification and those that demonstrated aptitude could be rated Petty Officer Air Fitter quickly. Those that showed the highest aptitude could be encouraged to apply for a twenty-five-week conversion course to become air artificers. Whilst this was undoubtedly good for both the man and the service in the long term, there was sometimes a reluctance on the part of commanding officers to recommend air fitters for the conversion course because they did not

Fairey Swordfish L7701, one of a batch of sixty-two ordered in 1937 and delivered in 1938, seen here armed with a practice Mark XII torpedo while serving with the Torpedo Trials Unit at Gosport. (Philip Jarrett collection)

want to lose a good man who, by then, probably had an important role to play in his squadron or AED.

The lowest grade was the air mechanic. These often had no previous engineering experience and joined the RN directly for an eighteen-week course which trained them to become 'semi-skilled maintenance ratings employed on minor inspection and repair by replacement'.[17] They wore the Class II 'square rig' of RN seamen and had a badge comprising a two-bladed propeller worn on the right arm. They sub-specialised into the same disciplines as air fitters and had the same letters under their badge. Advancement was by merit although, given the higher rates held by artificers and fitters after their extensive training, the opportunities for air mechanics to reach the higher rates were limited. Those who showed the greatest promise could seek to become fitters and, potentially, artificers. This was the grade into which volunteer hostilities-only ratings were absorbed in thousands as the war progressed. Artificers, fitters and mechanics all had their own tool boxes, appropriate to their sub-specialisation, which they took with them wherever they went, together with their kit bag and hammock. Artificers and fitters often made some of their own tools whilst under training but mechanics tended to use 'Pusser's issue' tools.

The opportunities for sideways recruitment were still there in this grade and some air mechanics were cross-trained from other branches, mostly what were still rather quaintly rated as stokers in the Marine Engineering Branch. The number of places on RAF courses was limited and until the Admiralty could set up its own permanent schools it took a number of imaginative steps to increase the number of student places so that volunteers could be taken up as quickly as possible. Typical of these was a contract signed in 1939 between the Admiralty and the Gas Light and Coke Company of Fulham to train apprentices as air fitters. This proved so successful that from 1940 another contract covered the training of unskilled men as air mechanics. After the outbreak of war the Government Training Centre at Watford was used to provide courses that would upgrade mechanics to air fitters.

Logistic and Administrative Duties

Unlike an RAF squadron, naval air squadrons were intended to be mobile and when they embarked in a carrier or disembarked to a naval air station the 'hotel services' needed to be augmented to cater for the extra numbers. The easiest way of achieving this was to draft officers' stewards, cooks, stores assistants and writers to the squadron itself so that they could embark and disembark with it. These came from the general service Navy but from 1938 many of those who served with the Air Branch effectively sub-specialised and they stayed with it. All these branches wore the Class III uniform of men not dressed as seamen and had a six-pointed star as a badge on their right arm. At its centre was a circle which contained the letters 'OS', 'C', 'SA' or 'W' to indicate the ratings' specialisations[18] mentioned above. The Stores Branch included several sub-branches, among them Naval, Victualling and Armament, and a new Air Stores Branch was added from 1938. Stores depots ashore were invariably run entirely by civilians and stores assistants served in ships and at naval air stations and establishments ashore. The civilian stores experts were the Principal Stores and Technical Officers (Naval) at the depots, some of whom embarked in ships of the Royal Fleet Auxiliary (RFA) as the war progressed.

All stores disciplines had an impact on the Air Branch. Stores assistants varied by qualification and experience from the basic, ordinary rate through Leading Stores Assistant and Petty Officer to Chief Petty Officer and Warrant Officer. The sub-specialisation was indicated by letters in brackets after the rate. Thus a victualling specialist would be a Leading Stores Assistant (V). Naval stores included, among many other things, tools, cordage, hardware and radio parts. Victualling stores included uniform clothing, food, rum, crockery and mess utensils. Senior victualling rates were also responsible for the preparation of menus.

The new Air Stores Branch had to learn quickly after 1938 and like the Air Engineering Branch relied on RAF stores experts to get it started. They were not helped by the fact that British industry and the armed forces had not yet produced

Swordfish of 820 and 821 NAS ranged aft on *Ark Royal*'s flight deck and running ready for launch during exercises in February 1939. (Author's collection)

an ideal system intended to make life easier for the end user in a naval air squadron. Thus an aircraft component intended for use as a replacement stores item would have a manufacturer's identity number; it would probably have been delivered to an air yard or dockyard where it would have been given a different naval stores number and in the specific aircraft maintenance manual it would, at least until 1943, probably have been identified by an RAF stores number which differed from the first two. To make matters worse, even if an air stores assistant opened an item's box he would probably be unable to recognise the contents and would have to rely on an air engineering officer or artificer to identify them for him. The introduction of American aircraft from 1940 brought a further layer of complication that needed to be resolved and the identification, codification, correct embarkation and stowage of air stores had still not been fully resolved in the aircraft carriers of the British Pacific Fleet in 1945. American aircraft also had screw threads, nut sizes and electrics that differed from the British system, and ratings who worked on them had to be issued with separate American, tool boxes.

Writers were effectively administrative clerks who worked in offices and dealt with pay, personnel records and the ship or squadron's official correspondence. Ashore they ran the drafting offices in the barracks, including Lee-on-Solent where drafts were worked out to form new naval air squadrons, replace men in existing ones as necessary and fill the air billets in warships. These were not new requirements but the branch needed to be expanded at the outset and to learn the needs and idiosyncrasies of the Air Branch as it found its feet.

Aircraft Procurement

A Directorate of Air Material (DAM) was established within the Admiralty in January 1938 tasked with forming staff requirements for new material, including aircraft, to meet Admiralty policy. It was composed of a mixture of executive officers with flying experience, some of the more senior members being observers, and technical officers and, unlike other Admiralty technical departments, it reported to an executive officer, ACNS (Air). Because the RN went to war in September 1939 with monoplane fighters of modest performance, the Blackburn Skua and Roc together with the biplane Gloster Sea Gladiator fighter and Fairey Swordfish TSR, many historians have assumed that the Air Ministry had forced the Navy to accept mediocre designs for the Fleet Air Arm. This is an over-simplification but the Air Ministry did have a pernicious impact on carrier-borne aircraft in a number of ways that are less obvious. However, given the length of time it took to develop new combat aircraft and their engines, the new DAM was formed too late to have a significant impact on the aircraft with which the RN went to war.

Chapter 10

Royal Navy Aircraft in 1939

The two principal aircraft in Royal Navy service in 1939 were the Fairey Swordfish TSR aircraft and the Blackburn Skua fighter-dive-bomber (FDB). A small number of Gloster Sea Gladiators were being procured as an emergency stop-gap because of delayed Skua production. Two other fighter types were in development, the Blackburn Roc and the Fairey Fulmar, both of which entered service in 1940. The biplane Swordfish was hardly at the forefront of design technology at its concept in the early 1930s and the Skua was markedly slower than the latest point-defence interceptor fighters in RAF service. These facts led many commentators to assume that the Air Ministry had passed its castoff or inadequate designs on to the Admiralty for use by the Fleet Air Arm but this criticism is not merited and deeper reasons have to be sought for the low performance of RN aircraft at the outbreak of war. Air Ministry policy did have a major impact on the aircraft procured for carrier operations but it was subtle and less direct than a deliberate attempt to provide designs that were mediocre or inadequate and it was to continue into the early war years.[1] From its inception in 1918 the Air Ministry had convinced politicians that all naval operations in the European theatre would be protected by RAF aircraft from shore bases and all attacks on enemy an enemy fleet in its anchorages would be carried out by shore-based RAF bombers. The Admiralty was, therefore, unable to make a case for carrier-borne fighters that could engage shore based enemy fighters on an equal footing. There was no incentive for the Royal Aircraft Establishment (RAE), to investigate the practicality of such aircraft or industry to build them. Worse, the Air Ministry view that all naval equipment fitted to aircraft must represent an unfortunate and performance-limiting overhead, on top of what it considered to be normal, led to the view in the RAE and industry that naval aircraft would always have to be inferior to their shore-based contemporaries. This was not the case in the USA and Japan where navies were unencumbered by a third, independent, service and realised from the outset that their aircraft would have to fight their way through every sort of air opposition. Knowing no better, the Admiralty assumed that all naval aircraft would suffer from the same inferiority and its own aircraft could, therefore, stand up to them in operations far from land. It is, therefore, at least arguable that the Admiralty had the aircraft it thought it needed in the late 1930s. It did not procure Skuas and Fulmars because of some sort of innate prejudice against modern high-performance fighters and strike aircraft but because it believed that, for the sort of war it expected to fight against the Imperial Japanese Navy in the open ocean, long-range and navigational capability were more important virtues than high speed. Ironically, high-performance aircraft were immediately recognised as important on the outbreak of war with the development of radar into an operational capability first demonstrated in 1939.

From the early 1920s the RN, like the US Navy, considered Japan to be the most likely future enemy and expected to have to fight a decisive sea battle against the IJN in the South China Sea at ranges from airfields ashore that were too great for land-based aircraft to become a factor. In such a battle, British naval aircraft would only be opposed by Japanese naval aircraft and if all carrier-borne aircraft suffered from the same inferiority, as the RAF emphatically claimed, they would not be opposed by anything beyond their own level of performance. The USN perspective, on the other hand, differed significantly as the result of realistic war-gaming and study at its tactical school. It assessed that its Pacific Fleet would pass within range of a number of Japanese-held islands as it moved west to close with the IJN battle fleet and would need aircraft capable of fighting land-based Japanese aircraft when they were encountered. This was a more realistic approach. After the Abyssinian crisis in 1935/36, the RN realised that it would also have to operate in the face of land-based air attack in the Mediterranean where there were so many Italian airfields. The armoured carriers of the *Illustrious* group were part of the Admiralty's response to this threat.

Carrier design was another factor that significantly influenced the number and type of aircraft that could be embarked, and this is an area where the RN found it a disadvantage to be first in the field after the Washington Naval Treaty limited total carrier tonnage. The early carriers took up a large part of that total but there was no question of building newer, more efficient ships. Some features of British carrier design had consequences,[2] especially the fully enclosed hangar design adopted to protect aircraft from wind and spray on the flight deck and the hull from the volatile avgas and oil fumes associated with aero engines and their maintenance. Piston-engined aircraft need to run up their engines for some minutes before launch to warm them through; in a closed-hangar ship this can only be done on the flight deck but in the open-hangar designs of the USN and IJN it could be done in the hangar before aircraft were ranged. The excessive after round-down and narrow width of British carriers limited the number of aircraft that could be ranged for take-off at any one time and the need to warm up successive ranges on deck severely limited the size of a strike that could be flown off. The need for a clear deck before every landing until the late 1930s was a further limitation on the size of a strike force, given the length of time some aircraft would have to wait for the aircraft ahead to be struck down into the hangar and the lift returned to flight-deck level. RN carriers, therefore, had to fly off their aircraft in small groups and had constantly to turn into wind for small launches and recoveries. Given the small air groups in *Hermes* and *Eagle*

N5500, the first Gloster Sea Gladiator, was ordered in 1938 and delivered to 801 NAS in February 1939. This photograph was taken in April 1939 when the unit was being re-equipped with Skuas at RNAS Donibristle. The Sea Gladiators were subsequently passed on to 769 NAS. (Author's collection)

this might just be acceptable but larger carriers such as *Courageous*, *Glorious* and especially *Ark Royal* were capable of operating far larger groups. Given its desire to absorb the bulk of British aircraft production for its own independent uses, the RAF had no incentive to find better ways of operating aircraft at sea in greater numbers or indeed at any greater level of efficiency.

In some respects, however, the Admiralty added to the inadequacy of Fleet Air Arm aircraft but it did so out of a desire to get more aircraft to sea and not, as some historians have supposed, because of a dinosaur-like rejection of new technology. The low numbers of aircraft that could be embarked in the small carriers led the Admiralty staff to consider embarking both fighters and strike aircraft in battleships and cruisers equipped with catapults. In consequence staff requirements for all naval aircraft included the statement that they were to have a minimum take-off speed of 60 knots to make them compatible with the catapult end-speed. This was relatively undemanding in the 1920s but it made a considerable difference when high-powered and heavy monoplanes were introduced in the late 1930s. The Admiralty did not fully realise this and the Air Ministry saw no reason to point it out. The requirement for a low take-off speed was probably the basis for selecting the biplane configuration for the Swordfish and it shows that by the mid-1930s the RN lacked the institutional capacity to evaluate the critical limitation of such a requirement and the independent RAF lacked a sufficiently co-operative outlook to explain it. Limited embarked capacity meant limited production runs of aircraft for the Fleet Air Arm, which resulted in a lack of interest from some manufacturers although Fairey, Blackburn and to an extent Hawker did specialise in meeting naval requirements.

Another of the Admiralty's decisions for making the best of its limited number of carrier-borne aircraft was to specify multi-purpose aircraft. The 1932 Mediterranean Fleet exercises had demonstrated that the two spotter flights embarked in the single carrier supporting the battle fleet could not provide the number of aircraft on task needed to spot ships' gunfire adequately. Numbers had to be made up with torpedo aircraft and this solution undoubtedly led to the specification of the aircraft that became the Swordfish as a torpedo-spotter-reconnaissance aircraft.

Aircraft Procurement After the Inskip Award and the 'Fighter Crisis'

The Admiralty request for an emergency batch of single-seat fighters from RAF stock gives an interesting insight into aircraft procurement for the RN in the months immediately after the Inskip Award and before full administrative control of naval aviation was transferred. In a letter dated 2 February 1938 the Admiralty wrote to the Air Council informing it that if, as at that time appeared likely, the Blackburn Skua and Roc 'proved to be aerodynamically unsound the fighting strength of the Fleet Air Arm would be almost negligible until the end of 1939 when the converted P4/34 was expected to be available'.[3] The Admiralty asked whether, if an emergency arose before that time, the Air Council would be prepared to supply 'the greatest possible number of Gladiators', modified as necessary to operate from carriers. On 15 February the Air Council decided that in an emergency it would try to meet the Admiralty's request 'but whether this could, in the event, be done would depend on the home defence situation and the Government of the day would have to decide on the relative priority of the requirements of the two Services'. They did decide, however, to order an additional fifty Gladiators to cover the probable shortage of fighters in the RAF in 1939 but also, partly, to meet the Admiralty's request. Following the government approval of aircraft procurement scheme L this order was increased to 350.

Even before the Air Council reply was sent, however, it received another letter from the Admiralty which pointed out that even if the Skua and Roc proved to be satisfactory there would still be a serious shortage of fighters in the Fleet Air Arm in the latter part of 1938. It was asked, therefore, if two squadrons of modified Gladiators with full reserves could be lent to the Fleet Air Arm as soon as possible and remain on loan until the shortage was overcome. The obvious urgency led to a meeting at which the Admiralty representative stated that the requirement was for twenty-four immediately operational aircraft with 150 per cent reserves. The Air Council agreed in principle but forecast that the aircraft could not be delivered before January 1939. This was still too late for the Admiralty which stressed the urgency of its request. At a meeting between 5SL, Vice Admiral Sir Alexander Ramsay,[4] and the Air Member for Supply and Organisation, Air Vice Marshal William Welsh,[5] it was pointed out that the agreed establishment of Fleet Air Arm fighter squadrons was, at the time, three squadrons with a total of thirty-three operational aircraft and a further fifty-two in reserve, a total of eighty-five. The commissioning of *Ark Royal* at the end of the year would increase that total by a further eighteen operational aircraft and twenty-seven reserves, a new total of 130 aircraft. Towards that total the RN had only thirty-seven Ospreys and twenty-four Nimrods, a total of sixty-one. Comparisons between agreed establishments and actual strengths were said to be as follows:

Date	*Establishment*	*Strength*	*Deficiency*
October 1938	85	61	24
January 1939	130	71	59
March 1939	130	65	65

When it was repeated that it would be impossible to provide Gladiators for the Fleet Air Arm in advance of those now earmarked except at the expense of home defence fighter squadrons, 5SL expressed the view that, given the international situation, the shortage of RN fighters had already reached the point where a decision would have to be taken by government between the conflicting demands. On 20 September Duff Cooper, First Lord of the Admiralty, wrote to the Secretary of State for Air, Sir Kingsley Wood, stating:

> as you are probably aware, owing to the delays in the production of new types, the Skuas and Rocs, the number of fighters in the Fleet Air Arm has now fallen to a figure which is catastrophic; we calculate that by the end of the year there will only be about 67 fighters remaining of the 134 required for first-line and reserves. When the squadrons are formed for HMS *Ark Royal* this shortage will be further accentuated … the Skua and Roc fighters which should have been in service a year ago are not yet fit for delivery and it seems unlikely that any useful numbers of them will be service before March 1939 at the earliest.

He ended by asking again whether special priority could be given to the contractors for the manufacture and delivery of sixty Sea Gladiators for the RN.

To its credit, the Air Council agreed in October, as an emergency and purely temporary measure, to make thirty-eight unmodified Gladiators available to the Fleet Air Arm rather than issuing them to Royal Auxiliary Air Force squadrons. They could be fitted with arrester hooks but would lack flotation gear and any

Sea Gladiator N5525 was serving with 802 NAS in *Glorious* in June 1939. Note the blister on the lower fuselage between the undercarriage legs; this was a dinghy stowage which, together with the tail hook visible further aft, distinguished the Sea Gladiator externally from its land-based counterpart. (Author's collection)

other modifications intended for the contracted production run of sixty Sea Gladiators. Subsequently referred to as 'Crisis Gladiators', these thirty-eight aircraft were new production aircraft with serial numbers allocated in the range N2265 to N2302 and were expected to be delivered from Gloster from November 1938 to January 1939. The Air Council reiterated, however, that there was no possibility of speeding up the production and delivery of Sea Gladiators because of the number of modifications needed to fit them for naval use which required the manufacture of new production jigs and the preparation of 240 new drawings. The sixty Sea Gladiators were given serial numbers in the range N5501 to N5574 and the differences from the standard RAF design included arrester hooks, catapult attachment points, an inflatable dinghy fitted in a fairing between the undercarriage legs and naval radio. The first three Crisis Gladiators were delivered on 9 December 1938 and the remainder in batches from 5 January 1939. Their time with the Fleet Air Arm was short, however, as sixteen were soon withdrawn to form a defensive fighter flight at Aden. On 3 May 1939 Air Member for Supply and Organisation (AMSO) wrote to 5SL asking for the return of the balance of twenty-two aircraft on the understanding 'that you have now received the full 60 Sea Gladiators'. 5SL replied two days later that he was happy to do so. The first Sea Gladiators were delivered to RNAS Donibristle in February 1939 where they replaced Nimrods and Ospreys in 801 NAS as a temporary measure until sufficient Skuas and Rocs were received. 802 and 804 NAS were re-equipped with Sea Gladiators in May and November 1939 respectively and operated in defence of Scapa Flow from RNAS Hatston and embarked in HMS *Glorious* during 1940. Other front-line units also operated the type, including a flight of 813 NAS in *Eagle* during 1940/41. Several second-line squadrons used Sea Gladiators, including those that formed part of the Fighter School at RNAS Eastleigh during the period covered by this book.

Gloster Sea Gladiator Details

Length:	27 feet 5 inches[6]
Wingspan:	32 feet 3 inches
Height:	10 feet 4 inches
Maximum weight:	5,420lb
Engine:	One 840hp Bristol Mercury IX
Fuel:	83 gallons[7]
Performance:	Maximum speed 223 knots at 14,500 feet; initial rate of climb 2,300 feet/minute; 9.5 minutes to 20,000 feet
Endurance:	2 hours at 185 knots
Armament:	4 x Browning 0.303-inch machine guns: 2 in the lower wings firing clear of the propeller arc, each with 400rpg,[8] 2 in the cowling forward of the cockpit, each with 600rpg, firing through the arc with an interrupter mechanism which slowed the rate of fire. With more rounds and a slower rate of fire the fuselage guns gave more prolonged fire than the wing guns.

Like so many British military aircraft, the Gladiator was the result of a private venture prototype funded by the manufacturer rather than an RAF specification. Gloster produced its prototype in 1934 but the type did not enter service until 1937. The RAF was, therefore, almost as slow getting its own aircraft into service as those intended for the Fleet Air Arm. The background to the Crisis Gladiator procurement shows that the Air Council was perfectly prepared to buy aircraft for naval purposes that were as good as those intended for its own independent operations, it just gave them a lower priority. While politicians talked with blissful ignorance about combined operations in which all three services worked together to achieve common aims, the RAF focus was on its own independent operations. The equipment of reserve air force squadrons had, at first, been given a higher priority than the aircraft equipment of the Home Fleet until this was challenged.

TSR1, TSR2 and the Fairey Swordfish

The only torpedo-spotter-reconnaissance aircraft in front-line service with the RN in 1939 was the Fairey Swordfish. A biplane with open cockpits, it too evolved from a private venture prototype and was considered by many to be obsolescent when it entered service in 1936. Its design evolved from a specification originally drawn up in 1930 but it continued to operate successfully in a variety of roles until 1945. It sank a greater tonnage of shipping than any other aircraft in the Second World War and must be seen, therefore, as an anachronism regarded by some as a prime example of the out-dated and mediocre aircraft procured for naval use by the Air Ministry. On the other hand, it actually proved to be an outstanding strike aircraft that was readily adaptable to the anti-submarine role and capable of landing on even the smallest aircraft carriers in the very worst of North Atlantic storm conditions far out at sea.

Its origins lie with an aircraft designed by Fairey to meet Air Ministry Specification S9/30 fitted with a steam-cooled Rolls-Royce Kestrel engine. Progress with the prototype, S1706,[9] known as the Fairey S9/30 was slow and it did not actually fly until 1934. By then the Fairey design team under Marcel Lobelle had produced an evolved design, identified as the TSR1, specifically intended to carry

The Fairey TSR-1 prototype in 1933. It was never allocated a British military serial number but its Fairey construction number F1875 can just be seen on the lower rear fuselage side. (Author's collection)

out the combined functions of torpedo bomber and spotter-reconnaissance aircraft for the Greek Navy.[10] Known on the shop floor as the 'Greek Job', no British airframe number was allocated to the TSR1 prototype which had the Fairey construction number F.1875. It first flew in March 1933 with company test pilot Chris Staniland at the controls powered by a 625hp Armstrong Siddeley Panther VI radial engine. Details of TSR1 were sent to the Air Ministry in the hope that it might be interested. Flying trials went well until 11 September 1933 when Staniland undertook a series of spinning tests, beginning at 14,000 feet. At first he could not induce a spin at all but at the second or third attempt F.1875 entered a spin which became very flat with the nose almost on the horizon and a fast, smooth rotation. Control inputs had no effect and attempts to stimulate rudder or elevator reaction by opening the throttle merely caused the aircraft to shake violently. After twelve turns Staniland decided that recovery would not be possible and attempted to bail out. Terrifyingly, he was blown into the rear cockpit on his first attempt but succeeded in getting out on his second attempt and the aircraft crashed at Longford in Middlesex. Notwithstanding TSR1's loss, test flying had revealed the aircraft's promise and a redesigned second prototype, known as TSR2, was manufactured to meet Air Ministry Specification S15/33, issued under Admiral Henderson's guidance for a combined torpedo-spotter-reconnaissance aircraft that could reduce the number of different aircraft types embarked in a carrier.

The prototype Swordfish, K4190,[11] was externally similar to the TSR1 but had an extra bay built into the fuselage and strakes ahead of the tailplane leading edges to aid spin recovery. Powered by a 690hp Bristol Pegasus IIIM3 radial engine, it flew for the first time on 17 April 1934, again with Staniland at the controls, from Fairey's Great West Aerodrome at Heathrow. Fairey's own test programme lasted about two months, after which K4190 moved to the Aeroplane and Armament Experimental Establishment (A&AEE) at Martlesham Heath for service trials, RAE Farnborough for catapult launch trials and HMS *Courageous* for deck landing trials. Finally it went to Fairey's factory at Hamble, where it was fitted with floats to be evaluated as a seaplane, flown for the first time in this guise by Staniland on 10 November 1934. In January 1935 it moved to the Marine Aircraft Experimental Establishment (MAEE) at Felixstowe, where it underwent service evaluation as a seaplane and then to Gosport where it was evaluated as a torpedo-armed strike aircraft. Unfortunately on 11 February 1935 K4190 suffered an engine failure while gliding in to land after a dive; the engine picked up and then failed again and it crashed into a hedge between barrack blocks.[12] This was not the end for this remarkable aircraft, however; it was rebuilt as a dual-control trainer and issued to the Fleet Air Arm pool at Gosport as such in February 1937. Its eventual fate is unknown. By then three prototypes[13] had been delivered which had continued the development programme. Overall the results of test flying were satisfactory although there was some initial criticism of the aircraft's stalling behaviour and slow recovery from some types of spin. As a seaplane, the water rudders at the after ends of the floats

Swordfish armed with practice torpedoes airborne for an attack on a target ship in the Firth of Forth from RNAS Crail. The lack of an observer or TAG in the rear cockpit of the aircraft in the foreground shows this to be a training sortie. (Author's collection)

were found to be inadequate at slow speeds in winds greater than 20 knots and had to be modified.

The first production contract, number 402278/35,[14] was for eighty-six Swordfish to meet Specification 38/34 and these began to be delivered from February 1936. After the outbreak of war, however, it was obvious that even with its new shadow factories, Fairey could not cope with the orders that were building up for the newer Albacore, Fulmar, Barracuda and Firefly if it continued Swordfish production in the required numbers. To solve the problem, the Admiralty's new Director of Air Material, Captain M S Slattery RN[15] proposed that Blackburn, another firm with naval aircraft experience, should take over all Swordfish production. Blackburn also had a heavy workload but was prepared to set up a new production centre in Yorkshire under the national industrial dispersal programme to reduce the bombing risk. The new plant was at Sherburn-in-Elmet between Leeds and Selby in Yorkshire and it was open by the end of 1940. V4288 was the first aircraft assembled there and it flew on 1 December 1940. Sherburn manufactured fuselages and assembled complete Swordfish but other companies in the Leeds area manufactured the wings, undercarriages, ailerons, fins, rudders, centre-section structure and cockpit floor assemblies. By the time it opened, Fairey built 692 Swordfish and Sherburn went on to make a further 1,699 by the time production ceased in 1944.[16]

The first squadron to re-equip with Swordfish was 825 NAS where they replaced Fairey Seal spotter-reconnaissance aircraft that had only been in service for three years. The unit embarked in *Glorious* and was still with her after the outbreak of war. By the end of 1936, 811 and 812 NAS had also been re-equipped, the former replacing Blackburn Baffin torpedo bombers and the latter Seals. When 810, 820 and 821 NAS replaced their Blackburn Shark torpedo bombers with Swordfish in 1938 the type became the only TSR aircraft in RN service and it was to remain so until its intended replacement, the Fairey Albacore, entered service in 1940. By September 1939 the RN had thirteen front-line Swordfish squadrons and another twelve were to be formed during the course of the war. One of the latter, 836 NAS, which provided flights for operation from MAC-ships (Merchant Aircraft Carriers) had over fifty Swordfish on charge in 1944 and was the largest naval air squadron at the time. A further twenty-three NAS used Swordfish for deployment as catapult flights, fleet requirements and training tasks. In 1939 Swordfish squadrons were embarked in all five operational carriers: *Ark Royal* with four; *Courageous* two; *Glorious* two; *Eagle* two and *Furious* two. The remaining squadron, 814 NAS, embarked in *Hermes* when she re-commissioned in October.

The Swordfish was obviously versatile and reliable but what did the naval aircrew who had to fly it think about it? A very good idea of a contemporary pilot's view can be gained from Lieutenant Commander Terence Horsley's book *Find, Fix and Strike*, published in 1943.[17] In it he said:

> perhaps once in the lifetime of every designer will come an inspiration which will result in an exceptionally good aircraft. It may be born of a pipe dream or merely the product of hard work blessed by the Goddess Good Luck but, whatever the origin, every pilot who lays his hands upon it will instantly know beyond all doubt that it is exceptional. Such an aircraft is the Fairey Swordfish … how extraordinary, you may say, that a biplane with a maximum speed of 132 knots continued to be a success in 1943, there must be something exceptional about it. Well, there is.

Reading through these words again in 2018 I was struck by the fact that the author used the word 'exceptional' three times in four sentences; one detects a genuine love and admiration for the aircraft he flew from a carrier's deck. I know of few other pilots who have written with such praise about the aircraft that they flew on operations and many who have expressed little but criticism. Horsley went on to say:

> in the beginning, before you start thinking about the 1,500lb of bombs or the 18 inch torpedo, you know that you have got a friend. And a friend, when you are fighting your way through the darkness towards a lurching flight deck, or are 100 miles out over an empty sea waste, is something worth having … it was only when I sat in the cockpit myself, made the … run towards the deck at a staggeringly slow speed and felt the firm and instant response to the controls, that I knew at last that I was flying the product of a designer's genius.

Horsley discovered that the Swordfish behaved itself even when subjected to the most violent manoeuvres and flown so badly that most other aircraft would have stalled and departed from controlled flight in a spin. In dive-bombing attacks the aircraft handled as easily in the vertical plane as it did in the horizontal; it could dive vertically from 10,000 feet without exceeding 200 knots and level out within a few hundred feet of the sea surface with a gentle backwards pressure on the stick. 'Translate that into terms of a night torpedo attack,' he said,

> and the pilot is relieved of half his worries – that of getting the aircraft out of the dive in time. He can concentrate on hitting his target, jabbing the rudder bar or man-handling the control column in the sure knowledge that he's virtually safe from a high-speed stall … that is why when high-speed is not vital for getting away, that the Swordfish is still the greatest torpedo bomber in the world in the eyes of the pilots who fly them. And this is an aircraft which has neither flaps, retractable undercarriage or variable pitch airscrew - in fact none of the things which are accepted as part of modern war planes.

The reader might now reflect that there was, after all, some merit in the Admiralty's insistence on good low-speed handling qualities for its aircraft.

The classic RN aerial torpedo attack did not involve a long, low approach like that employed by the USN. It involved radical changes of height and bearing intended to make an enemy ship's anti-aircraft gunfire control solution more difficult to achieve; it did, however, make the attack itself more difficult, and the technique required extensive training and constant practice. The approach to the target by a twelve-aircraft squadron was made at about 10,000 feet in four flights of three aircraft, each in 'V' formation. They would set themselves up to attack from different directions so that whichever way the target ship turned, it would find it difficult to evade every torpedo once they were running. The leader would manoeuvre into a position a mile or two ahead of the target and order his own numbers 2 and 3 into line astern by hand signals. They would drop back into positions 300 and 600 yards behind him and when they had taken up their positions they would dive, in sequence, vertically onto the target. The other flight leaders would take up positions at 90-degree intervals around the target and carry out similar diving procedures in synchronisation with the

Fairey Swordfish L7701 served with 820 NAS in *Ark Royal* from August 1939 after several months with the Torpedo Trials Unit. It is seen her carrying out a diving attack profile with a practice torpedo. (Philip Jarrett collection)

A Swordfish from the Torpedo Trials Unit, Gosport, dropping a Mark XII torpedo under ideal conditions. (Philip Jarrett collection)

overall leader. From roughly 2 miles high the descent took about half a minute, during which time individual pilots had to maintain their position relative to their leaders, identify the target and estimate its course and speed and make the torpedo ready for release. Below 1,000 feet pilots would ease their aircraft out of the dive, retrimming as necessary, and use the sights to aim-off before release to allow for target movement as the weapons ran towards it. The ideal release point was at about 1,000 yards, half a nautical mile, from the target. At the moment of release the aircraft had to be at about 200 feet, straight and level with no side-slip so that the weapon entered the water cleanly with no risk of breaking up. If the squadron attack was perfectly executed, the target ship would move into the tracks of at least three torpedoes no matter how it tried to evade. Throughout the attack, pilots had to maintain station on their leaders and, after weapon release, turn hard away to avoid enemy anti-aircraft fire.

The Mark XII airborne torpedo carried by the Swordfish in 1940 weighed 1,610lb and had a warhead containing 388lb of TNT[18] but later Marks had warheads containing 545lb of Torpex, an explosive designed specifically for torpedoes. All Marks were propelled by 'burner-cycle' engines, semi-diesels that developed 140hp. When the pilot dropped the weapon, high-pressure air from a chamber within the torpedo was released into an igniter where it mixed with a small amount of atomised kerosene to produce a pressurised air/gas mixture at 1,000 degrees Centigrade which was fed into the engine cylinders via poppet valves. More fuel was injected into the cylinders themselves which ignited spontaneously to run the engine. Before release the pilot could change the engine setting to either give a run of 40 knots out to 1,500 yards or 37 knots out to 3,500 yards. The former was preferred against a single target as it gave the enemy less time to evade when dropped from the ideal distance; the latter was used against multiple targets in close proximity. As the compressed air ran out, the engine would slow and then stop. Fuses were fitted to the warheads that detonated them either on contact with the target or by its magnetic signature as the torpedo passed under it. The latter was the better option as the explosion would break the target's back, ensuring its destruction, although the impact fuse was generally considered to be more reliable. In the Second World War the airborne torpedo proved to be the RN's most effective anti-ship weapon in terms of percentage hits; 609 'war-shot' weapons were dropped which scored 167 certain and 37 probable hits, a success rate of 33.5 per cent. By comparison destroyers launched 606 with a success rate of 16.2 per cent; submarines 5,121 with a success rate of 22.2 per cent and motor torpedo boats 1,328 with a success rate of 26.7 per cent.[19] British airborne torpedoes proved to be robust and reliable unlike the USN Mark 13 which was slower at 33 knots although it did have a longer range at 4,000 yards. Its chances of hitting were proportionately lower and made worse by its unreliability, with only 30 per cent of early models running effectively when dropped. Unlike British torpedoes, USN Mark 13s had to be dropped low and slow at 50 feet and 110 knots.

Another remarkable fact about the Swordfish is that the Mark I version which first flew in 1934 remained in production virtually unaltered until 1943. Even then the Mark II version that replaced it only differed in having metal-skinned under-surfaces on the lower wings to allow 3-inch rockets to be fired from rails under the wing against surfaced U-boats. A Mark III version joined the Mark II in production in the same year; this was fitted with ASV X radar in a radome fitted between the undercarriage legs which prevented the fitting of a torpedo although depth charges, rockets and bombs could be carried on under-wing pylons. No Mark IV variants were built as such but the description was applied to Mark IIs built with enclosed cockpits for use as training aircraft in Canada. Later Mark IIs and all Mark IIIs had the up-rated Pegasus 30 engine delivering 750hp.

Fairey Swordfish Mark I Details

Length:	36 feet 4 inches (40 feet 11 inches with floats)
Wingspan:	45 feet 6 inches (17 feet 3 inches folded)
Height:	12 feet 10 inches (14 feet 7 inches on floats)
Maximum weight:	9,250lb
Engine:	One 690hp Bristol Pegasus IIIM
Fuel:	155 gallons avgas main internal tank; 12.5 gallons avgas internal gravity-fed tank; 60 gallon avgas overload tank could be fitted in rear cockpit; 69 gallon avgas overload tank could be fitted to torpedo crutches.
Performance:	Maximum speed in level flight 125 knots
Endurance:	Over 4 hours at 90 knots
Armament:	1 x 1,610lb torpedo on centreline crutches; up to 1,500lb of bombs or depth charges on centreline and under-wing hard points; 1 x fixed Vickers 0.303-inch machine gun to the right of the pilot's cockpit with 500rpg and 1 x 0.303-inch Lewis machine gun on a Fairey high-speed mounting in the rear cockpit with a number of 47-round ammunition drums (or trays).
Notes:	In September 1939 the Swordfish was one of only 2 British aircraft types capable of laying sea mines, the other was the Bristol Beaufort operated by the RAF.

Blackburn Skua Mark II

Like the Swordfish, the Skua had become something of an anachronism by the time it finally entered service, but when its specification was first drawn up to meet an Admiralty requirement, it represented a very great advance over the aircraft it was intended to replace.[20] Air Ministry Specification O27/34 was written

Blackburn Skuas of 803 NAS from *Ark Royal* in June 1939. A7F, flown by the CO or a flight commander, has a striped tailplane so that wing-men can see and identify it in action. It can be seen in the middle of the 5 aircraft in this posed photograph. Apart from the blue and red fuselage band which showed them to be from *Ark Royal*, the aircraft are still in the pre-war silver finish in which they had been delivered a few months earlier. (Phillip Jarrett collection)

around the requirement and Blackburn's B-24 designed by G E Petty was selected in preference to designs submitted by Avro, Boulton Paul, Hawker and Vickers. With the end of the depression these firms were keen to obtain any orders they could after several years of limited production. Petty's design was to be the Fleet Air Arm's first carrier-borne fighter to be constructed entirely of metal, the first cantilever monoplane, the first to have a retractable undercarriage and the first to have a variable-pitch propeller. Under the Admiralty's new policy of procuring multi-role aircraft to produce the most flexible capability from small carrier air groups, the B-24 was to serve as both a fighter and a dive-bomber. Two prototypes, effectively Skua Mark Is, were ordered in April 1935 and their construction only proceeded at a slow pace since Blackburn was committed to a number of other projects, including the B-26 Botha reconnaissance bomber which was given the highest priority by the RAF for Coastal Command. The first aircraft, K5178, was flown for the first time at Brough on 9 February 1937 by the company's chief test pilot A M 'Dasher' Blake powered by an 840hp Bristol Mercury IX air-cooled radial engine. The aircraft followed the usual process of company testing followed by service trials culminating at the RAE Farnborough in December 1937. The

Skua L2875 photographed at the Central Flying School, Upavon, in December 1938, where it had been used to develop pilots' notes for the type and other procedural manuals before being issued to 803 NAS in February 1939. The three men beside it give an idea of the aircraft's size. (Author's collection)

former were slowed by the unfortunate death of Blake in October and the latter by the discovery that the aircraft was longitudinally unstable at low gliding speeds.[21] The Admiralty had hoped to get the aircraft into service by 1937; it was already late, therefore, but had to wait until the problem was resolved. It manifested itself as a sudden wing-drop without previous buffet or any other warning at deck landing speed and wind tunnel tests showed the aircraft was not capable of recovering from spins using the standard recovery method.

By 1938 the Air Ministry was complaining that continuing work on the Skua was holding up both the Botha and the Roc and there were doubts about whether it was worth continuing with the Skua at all. As we have seen, these led the Admiralty to ask for the 'Crisis Gladiators' to partially fill the gap and to order the Fairey Fulmar off the drawing board in an attempt to get it into service as quickly as possible. Work on the Skua did continue, however, and the type's stalling characteristics were examined by gluing wool tufts to the upper surface of the prototype's wings and filming them in flight to observe the airflow pattern at and near the stall. Modifications were incorporated which cured the problem although intentional spinning was 'universally and totally forbidden'.

Other modifications were incorporated to the design during the development phase and the second prototype, K5179, was given a nose lengthened by 2 feet 4.75 inches which effectively made it the prototype Mark II. Production was also delayed by the need for further development after the Air Ministry insisted that the prototype's Mercury engine be replaced by an 890 hp Bristol Perseus XII because all Mercury engines were to be used in expanded production of Bristol Blenheim bombers. The RN needed the Skua so badly that it agreed to a production batch of 190 being ordered off the drawing board to Specification 25/36 in July 1936, six months before the type's first flight. The first production Skuas, beginning with L2867, were used for development work but here again there were problems caused by 3 aircraft suffering accidents, one of them during deck trials on *Courageous* in the Firth of Forth during December 1938. Blackburn did everything it could to hasten production. Some fuselages were sub-contracted to General Aircraft Ltd at Hanworth and wings were manufactured in the old Olympia Works in Leeds. Despite this effort the first aircraft were not delivered to the RN until October 1938 when 800 NAS began to re-equip at RNAS Worthy Down in Hampshire. Even then deliveries were slowed by bad weather which affected the runway at Brough, forcing Blackburn to transport Skuas by road to RAF Leconfield for air test and delivery. The name Skua was bestowed on the type by the Air Ministry on 17 August 1937.

The Skua Mark II had a flush-riveted Alclad fuselage incorporating two watertight compartments, one under the pilot's floor and the other in the rear fuselage behind the gunner's compartment, intended to provide buoyancy if the aircraft ditched. The cockpit was also watertight up to the level of the cockpit canopy. It was stressed for both catapult launching and arrested recovery and the hook was fitted with a hydraulic damping device to prevent bounce as the bill struck the deck. The wings were also made with Alclad and built in three units with the two-spar, heavy-duty centre section bolted under the fuselage to form the bottom of the front watertight compartment. The folding outer wings tapered in both plan and thickness and ended in detachable, turned-up tips. The space between the main spars forward of the ailerons was sealed to provide additional watertight compartments and recesses in the rear under-surface of the inboard part of the wing housed the Zap flaps, which also acted as dive-breaks to limit speed in steep dives. The wings were folded manually by being moved aft about an inclined hinge housed internally, twisting as they moved so that in the folded position they lay parallel to the fuselage with the leading edge uppermost. Latch pins were then inserted or withdrawn through linkages operated by a small hand lever and gear box in the wing root. The crew of two, pilot and observer or TAG, sat under a glazed cockpit supported internally by strengthened frames which acted as a roll bars if the aircraft turned upside down after crashing on land. The pilot had a sliding hood which was opened for take-off and landing and had a comfortable seat in line with the wing leading edges which gave him a good view ahead and down. The observer/gunner sat further aft under a tilting canopy which was opened to deflect the slipstream when the Lewis gun was brought into action. The wireless compartment was just aft of the pilot; messages were transmitted and received in Morse although after the outbreak of war front-line Skuas began to be fitted with VHF radio sets that allowed voice communication between the pilot and the carrier over short line-of-sight distances.

No further orders were made for Skuas beyond the initial 190 because by the time the last was delivered in March 1940 more advanced fighters were coming into service and there was insufficient space on carrier decks for the type as a specialist dive-bomber, despite its undoubted usefulness in the role. Almost all Skuas were delivered in 1939, with quantities as follows:

October 1938	3	June 1939	17
November	3	July	26
December	6	August	14
January 1939	9	September	11
February	15	October	16
March	15	November	5
April	23	December	3
May	23	March 1940	1

Work to complete service acceptance of the new aircraft was not finally completed until January 1939, by which time aircraft were beginning to be issued to front-line squadrons. Despite the late arrival of the Skua in squadron service, Blackburn had done well to get it into service at all given the number and variety of competing pressures the firm was under. Although modest by comparison with production numbers achieved soon afterwards under the shadow scheme, the quantities delivered in mid-1939 were high by recent peacetime standards. 800 NAS was the first unit to re-equip with Skuas in October 1938, followed by 803 NAS in early 1939. 801 and 806 NAS subsequently re-equipped with the type and it went to serve with a number of training, second-line and fleet requirements squadrons.

Captain Eric 'Winkle' Brown CBE DSC AFC RN, under whom I served briefly and grew to know well when I was curator of the Fleet Air Arm Museum at RNAS Yeovilton, flew Skuas of 759 NAS during his time in the RN Fighter School at Yeovilton in 1940. He left an accurate account of what the aircraft was like to fly in his 1980 book *Wings of the Navy*.[22] He described the take-off performance from a runway as 'somewhat lumbering' after which, with the undercarriage and flap retracted, the gills fully open and the propeller in course pitch the initial rate of climb was about 740 feet per minute in a fully loaded aircraft, increasing to about 930 at 6,000 feet. He noted that 'the Skua was credited with an initial climb in excess of 1,500 feet per minute but felt that if that had ever been achieved, 'the aircraft must have been very lightly laden indeed'. Flat-out at full throttle with 2.5 inches of boost and the Perseus turning at 2,750rpm (which was only permissible for five minutes in any flight), the Skua 'could achieve a stately 195 knots. If the engine cooling gills were opened this immediately fell to about 176 knots.' The tendency to drop a wing on the stall was never fully corrected and production aircraft had a tail chute for use if the pilot could not recover from an inadvertent spin. If still spinning at 3,000, instructors briefed their students to bail out rather than make further attempts at recovery. In normal flight the aircraft was an average performer, if somewhat heavy on the controls but it was in the dive that the type really excelled. The dive-bombing technique Brown and his contemporaries were taught was:

> to approach the target at about 8,000 feet at right angles [to the fore and aft line of the ship], keeping it in sight until it disappeared under the leading edge of the wing tip, pulling up until it reappeared at the trailing edge and then winging over into a 70 degree dive, extending the Zap flaps fully and keeping the target in sight at the top of the engine cowling. Release height was 3,000 feet and pull-out was commenced, simultaneously retracting the flaps, to complete at about 1,500 feet to avoid the bomb blast and any light flak. The elevator force required to pull out was heavy.

Subsequently, Brown flew a number of different US and German dive-bombers in his role as a test pilot and, significantly, he considered the Skua to 'match up well with the best of these as regards diving characteristics' but the two-position propeller tended to over-speed before terminal velocity was reached. However, he thought, a screaming propeller could be considered a psychological advantage for any attacking dive-bomber. He noted that the Skua had a poor reputation as a deck landing aircraft, which was put down at first to pilots' lack of familiarity with monoplane handling characteristics. In truth, Brown believed, the Skua did not have very good deck landing characteristics:

> The approach was normally made with some engine to flatten the gliding angle and the recommended circuit speed was 120 knots, turning into wind for a straight approach at not less than 500 feet, maintaining a speed of not less than 80 knots and flattening out before closing the throttle. The view from the cockpit was not ideal and the long-stroke Vickers oleo-pneumatic shock-absorber legs were of the bouncy type, which, combined with the fact that the Skua was nose heavy, meant that on cutting the engine one tended to land on the main wheels rather than make a three-pointer. On a carrier deck the arrester hook was prone to missing the arrester wires with the inevitable result of a barrier crash. The Dunlop pneumatic brakes had to be applied with the utmost care and then only in an emergency, for harsh braking during taxiing or the landing run would tip the Skua over on its nose.

Blackburn Skua Mark II Details

Length:	35 feet 7 inches
Wingspan:	46 feet 2 inches (15 feet 6 inches folded)
Height:	12 feet 6 inches
Maximum weight:	8,228lb
Engine:	1 x 890hp Bristol Perseus XII
Fuel:	163 gallons avgas
Performance:	Maximum speed 198 knots; initial rate of climb 1,580 feet per minute; service ceiling 20,000 feet
Endurance:	4 hours 20 minutes at 165 knots
Armament:	1 x 500lb semi-armour piercing (SAP) bomb semi-recessed under the fuselage centreline with ejector arms to swing it clear of the propeller arc on release; 4 x 0.303-inch Browning machine guns, 2 in each wing firing clear of the propeller arc, each with 600rpg. 1 x 0.303-inch Lewis Mark IIIE or Vickers gas-operated machine gun in the rear cockpit with several 47-round drum magazines. Light series carriers under the wings could each carry 4 x20lb bombs or flares.

History has not been kind to the Skua because of its low top speed in the fleet fighter role. By the time it entered service, engines in the 1,000hp class were already equipping front-line fighter squadrons in the RAF with considerably more powerful engines in development. However, even with these engines aircraft such as the Supermarine Spitfire relied on light airframe weight to achieve high performance and were incapable of the multi-tasking capability or the radius of action offered by the Skua. It is also interesting to observe that the Admiralty saw the type originally as a dive-bomber with fighter capability against reconnaissance aircraft in the open sea and this was effectively what it became. In comparison, the IJN's D3A1 'Val' dive-bomber, which first flew in 1937, had a top speed of 209 knots and a maximum weight of 8,047lb, both closely comparable with the Skua. It carried a 551lb bomb under the fuselage and had two 0.303-inch front guns. Somewhat later the USN procured the Douglas SBD Dauntless which entered service in 1941 and doubled as both a dive-bomber and reconnaissance aircraft. Fitted with a more powerful 1,200hp Wright R-1820 engine, it had a maximum speed of 215 knots, not that much greater than the Skua, but the more powerful engine allowed it to carry a 1,000lb bomb over a greater radius of action. It had two 0.5-inch front guns. Both 'Val' and Dauntless earned praise for engaging enemy aircraft as fighters when necessary and it is difficult to escape the conclusion that the Skua has been somewhat under-rated by British historians. It was what it was: a very good dive-bomber that could act as a fighter when necessary even, as the Norwegian campaign was to show, against sophisticated opposition but not against land-based fighters after 1939.

Blackburn Roc

In the early 1930s the Admiralty stated a requirement for a pure fighter with long endurance capable of defending spotter aircraft from enemy interference during a fleet action or of breaking up formations of enemy bomber aircraft attempting to attack the fleet. The Air Ministry drew up Specification O.30/35 to meet the requirement and, after calling for competitive designs, selected the Blackburn B-25 designed by G E Petty. It followed the concept then very much in vogue with some senior RAF officers that a group of aircraft with power-operated gun turrets would offer considerable flexibility in engaging bombers with the minimum need to manoeuvre. The idea was actually quite out-dated and the officers concerned must have remembered the success of two-seat fighters such as the Sopwith One-and-a-Half Strutter and Bristol F2B in the First World War and, more recently, Hawker Demon in 1930. The introduction of powered gun turrets in the mid-1930s had two applications in the RAF: first in bombers where the Air Council thought that they would give such powerful defensive fire that fighter escorts would no longer be needed for them and, secondly, they were expected to give fighters the ideal weapon to act as 'bomber-destroyers', bringing concentrated fire to bear on unescorted bombers from almost any angle with little need for the fighter to manoeuvre. Neither concept was tested realistically and both were found to be deeply flawed when exposed to real operations in 1940. The RAF equivalent was the Boulton Paul Defiant, fitted with the same type of turret, but this proved no more successful as a day fighter although it did enjoy slightly more success as a night fighter in 1941. 'Mixing it' with fighters armed with front guns, neither Defiant nor Roc stood much chance because of the difficulty of co-ordinating the pilot's hard manoeuvring with the gunner's need to train his turret and aim-off to hit a fast, turning target. Single-seat pilots aiming their front guns found their own spatial awareness much easier to master.

The power-operated turret in question was the Boulton Paul Type A Mark II which was fitted with four 0.303-inch Browning machine guns, each with 600rpg, mounted in pairs with the breeches either side of the gunner. It could rotate through a full 360 degrees with 85 degrees maximum elevation, control being by the movement of a single 'pistol-grip' control to the gunner's right. Hydraulic power was provided from an electrically driven pump and the guns were fired electrically by a button on the control grip with automatic interruption of the firing circuit if the tailplane or propeller disc came into the line of fire. Broadly, the Roc was similar in design to the Skua and the turret fitted over the W/T compartment forward of a continuation fairing which ran towards the tail.[23] A device at the bottom of the turret lowered this fairing into the fuselage when the guns were pointing in an after direction. Naval equipment and an inflatable dinghy were carried in the rear fuselage and there was provision for a 250lb bomb to be carried on the centreline to give a strike capability. However, with the extra weight of the bomb the aircraft's mediocre performance deteriorated still further and, as far as I have been able to make out, no bomb was ever carried operationally. Unlike the Skua, provision was made for a 70-gallon overload fuel tank which could be fitted under the fuselage centre section. Again this added weight and was seldom, if ever, fitted to aircraft operating in the fighter role.

A contract for 136 Rocs was placed with Blackburn on 28 April 1937 but by then the firm was so committed to Botha construction that the work was sub-contracted to Boulton Paul at Wolverhampton; sub-assemblies were further sub-contracted to General Aircraft Ltd at Hanworth who made complete tail assemblies. There were no prototypes and the first production Roc, L3057, flew for the first time on 23 December 1938 with Blackburn test pilot H J Wilson at the controls. Company trials were followed by evaluation at the A&AEE and the first three Rocs were among the earliest aircraft to move from Martlesham Heath to Boscombe Down on 19

Blackburn Rocs of 759 NAS, the fighter training school from RNAS Eastleigh, in formation. The nearest aircraft has its power-operated gun turret trained forward with the barrels at maximum elevation. The third aircraft's turret gunner has his guns pointed directly at the cameraman. All four aircraft are painted in an early wartime camouflage scheme with the port lower wing painted black and the starboard white as a recognition feature adopted by all British fighters in 1940. (Philip Jarrett collection)

September 1939. From the outset performance was described as 'disappointing' and different propellers were fitted in an attempt to gain more speed. With the same low-powered engine as the Skua and the greater weight and drag of the gun turret and its systems, there was little that could be done, however, and it soon became obvious that the Roc would fall into the category of 'prey' rather than 'hunter' against anything but the most benign air opposition. In flight, Captain Brown said of the Roc, 'the impression of being underpowered was even more marked than with the Skua',[24] which really says it all.

Unlike the Skua, the Admiralty had always wanted the Roc to be capable of operating as a seaplane as well as with a conventional, wheeled undercarriage. Specification 26/36 was drawn up to meet the requirement. Two Rocs, L3057 and L3059, were sent to the Blackburn factory at Dumbarton in October 1939 for conversion; they were fitted with Blackburn Shark-type interchangeable Alclad floats mounted on close-set 'N' struts amidships and single front struts with a spreader bar. Water rudders were operated pneumatically from the aircraft's braking system and the tailwheel was replaced by a mooring ring. In that month the MAEE moved from Felixstowe to Helensburgh, only 10 miles from Dumbarton so the aircraft did not have far to travel for evaluation. L3059 was tested in seaplane configuration from November 1939 but showed such marked directional instability that it crashed shortly after take-off on 3 December. Tests on the other aircraft were commenced in April 1940 with an additional fin below the tailplane which, it was hoped, might cure the problem. Without it, turns at low altitude were described as hazardous; with it the aircraft was more stable but care was still needed to avoid inward sideslip in low turns. Put simply, the Roc seaplane was a failure and the concept was taken no further.

The Roc never fully equipped a front-line squadron but L3141 was evaluated by 778 NAS, the Service Trials Unit at RNAS Lee-on-Solent, and four were allocated to 806 NAS, together with eight Skuas in February 1940. Further Rocs supplemented the Skuas in 801 and 803 NAS for brief spells in March and April 1940 with some of the latter embarking, briefly in *Glorious*. Basically, the Roc was found to be useless in its intended role and was soon withdrawn from it but did find subsequent use, with the turret removed, in fleet requirements squadrons as a target-tug until 1943 when supplies of spares ran out. Production ceased in August 1940 when the last of the original order for 136 aircraft was delivered.

Blackburn Roc Mark I details

Length:	35 feet 7 inches (15 feet 6 inches folded)
Wingspan:	46 feet
Height:	12 feet 1 inch
Maximum weight:	8,800lb

Engine:	1 x 890hp Bristol Perseus XII
Fuel:	163 gallons avgas internal; 70 gallons in optional external tank
Performance:	Maximum speed 170 knots; 6.5 minutes to 5,000 feet; service ceiling 14,000 feet
Endurance:	4 hours at low speed
Armament:	4 x 0.303-inch Browning machine guns, each with 600rpg, in a power-operated turret. provision for 1 x 250lb bomb on centreline.

Aircraft in Front-Line RN Air Squadrons 1939-40[25]

	Sept 1939	*April 1940*	*Sept 1940*
Swordfish	140	137	139
Walrus[26]	45	48	58
Skua	18	31	33
Roc	6	10	0
Sea Gladiator	12	18	15
Sea Fox[27]	11	8	5
Albacore	0	12	30
Fulmar	0	0	30
Total	232	264	310

These figures show the very low numbers with which the RN was expected to undertake the Norwegian campaign in April 1940. After years of having a misguided government policy inflicted on it, it had to face a German air force that had both qualitative and quantitative superiority, relying on the courage and steadfastness of its aircrew and their newly recruited maintenance personnel to make the best of the situation that they could.

Aircraft Being Developed in September 1939

The Swordfish and Skua were only thought of as stop-gaps on the outbreak of war and the Admiralty was relying on new aircraft types which it wanted to get into service as quickly as possible to replace them.

Fairey Albacore

The Albacore was intended as a Swordfish replacement but eventually only supplemented the earlier type and was actually withdrawn from service before it in 1943. It was a rather conservative fusion of two separate requirements, M.76/36

A Supermarine Walrus being catapulted from a cruiser. (Author's collection)

for a replacement TSR and S.41/36 for a dive-bomber-reconnaissance (DBR) aircraft. Both were to operate in the 58–183 knot speed range and suffered from the incorporation of catapult launch and seaplane modification requirements. The Admiralty specifically requested that Fairey Aviation should be awarded the contract for the DBR to save time by dispensing with the normal tender design procedures but other firms were invited to tender for the TSR. Eventually the TSR tender was withdrawn and Fairey was given the task of producing a combined DBR/TSR. Both monoplane and biplane designs were offered but the Air Ministry considered a monoplane to represent too radical an approach and advised the Admiralty to accept the biplane. The first 100 Albacores were ordered off the drawing board to save time, with the first two to act as prototypes. The first of these, L7074, piloted by F H Dixon flew for the first time from Fairey's Great West Aerodrome[28] on 12 December 1938 and both were flying by April 1939. They were subsequently tested at A&AEE Boscombe Down in the summer of 1940 where the controls were found to be heavy and the aircraft less manoeuvrable than the Swordfish. They did, however, have the advantage of an enclosed cockpit with a heating system, flaps and a variable-pitch propeller. Eventually 800 Albacores were produced, powered by the 1,065hp Bristol Taurus II engine although late production examples had the 1,130hp Taurus XII. Armament was similar to the Swordfish.

Fairey Fulmar Mark I

The Admiralty's desperate need for an effective carrier-borne fighter led to Specification O.8/38 being drawn up around a navalised version of Fairey's P4/34 light bomber design which had not been adopted by the RAF. It had the second seat for an observer considered essential at the time to navigate for considerable distances away from the carrier over the open ocean but the same eight fixed-gun armament as the RAF's Spitfire and Hurricane interceptor fighters. A reflector sight assisted pilots' assessment of the ideal aim-off against manoeuvring targets, and the controls were light and well harmonised. The Fulmar was to prove popular with pilots and was described as being 'easy and pleasant to fly' by A&AEE Boscombe Down. Deck landing trials, carried out in the new *Illustrious*, went well although it was found advisable to maintain a lot of power approaching the deck at low speed so that the slipstream would maintain rudder and elevator effectiveness. The Mark I Fulmar was fitted with the 1,080hp Rolls-Royce Merlin VIII engine. An instruction to proceed was given on 5 May 1938, when the name Fulmar was allocated and it was decided to manufacture the type at Fairey's new Heaton Chapel, Stockport, factory with final assembly at Manchester's Ringway Airport. 250 Mark Is were built, followed by 350 Mark IIs, the last of which was delivered in 1943. The eight 0.303-inch Browning machine guns were fitted with four in each wing, slightly staggered to provide space for the ammunition feeds. They each had stowage capacity for 500rpg.

The prototype Fulmar, N1854,[29] flew for the first time at Ringway on 4 January 1940 piloted by Duncan Menzies. The first unit to equip with the type was 808 NAS at RNAS Worthy Down in June 1940 after a period in development that was commendably quick after the experience with the Skua and Roc. With a maximum level speed of 250 knots the Fulmar was a significant improvement over the Skua and Sea Gladiator and went on to do well against the Italians in the Mediterranean but it was outclassed by the Luftwaffe's single-seat day fighters. Terence Horsley summed up the Fulmar well in *Find, Fix and Strike*[30] in which he said:

> there was never anything wrong with the eight-gun Fairey Fulmar. It was a fine aeroplane, manoeuvrable, with a good take-off, a moderate rate of climb and plenty of endurance. It satisfied the demand for a navigator's seat and several wireless sets considered essential for fleet work. It merely lacked the fighter's first essential quality – speed … [It had] good fire power but unless the pilot could make his attack from above, and unless his first burst made a kill, he rarely got a second chance unless the enemy gave it to him.

In 1940 the Fairey Barracuda and Firefly were also in development but since neither of them entered operational service until 1943 their story falls outside the scope of this chapter.

Chapter 11

Squadron Command

Naval air squadrons were complemented to fit into the command structure of both aircraft carriers and naval air stations and were expected to move between the two at short notice with the minimum of disruption. Every element of the squadron's existence – from the office filing system, through aircraft logs to personnel with their tools and baggage – had to be capable of being packed up and transported by road, rail and floating tender. Both carriers and air stations had senior captains RN as commanding officers (COs); these were all executive officers in 1940 but could be gunnery, navigation, torpedo or submarine specialists. Few pilots or observers were senior enough in 1939 to achieve big ship or shore establishment command and under dual control the RN had not been permitted to train senior officers to fly as the USN had done.[1] Unlike in the USN, therefore, British aircraft carriers were not commanded by aviation officers until the very end of the Second World War.

The senior aviation officer in both carriers and naval air stations was a Commander RN with extensive experience as a pilot or observer who was known as Commander 'Air', responsible directly to the captain for all matters to do with aviation and the employment of the squadrons under his command. Under him there were two officers who implemented and devised the flying programme for the embarked squadrons, known loosely as the air group. These were Lieutenant Commander 'Flying', familiarly known as 'Little f', who ran all flying in the vicinity of the ship or air station, the launching and recovery of aircraft, their ranging and movement on deck and movement to and from the hangar. His equivalent was the Operations Officer, known as 'Ops', usually a Lieutenant Commander observer, although early in the war years some operations officers were commanders. He was responsible for drawing up operational plans and for creating the basis of the ship or station flying programme that the squadrons would be tasked to carry out. He was assisted by one or two assistant operations officers who worked on the detail of programmes and briefings; these were usually experienced Lieutenant observers. 'Little f' was assisted by the Deck Landing Control Officer (DLCO) – the 'batsman' who controlled every deck landing – and the Flight Deck Officer who supervised every aircraft movement and launch on deck. Both of these were usually experienced Lieutenant pilots. As the Air Branch expanded rapidly there was a steadily growing need for experienced aircrew officers to fill administrative and command posts such as these, which were essential but had previously fallen to RAF officers who may or may not have had a great deal of knowledge about naval air matters. Added to the urgent need for pilots and observers to fill appointments in the expanding number of squadrons, carrier and air station appointments were not always easy to fill with the best men but widespread enthusiasm for the new branch was a great help. Vacant appointments requiring qualified pilots to fill them could only be filled in the short term by taking men like Bill Lucy from non-flying billets. As with Bill, these had been intended to refresh their ship-handling and watch-keeping skills to fit them for higher command in due course but the exigencies of the service came first and they were quickly recovered after September 1939 to fill flying appointments.

Naval Air Squadrons Described

Naval air squadrons were usually commanded by a Lieutenant Commander RN or Major RM although it was not uncommon for a senior Lieutenant RN or Captain RM to be given command in early 1940, especially if they would soon be due for promotion by seniority.[2] Immediately subordinate to the commanding officer was the senior pilot, an experienced officer who would have completed at least one front-line tour and who would be expert in the squadron's intended role, even if its aircraft were new, as in the case of Skua and Roc squadrons in 1940. His primary task was the maintenance of the standards and practices of all the squadron's pilots at the highest level, ensuring that skills such as air-to-air gunnery in a fighter squadron or torpedo attack in a TSR squadron were regularly practised and fully understood. In squadrons with multi-seat aircraft his equivalent was the senior observer, whose task it was to oversee the observers' skills and techniques. The senior pilot was usually the squadron second-in-command unless the senior observer had greater seniority. The CO could be a pilot or observer although it was more usual for fighter squadrons to have pilots in command. It was normal for the senior pilot to work out the daily flying programme to meet the tasking produced by the operations officers and for the senior observer to write up post-action or exercise reports that debriefed squadron activities.

Crews tended always to fly together to maintain familiarity and close co-operation. When the CO was a pilot it was usual for him to fly with the senior observer. On the other hand, the senior pilot often elected to fly with the most junior observer to give him encouragement and help him gain experience.[3] The remaining aircrew would be 'paired up' when they joined the squadron and would often remain together throughout their time in the unit. In TSR squadrons which had TAGs as well as observers there would be a senior TAG, usually a Chief Petty Officer or Petty Officer with previous experience in the role. The majority of the remainder would be Leading Airmen. In squadrons which had rating pilots and observers it was the senior pilot and observer's duty to ensure that they got as much information as their rate would allow and were able to achieve adequate briefing

Manchester fitting out at Hawthorn Leslie's shipyard at Hebburn-on-Tyne. She was completed on 4 August 1938 in the white-and-buff colour scheme seen here and subsequently served with the 4th Cruiser Squadron on the East Indies Station in 1938/39. (John de Lucy collection)

Bill Lucy, second from the right, on the quarterdeck of *Manchester*. His original caption for this photograph does not, unfortunately, name the men with him but his own more formal uniform probably indicates that he was the ship's Officer of the Day. He appears not to be wearing his 'wings' over the left breast pocket of his tunic, probably because he was not appointed to the ship for flying duties. (John de Lucy collection)

for sorties. Although this sounds simple, it was sometimes difficult to allow rating aircrew to have access to briefing material, which was often marked 'Officers Only'. As the war progressed this problem became less acute as it was recognised that material needed to be made more widely available and the majority of rating aircrew were promoted to at least Warrant Officer. Each RN member of aircrew has always had to keep a log book in which details of every sortie are entered. Senior pilots and observers kept an eye on these to see that their people's drills, qualified flying instructor (QFI)[4] checks and annual medical examinations were up to date and that they were correctly filled in. At the end of every month they would be collected in for signature by the CO; at the end of every quarter the Commander 'Air' of the ship or air station at which the squadron was serving signed a quarterly summary and at the end of every year an annual summary was signed by the captain. The squadron's reputation could be diminished if log books were found by senior officers to be badly or inaccurately filled in.

One of the squadron's more senior lieutenants would be designated the unit's first lieutenant, an executive task that involved a whole range of duties that often had little to do with his flying. First and foremost among these was the welfare of the squadron's sailors. They would have arrived in a carrier with their regulation kit-bag, a small attaché case for their most private and personal possessions and their hammock, tightly secured with customary seven turns, containing their mattress and bedding[5] together with their neatly folded raincoat if they were not wearing it. They would be allocated a mess deck by the ship's Master-at-Arms and in an aircraft carrier this could be a vast 'cavern' with hanging rails for a hundred or more hammocks. Since the Air Branch was new it had fewer long-serving sailors – men with three good conduct badges and leading hands known as 'killicks' after the rate badge worn on their left arm – than the older branches and even in 1939/40, a number of men would be going to sea for the first time. Slinging a hammock, stowing kit away in the minimal space available and finding their way around would be a whole new experience for them and it was up to their officers to make sure that they coped. The squadron scheme of complement produced by the drafting organisation at Lee-on-Solent allowed more men per unit than were strictly needed for its task so that a small percentage was always available to fulfil ship's communal tasks with men from every other department. These included 'mess-men' who waited on senior ratings in their messes, and squadrons also had to provide mechanics to supplement the AED staff in workshops to work on deep engine, instrument and radio repair. From the CO downwards good officers took time to visit their men working on aircraft in the hangar and those working on communal duties. It was noticeable that the men worked better when they knew what their officers were doing and how their aircraft were standing up to pressure. The men took an intense pride in their squadron's achievements and there was always a healthy rivalry between different units with the same type of aircraft embarked in a carrier.

Among the communal tasks at this period was that of 'mess cook'. Within the mess deck area the men would be divided in numbered messes of twelve or fourteen, each with a leading hand in charge. This was the era of 'broadside messing' before British warships had dining halls, and every day two mess members from every mess were detailed off to draw meat and vegetables for their mess prior to each meal. These were prepared as a stew or whatever else the 'mess cook' specified and taken to the galley in suitable containers known as 'fannies' for cooking prior to every meal. They would also be expected to produce some sort of pudding such as a 'spotted dick' or other suet pudding in the same way. While the food was being cooked they would clean the mess and ensure that all hammocks were neatly stowed. They would also draw their mess-mates' tots of grog in a suitable container when the bugle call for 'up spirits' was made and would dish both tots and food out at the midday meal. While it was normal for different 'mess cooks' to carry out the task every day, it was sometimes the case that men who were particularly good at it would volunteer to do the job on a semi-permanent basis while their mess-mates worked on aircraft. Every evening rounds of mess decks and their adjacent heads and bathrooms were carried out by the ship's executive officer or another senior officer. Every month the captain would carry out mess deck rounds and the squadron CO would be present if possible to see how his men had done. A good squadron first lieutenant or executive officer would have been closely involved in supervising the preparation for rounds, making sure that the work of cleaning, often late at night by men who were already tired, was appreciated.

Most officers also had secondary duties, acting as the focal points for specialised matters within the squadron's activities. Among these would be the armament officer, who would follow the work of the ordnance ratings and make specialised inputs to suit the unit's unique requirements, and the map and chart officer who had to ensure that the ship carried everything his unit might need. The diary officer maintained a diary of everyday events with lists of personnel and achievements. Some were just handwritten notes in an exercise book, others were beautifully typed and supported with maps, drawings and photographs. They were usually signed by the CO monthly[6] and later proved to be valuable historical documents.

One of the most important secondary duties was that of divisional officer. This involved an officer taking responsibility for the administration of a small number of sailors, typically ten to twenty within a squadron. He would hold their service documents, ensure that they were up to date and correctly filled in. He would ensure that men who were due for advancement or further technical training took the necessary request action and speak up for them if they committed an offence against the Naval Discipline Act which was brought before the ship's executive officer or captain for summary punishment. The RN divisional system had many advantages: it kept officers close to their men and helped them to understand their ambitions, cares, worries and shortcomings where there were any. It also gave the men access to the officers under whom they worked. Wherever possible the men in

Bill Lucy on the right with guests on *Manchester*. Unfortunately he did not name the others when he put this photograph into his album but this section was headed 'Visits to India'. The photograph may, therefore, have been taken at Bombay in October 1938, Madras or Calcutta in February 1939, all of which were visited by *Manchester* to boost regional confidence that the RN was ready to defend Great Britain's eastern Empire. (John de Lucy collection)

Bill Lucy's caption for this photograph read 'Captain Dick Partridge RM and self at the RN and RM Tennis Tournament in 1937 – Won the Singles' Plate'. The long friendship between these two outstanding officers helped them both when they commanded fighter squadrons that operated together in 1940. (John de Lucy collection)

Bill Lucy with his mother, centre, and Betty Scott photographed at the 1937 RN and RM Tennis Tournament at Wimbledon. (John de Lucy collection)

a particular officer's division were from a trade with which he was associated, thus the parachute officer was divisional officer for the safety equipment ratings; the armament officer was divisional officer for ordnance ratings and the squadron air engineering officer was divisional officer for senior ratings who worked under him in charge of the various watches.

Like most of the rest of the ship's company, the sailors in a squadron were divided into watches. On embarking, the squadron regulating CPO would issue every rating with a station card which would identify their action, defence and abandon ship station and their place in a both a two-watch and three-watch routine. The two-watch routine, usually designated port and starboard, involved four hours on and four off, thus more men were available at any one time but after a few days exhaustion would become a factor. A three-watch system meant four hours on and eight off, which could be sustained for longer but gave fewer men available at any one time. In practice the working routine of squadron mechanics was dictated by the flying programme and the number of serviceable aircraft that were available to meet it. Men would work in the hangar for as long as it took to get the aircraft ready and on deck until they were fuelled, armed and ready to be manned. A good CO would ensure that his officers visited their men while they were working, including those that were lent to other parts of the ship, and told them what their aircraft were achieving and how well the squadron was achieving its allotted tasks. A well-led squadron took great pride in its achievements, especially when it could put all its aircraft into the range fully serviceable and other embarked units failed to do so. Team spirit was hard to maintain, easy to lose in adversity, but always the hallmark of a good commanding officer when it inspired his men to do their best.

Apart from maintaining his own flying currency and the skills needed to lead his unit into action, there were many other facets to the tasks that squadron COs needed to be good at. First they were commanding officers of commissioned units within the RN in their own right but in an aircraft carrier or air station they formed part of the Air Department with Commander 'Air' as their head of department (HOD). The deputy HODs were referred to as the senior something, for instance the senior engineer in the Marine Engineering Department. In the same way squadron COs had their senior pilots and observers and could be described as mini-HODS within the overall Air Department. Their status in command made it relatively easy for them to move from one carrier to another or to an air station ashore with the minimum of administrative fuss.

One task that could not be delegated was writing all his officers' confidential reports on form S206. These took the form of both a narrative report and marks

Fighter pilots need excellent hand/eye co-ordination. Bill Lucy helped himself to develop this skill in a number of ways including sport. He played tennis, rugby and golf and was also an excellent clay-pigeon shot. He is seen in this photograph practising the latter on *Hermes*' flight deck while she was in the Far East. Note the pile of clays on the deck and his spent cartridge cases. (John de Lucy collection)

An RN exhibition rugby team from *Cornwall* at Surabaya, Java, in 1937. Bill Lucy is fifth from the right, wearing a scrum cap, and his caption read, 'Davis, Chas, Charlton, Spalding, Partridge, self, Wood and Wart'. (John de Lucy collection)

on specific aspects of an officer's performance and were, ultimately, the basis on which the decision to promote a particular officer rather than another would be based. They would be passed up the chain of command, through Commander 'Air' and the captain to the ship or air station's administrative authority and from the Admiral to the Naval Secretary's Department within the Admiralty, where they would be read carefully by promotion boards. Whilst allowance would be made for an individual officer's reporting technique or tendency to mark high or low, the report of a CO of a front-line squadron on one of his officers would count for lot, especially if both had seen action. From 1941 onwards a number of good RNVR pilots achieved rapid promotion from Sub Lieutenant to Lieutenant Commander in little over two years. By 1945 the majority of squadrons in the much-expanded Air Branch were commanded by RNVR officers who had learnt quickly and shown themselves ready for the task both in the air and, administratively, embarked in a carrier.

RNVR aircrew began to join squadrons from 1940 and had the potential at first to add to the CO's burden since almost all of them lacked any naval knowledge. They had to be eased into the squadron way of life, for which nothing in their flying training with the RAF could have prepared them, but at least they gained some advantage having joined as ratings and carried out a six-week course at HMS *St Vincent*, a former boys' training establishment in Gosport where they learnt some of the harsh realities of the naval way of life their men would undergo. On the other hand, they were only commissioned as officers on being awarded their flying badges, or 'wings', and had only two weeks at RNC Greenwich and their operational flying training at RN Air Stations Yeovilton or Crail as officers when they were appointed to their first squadron. Wardroom life in a carrier would be quite strange for them at first. Fortunately the majority were keen and wanted to play their part well.

As the war developed, a further task fell to squadron COs, that of recommending men who merited the award of gallantry medals, honours and decorations. The paperwork went through the same channels as officers' confidential reports and again the reports of COs who had often seen their men in action and could render or endorse at first-hand accounts of their actions counted for a lot. It was usual for a Mention in Despatches (MID) to be requested for an action that was clearly above and beyond the normal expectation of duty. The Distinguished Service Cross (DSC) usually reflected a successful action against the enemy – such as shooting down enemy aircraft or sinking a U-boat – and the Distinguished Service Order (DSO) reflected gallantry against the enemy with a significant element of leadership involved. For ratings there was the Distinguished Service Medal (DSM) in the face of the enemy. As for all British service personnel the Victoria Cross (VC) was the highest award for gallantry in the face of the enemy. Only the VC and

Recreational activities available to the officers of HM ships when they visited ports in the Far East during the 1930s were many and varied. Bill Lucy's caption for this image read, 'In hostile country, Amoy, 1936 - Tiger shooting – Tibbits left and self'. (John de Lucy collection)

759 NAS in 1939 photographed in front of a Blackburn Shark. Note that the majority are wearing gas mask bags smartly slung across the body from the right shoulder. These would have become everyday items on the outbreak of war. Both Bill Lucy and the CO, Lieutenant Commander Saunt, have their names stencilled in white on their gas mask bag straps. Note the number of RAF personnel still serving with what was now an RN squadron. Bill Lucy is seated eleventh from the left with Lieutenant Commander Saunt on his left. (John de Lucy collection)

MID could be awarded posthumously. The George Cross (GC) and George Medal (GM) could be awarded to any person or group, service or civilian, for gallantry that was not in the face of the enemy. Another, more difficult, duty was the need to write to the next of kin after a member of the squadron was killed in action or listed as missing. As we shall see later it was important to keep the wider squadron family involved and this would mean that the CO might often have to write these most difficult letters.

Just as a good CO could lead his squadron to achieve the best results possible, good Commanders 'Air' and captains could help him achieve the highest standards. Bad ones could make his life, and that of all the squadrons under their command, a miserable experience but fortunately the latter were in a tiny minority.

Lieutenant W P Lucy RN
Appointed in Command of 803 Naval Air Squadron

After just over six months in the cruiser *Manchester* serving on the East Indies Station, Bill Lucy was, in his own words, abruptly recalled to resume flying duties at home.[7] His time in the ship was just enough to restore his credentials as an executive officer and his confidential report showed that during his time in the cruiser he had served to his captain's entire satisfaction. Fortunately, Bill Lucy kept a handwritten journal at this time and his entries tell not only where he was and what he was doing but also his thoughts. He travelled back to the UK in the troopship *Lancashire* in which he observed 'crowds of nervous passengers scanning press reports about the deteriorating situation in Europe and discussing the possibility of war. When the ship passed through the Suez Canal on 20 April 1939 there were fears that an Italian attack could be launched on that day against British interests in Egypt, and passengers who had hoped to speed their journey back to the UK by air found this to be impossible. The ship eventually arrived safely in England on 2 May 1939 and Bill Lucy reported to the Admiralty where he was told to hold himself at instant readiness for a new appointment. He went to his family home at Sutton Valence near Maidstone in Kent where he 'enjoyed a few quiet days at home' but soon grew restive and rang the Naval Air Department in the Admiralty twice to ask about his new appointment. He was eventually contacted by telegram and told to report to what was still an RAF airfield at Eastleigh outside Southampton; things were still in a state of flux after the Admiralty had resumed full administrative control of what was now the Air Branch in May, but now events did begin to move quickly. On 1 July the airfield was transferred to the RN, commissioned as HMS *Raven* and the white ensign was hoisted. On the same day 759 NAS at Eastleigh was renumbered as 758 NAS for duty as a TAG training squadron[8] equipped at first with thirteen Blackburn Sharks and six Hawker Ospreys, forming part of Number

803 NAS Skuas and a Swordfish starting up at RNAS Hatston in 1940. (Author's collection)

2 Air Gunners' School. Lieutenant Commander W H G Saunt RN was appointed in command with Bill Lucy as one of his most experienced pilots. TAG training began in earnest on 1 August and he described life as being enjoyable with plenty of flying, long weekend leave, tennis and garden parties. He was selected for the Staff Course at Greenwich and was looking forward to 'a pleasant 18 months ashore' after spending most of his time as a Lieutenant at sea. It was not to be, however, and rather than try to transcribe an abridged version of Bill Lucy's journal here, I think it would better to quote from it to give his impression on the outbreak of war on 3 September 1939.

> Towards the middle of August, tension between this country and Germany was growing most alarmingly and the war between China and Japan drifted into the background. The reserve fleet became a regular unit and by the end of August England was organised almost on a war footing. Germany continued in her domineering manner and in spite of absolutely definite statements by Britain and France she marched into Poland on 1 September 1939. 3 September was a Sunday. For some reason our entry into the war was delayed and it was not until that forenoon that a state of war was declared. We were all congregated in the mess to listen to our premier, Mr Chamberlain, speak at 1115. When the fateful message was broadcast we were all, in spite of previous events, somewhat staggered. All of us rather older officers realised the immense gravity of the announcement; some of the younger members broke out with cheerful jests. A parade was organised and the ship's company was addressed by the Captain who ordered all the air station's passive defence measures to be put into full operation'.

Much of the rest of his journal described his views on the early war situation, briefly mentioning the loss of the aircraft carrier *Courageous* on 17 September and the battleship *Royal Oak* on 14 October. He mentioned that his long-standing friend Captain Dick Partridge RM had been appointed to 803 NAS with its new Skuas but that he had 'made great friends with Ralph Richardson, the famous actor who was now an RNVR pilot in 758 NAS', with whom he played squash two or three times a week. Richardson had gained a pilot's licence in the 1930s but acquired the nickname 'Pranger' in the Air Branch because of the number of aircraft he damaged. Skuas began to arrive in 758 NAS from October 1939 and Bill Lucy and his colleagues would soon have become familiar with them. Bill's journal made no mention of them but his friend Dick Partridge described them in his autobiographical *Operation Skua*[9] as being an 'easy aircraft to handle and a first-class dive-bomber but sadly lacking in speed and performance as a fighter'. He also said that 'it tended to be unstable fore and aft when fully loaded with front guns and their ammunition, rear gun and ammunition, one 500lb bomb, eight 20lb bombs and fuel for 4.5 hours in the air'. The appointing situation was still fluid, however, especially for the more senior officers who were needed to fill the rapidly growing

803 NAS badge. Its motto is 'CAVE PUNCTUM' which translates into English from the Latin as 'Beware of the Sting', most appropriate for a fighter squadron. (Crown Copyright).

number of squadron and staff appointments as the RN was mobilised onto a war footing. After only a few weeks in 803 NAS Dick Partridge was appointed to form and command 804 NAS with 'crisis' Sea Gladiators at RNAS Hatston to defend the Home Fleet anchorage at Scapa Flow against enemy air attack.

Bill Lucy did not spend much longer with 758 NAS himself. He left the unit on 14 January 1940 to take up a new appointment as commanding officer of 803 NAS, which was equipped with nine Skuas and three Rocs based temporarily ashore at Wick under RAF Fighter Command orders as part of the Scapa Flow defences. He replaced Lieutenant Commander D R F Cambell RN who was later to earn a place in history by inventing the angled deck while serving in the Admiralty after the war.[10] Cambell's confidential reports described him as an exemplary officer and pilot and it is clear that the Naval Secretary would only have chosen an outstanding officer to replace him, the more so since Bill Lucy was not due to be promoted to Lieutenant Commander until 1 August 1940. At the time he was 29 years old and had not married[11] but always found the time to write to his parents and family. It would probably be fair to say that he was devoted to the Navy and had given little thought to starting his own family. His confidential reports spoke of him as a talented officer of great ability, a gentleman who came to the attention of senior officers, was admired and respected by his peers and looked up to by his men who would have followed his orders at any cost.

Bill Lucy was also a keen sportsman. Like many fighter pilots he was an outstanding marksman and clay-pigeon shot – things he could practice on the flight deck of an aircraft carrier when there was no flying.[12] He was a tennis player of considerable ability who represented the Royal Navy and played at Wimbledon on a number of occasions. He also regularly played squash[13] and golf with his squadron contemporaries ashore, and during non-flying periods on board he would have played lift-well volleyball and flight deck hockey which remain popular aircraft carrier pastimes in the twenty-first century. In retrospect, his time in 758 NAS was a period of refresher flying intended to prepare him for the squadron command the Admiralty planned for him despite the fact that he was not yet a lieutenant commander. It gave him the chance to settle into the new Air Branch as it evolved rapidly after 24 May and to become familiar with the Blackburn Skua. He must also have flown its stablemate the Roc and formed an opinion about it but he makes no mention in his short journal of having done so and neither I nor his nephew John de Lucy have been able to trace his log book. 758 NAS also gave him the chance to instil his own dynamic form of leadership and airborne aggression into new pilots as they joined and the TAGs that they trained. Nothing but the best would have been good enough for him; others knew this and would have tried their hardest to achieve it for him.

Bill Lucy's time in command of 803 NAS was to be short but from the outset his achievements were memorable. They will be covered in detail in the following chapters.

Chapter 12

Naval Aviation in the First Months of the Second World War

THE SITUATION IN WHICH the Royal Navy and its Air Branch found itself on the outbreak of the Second World war on 3 September 1939 in some ways resembled that of 4 August 1914.[1] Germany was again the enemy and, initially, it had no important naval ally.[2] Again France was Great Britain's ally and the United States was a friendly neutral. The despatch of the BEF to France was the first military operation and the defence of British sea-borne trade and the convoys transporting large numbers of troops to the UK from Australia, Canada and New Zealand were immediate and important naval commitments. In the material field, however, there were significant differences and it was widely believed that the Luftwaffe would counter-balance the naval supremacy of the UK and France. Exercises and experiments had given some indication of how the fleet could best defend itself against air attack but nobody knew for certain what would happen under real conditions in war. In one important respect, however, the situation was better than 1914 in that warships were being fitted with radar, a game-changing technology that was capable of detecting enemy aircraft at sufficient range for fighters to be directed towards them with a reasonable chance of intercepting them. Unfortunately, the full implications of this new technology had not yet been absorbed by Admiral Forbes, Commander-in-Chief Home Fleet, and his staff either through exercises or realistic game play, and at first they held the view that anti-aircraft gunnery stood a better chance of driving off enemy bombers than fighters.

The Admiralty believed that its air arm had 'kept broadly in line with the requirements of the Navy' within the quantitative, qualitative and economic limitations forced upon it but this soon proved to be an unduly optimistic opinion. It had not yet appreciated the impact that the Air Ministry's long-standing view that naval aircraft would not need to be capable of matching land-based air opposition would have on actual operations. The Norwegian campaign would shortly banish that unfortunate concept forever as well as highlighting another important shortcoming which the Air Branch shared with the whole of the RN. In 1939 it was trained and equipped for the war that the Chiefs of Staff thought would happen, a view with which the Admiralty obviously concurred, and was not ideally trained or equipped to fight the war that unfolded in early 1940. The greatest part of pre-war naval training had

Ark Royal anchored at Spithead in June 1939. Note that the two octuple 2-pdr pom-pom mountings have not yet been fitted to their port-side sponsons amidships. The dustbin-shaped object at the masthead is a Type 72 aircraft homing beacon. (Author's collection)

been directed towards an action between main fleets on the open sea far from interference by land-based enemy aircraft, in effect a second Jutland-style battle. The war's opening moves actually involved widely dispersed actions by relatively small naval forces.

On the outbreak of war German U-boats and some surface raiders had already taken up their war stations and the liner *Athenia*, outbound from Liverpool to Montreal 200 miles west of the Hebrides, was torpedoed by U-30 on the day war was declared with the loss of over 100 lives.[3] The Home Fleet had taken up its war station at Scapa Flow on 24 August 1939 and on 1 September heavy units, including *Ark Royal*, were patrolling between the Shetland Islands and Norway. Unfortunately, a Swordfish encountered difficulties in the prevailing bad weather and came down in a Norwegian fjord. The crew managed to get ashore in their dinghy and found themselves near an airfield from where the Norwegian Air Force helpfully flew them to Bergen in time to take passage on a ship to the UK a few hours before war was declared. On 3 September the flagship *Nelson* with *Ark Royal*, *Rodney*, *Repulse*, *Sheffield*, *Aurora* and ten destroyers was off the Norwegian coast in thick fog searching for enemy shipping.

Broadly, naval air operations in the first months of the war can be divided into several distinct aspects, from each of which lessons were learnt which had to be quickly digested. It soon became apparent that the pre-war generation of aircraft were not available in sufficient numbers and in some cases they were totally unsuitable and could generally be classed as obsolescent. The aspects were:

1. Anti-submarine patrols of geographically limited areas by aircraft carriers which began on the first day of the war and ended abruptly with the loss of *Courageous*.
2. Short-notice deployments of fighters to defend the Home Fleet and UK coastal shipping against enemy air attack and air support for the convoy focal point off West Africa.
3. Embarked operations against enemy raiders in the Atlantic and Indian Oceans.
4. Spotting and reconnaissance operations by catapult flight aircraft against enemy raiders brought to action.
5. The German invasion campaigns in 1940 in which carrier-borne aircraft were employed in strike, air defence and army support operations that had not been anticipated before the war.

It is interesting to note that in aspects 1 and 2, naval aircraft had to fill gaps left by the inadequate number of RAF aircraft available to perform tasks allocated to them by the Chiefs of Staff in pre-war joint plans. Far from the RAF providing vital air support for what had been regarded since 1919 as joint maritime operations, naval aircraft had to be used to fill important gaps in land-based air coverage over the sea. It is also worth noting that while the aircrews of RAF Coastal and Bomber Commands had received some training in maritime reconnaissance techniques, neither had received any training in anti-submarine tactics and the 100lb bombs with which both RAF and RN aircraft were armed proved to be useless against U-boats, even when they fell in close proximity. The number of aircraft available to Coastal Command for the protection of shipping approaching choke-points to the west of the UK before the full introduction of the convoy system was extremely limited and flotillas of anti-submarine vessels were not immediately available to protect shipping as it made for port. Winston Churchill had been appointed as First Lord of the Admiralty in Chamberlain's War Cabinet and, as in 1914, his enthusiasm for what seemed to him to be offensive action was immediately apparent. In *The Second World War* he described the decision to use aircraft carriers to fill the gaps as giving 'some freedom in helping to bring in the unarmed, unorganised and un-convoyed traffic which was then approaching our shores in large numbers. This was a risk which it was right to run.'[4]

Offensive Anti-Submarine Patrols by Aircraft Carriers

The aircraft carriers *Courageous* and *Hermes* were placed under the orders of the C-in-C Western Approaches to provide aircraft to fill the gaps in specific areas. *Courageous* operated west of 12° W, *Hermes* to the east of it. *Ark Royal* operated in the North West Approaches under the orders of the C-in-C Home Fleet on similar duties with 800 and 803 NAS embarked with Skuas together with 810 and 820 NAS embarked with Swordfish.

Unfortunately, it soon became clear that under real conditions the ability of their Asdic-fitted escorts to form a barrier that would prevent U-boats from getting into an attacking position against high-value units had been over-estimated. On the morning of 14 September 1939 the British merchant ship *Fanad Head* transmitted a distress message to say that she had been torpedoed by a U-boat in a position roughly 200nm to the south-west of *Ark Royal.* On receipt of the message, the carrier increased speed, altered course to close *Fanad Head*'s reported position and ranged a striking force of three Skuas on deck. At 1440 she turned into wind to launch the aircraft without being aware that this manoeuvre put the U-39 into an ideal firing position. The boat was dived and its CO had been following *Ark Royal*'s movement through his periscope; he fired a salvo of three torpedoes with magnetic pistols and went deep. Lieutenant Vincent Jones on the carrier's quarterdeck saw one of the torpedoes break surface as it 'porpoised' after firing and he ran to the nearest telephone[5] to warn the compass platform. Unfortunately he was given a wrong number but Leading Signalman J E Hall on the compass platform also saw the tell-tale tracks and shouted a warning the officer of the watch, Lieutenant Rodd RN who ordered the rudder hard to port in sufficient time to avoid them. Two of the torpedoes passed astern and one of them detonated in the wake; this was the first that the escorting destroyers knew about the attack and *Faulkner, Foxhound* and *Firedrake* closed the likely firing position to launch a counter-attack. They soon gained Asdic contact and dropped a pattern of depth-charges that blew the U-boat's diesel engines off their beds. A second pattern blew her to the surface in a sinking condition and she was identified as U-39. All three destroyers opened fire but checked when men were seen to be abandoning ship. The U-boat's whole crew, forty-three men, got clear as it sank and were rescued by *Faulkner*. It was the first U-boat to be destroyed in the Second World War.

The three airborne Skuas located *Fanad Head* about 100nm away, lying stopped in the water with passengers and crew nearby in lifeboats. The sea was flat calm and a U-boat could be seen on the surface trying to finish her off with gunfire; she was in the middle of a patch of oil some 50 feet in diameter. On seeing the Skuas she dived immediately, so quickly in fact that two of her gun's crew were left treading water in the oily patch of sea. The Skuas carried out an urgent attack and released their bombs as the conning tower slid beneath the surface but, unfortunately, two of them were so low when they did so that bomb-blast shattered their tailplanes, killing their TAGs and causing them to crash into the sea. The pilots survived, however, and saw the third aircraft continuing to orbit the scene. Twenty minutes later the U-boat, subsequently identified as U-30, resurfaced on *Fanad Head*'s starboard quarter and the remaining Skua made a single diving attack with its front guns, expending 1,150 rounds in a single, prolonged burst during which the boat dived again. The Skua then returned to *Ark Royal* alone but six Swordfish arrived on the scene just as a torpedo hit *Fanad Head* amidships and finally sank her. All six subsequently attacked the vague outline of the U-boat with bombs and they believed that they had sunk her but it was later learnt that U-30 returned to Germany, taking the pilots from the ditched Skuas with her. They were the first RN personnel to be taken prisoner in the new war. One of them, Lieutenant G B K Griffiths RM, subsequently wrote from his prisoner of war camp with a full account of the incident and his statement is reproduced in full as it gives a good idea of the state of naval aviation training on the outbreak of war.[6]

Lt G B K Griffiths RM
OFLAG IXA
Germany
2 November 1939

c/o Agence de Prisonniers de Guerre
Palais du Consul General
Rouge Croix
Geneva
Switzerland

Dear —

I am writing from our prison camp in Germany, to which we were moved nearly two weeks ago. I was taken prisoner on 14 September 1939 whilst on a bombing raid. I went out in my machine to look for a submarine which was supposed to have sunk one of our merchant ships about 500 miles out from Ireland in the North Atlantic. Three machines went out and I searched for the sub., but failed to find it and started back for the ship. My observer, a Chief Petty Officer, suddenly shouted to me 'there's a merchant ship on the horizon, let's look at it'.

Well it was about 20 miles away, but away we went. When we were almost on it my chap said 'go low so that I can see its name' so down I went to sea level and slowed down. Suddenly, just as I got alongside the ship, I spotted the sub. alongside the far side of the ship! Up I went but the sub. had already got half submerged leaving me no time to get to a safe height to bomb from. So I took a chance and bombed from a low height in order to hit. My first bomb missed by about 20 feet and my next blew me up with the blast! I hit the sea at 200 mph at a steep dive and went straight down without stopping. I tried to get out of the cockpit but was jammed in with a stuck roof. When I was almost out of breath, I managed to break free and came to the surface. My observer was killed at once, for I never saw him again. I looked for him but with no luck. I then found that I was nearly a mile away from the merchant ship, in very cold water, with flying clothes on and not a little knocked about. Somehow I got there and clambered aboard the merchant ship. On board were some of the submarine's crew who were collecting the ship's papers when I had arrived. On board was also one of my squadron who had done almost the same thing as I had. A few minutes later up came the submarine, we were taken prisoner and the ship was torpedoed almost at once and once more we were submerged. We also had to swim to the sub.

Well, we spent a fortnight on that sub., before finally returning to Germany on 27 September. We were then lodged at the local naval jail for a fortnight, followed by a fortnight with Poles and then moved on to this place.

I wrote home as soon as I could and have since written again, but although that was over four weeks ago, I have not heard from any of them, although it may be here any day. English RAF prisoners have slowly joined us and now we are 1 Navy and 1 RM, 10 RAF officers and quite a few French also. This place is high up in the hills and is a very old castle surrounded by a moat and some 'obstacles'.

In the centre is a courtyard where we take our exercise, or walk around the walls of the moat in the inside. The moat is inhabited by 3 wild boars and is a most unsafe place indeed. Well, that is all the local news I am able to tell you. I expect that I shan't leave this place until the war ends, whenever that may be.

GBKG

The directions given by the Swordfish observers enabled destroyers to pick up the passengers and crew of the *Fanad Head* that same evening. *Ark Royal* returned to harbour on 17 September.

Courageous had re-commissioned after a refit on 31 July 1939 and formed part of the force that escorted the first elements of the BEF to France[7] before being ordered into the Western Approaches for an offensive anti-submarine patrol. Her air group comprised 811 and 822 NAS, both equipped with twelve Swordfish, and which had had little time to work up with the ship. The German wireless intelligence service was able to estimate correctly that she was working in the Western Approaches but was unable to deduce a position that was accurate enough to direct U-boats onto her. The War Diary of U-29 leaves no doubt that when *Courageous* was sighted through her periscope at 1800 on 17 September 1939 the encounter was entirely unexpected.[8] It was nearing the end of the U-boat's time on patrol and it had actually been trying to intercept a convoy reported by another U-boat. It took nearly two hours to get into an attacking position and then a firing solution was only made possible by the carrier turning onto a flying course to recover aircraft and placing itself in the U-boat commander's sights. At the time she was only screened by two destroyers, *Impulsive* and *Ivanhoe*, another two having been detached to go to the

Courageous sinking on 17 September 1939. (Author's collection)

aid of a merchant ship that had been attacked. An unlucky chain of circumstances, therefore, placed this valuable warship in a position of great danger which U-29 exploited to the full. She was hit at 1958 on the port side by two torpedoes fired at a range of about 2,500 yards in position 50 10N 14 50W to the south-west of Ireland,[9] sinking soon afterwards at approximately 2017. All her aircraft were lost, as were a number of aircrew, reducing still further the numbers available for the expansion of the Air Branch.

A Board of Inquiry into the loss was convened on 26 September by the C-in-C Western Approaches which questioned the carrier's failure to launch an air patrol to replace the detached destroyers. They felt obliged to comment that, had she done so, it would have been quite possible that the aircraft would have detected the presence of the U-boat at about 1900 when the force was steaming to the west at just over 26 knots, a speed that would have caused 'quenching' of the destroyer's lowered Asdic hull outfits that would have made contact impossible. With a reduced escort, the Board felt, it ought to have been imperative to use all means available for the detection of U-boats. *Ivanhoe* had subsequently obtained sonar contact and attacked while *Impulsive* was ordered to stand by *Courageous*. The Board felt that on the available evidence, these attacks stood a 60 per cent chance of having been successful.

Initial flooding in *Courageous* took place between frames 40 and 80 where the torpedoes hit and she took on an immediate 20-degree list to port but the Board found no evidence from witnesses that bulkheads had collapsed outside this area. The electrical ring main had not been split into sections and was severed by the initial explosion, causing a complete electrical failure within the hull; in turn this led to the loss of all lighting, telephone and main broadcast systems. There was no secondary lighting. Noises heard by survivors as the ship rolled to port were believed to be from aircraft and equipment in the hangar breaking loose and the Board regretted to come to the conclusion 'that the rapid sinking of the ship was due to the majority of [watertight] doors other than "X" doors being open. Even some of the "X" doors were not closed and all ventilation was open. There was thus almost a free run of water throughout the ship as the list increased.' A number of recommendations were made, notably that watertight doors should only ever be opened for urgent work at sea and that the number so opened should be strictly limited. Personal life-jackets should be issued as soon as possible to every officer and rating and, interestingly, anything liable to float to the surface after a ship sank should be securely lashed down. 'If wood is required for life-saving it should be put over the side before the ship sinks.' The Board was certain that a number of men were killed by flotsam surfacing after *Courageous* went down. In all, 518 men were lost, including her captain, Captain W T Makeig-Jones RN, out of a ship's company of 1,260.

She was the first British warship to be sunk in the conflict and the lesson was immediately learnt that hopeful patrolling without up-to-date intelligence of the enemy or specialised anti-submarine training was as unproductive as it was dangerous.[10] Operating an aircraft carrier continuously in a circumscribed area with constant, predictable, turns into wind steaming a straight course to operate aircraft in an area that was likely to have several U-boats on task was not a sensible idea and after the loss of *Courageous* it was not repeated. It was actually the War Cabinet that advised the withdrawal of aircraft carriers from submarine-hunting work and their employment on such a hazardous task with an inadequate escort reflects little credit on either the Naval Staff of the new First Lord, who was anxious to see offensive measures undertaken without considering their likely effectiveness or danger. In *The War at Sea*, Roskill commented that it now seems 'surprising that they should have been risked on that type of duty',[11] and it would be difficult to argue against his point of view. A valuable ship, a lot of valuable trained men and a significant number of front-line aircraft were lost for no gain. *Hermes* had re-commissioned on 24 August 1939 after a period in reserve[12] and embarked the Swordfish of 814 NAS. She was further east than *Courageous* and was not attacked but none of her aircraft had located a U-boat either; she returned to Devonport on 27 September.

Further Afield

On 25 August 1939 the seaplane carrier *Albatross* was re-commissioned for a slightly different form of anti-submarine duty;[13] she embarked the nine Walrus amphibians of 710 NAS and sailed for Freetown in Sierra Leone where she acted as a depot ship for her aircraft while they protected ships at the focal point of the West African convoy routes. She was moored near Hastings while a naval air station was constructed ashore. Again, there were no RAF maritime patrol aircraft within 1,000 miles of this area[14] and 710 NAS had filled an important gap by providing, at short notice, the numerically largest concentration of maritime patrol aircraft outside the UK, illustrating the importance that the Admiralty placed on the protection of merchant shipping in this area. Prior to the French collapse in June 1940, a detached flight operated from Dakar in French Senegal and another from Bathurst in the British colony of Gambia until RAF flying boats eventually arrived to relieve them. *Albatross* and 710 NAS continued their task until well into 1941. The original idea had been for the Walrus to search for enemy surface raiders but their principal value proved to be in anti-submarine work as the U-boats extended their operations southward. Their presence undoubtedly prevented merchant ship casualties in the area and must be judged a success. Naval aircraft were also deployed to airfields where they could cover the lack of RAF aircraft to defend naval bases at Scapa Flow, Gibraltar and Alexandria against air attack as well as convoys in their immediate proximity.

Carrier Operations with the Home Fleet

After her spell of offensive anti-submarine operations *Ark Royal*'s next sortie began on 25 September when the C-in-C Home Fleet, Admiral Forbes, learnt that the 'S' class submarine *Spearfish* had been damaged by a German depth-charge attack off the Horn Reef and was unable to dive. The 2nd Cruiser Squadron comprising *Southampton*, *Glasgow*, *Sheffield* and *Aurora* with six destroyers was given the task of extricating her and heavy cover was provided by the flagship *Nelson* with *Rodney* and the battlecruisers *Hood* and *Repulse* together with *Ark Royal* and escorting destroyers. *Rodney* and *Sheffield* had been the first two RN warships to be fitted with air warning radar, Type 79Y.[15] By September 1939 their sets were capable of detecting aircraft at 10,000 feet at a range of about 70 miles and higher aircraft at even greater ranges. On the morning of 26 September the force was about 180nm east of Aberdeen, *Spearfish* had been rescued and was heading for Rosyth; the heavy units were heading back to Scapa Flow at about 1100 when there was a report from one of two Swordfish on anti-submarine patrol that a Dornier Do 18 flying boat was shadowing the fleet about 10nm to the south-east. *Rodney*'s radar also detected a further two or three groups of enemy aircraft about 80nm to the south-east. Action stations were sounded and *Ark Royal* ranged a total of nine Skuas which were started and warmed up by mechanics as the aircrew were briefed. They were launched in three groups at intervals of about thirty minutes to drive off the shadower; the first flight comprising aircraft of 803 NAS led by the CO. With no other information they had to carry out a visual search for the shadower which proved difficult because it had a dark camouflage paint scheme and was flying low over the sea. It was seen and engaged, however, at 57 36N 02 53E but immediately made off when attacked by the Skuas. The flight comprised:

Pilot	Observer
Lt Cdr D R F Cambell	Lt M C E Hanson
Lt A T J Kindesley	LA R F Hurford
PO J A Gardner	NA P J Busby[16]

It was subsequently learnt that *Rodney* held the enemy aircraft on radar and had passed ranges and bearings to the C-in-C in *Nelson* by flag signals but they had not been passed on to *Ark Royal*. Captain Syfret of *Rodney* subsequently commented that his reports had not been given sufficient importance by the fleet command[17] and it appears that the scope of this new technology had not yet been fully grasped, perhaps because of the tight security that surrounded anyone with knowledge of radar's capabilities. For whatever reason, Admiral Forbes and his staff seemed to lack the situational awareness they would need to fight while within range of a powerful enemy air force.

The Dornier Do 18G-1 in service with the Luftwaffe in 1939 was a development of a type designed originally as a transatlantic mail carrier with a maximum range of over 2,000nm. It was powered by two 880hp Junkers Jumo 205D six-cylinder double-opposed liquid-cooled engines in a unique nacelle arrangement over the wing with one engine pulling and one pushing. It was intended mainly for reconnaissance but could carry four 110lb bombs. The defensive armament comprised a single 13mm MG131 machine-gun on a pillar mounting in an open hatch at the bow and a single 20mm MG151 cannon in a dorsal turret. It had a crew of four and a maximum level speed of 145 knots which gave the Skua, which was about 50 knots faster, a reasonable chance of overtaking it in a tail chase. The turret-mounted cannon was a concern, however, and fighter pilots would not want to give its gunner a low deflection shot astern if possible. The best method of attack would be from behind and below and this is no doubt why the Dornier remained low over the sea. Like all British fighters of the period, the Skua was limited by the rifle-calibre ammunition of its front guns, which needed to hit something vital such as the target's engines or its pilot to bring it down.

As the shadower made off to the south-east the Skuas fired several bursts which they claimed to have damaged it. A report was subsequently received by the Admiralty that a damaged Do 18 had landed in Dutch territorial waters after failing to get back to its base at Borkum Island off the mouth of the Ems River. At about 1130 a second flight was launched which comprised:

Pilot	Observer
Lt B S McEwen	PO B M Seymour
Lt C L G Evans	PO H Cunningham
Lt W A Robertson	LA A Ashby

This flight was actually directed towards a second group of shadowers by an improvised system that now made use of *Rodney*'s radar. Ranges and bearings of the contact were passed by visual signals from *Rodney* to *Ark Royal* and immediately relayed to the aircraft by W/T. Although somewhat stale by the time it reached the fighters, the information at least pointed them in the right direction and the lack of height information did not matter because the shadowers were likely to be at very low level to maintain visual contact with the fleet. Once the enemy aircraft were seen, things happened very quickly and the flight split up to engage individual aircraft. The Do 18s had apparently not seen the Skuas coming and McEwen selected one aircraft which was flying near the surface and 'swept down on it for the first burst'.[18] As he positioned his aircraft for a second firing pass he saw 'the flying boat down on the water, its pilot waving his [white] flying overalls as a distress signal'. The four crew members were subsequently picked up from the dinghy by the destroyer *Somali* which then sank the aircraft with a single 4.7-inch round. This was the first German aircraft to be shot down by any British Empire or Allied fighter in the Second World War.

German shadowers continued to probe the force and a third flight, this time from 800 NAS, was launched that intercepted another Do 18 at about 1230. This comprised:

Pilot	**Observer**
Lt E D G Finch-Noyes	PO C J E Cotterill
PO H A Monk	LA M Hall
Lt K V V Spurway	AC1 G G Thomas

Between them the flight chased the enemy away from the fleet and fired out all their front-gun ammunition. The Dornier evaded successfully by making a series of very tight turns at sea level every time that a Skua made a firing pass and succeeded in returning to its base but was later assessed as having been damaged. This flight had also been vectored onto its target by visual signals from the battleship transcribed into W/T messages from the parent carrier, a method that was to be refined and improved over the months ahead. Surprisingly, *Ark Royal* herself was never fitted with radar.[19]

Admiral Forbes signalled his congratulations to *Ark Royal* but although the shadowers had been driven off, they had succeeded in reporting the fleet's position and an attack by bombers followed at about 1420. Fortunately, these were neither well prepared nor executed and the Luftwaffe appeared to be hesitant in deciding how best to use aircraft in action against ships. Before the advent of radar, the Admiralty had decided that no affordable aircraft carrier could carry sufficient fighters to maintain constant daylight combat air patrols against aircraft that could attack from almost any direction. It had decided, therefore, that gunfire offered the most practical protection against aircraft. Whilst regrettable, one can see sense in

The Dornier Do 18 shot down by Lieutenant McEwen and Petty Officer Seymour of 803 NAS on 26 September 1939 photographed from the destroyer *Somali*. After rescuing the aircrew, *Somali* sank the aircraft with her 4.7-inch guns. (Author's collection)

this viewpoint, which had already led to the design and construction of armoured carriers capable of continuing to operate aircraft even after damage. However, radar changed everything and from 1938 the Admiralty should have used war-gaming at the Tactical School and sea exercises to evaluate its potential use more effectively. There was just too much else going on at the time, however, and the use of radar was not given the priority it should have received. Extemporised methods of fighter control were developed later by the Home Fleet and Force H that led directly to our modern conception of situational awareness and fighter control. It would be fair to say that from 1942 the RN led the world in this discipline and maintained that lead into the early 1970s. In 1940, however, the Admiralty had not yet fully appreciated the improvements that command and control of carrier-borne interceptor fighters would bring to the air defence of a fleet. Admiral Forbes had certainly not appreciated it and both he and his staff retained the pre-radar dogma that placed gunnery before fighters as a means of driving off enemy air attack. Therefore, he ordered *Ark Royal* to strike down all aircraft into the hangar, including her fighters, and drain them of fuel to reduce the risk of fire. Coming so soon after McEwen's success this came as an unpleasant surprise in the carrier but there was little that could be done about it and she was ordered into line with the battleships to use her anti-aircraft guns as part of the fleet's barrage fire. The CO of 803 NAS at the time later spoke about this incident in 1957, after his promotion to Rear Admiral, in a lecture to the Royal Aeronautical Society at Brough where the new Buccaneer strike aircraft were being developed. Asked when the RN had changed its mind and begun to believe in aviation, he referred to the fighters being struck down on 26 September 1939 rather than flown off against the enemy to their very great frustration. The change in attitude came, he suggested, 'when the bombs began to fall'.[20]

Five Heinkel 111 bombers approached the fleet at about 1420, flying at about 6,000 feet using cloud cover. Four of them dropped their bombs outside the barrage and withdrew but one, flown by Lieutenant Adolf Francke, singled out *Ark Royal* for a glide-bombing attack with his single 1,000kg bomb. It was a near miss and although Francke made no claim to have done so, the attack led the German propaganda organisation to make the first of many false claims to have sunk her. Other attacks followed and *Hood* received a glancing blow on the quarter from a bomb which caused no damage. The cruisers were subjected to high-level attacks from about 12,000 feet but received no hits. Like the earlier attack on *Ark Royal*, these attacks were not well co-ordinated and no attempt was made to single out high-value units. The anti-aircraft fire proved to be as ineffective as the bombing and Admiral Forbes noted in his subsequent report that 'control personnel were obviously unprepared'.[21]

Raider-Hunting Groups

During the early months of the war covered by this book the Germans used U-boats, aircraft and mines to attack shipping in the approaches to UK ports; the U-boats were not yet numerous or capable enough to deploy into the open oceans and the primary threat to merchant ships in these areas was expected to come from the enemy's powerfully-armed 'pocket battleships'. Armed merchant cruisers specially modified for extended raiding operations were not yet a threat because German policy had been to avoid arousing suspicion by starting work on them in peacetime.[22] Eventually, however, the German naval command planned to modify twenty-six ships for the role and intended to use them mainly in the Indian Ocean. One ship was fitted out at Murmansk near which the Russians had given their new ally the use of a base and it was ready to commence operations in February 1940. In November 1939 Hitler approved an approach by the German Navy to Japan asking for the use of bases by merchant raiders and U-boats operating in the Far East. The Admiralty was right, therefore, to regard surface raiders as a potentially serious worldwide problem. The threat they posed involved not only ship sinkings but the disruption of the flow of shipping their presence, or even the suspicion of their presence, would cause in an area. Countering them would necessitate a redisposition of forces, which might weaken the Home Fleet's superiority in the North Sea. Admiral Raeder had decided to use his pocket battleships as raiders from the outset and *Admiral Graf Spee* sailed to take up a position in the mid-

Atlantic on 21 August 1939. Her sister-ship *Deutschland* followed on 24 August to take up station in the North Atlantic.

The Admiralty learnt that a raider was definitely at large in the South Atlantic on 1 October 1939 when the crew of the British merchant ship *Clement* reached South America having been rescued by another ship after she became *Graf Spee*'s first victim. They reported, however, that they had been sunk by *Admiral Scheer*. The presence of a second raider was discovered on 21 October when the crew of the Norwegian *Lorentz W. Hansen* reached the Orkney Islands in another ship that had rescued them and reported having been sunk by the *Deutschland* on the 14th. Admiralty reaction to the threat was prompt and eight powerful hunting groups were formed from 5 October, some of them containing French warships after consultation with the French Ministry of Marine. They were identified by letters and comprised the following ships:

Force F	*Berwick*	2 Walrus[23]	North America and West Indies
	York	1 Walrus	
Force G	*Exeter*	2 Walrus	South-east coast of South America
	Cumberland	3 Walrus	
	Ajax	2 Seafox	
	Achilles	1 Walrus	
Force H	*Sussex*	1 Walrus	Cape of Good Hope
	Shropshire	1 Walrus	
Force I	*Cornwall*	2 Walrus	Ceylon
	Dorsetshire	1 Walrus	
	Eagle	813 and 824 NAS, Swordfish	
Force K	*Renown*	2 Swordfish	Pernambuco, South Atlantic
	Ark Royal	800 and 803 NAS, Skuas	
		810 and 820 NAS, Swordfish plus 1 Walrus	
Force L	*Dunkerque*	4 seaplanes	Brest
	Bearn	25 aircraft	
	3 French cruisers		
Force M	2 French cruisers		Dakar
Force N	*Strasbourg*	4 seaplanes	West Indies
	Hermes	814 NAS, Swordfish	

A Skua being prepared for launch from *Ark Royal*'s port catapult while the ship formed part of Force K hunting for German raiders in the South Atlantic. One Swordfish is being launched from the starboard catapult with another waiting its turn astern of it. The calm sea indicates a complete lack of natural wind, making the catapult launches a necessity for fully loaded aircraft. (Author's collection)

Lieutenant B Paterson RN in shirtsleeves next to Sea Gladiator N2272 of 804 NAS at RNAS Hatston in early 1940. The officer sitting on the cockpit sill is Lieutenant W E G Taylor RN, an American citizen who had joined the Air Branch before the outbreak of war. (Author's collection)

An officer being transferred from *Glorious*' quarterdeck to a destroyer, from which this photograph was taken, by light jackstay. It shows details of the quarterdeck, including the door into the lower hangar and the two seaplane cranes in their stowed positions. The quarterdeck was designed with a low freeboard to facilitate moving seaplanes onto the water with the minimum swing when suspended beneath a crane. Note also the two single 4.7-inch guns and the ship's badge on the after hangar bulkhead. (Author's collection)

In addition to these groups the Admiralty allowed the C-in-C South Atlantic to retain four destroyers that had previously been ordered back to the UK, and several heavy units were deployed to Halifax from where they were to escort homeward-bound Atlantic convoys. These initially included *Resolution* with one Swordfish, *Revenge*, *Enterprise* and *Emerald*, followed later by *Repulse* with two Swordfish, *Furious* with 801 NAS (Skua), 816 and 818 NAS (Swordfish) and *Warspite* with two Swordfish. *Malaya* with two Swordfish and *Glorious* with 802 NAS (Sea Gladiator), 812, 823 and 825 NAS (Swordfish) embarked. In fact Force F never worked together as a hunting group because its ships were re-allocated to the Halifax escort group when the presence of *Deutschland* in the North Atlantic was discovered. Forces G, H and K were placed under the operational control of the C-in-C South Atlantic, Admiral G H d'Oyly Lyon and the searches for *Graf Spee* fell to these groups.

Apart from the carriers and their air groups, the listing above shows that the various battleships, battlecruisers and cruisers embarked a total of thirty-three catapult aircraft, and these made a huge difference to the areas of sea that could be

A later stage in the jackstay transfer showing the lieutenant in the tray happily giving a thumbs-up to show that all is well. More external detail of the ship is visible including the fog buoy to the right of the lieutenant's hand. This would have been streamed astern in conditions of low visibility for the next ship astern in a formation to judge its exact distance from the streaming ship. This could be as short as 200 yards, leaving little room for error by either ship. (Author's collection)

searched by the forces. The Germans also found to their cost that the deployment of pocket battleships as raiders not only weakened the Home Fleet but also weakened their own forces available in the North Sea. Whilst *Deutschland* succeeded in getting home, *Graf Spee* would have had to evade several hunting forces and their air searches in order to get home, and this would have been no easy task. The fact that he believed *Ark Royal* to be waiting for him off the River Plate was a major factor in Captain Langsdorf's ultimate decision to scuttle *Graf Spee* rather than try to fight his way back to Germany.

The ability of the hunting forces to be in the right place at the right time depended to a great extent on the ability of an attacked merchant ship to send a raider report – RRR followed by a position – as soon as the enemy was identified and instructions to do so were sent to all masters. Aware of this, raiders threatened to sink ships without giving their crews the chance to abandon them, but the majority did manage to send reports at grave risk to themselves. The hunting groups in late 1939 did succeed in locating and intercepting three enemy merchant ships before

A Skua carrying out a practice quarter attack on another Skua over the Orkney Islands in 1939. This photograph shows just how vulnerable the Skua was to return fire in the final seconds of an attack from astern if it had no speed advantage over the target. (Author's collection)

three cruisers of Force G under Commodore H Harwood located and brought *Graf Spee* to action on the morning of 13 December 1939. These were the *Uhenfels* on 5 November, located by *Ark Royal* and her attendant destroyers, *Adolph Woermann* located by *Neptune* off Ascension Island on 22 November and *Emmy Friedrich* in the Gulf of Mexico by *Caradoc*.

The Battle of the River Plate

The overall conduct of the battle falls outside the immediate subject matter of this book but one aspect does merit inclusion: the use of catapult aircraft to spot the fall of shot. *Graf Spee* and the three British cruisers all carried catapult aircraft but none of them was airborne when the first encounter took place. *Graf Spee* saw the British ships at 0552 on 13 December 1939; in turn she was seen at 0616 by *Exeter* and all three British ships sounded action stations. The German ship opened fire on *Exeter* at 0617 and fired was returned at 0621 with *Exeter* straddling *Graf Spee* with her third salvo. *Ajax* launched a single Seafox at 0637,[24] twenty minutes into the action, which proved to be the only aircraft to take part in the battle. Others, including the Arado on *Graf Spee*, were all damaged on their catapults.

The pilot was Lieutenant E D G Lewin RN, who had been a member of Number 31 Pilots' Course at Leuchars, qualifying in December 1935; the observer was Lieutenant R E N Kearney RN, who had been a member of 27 Observers' Course, qualifying at Lee-on-Solent in July 1935. Both were, therefore very experienced and their flight, which was part of 718 NAS, had been deployed with their ship for some months. They were briefed to fly at 3,000 feet on the disengaged side of the cruiser and spot her fall of shot, making corrections as necessary to straddle the enemy. This was precisely what catapult flights were intended to do and given the time that the flight had spent on board, they and the ship's gunnery direction officers should have formed a well-drilled team. In fact things started badly before effective results were obtained. No doubt for good reasons, Kearney informed personnel on the cruiser's flag deck that once airborne he intended to use the reconnaissance radio frequency and not the spotting frequency. His message was not relayed to the bridge wireless office, however, and it listened for him on the spotting frequency. In consequence there was no communication between aircraft and ship for twelve minutes at the height of the battle, at a time when the light cruisers' fire was scattered after some confusion over whether they were concentrating their fire or not. By 0720, however, things had improved and Kearney was able to signal 'good shot' repeatedly to *Achilles*. Later they reported torpedo tracks that would pass ahead of the light cruisers although there is no record in *Graf Spee*'s report of any being fired at this time. Despite the errors, the Seafox crew had achieved what was required of them. Lewin was subsequently awarded the DSC and Kearney was mentioned in despatches.

Naval Air Squadrons Operating Fighters Ashore

As related in the last chapter, 803 NAS disembarked its Skuas to RNAS Hatston near Kirkwall in the Orkney Islands on 1 October to provide air defence for the fleet since RAF Fighter Command was unable to do so within its own resources. At the First Lord's instigation, Dick Partridge had left 803 to form 804 NAS with Sea Gladiators, also at Hatston, at the end of November 1939 to further increase the air defences of Scapa Flow. In 1940 several disembarked naval air squadrons added to air defences in the northern UK. From 16 February 1940 800 NAS operated from Hatston providing air escorts for coastal convoys and later striking at targets in the Norwegian littoral. 801 NAS operated at RAF Wick and RNAS Hatston from 25 March 1940 to provide fighter protection for ships of the Home Fleet anchored in Scapa Flow, escorts for coastal convoys and, later in the period, strikes against targets in the Norwegian littoral. 803 NAS also operated from RAF Wick and RNAS Hatston, working with 800 NAS. These three squadrons were all Skua units but 804 NAS operated its Sea Gladiators at RNAS Hatston until 5 September 1940 in defence of the Home Fleet. For immediate operational control, these units came under 14 Group RAF which had a sector headquarters at Wick.[25]

Dick Partridge described 804 NAS after its hasty formation in *Operation Skua*, giving a good idea of what life was like in a shore-based unit at the time:[26]

> after a few days I was able to tell the station commander that I had 6 aircraft operational and that soon the squadron would be completed. There was no accommodation for the ground crews at the field and they were housed in large buildings such as the Town Hall in Kirkwall. I visited them from time to time to do what I could for their well-being and to encourage them. They were a fine, cheerful, loyal and willing lot, sleeping in spartan conditions, mostly on the floor.
>
> Now and again the odd German aircraft or two used to appear, usually Heinkel HeIIIs at great height, probably on reconnaissance, but occasionally a stick of bombs was dropped near the aerodrome and the enemy were then chased off by us … .804 was equipped with Sea Gladiators, the last of the biplane fighters … they were not in the Spitfire or Hurricane class but they were rugged, easy to fly and very manoeuvrable. They had an excellent rate of climb and I can remember that one day when I had tried to chase after a reported 'Peacock' [brevity code for an unidentified aircraft] to 30,000 feet when visibility was maximum I could see the Orkney and Shetland Islands, Fair Isle and practically the whole of Scotland. Unfortunately the only thing I didn't see was the Peacock.
>
> With the squadron acting in this fighter role we obviously had to have at least some aircraft at immediate readiness and I found that with the pilots accommodated in a hotel a mile or more from their aircraft the delay between the alarm and getting to those aircraft was unacceptable. There was a large, long hut on the airfield used for storage and I managed to convince the Captain that that this must be converted into living quarters and a Mess for the pilots of 804 NAS. This was very successful and we now lived 'on the job' and really were available. Of course, we sacrificed some comfort, sleeping in dormitories and eating issue rations but nobody minded and it did a lot to build the squadron into a really close team. Our usual routine was one sub-flight of 3 at immediate readiness, one at readiness and one at stand-by. The fourth was off-duty unless it was known that something special was expected. When no aircraft were airborne on patrol we always had one machine manned and warmed up at the end of the duty runway ready for instant take-off.

In early December Dick Partridge became ill with tonsillitis and was sent on sick leave to convalesce. His appointment in command of 804 NAS had only been temporary and while he was away Lieutenant Commander J C Cockburn RN took over command of the squadron. After Christmas 1939 Partridge returned to the squadron as senior pilot. His journey north was of interest: he travelled by train to

Inverness and then flew in a de Havilland Dominie of Scottish Airways to RNAS Hatston. He recalled,

> these Dominie trips always used to amuse me because if the pilot had a full load of passengers, about 7 or 8 I think, he used to taxi out to the end of the duty runway and when in position for take-off he would turn around and casually ask the rear 4 passengers to come forward and kneel in the passageway just behind him so that it would be easier for him to get the aircraft tail up when taking off. Of course, as soon as [we were] airborne, the 4 passengers returned to their seats.

The first three months of 1940 were spent on routine local defensive flying, mostly investigating radar reports of incoming unidentified aircraft. On 16 March there was an enemy air attack on Scapa Flow beginning at 1950 and the whole of 804 NAS got airborne but failed to make contact with the enemy in the gathering gloom. Landing back on the airfield was made difficult by the lack of any lighting or flares as a precaution against its being seen by enemy aircraft.

On 1 April 1940 an Admiralty signal appointed Partridge in command of 800 NAS on 3 April, replacing Lieutenant Commander G N Torry RN who had commanded the unit since November 1938. 800 NAS had been disembarked from

A Sea Gladiator photographed practising a slashing attack on the photographer's Swordfish over Scapa Flow. The Sea Gladiator was a compact and very manoeuvrable fighter. (Author's collection)

Swordfish ranged on the main hard-standing at RNAS Hatston armed with practice torpedoes or mines. St Magnus Cathedral in Kirkwall is visible in the distance over the furthest hangar. (Author's collection)

Survivors from *Fanad Head* being over-flown by a Swordfish from *Ark Royal* on 14 September 1939. (Author's collection)

its parent carrier, *Ark Royal*, to Hatston since 15 February and his senior observer was Lieutenant Robin Bostock who had qualified with Number 31 Observers' Course in December 1937. He described him as 'a quiet personality but immensely experienced and capable as a Fleet Air Arm observer'. They got on well together and Partridge had complete faith in his professional ability; he liked to think that Bostock had the same faith in him as a pilot.

The other Skua squadron disembarked at Hatston at this time was 803 NAS which had moved up from Wick on 11 February. Partridge noted that it was commanded by 'an old friend of mine, Lieutenant William Lucy RN'. Bill Lucy and he had been together for many years both in the UK and in the Far East and Mediterranean and they had played tennis together in the first days of the war at Eastleigh. Partridge described Bill as 'a fine officer and pilot and, as far as I could see, completely fearless'.[27] 800 and 803 NAS settled into a routine of convoy patrols, investigating reported enemy air attacks on merchant ships and a variety of similar tasks.

Lieutenant Lucy's First Weeks in Command of 803 NAS

Bill Lucy was well aware that flying under-powered dive-bomber/fighters against enemy aircraft with a superior performance either from the deck of an aircraft carrier or from a naval air station ashore would be a dangerous task but he was determined from the outset to take the fight to the enemy. He assumed command of 803 NAS on 8 February 1940 while the squadron was based ashore at RAF Wick and lived, with other officers, at Mackay's Hotel. On 10 February the squadron moved to RNAS Hatston and accommodation was found for him and his officers in the Ayre Hotel Orkney. The sailors lived in a mixture of temporary and tented accommodation while more permanent buildings were constructed at the air station. He found the time to write a letter to his family which was to be opened if he failed to return from a sortie and this was subsequently retained and treasured by them. Written on notepaper from RNAS Eastleigh, Southampton, with the address crossed through and dated 19 February 1940, it tells us something of his inner thoughts:-

> My dear Family,
>
> A chance has come to fight for justice, freedom and peace. If it should happen that I do not return this is my farewell.
>
> I have tried to live a Christian life and as a Christian I look forward to the life to come. Thank you all very much for all the happiness you have brought to me and shared with me.
>
> With Love
> Bill

When it was eventually opened it must have brought comfort to his family, especially his mother, to know how sincerely he believed in what he was doing.

803 NAS soon developed a routine and flew a number of hours, mostly on defensive patrols lasting up to four and a half hours out of sight of land over the sea.[28] Bill always flew with the squadron's senior observer, Lieutenant M C E Hanson RN. Other pilots flew with rating observers or TAGs. They were occasionally directed to the aid of lone merchant ships being attacked by a Heinkel He 111 bomber and were usually able to chase it off but their lack of performance prevented them from catching it. It was rewarding, however, to be able to return to the ship to see the crew coming out onto the deck and waving their thanks. Bill Lucy seemed to be more successful than the other Skua pilots and when Dick Partridge asked him why this was he explained that he 'always patrolled either at 12,000 feet or as high as the cloud base would allow so that, hopefully, he would have height advantage over any enemy aircraft and catch up with it in the ensuing dive'. He then added quite casually that he 'never opened fire until he was just about to collide with the enemy'. This sounded a hazardous form of attack to Dick Partridge but when he suggested to Bill that one day a rear gunner was going to get him first he smiled, shrugged his shoulders and said that he was sure it was the best way of 'blasting the buggers out of the sky'. Any suggestion of opening fire with a short burst at about 300 yards and closing in with short bursts until the final kill cut no ice with Bill. Nor would he concede that the enemy rear gunner's aim and peace of mind might be affected by the sight of tracer coming towards him.

Bill Lucy's method of attack was a variation on the classic 'perch' method in which the fighter pilot could use height advantage to set himself up high on his target's beam. He then turned towards the target and dived, reversing the turn as he closed in and steadying as he opened fire at close range. This technique had the advantage that the fighter offered the gunners in the enemy aircraft a crossing target that also had a high but varying rate of descent throughout the attack; it was thus made difficult for them to estimate the correct amount of lead, both in elevation and bearing, to score hits on the fighter. The Skua had a reflector gunsight which enabled the pilot to estimate the right amount of aim-off as he opened fire to put his bullets where the target would be at the end of their time of flight. Obviously the closer the fighter was to the target, the shorter the time of flight and less aim-off, or lead, needed to be applied. In level flight the He 111 was capable of 225 knots, about 25 knots faster than a Skua and so the Skua could only make one firing pass before losing its advantage from the dive and dropping astern; this was another reason for firing at close range to minimise the need for aim-off and make every bullet count. Here too the Skua was at a disadvantage with only four Browning 0.303-inch front guns. These were the standard British fighter armament in 1940; they weighed less than 25lb each and fired about 1,200 rounds per minute giving the Skua twenty-five seconds of fire but the rifle-calibre bullets had to hit something vital to bring an aircraft down or even cause serious damage. It was usual to put the point of aim

Skuas of 806 NAS from RNAS Eastleigh in 1940. Note the differing styles of fuselage roundel; several variations were in use at this time. (Author's collection)

on the bomber's cockpit, hoping to incapacitate the pilot, but hits on the engines or their liquid cooling systems could be effective.

In fighter-versus-fighter combat the classic manoeuvre was the 'scissors' in which the attacking pilot tries to get into a firing position astern of his opponent. On seeing him getting into a position in his 'six o'clock',[29] the defending pilot would turn as hard as possible to the left or right. To achieve the necessary aim-off to hit him, the attacking pilot must pull even harder but the defending fighter's turn will cause its speed to wash off, making its turn tighter and causing the attacker to slide outside his turn radius. As soon as the defender sees this happen he will snap roll into a turn the other way putting the two fighters cockpit to cockpit in a 'scissors' manoeuvre which the attacker must attempt to follow. If the defender can force a succession of overshoots from the attacker he will gradually work successive 'scissors' until he gets behind the original attacker and can have a shot at him. Where one of the fighters has a speed advantage it can pull high in the 'scissors' to over-bank and tighten its turn; a manoeuvre known as a 'yo-yo'. Differing fighter performances allow other variations on the basic 'scissors' and 'yo-yo' but these had little application for the Skua, which was slower than virtually all the enemy aircraft it had to intercept. The only exception was the Arado Ar 196 floatplane carried by German battleships and cruisers which was only capable of 170 knots at 13,000 feet. Bill Lucy never hung back when there was a chance of engaging an enemy aircraft and always took every opportunity to take the fight to the enemy. Two Skuas of 800 NAS were carrying out a combat air patrol over convoy ON21 to Norway on 20 March 1940 when it was attacked by 10 He 111s at about 1850. The section comprised:

Lt E W T Taylour RN	Lt R S Bostock RN	in L3028
PO H A Monk	LA M Hall	in L3025

Taylour fired 1,860 rounds and succeeded in driving the enemy bombers off, possibly damaging one of them. Monk only fired 300 rounds with one gun jammed but helped to drive the enemy off. At about 1940 Bill Lucy was returning from another convoy escort sortie with Michael Hanson in L2963 when he encountered a single He 111 which was machine-gunning a merchant ship off Copinsay Island. He attacked it immediately and managed to carry out two attacks in which he fired 1,600 rounds but the enemy managed to evade into cloud. However, its wheels were down and Bill Lucy's windscreen was covered in oil from the enemy bomber. 18 Group of RAF Coastal Command signalled a day later[30] that 'the AOC-in-C had learnt that the German wireless was calling in vain up to midnight on 20 March for the return of a missing aircraft. This is probably the result of action by the Skuas and he sends his congratulations on this success.' Lucy was informed that his He 111 was a probable kill and received another signal on 21 March, this one from the AOC of 13 Group Fighter Command which was responsible for the sector operations centre at Wick; it said, 'congratulations on your successful air action yesterday'. At 1709 on 21 March a further signal was received from the Admiralty, repeated to the C-in-C Home Fleet, RANAS, Vice Admiral Aircraft, *Ark Royal* and Hatston. It said that 'their Lordships have heard with great pleasure of the successful manner in which Fleet Air Arm Skuas protected the ON convoy yesterday in [the] face of larger numbers of enemy aircraft'. An Admiralty communiqué was taken up by the *Daily Telegraph* and other newspapers and printed on 23 March. Under the headline 'Three British 'Planes Rout Ten Nazis' the *Telegraph* told readers on its front page that 'only three British fighters were responsible for the rout of 10 German bombers which attacked a convoy consisting almost entirely of neutral ships off the north-east coast of Scotland … one enemy 'plane was shot down and, according to the Admiralty, others hit'. Under Lucy's inspirational leadership, 803 NAS was showing what could be achieved, even with aircraft that were out-performed by those of the enemy. He was able to write to his father saying that now he had been in action, it was an exciting feeling that was almost worth being at war for.[31]

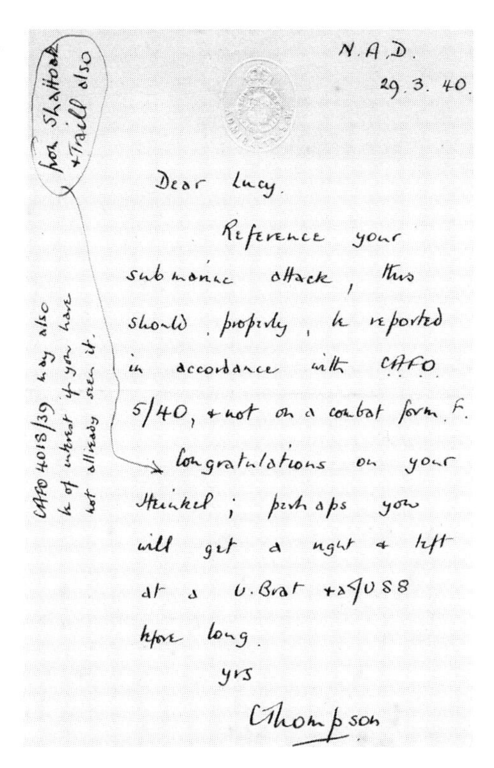

N.A.D.
29.3.40.

Dear Lucy.

Reference your submarine attack, this should, properly, be reported in accordance with CAFO 5/40, & not on a combat form F.

Congratulations on your Heinkel; perhaps you will get a right & left at a U.Boat + a JU88 before long.

yrs
C Thompson

from Shattock + Traill also

CAFO 4018/39 may also be of interest if you have not already seen it.

Bill Lucy's letter from Captain Thompson of the Admiralty's Naval Air Department. (John de Lucy collection)

Although Dick Partridge did not mention it in his recollections, Bill Lucy must have told his aircrew to keep their eyes open for targets on the sea surface as well as in the air. On 29 March 1940 he received a handwritten, personal letter from Captain C Thompson RN of the Naval Air Department in the Admiralty:

> Dear Lucy,
>
> Reference your submarine attack, this should, properly, be reported in accordance with CAFO 5/40 and not on a [air] combat Form 'F'.
>
> Congratulations [from Shattock and Traill also added in the margin] on your Heinkel; perhaps you will get a right and left at a U-boat and a Junkers 88 before long
>
> Yours
> C Thompson

The mild, almost humorous, rebuke about filing his combat report on the wrong sort of form does not disguise the fact that the Air Department obviously held him in high regard and looked to him as a CO who could achieve the results they wanted. His leadership ability was, thus, recognised just as the period that American journalists had referred to as 'the phoney war' came to an end.

Chapter 13

The German Invasion of Norway and Strike Operations from RNAS Hatston

THE IMPORTANCE OF THE Norwegian littoral was recognised in both the UK and Germany. As early as 29 September 1939 the new First Lord of the Admiralty, Winston Churchill, drew the Cabinet's attention to the importance of Swedish iron ore to German industry; in the summer months this was shipped across the Baltic from Lulea but in the winter it was taken by rail to the Norwegian ice-free port of Narvik and shipped from there to Germany.[1] In Germany, study between the wars had shown the potential importance of Norwegian harbours to give U-boats greater access to the Atlantic shipping routes than they had enjoyed in the Great War if they were seized and there was an awareness, through intelligence sources, that the British might attempt to interrupt the ore traffic. Norway itself was resolutely neutral but, with a king related to the British royal family, was sympathetic towards the British cause. Merchant shipping was protected by the Home Fleet from the UK to Norway in a series of ON convoys outbound and HN convoys inbound. As we saw in the last chapter, these were protected by naval fighters from Hatston as well as surface escorts.

German imports of iron ore in 1938 were known to have amounted to 22 million tons but it was estimated that some 9 million tons had already been cut off after September 1939 by the blockade implemented by the Royal Navy on the outbreak of war.[2] About 9 million tons was estimated to have reached Germany from Sweden and, as winter approached, Churchill continued to press for this supply to be intercepted, frustrated that enemy merchant ships carried out almost the whole journey through Norwegian territorial waters known as the Indreled or Inner Leads, a passage he described as 'the covered way'. It was also becoming apparent that German blockade runners from the outer seas were using this route, entering in the far north and continuing almost as far south as Stavanger. His solution was to mine the Inner Leads and drive German shipping out into the open sea where it could be intercepted, but the War Cabinet refused to agree and the French were at first opposed to the idea for fear of reprisals. The Winter War between Russia and Finland complicated matters for some months but eventually, in February 1940, the Cabinet agreed that mining preparations could be made but then withdrew its permission ten days later. Eventually the French government agreed at the Supreme War Council on 28 March 1940 that mining could proceed and the British Cabinet gave the Admiralty permission on 3 April to begin mining in what was now known as Operation Wilfred. A number of good pretexts had been cited, not the least of which was the rescue, by the destroyer *Cossack*, of British prisoners from the German tanker *Altmark* anchored inside the Leads.[3] Churchill summed up the vacillation succinctly in Volume I of *The Second World War* in which he said that the War Cabinet's 'vain boggling, hesitation, changes of policy, arguments between good and worthy people unending, we had at last reached the simple point on which action had been demanded 7 months before. But … now Hitler was ready, and ready with a far more powerful and well prepared plan.' This brief summary gives the background to the Norwegian campaign which was to see the first prolonged clash between the British and German Navies in the Second World War. The war at sea was to be fought in three dimensions with aircraft of the Royal Navy acting as an integral part of the fleet in its operations. In 1918 the RN had planned to use carrier-borne aircraft to attack the German fleet in its harbours[4] but the Armistice ended hostilities before the strikes could be flown. It therefore fell to the generation of naval aircrew in 1940 to carry out many new aspects of naval air operations over the sea for the first time in history. The possession of naval aircraft, operating from both ships and shore bases, gave the C-in-C Home Fleet and his subordinate commanders and captains options in the third dimension that their predecessors had not enjoyed. They were not always used to their best advantage but lessons were learnt which informed the later conduct of the war in both the Royal and United States Navies. There were no air operations carried out in the Home, Mediterranean, East Indies and British Pacific Fleets that had not already been at least attempted in the brief, but ultimately unsuccessful, Norwegian campaign of April to June 1940. It is, therefore, worth studying in some detail.[5]

The German Invasion of Norway

The German invasion plan, finalised in early March 1940, hinged on surprise and Admiral Raeder assessed the operation as being 'contrary to all principles in the theory of naval warfare' since it was to be carried out in the face of a vastly superior British fleet.[6] However, the bulk of the invasion force crossed the Skaggerak where the Germans did have local superiority. North of Bergen the operation comprised a series of synchronised raids landing assault troops who were not to be relieved by sea but by transport aircraft that relied on control of the air by the Luftwaffe and the advance of the main force overland from Oslo. Even the raiders heading for the far north could shelter to some extent in the Leads to avoid British air patrols. Roughly 800 German aircraft were allocated to the operation which included 300 transport aircraft and 500 other front-line aircraft including those of Fliegerkorps X which had been trained for anti-shipping operations by squadrons that had originally been intended for deployment to the German aircraft carrier *Graf Zeppelin*, which had not yet been completed. The initial assault included sea-borne landings at

Oslo, Arendal, Kristiansand (south), Egersund, Bergen, Trondheim and Narvik. The attack on Oslo was to include some of the first assaults by parachute forces ever carried out, intended to seize the King and his government but fortunately they failed to achieve their aim. The battlecruisers *Scharnhorst* and *Gneisenau* and the heavy cruiser *Hipper* were to patrol the southern part of the Arctic Sea after the initial assault to provide distant support and, it was hoped, draw off the Home Fleet. In this they succeeded both on a strategic level as the focus of Admiralty attention and on a tactical level. All air support was to be provided by the Luftwaffe but the divided German command structure proved less than ideal. It had originally been intended that aircraft would lay mines in Scapa Flow from 28 March to disrupt the Home Fleet but, much to Raeder's annoyance, this operation was cancelled by the Luftwaffe on 27 March without reference to the Naval Staff.

Follow-up forces for Norwegian ports from Bergen to the south and Copenhagen were embarked in the fifteen ships of the 1st Sea Transport Division which between them carried 3,761 troops, 672 horses, 1,377 vehicles and 5,935 tons of ammunition and stores. They were disguised as ordinary merchant ships and sailed singly to arrive at their destinations shortly after the assault forces. Follow-up forces could not be sent to Trondheim or Narvik because of the risk of interception by the Home Fleet but *Rauenfels*, *Alster* and *Barenfels*, also disguised as merchant ships, were despatched early to Narvik to await the arrival of the assault force. *Sao Paulo*, *Main* and *Levante* were sent ahead to Trondheim and the tanker *Jan Wellem* was sent to Narvik from Murmansk to refuel the assault warships for their journey back to Germany. The tanker *Kattegat* was sent to Trondheim from Germany for a similar purpose.

Operation Wilfred

The Admiralty planned to declare three areas as mined although not all of them would be at first. One was to be in Vestfjord, another off Bud further south and one off Stadlandet still further south. Destroyers of the 20th Flotilla were to lay the field in Vestfjord and the minelayer *Teviot Bank* was to lay the field off Stadlandet. No mines were to be laid at Bud. Orders were given that should the Norwegians use force to protect their neutrality, minelaying was to be abandoned rather than risk provoking an incident with a Norwegian patrol vessel. However, Allied troops were made ready under what was designated Plan R4 to land at the ports of Stavanger, Bergen, Trondheim and Narvik if German forces violated Norwegian neutrality or gave clear evidence that they intended to do so. Stavanger and Bergen were each allocated two infantry battalions which were to sail in cruisers. A single battalion for Trondheim was to travel in a troop transport, arriving two days after the cruiser-borne forces. A much larger operation was planned for the key iron-ore port of Narvik. A single infantry battalion was to carry out an initial landing in a

A Blackburn Skua in flight low over the North Sea in 1940. The high demarcation, known as the 'waterline', between the dark sea grey/slate grey upper camouflage and the lower Sky Type 'S' is typical of the early 1940 period. This aircraft is not armed with a 500lb bomb but has light-series carriers under the wings. (Author's collection)

transport escorted by two cruisers under Admiral Sir Edward Evans. They were to be followed by a British brigade and French Alpine troops with a combined total of 18,000 men. A striking force of two cruisers and three destroyers under Vice Admiral Sir George Edward-Collins, CS2, was to be kept in readiness at Rosyth 'to deal with any sea-borne expedition the Germans may send against Norway'. A second group comprising two ships of the 18th Cruiser Squadron under Vice Admiral Layton was nominated as a striking force by the C-in-C Home Fleet but until required for a specific task they were to act in support of ON convoys to Norway as needed. Heavy cover was to be provided by *Rodney*, flag C-in-C Home Fleet (HF) – replacing *Nelson* which was being repaired after damage caused by a mine – *Valiant*, *Renown* and *Repulse* screened by ten destroyers but, surprisingly, at the time the Home Fleet had no operational aircraft carrier. *Ark Royal* had joined *Glorious* in the eastern Mediterranean where they were being used to train new Swordfish aircrew in torpedo attack profiles and deck landing. Her Skua squadrons had remained disembarked at Hatston while she was away to provide air cover for Scapa Flow and the Norwegian convoys and it was fortunate that they had done so. *Furious* was nominally part of the Home Fleet but had just completed a refit in Devonport and in early April was in the Clyde, not yet operational, with her squadrons ashore working up.

These dispositions covered a range of possible moves by the enemy but attention in the Admiralty War Room was still fixed on the possibility of a break out by the German fleet to attack convoys in the Atlantic. This fixation ran like a strand through the days that followed and limited the degree of success achieved by the Home Fleet in action. The British system of command also left something to be desired and at this stage the operations of both RAF Bomber and Coastal Commands were independent of naval operations and of each other, reporting through their own chains of command with little knowledge of or regard for the whole picture. Neither the German nor the British plans went entirely as expected as both sides sought to use their tactical aircraft in new ways. On 4 April 1940, the day after the Cabinet took its final decision to proceed with Wilfred, Admiral Evans hoisted his flag in the cruiser *Aurora* in the Clyde where the Narvik force was to assemble prior to sailing on 8 April. His second cruiser, *Penelope*, was ordered to leave the Norwegian convoy she was protecting and proceed to Scapa Flow to refuel on 6 April. The ships for Stavanger and Bergen assembled in the Firth of Forth under Admiral J Cunningham, CS1. Troops and stores were embarked ready in *Devonshire*, *Berwick*, *York* and *Glasgow*. The cruiser *Birmingham* and the destroyers *Hostile* and *Fearless* were ordered break off a search for German fishing vessels in the north and join Vice Admiral Whitworth's force comprising the battlecruiser *Renown* with the destroyers *Greyhound*, *Glowworm*, *Hyperion* and *Hero* that were to cover the Vestfjord minelayers.

On the morning of 6 April Admiral Whitworth's force was joined by the minelaying destroyers *Esk, Impulsive, Icarus* and *Ivanhoe* under Captain J G Bickford RN, D20, and their close escort the destroyers *Hardy*, *Hotspur*, *Havock* and *Hunter* under Captain B A W Warburton-Lee RN, D2. The latter were instructed to patrol in the vicinity of the minefield once it was laid. However, the weather was rapidly becoming stormy and *Glowworm* lost a man overboard, heaved to to search for him and lost touch with *Renown*. Two other destroyers were detached to refuel and, on completion, to pretend to lay a minefield off Bud. Admiral Whitworth intended to rendezvous his depleted force with *Birmingham* and her destroyers on the evening of 7 April. With increasing pressure being placed on Norway by the Allies, RAF reconnaissance sorties were flown to seek evidence of German reaction. Two high-flying Spitfire photographic-reconnaissance (PR) aircraft photographed *Scharnhorst*, *Gneisenau* and *Hipper* together with many other vessels in Wilhelmshaven during 6 April. The main enemy forces actually sailed that night and *Hipper* was spotted to the north of Heligoland by a Bomber Command Handley Page Hampden of 83 Squadron. A further PR Spitfire, flown by Flight Lieutenant Longbottom, detected a concentration of shipping in Kiel, extensive road traffic and dense concentrations of aircraft on nearby airfields. Many of the latter were identified by analysts as Junkers Ju 52 transports.

7 April

As the British and German plans evolved on opposite sides of the North Sea, both sides lacked a clear picture of enemy movements. The Admiralty requested extensive air searches to locate any German forces at sea and 18 Luftwaffe Dornier Do 18s of KuFlGr 406 (KustenFliegerGruppe, a Luftwaffe coastal flying force) searched the sea areas between Peterhead and the Shetland Islands for signs of a British reaction to the German plan. At 0848 an RAF Hudson of 220 Squadron piloted by Flying Officer Bruce reported an enemy cruiser and two destroyers about 150 miles south of the Naze, the southernmost tip of Norway, steering north. He was driven off by anti-aircraft fire but six Messerschmitt Bf 109 fighters of II/JG 77 (JagdGeschwader, a Luftwaffe hunting wing) scrambled to intercept him failed to gain contact. Bruce's enemy contact report was sent to his Coastal Command Group headquarters at Pitreavie near Rosyth, from there to the operations room of the C-in-C Rosyth and from there to the Home Fleet broadcast. The C-in-C Home Fleet did not receive the message until 1120, by which time Bomber Command had sent two separate groups of bombers, one of Blenheims and one of Wellingtons, to attack the enemy force. Neither achieved any success and two Wellingtons were shot down in flames by Bf 110 fighters of I/ZG 1 (ZerstorerGeschwader, a Luftwaffe destroyer wing). At 1420 the C-in-C Home Fleet received signal 1259/7 from the Admiralty which stated:

> Recent reports suggest a German expedition is being prepared. Hitler is reported from Copenhagen to have ordered un-ostentatious movement of one division in ten ships by night to land at Narvik with simultaneous occupation of Jutland. Sweden to be left alone. Moderates said to be opposing the plan. Date given for arrival in Narvik was 8 April.
>
> All these reports are of doubtful value and may well be only a further move in the war of nerves. Great Belt opened for traffic 5 April.

In the light of subsequent events, the C-in-C later observed that it was most unfortunate that the second paragraph had been added as it did nothing but confuse a situation which might, otherwise have been clarified.

Three Days of Confusion

There had indeed been a number of indications that a large-scale operation was being set in train by the Germans. After the second week of March all U-boat activity against British trade routes had ceased abruptly, a clear sign that some alternate use had been ordered. Minelaying by destroyers and U-boats had also ceased. RAF reconnaissance aircraft continued to photograph extensive concentrations of ships, vehicles and aircraft in northern Germany and German W/T activity was particularly intense from the evening of 6 April. They also reported unusual activity during the night of 6/7 April in the ports of Kiel, Eckenforde, Hamburg and Lubeck where wharves were seen to be brightly floodlit and long convoys of motor vehicles were moving with undimmed headlights. Cumulatively the weight of intelligence material indicated an imminent attack on Denmark and Norway but this was not the assessment made in the Admiralty War Room where the continuing focus was on bringing German surface ships to action once their numbers and position were confirmed beyond doubt. On receipt of the Admiralty's signal 1259/7 Admiral Forbes ordered the Home Fleet to come to one hour's notice for steam. At 1546 he ordered four destroyers near Rosyth with convoy HN24 to refuel, keep steam up and await further orders. At 1558 *Sheffield* and four destroyers were ordered to raise steam and at 1607 Vice Admiral Edward-Collins was ordered to proceed with *Galatea*, *Arethusa*, the four destroyers from HN24 and four further destroyers to arrive in position 58 30N 03 30E by 1700 on 8 April if possible, after which they were to sweep to the north searching for the enemy. A further Admiralty signal, 1720/7 was received at 1727 which revealed that at 1325 RAF aircraft had sighted two cruisers, one large warship possibly of the *Scharnhorst* class, and ten destroyers in position 56 48N 06 10E steering 320. This was the first indication of German heavy units being at sea to reach the C-in-C and he assessed that the forces sighted at 0848 and 1325 must be the same. It was actually *Gneisenau*, *Scharnhorst*, *Hipper* and twelve destroyers which had left harbour in time to rendezvous at 0300 on 7 April. The vital information contained in 1720/7 had originally come from a force of eighteen RAF Blenheim bombers that had attacked the enemy warships between 1322 and 1327 without result. A W/T message to Bomber Command by their leader was not received and it was not until the force landed between 1612 and 1652 that the composition of the enemy force became known and the information passed to the Admiralty.

On receipt of this signal, Admiral Forbes ordered all the ships in Scapa Flow to raise steam immediately and at 2015 on 7 April his heavy units sailed, followed an hour later by the Rosyth striking force. The Admiralty took the decision to abandon the minelaying operation off Stadlandet but no change was made to the plan to lay mines off Vestfjord. It had proved impossible to deliver any photographs of the enemy force to the C-in-C but he and his staff assessed that the enemy force's composition, position course and speed were consistent with an attempt to intercept Norwegian convoys, attack ships of the Northern Patrol or break out into the North Atlantic to attack shipping. They were, he thought, following the pattern of many similar excursions in the First World War, differing only in scale. He signalled the Home Fleet, 'We are endeavouring to intercept enemy ships reported by aircraft at 1325 to be in position 56 50N 06 10E, course 320 speed 17 knots. One battlecruiser, one pocket battleship, 3 cruisers and about 12 destroyers'. Admiral Forbes had with him the capital ships *Rodney*, *Valiant* and *Repulse*, the cruisers *Sheffield*, *Penelope*, the French *Emile Bertin* and the destroyers *Codrington* (Captain D1), *Griffin*, *Jupiter*, *Electra*, *Escapade*, *Brazen*, *Bedouin*, *Punjabi*, *Eskimo* and *Kimberley*. Unfortunately, the *Emile Bertin* had only arrived in Scapa Flow that afternoon, lost contact soon after sailing and returned to its anchorage. Forbes' initial plan was to steer for 61 00N 01 00E at 19 knots, increasing to 20 knots at midnight.

A complicated picture had begun to emerge in which experience of the way in which German operations had evolved in the Great War was not necessarily a good thing as it led to preconceived ideas. *Renown* and her escort were approaching the coast of Norway to support the Vestfjord minelayers and *Birmingham* was on her way to join her. Convoy ON25 had sailed from Methil on the morning of 5 April escorted by the radar-equipped anti-aircraft cruiser *Curlew* and the destroyers *Javelin*, *Janus*, *Juno* and *Grenade*. Two further cruisers, *Manchester* (flag Vice Admiral Layton) and *Southampton* had sailed from Scapa Flow on the morning of 7 April to act in support of both ON25 and HN25 which was about to sail from Bergen. The latter was instructed by the Admiralty not to sail but, fortunately, did so on its own initiative and thus managed to avoid the invading German forces. Once clear of the coast, the Guide of the Convoy, Captain J S Pinkney Master of the ss *Flyingdale*, sighted the German tanker *Skaggerak* on its way to Trondheim and learnt on 9 April from a Swedish ship that the Germans had landed in Bergen. He took charge of the convoy and headed for Rosyth, eventually being joined by destroyers sent by the C-in-C Home Fleet to support him. Captain Pinkney was subsequently awarded the OBE for his initiative. ON25 did not fare as well. Admiral Layton's force joined it 15nm north-east of Muckle Flugga but after the report of German heavy units at sea, Admiral Forbes ordered it to turn back to British waters. In the mounting seas of the developing north-westerly storm, however, twenty-four ships lost contact and continued their voyage. Of these thirteen were eventually captured or sunk by the enemy. Admiral Layton received a signal from the C-in-C timed at 1934/7 which gave him the position at which the Home Fleet was to rendezvous at 0800 on 8 April but he felt uncertain of the C-in-C's location or intentions and continued to steam along the general route intended for the convoy.

The Vestfjord minefield was laid between 0430 and 0530 on 8 April while *Renown* with *Greyhound*, the only destroyer left in her screen, patrolled 30nm to the west of the entrance to the fjord and 100nm from the minefield. At 0600, three Sunderland flying boats from Sullom Voe in the Shetland Islands were ordered to search for the German force located the day before but the next contact with it was actually made by *Glowworm*, which had been isolated by the search for its man overboard. She sighted two German destroyers in about 65 04N 06 04E and signalled the Vice Admiral Battlecruiser Squadron (VA BCS), Admiral Whitworth in *Renown*, with an enemy sighting report at 0759. *Glowworm*'s CO, Lieutenant Commander G B Roope RN, elected to follow the enemy in the expectation that they would lead him to any heavy unit they might be screening. On receipt of the first signal Admiral Whitworth turned towards the reported position at his best speed to provide support. Admiral Forbes was about 300nm to the south-west but ordered *Repulse*, *Penelope* and four destroyers to close *Glowworm* at their best speed but his staff noted that if these destroyers were from the enemy force located the day before they would have to have made good about 27 knots. While this was not impossible, it was unlikely in the stormy sea conditions and it was subsequently learnt that the position given at 0759 was 60nm too far to the north. The Germans placed the encounter at 64 05N 06 18E.

The details of the gallant action that followed did not become known to the Admiralty until after the war when survivors who had become prisoners were released. It appeared that when Lieutenant Commander Roope identified the *Hipper*, he estimated that he could not outrun her and nor were the storm conditions suitable for a torpedo attack. He decided, therefore, to ram the enemy cruiser and caused significant damage to it in doing so. *Glowworm* then broke free, turned upside down and sank. *Hipper* rescued forty survivors including one officer from the water; Roope was being hauled aboard and had just reached the cruiser's deck when exhaustion caused him to let go the rope he had been clinging to and he fell into the sea and was drowned. When the survivors eventually told their story in 1945, King George VI immediately approved the posthumous award of the Victoria Cross to Lieutenant Commander Roope for his gallant action. The damaged *Hipper* made slowly for Trondheim and flew off her Arado Ar 196 catapult floatplane to see if other British warships were in the vicinity. Short of fuel, the pilot eventually landed in Kristiansund at 1950, a small port just south of Trondheim not to be confused with the larger Kristiansand further south. The aircraft and its aircrew were arrested and interned by the Norwegian Navy.

When signals from *Glowworm* ceased after 0855 it had to be assumed that she had been sunk and Admiral Whitworth reduced speed though continuing to make progress through heavy seas to the south. At 1045 the Admiralty instructed the eight destroyers of the Vestfjord minelaying force to join *Renown*, leaving the approach to Narvik open to the enemy with no British forces patrolling it, a decision that was to have disastrous consequences for the subsequent British conduct of the Norwegian campaign. At this point, Admiralty attention still seemed to be focused on a potential fleet action but then at 1114 a further signal was sent to the C-in-C advising him that the substance of 1259/7 was now believed to be true and that German landing forces could well be at sea. Admiral Whitworth appreciated that he was in a position to intercept the line of advance of an enemy force heading for Narvik at about 1330 and headed for this point. However, visibility was reduced to 2 miles in mountainous seas and he headed north-east to rendezvous with the destroyers leaving Vestfjord. At noon on this eventful day the Polish submarine *Orzel* intercepted the German ss *Rio de Janeiro* off Kristiansand (south) just outside territorial waters. In accordance with the Rules of Engagement in force on that day, the Germans were given the opportunity to abandon ship before it was torpedoed and sunk and a Norwegian destroyer and local fishing boats found themselves rescuing hundreds of German soldiers who told them that they were on their way to Bergen to protect it against the British and French. This might have compromised the whole invasion plan if the correct conclusions had been drawn but they were not. The Norwegian Storting (Parliament) learnt of the event that evening but failed to give it credence and the Navy and coastal defences were not alerted. At 2030 news of the sinking was broadcast by Reuters from Oslo and the German Naval Staff noted in their War Diary that surprise had been lost.

In the Admiralty it was appreciated at last that the presence of soldiers in the *Rio de Janeiro* probably did confirm the German intention to invade Norway but attention continued to focus on bringing *Scharnhorst* and *Gneisenau* to action. Admiral Raeder's bait had worked. The information about probable invasion shipping was, however, broadcast to British submarines whose patrols were relocated to improve their chances of intercepting enemy warships. Incredibly, this information was not passed to Admiral Forbes until 2255. At 1300 he had received Admiralty signal 1216/8 which informed him that the cruisers loaded with troops for Plan R4 had been ordered to disembark them and sail from Rosyth at 1400 heading north. *Aurora* and the destroyers in the Clyde were to leave at 1300 and head for Scapa Flow. A further signal, 1317/8 received at 1400, informed him that *Emile Bertin*, *Manchester*, *Southampton* and the four destroyers that had been intended to support the minelayer *Teviot Bank* off Bud had been placed at his disposal. The arbitrary abandonment of R4 greatly surprised Admiral Forbes who was now in no doubt that the very German operations it had been designed to counter were taking place. Had Vice Admiral Cunningham's force been sailed with its troops as soon as the Admiralty received news of the *Rio de Janeiro* incident, they could have reached Stavanger – which, with its airfield, was to prove the key to the whole campaign in central Norway – before the Germans. It is difficult, even with the wisdom of hindsight, to see why the Admiralty abandoned R4 in such haste. It should have been obvious that any German raid intended to seize a Norwegian port would have been supported by heavy warships and even without the reinforcements ordered by these two signals the C-in-C Home Fleet had at his disposal more warships than the entire German fleet.

At 1400 one of the Sullom Voe flying boats, aircraft 'B' flown by Flight Lieutenant E L Hyde, spotted a group of ships he identified as a battlecruiser, two cruisers and two destroyers off Trondheim heading west. The aircraft was damaged by anti-aircraft fire and driven off before making its report and lost contact with the enemy. This force was in fact *Hipper* and four destroyers but the report added to confusion since it appeared to confirm that the force was heading to break out into the Atlantic and, thus, continued to draw attention in the Admiralty War Room towards the possibility of a fleet action rather than countering an invasion of Norway. In fact the westerly course had been nothing more than a random choice to fill in time before moving into Trondheim on 9 April. This sighting also complicated Admiral Forbes' plot and he ordered his force onto a northerly heading to intercept it. At 1715 Admiral Whitworth in *Renown* joined the Vestfjord destroyers 20nm south-west of the Skomvaer Light. He too had received the aircraft report and formed a plan for the destroyers to search southward from the Skomvaer Light after dawn, keeping *Renown* in support to the north of them.

At 1915 Admiral Whitworth received 'Most Immediate' Admiralty signal 1850/8 which instructed him that the force under his orders was to concentrate on preventing any German forces from proceeding to Narvik. The Admiral, however, saw his first duty as maintaining his ships in 'a condition of sea-going fighting efficiency' in the appalling storm conditions now being experienced. At 2100 he ordered a westerly heading but the destroyers found themselves unmanageable in the sea conditions and so he altered to north. *Birmingham* had still not joined him and nor had *Repulse*, *Penelope*, *Bedouin*, *Eskimo*, *Punjabi* or *Kimberley* detached from the C-in-C that morning to assist *Glowworm* and subsequently ordered to join Admiral Whitworth. Accordingly at 2200 on 8 April he signalled his position, course and speed as 67 09N 10 10E, course 310, speed 8 knots, wind NW Force 10, nine destroyers in company. *Birmingham* was still 80 miles away with a single destroyer and they were ordered to Scapa Flow to refuel. At 1843 *Rodney* launched a Walrus to search for the enemy but it failed to locate them. By then Admiral Forbes was so certain that a German invasion of Norway was imminent that he personally briefed the pilot that he was to allow himself enough fuel to reach Norway and then give himself up. He would be free the next day, since Germany was going to war with Norway, when he was to get hold of enough fuel to fly back to the Shetland Islands. This was exactly what subsequently happened.

At about 1930 Admiral Forbes reviewed the situation. By then he should have intercepted the enemy force reported that afternoon by RAF reconnaissance if the report been anything like accurate but he had not done so. There appeared to be at least one enemy battlecruiser with its escorts in the north and intelligence reports from the Naval Attaché in Copenhagen routed to him via the Admiralty reported extensive movements in the Kattegat. The submarine *Triton* had just reported what it believed to be *Gneisenau*, *Emden* and several destroyers passing the Skaw at 1800 heading west. This group was in fact *Blucher*, *Lützow*, *Emden* and several torpedo boats which had left Kiel at 0200 on their way to occupy Oslo. The C-in-C Home Fleet's own task force now comprised *Rodney*, *Valiant*, *Sheffield* and their screening destroyers at 64 22N 03 40E heading 195 degrees to intercept German forces reported to the south. He left *Repulse* and her task force to join *Renown* and ordered the cruiser striking groups under Admirals Layton, Cunningham and Edward-Collins to carry out a series of sweeps in order to find the enemy. This order was immediately annulled by the Admiralty because it feared that 'dispersed and weaker' forces might be caught by superior enemy forces with heavy units of the Home Fleet too far away to help. Instead they were ordered to concentrate at 59 30N 02 30E at 0500 on 9 April and thence to steer as necessary to join the C-in-C. The prospect of a fleet action still seemed to be irresistible in the Admiralty War Room despite recognition of the evidence that an invasion of Norway was imminent.

Up to this point operations had followed the pattern established in the First World War and the potential value of air reconnaissance had been negated by the storm affecting the North Sea. Every attempt by the RAF to attack the German ships it had located failed and without an aircraft carrier Admiral Forbes' own air assets were limited to the catapult aircraft embarked in his capital ships and cruisers. Their use was limited by the inability of ships to recover them in the prevailing sea conditions. Thus far the Luftwaffe had played no significant part in events because of the absolute need to achieve surprise on 9 April. Once Fliegerkorps X did begin operations on that day, however, the Home Fleet was exposed to a scale of air attack that was unprecedented in the history of naval warfare. Fortunately, both *Ark Royal*'s fighter squadrons were still at Hatston, just within range of Bergen and they were to play a significant role in the campaign that was about to start

803 and 800 NAS Sink the Cruiser Königsberg

From midnight into the early hours of 9 April reports arrived in the Admiralty revealing that a German invasion of Norway was happening. By dawn it was clear that the Germans were seizing all the ports that the Allies had hoped to keep from their control by implementing Plan R4. At 0630 Admiral Forbes asked the Admiralty for news of German strength in Bergen as he wanted to use Admiral Layton's cruisers to attack enemy warships in the port. The Admiralty's reply, contained in signal 0820/9 gave no enemy strength but instructed the Home Fleet to prepare plans for attacking enemy warships and transports in both Bergen and Trondheim, assuming that coastal artillery positions were still in the hands of the Norwegians. The approaches to both ports were to be controlled. If sufficient forces were available to attack both ports, Bergen was to be given priority. The Admiralty also ordered the approaches to Narvik to be watched and enquired as to when the attack on Bergen and Trondheim could be expected to begin. Now the possible fleet action seemed to have been forgotten and a series of Admiralty signals were sent to Admiral Forbes. Signal 0935/9 informed him that RAF reconnaissance aircraft reported 'at least one *Köln* class cruiser in Bergen; 1010/9 sanctioned an attack on Bergen by cruisers and destroyers; 1132/9 cancelled any attack on Trondheim until the German battlecruisers were located 'as it would entail dispersion of forces'. Signal 1211/9 conceded that shore batteries must now be assumed to have fallen into the hands of the enemy.

Admiral Forbes responded to 0820/9 at 1020 by signalling that striking forces could go into the fjords north and south of Bergen in three hours from the executive order to proceed. By then the Rosyth cruisers had joined him and Admiral Layton's force was strengthened to include *Manchester*, *Southampton*, *Glasgow* and *Sheffield* with the 7 destroyers of the 4th and 6th Flotillas. They detached from the main force at 1130 with orders to destroy enemy forces in Bergen, including the *Köln*-class cruiser, and to report on the situation ashore. Three or four destroyers were to enter by Fejeosen Fjord, the remainder by Kors Fjord with the cruisers in support at both entrances. The possibility of U-boats being present was to be taken into account. Admiral Forbes clearly had doubts about the risk of using surface forces in the narrow fjords and in the same signal he stated that in his opinion 'the best chance of success' lay with a torpedo attack by carrier-borne aircraft if the Germans had taken over the coast defence artillery. The Admiralty agreed that the third dimension offered better prospects but although *Furious* had sailed on 8 April, she could not join Admiral Forbes' force and launch strikes for another two days. In the absence of a carrier, the Admiralty asked the RAF to attack shipping in Bergen on the evening of 9 April and ordered RNAS Hatston to prepare a strike by the Skuas of 800 and 803 NAS on the morning of 10 April.

To further complicate matters, an attack by surface ships 'three hours from the order to proceed' proved unduly optimistic since the ships in question had steamed south throughout the forenoon with the result that by 1130 Fejeosen Fjord lay some 80nm to the north-east and Kors Fjord only 12nm closer. With storm force winds from the north-west and rough sea, the destroyers could only make 16 knots and it would take them five hours to reach an attacking position. At 1408 another aircraft reconnaissance found that there were two cruisers, not one, in Bergen and with only seven destroyers planned to enter the harbour the prospect of success appeared to have diminished. Admiralty telegram 1357/9 ordered the attack by surface ships to be cancelled, a measure typical of the Admiralty's close control of operations at this stage and subsequently regretted by the First Lord, who admitted that the British had been 'forestalled, surprised and outwitted'.[7] The Home Fleet turned back to the north at noon; by then cloud cover had cleared and German aircraft had shadowed the fleet since about 0800.

Attacks by both medium-level and dive-bombers began at about 1430 and continued in small groups until 1800. Significantly, the first attacks were against Admiral Layton's force, which had approached sufficiently close to Bergen to be located by the enemy, provoking a strong reaction from Fliegerkorps X as it withdrew from the coast. This became the first sustained battle between aircraft and ships in history and over a period of three hours forty-seven Junkers Ju 88s and forty-one Heinkel He 111s attacked Admiral Layton's force[8] and near misses damaged *Southampton* and *Glasgow*. The sea conditions were extremely rough with spray limiting the effectiveness of the ship's anti-aircraft direction systems and making the work of the gun crews difficult, especially in the destroyers. One of these, the *Gurkha*, was commanded by Commander A W Buzzard RN, a gunnery specialist who was determined to gain the best results from his guns. Presented with live targets for the first time and enraged by his guns' apparent inability to hit them, he turned his ship away from wind and sea to improve conditions but this manoeuvre isolated *Gurkha* from the mutual fire support provided by the remainder of the force. She formed part of the 4th Destroyer Flotilla and Captain P L Vian RN, her Captain (D), wrote afterwards,[9] 'this involved leaving the cruiser screen and I should have recalled him at once; but in those very early days of air attack on ships, the tactics to be pursued by surface forces were still being worked out and there was no set policy. Buzzard's manoeuvre cost him his ship and very nearly the lives of his crew.' Since he was now steaming at 25 knots in one direction whilst the cruiser squadron and screen were steaming at high speed in another, he was quickly over the horizon and so became detached. As such, he attracted immediate attention from the Luftwaffe and *Gurkha* was soon overwhelmed, stopped and left in a sinking condition. As night drew on Buzzard's predicament became very serious but was saved by his firing high-explosive shells into the sky. One of the bursts was observed by the cruiser *Aurora* who closed from a distance to investigate, found *Gurkha* and took off her crew before she foundered and sank, becoming the first significant warship to be sunk by aircraft in the Second World War. Once Admiral Layton's force joined the remainder of the Home Fleet, the situation improved, partially because the bombers had more targets to attack and partially because there was a greater volume of fire to deter them.

Both sides drew lessons from the battle which had not produced results they had anticipated. The disjointed German attacks had lacked cohesion and the absence of a strike co-ordinator meant that aircraft had attacked the first ship they encountered, not necessarily the high-value units, although one of the last aircraft to attack, a solitary bomber, managed to hit *Rodney* with a single 500 kg bomb which was defeated by the deck armour and caused little damage. The British learnt the hard way that anti-aircraft gunnery was not the best answer to air attack and that carrier-borne fighters would have been the best way of breaking up the enemy attacks. Some ships had used up 40 per cent of their ammunition but only four enemy aircraft were known to have been shot down. Admiral Forbes was shaken by the experience and decided that his fleet could not operate this far south in the face of the battle-space superiority the Luftwaffe had established without his own fighter cover. Other senior officers merely concluded that there was an obvious requirement for fighter protection and better anti-aircraft gunnery.

The ill-considered decision to sail *Furious* without her fighter squadron was already apparent and will be described in the next chapter. Admiral Forbes also doubted her ability to operate safely in these latitudes and sent a revised evaluation of the situation to the Admiralty in his signal 2231/9. In it he stated that in view of the severity of that day's bombing attacks he would not attempt to strike the enemy warships in Bergen with *Furious*' aircraft but would, instead, use the Skuas disembarked at Hatston to attack them. Whilst these squadrons were not embarked in a carrier, he still regarded them as being an integral part of his fleet and they were, after all, naval units trained to locate, identify and attack warships. His three-dimensional appraisal ended by stating that enemy warships in Stavanger, Kristiansand and Oslo would be left for patrolling submarines to intercept and attack.

By sunset on 9 April, three separate plans to attack enemy warships known to be in Bergen had been ordered by the C-in-C: the first using a cruiser/destroyer surface striking force, the second using Swordfish armed with torpedoes from *Furious* and lastly by dive-bombers operating at extreme range from RNAS Hatston in the Orkney Islands. Their diversity shows the lack of any preconceived plan for attacking enemy warships in confined coastal waters dominated by enemy aircraft although the use of naval aircraft in two of them together with the employment of submarines further south does show that Admiral Forbes and his staff thought in three dimensions.

Pre-war plans in the Mediterranean Fleet had included the use of carrier-borne aircraft to attack enemy warships in their harbours but there was no similar plan in the Home Fleet because the issue was complicated by the existence of RAF Bomber Command which had responsibility for all air attacks from the littoral inland. The Fleet Air Arm was not expected or equipped to fly such missions in the face of the inevitable enemy air defences, but on the other hand, Bomber Command had concentrated on what it saw as its primary role of attacks on fixed sites in continental Europe that were not time sensitive. No common policy had been agreed between the Admiralty and Air Ministry and nor had the War Cabinet asked for one. The services themselves had divergent views on how best to destroy the enemy fleet and this showed a lack of progress since the Admiralty's plan to attack the High Sea Fleet in its harbours as far back as November 1918 using carrier-borne Sopwith T1 torpedo aircraft. Bomber Command had, in fact, carried out several attacks against German warships since the earliest days of the war but had produced negligible results for very heavy losses. By April 1940 the Command had asked for naval observers to be lent to it capable of identifying German warships and advising on their likely tactics in action. The type of level bombing from medium altitudes RAF aircrew were trained in proved to be an ineffective method of attacking ships both in harbour and under way at sea, and aircrews who had only been trained to bomb static targets ashore found themselves at a disadvantage in a type of warfare that was unfamiliar to them. To be fair, the level bombing results achieved by the German and Italian air forces were little better. Notwithstanding its earlier failures, Bomber Command did respond positively to an Admiralty request for an attack on Bergen on the evening of 9 April, thus introducing a fourth strike option during this remarkable day. Twelve Wellington bombers from 9 and 115 Squadrons took off at 1510 followed by twelve Hampden bombers from 50 Squadron at 1600. They attacked the crowded harbour at Bergen from 1800 but failed to score any bomb hits; some aircraft descended to low level and strafed the cruiser *Köln*, however, killing three sailors and wounding another five. One Wellington was shot down.

The German force that had seized Bergen comprised Assault Group 3 under the command of the Flag Officer Scouting Forces, Rear Admiral Schmundt, flying his flag in *Köln*. With her were the cruiser *Königsberg*, the gunnery training ship *Bremse*, the torpedo boats *Leopard* and *Wolf*, the 1st E-boat Flotilla and the depot ship *Karl Peters*. Between them they had landed 900 troops to capture the port, but as they had made their approach the Norwegian coast defence battery at Kvarven – despite having received no prior warning from the government – opened fire. *Bremse* was hit by a single 8-inch shell and *Königsberg* by three, one of which was on the waterline, causing sufficient damage to convince her captain that repairs by the ship's engineers were needed and that he could not, therefore, return to Germany as planned that night. In fact, *Köln* did not get far that night either. Alerted by the volume of traffic sent by British cruisers off Bergen, Admiral Schmundt elected to anchor at the head of Mauranger Fjord during the daylight hours of 10 April where he remained unseen by British reconnaissance aircraft. After sunset he slipped through the Leads and returned successfully to Germany with a CAP provided by long-range Bf 110 fighters from sunrise on 11 April.

A Coastal Command squadron had been tasked with carrying out a close reconnaissance of the Norwegian coast on 9 April and, uncertain of its own aircrews' ability to identify enemy warships, had been lent several naval observers. Lieutenant Commander Geoffrey Hare RN was in an aircraft that flew over Bergen early in the day and he correctly identified *Köln*, *Königsberg* and *Bremse* and instead of routing his report through the tortuous Coastal Command chain, he signalled the information direct to the C-in-C Home Fleet in *Rodney*. In doing so he demonstrated what could be achieved in providing time-sensitive information to the fleet command with a better system of communications. As he climbed out of his aircraft shortly after landing at RAF Lossiemouth, Hare was rushed to a waiting transport aircraft and flown to Hatston, where he briefed the CO on what he had seen.[10]

At RNAS Hatston on 9 April all flying was precluded by mist and low cloud swirling over the islands.[11] Dick Partridge described the bad weather as a 'heaven-sent lull when one could relax with a clear conscience' but not so Bill Lucy. According to Dick, when Bill was not flying he would pace the operations room reading every signal that came in, monitoring the weather forecasts and praying for a clearance so that he could get at the enemy. To what extent the initiative for planning a dive-bomber strike against the ships in Bergen lay with the C-in-C, the CO of Hatston, Hare or Bill Lucy will probably never be known for certain. Dick Partridge certainly though it was Bill's idea and in *Operation Skua* he wrote, 'an excited Bill Lucy shattered my peace with a most outrageous plan. He told me that in the operations room he had just seen an RAF reconnaissance report that said a German cruiser was lying alongside in Bergen harbour and, if I agreed, he proposed taking both squadrons across and dive-bombing her.' In 1988 Dick wrote in his recollections of Bill for his family that he 'was having a quiet and peaceful

lunch when Bill burst in excitedly saying "there's a German cruiser alongside in Bergen harbour and the Met men say the weather will be clearing shortly … let's take both squadrons over and dive-bomb the cruiser at dawn tomorrow morning.'" Regardless of whether the idea came from Admiral Forbes, Commander C L Howe RN who commanded RNAS Hatston, Lieutenant Commander Hare or Bill Lucy himself, what is certain is that Lucy was in on it from the outset and was the driving force behind its planning and execution with the assistance of Hanson, Partridge and Hare. In his 1988 narrative, Dick Partridge recalled that with his quiet lunch in ruins, he pointed out to Bill that

> 'in still air Bergen was 2 hours' flying time away and 2 hours back and that the Skua's endurance was only 4 hours and 20 minutes. A head wind, a forced diversion or a tangle with enemy fighters and we would never get back. Bill would have none of this and merely said that even if some of us had to ditch on the way back it would be worth it if the raid was successful. Bill's daring and complete dedication to the prosecution of the war was infectious and there was no doubt that such a raid would have the invaluable advantage of surprise.

After the shocking realisation on 9 April that the German aim had been to invade Norway and not to break out into the Atlantic shipping routes with all the changes of plan that had followed the first air/sea battle, it fell to a force of Skua

Sequence running from far-left image on opposite page:

Königsberg on fire alongside the Skoltegrund Mole photographed by a brave Norwegian civilian minutes after the last Skua had carried out its attack and departed. The merchant ship visible to the right is the American SS *Flying Fish.* Note the vertical column of smoke, indicating no natural wind – ideal for the Skuas' long flight back to Hatston. (John de Lucy collection)

Several minutes after the previous photograph was taken, *Königsberg* is clearly down by the bow and listing to port. The smoke column is noticeably more dense. (John de Lucy collection)

Now burning extensively, *Königsberg* has rolled away from the mole onto her port beam ends and is going under. (John de Lucy collection)

The smoke thins as *Königsberg* disappears below the surface. (John de Lucy collection)

Gone. *Königsberg* has sunk and the pall of smoke is beginning to clear. (John de Lucy collection)

dive-bombers disembarked from their parent carriers at Hatston to attack the German ships at Bergen at dawn on 10 April. Weather for the strike was briefed as a half cover of cloud at 8,000 feet with a visibility of 20nm below it. The surface wind was north-westerly at 10 knots veering to northerly and 16 knots at 3,000 feet, giving a slight tail wind component on the way out and no head wind on the way back, perfect conditions considering the aircraft would be operating to the limit of their endurance. IFF (Identification Friend or Foe) equipment was removed from the aircraft because of the risk that the enemy might recover it from aircraft that were shot down. There was to be W/T silence on the outbound flight to the target but the results of individual attacks were to be transmitted to Hatston as soon as possible after the attack. Each aircraft was armed with a single 500lb SAP bomb in addition to the usual four fully loaded front guns and extra ammunition for the TAG's gun in the rear cockpit.

800 and 803 NAS, *Königsberg* strike, 10 April 1940

Section	*Pilot*	*Observer/TAG*
803 NAS		
Blue Leader	Lt W P Lucy	Lt M C E Hanson
2	Capt. E D McIver RM	LA A A Barnard
3	Lt A B Fraser-Harris	LA G S Russell
Green Leader	Lt H E R Torin	Mid (A) T A McKee
2	Lt L A Harris RM	NA D A Prime
3	Lt W C A Church	PO B M Seymour
Red Leader	Lt B J Smeeton	Mid (A) F Watkinson
2	Lt C H Filmer	NA F P Dooley
3	PO T F Riddler	NA H T Chatterley
Spare Leader	Lt K V V Spurway	PO C J E Cotterill
2	PO J A Gardner	NA A Todd
800 NAS		
Yellow Leader	Capt. R T Partridge RM	Lt Cdr G Hare
2	PO H A Monk	LA L C Eccleshall
3	PO J Hadley	LA M Hall
White Leader	Lt E W T Taylour	PO H G Cunningham
2	Lt J A Rooper	PO R S Rolph

The briefed objective was the destruction of the two *Köln*-class cruisers believed to be in Bergen, and Lieutenant Commander Hare was to fly with Dick Partridge to bring his knowledge of what he had seen on the morning of 9 April to the fight. 800 NAS's senior observer, Lieutenant Robin Bostock was, in any case, one of the observers lent to RAF Coastal Command and, to his great regret, could not have returned in time to fly the mission. The take-off was to be at 0515 so that the aircraft would be over Bergen shortly after dawn and the squadrons were to fly in two groups, keeping within sight of each other. The first was to comprise nine Skuas of 803 NAS led by Bill Lucy; the second was to comprise five Skuas of 800 NAS with the two spare aircraft of 803 NAS added to them led by Dick Partridge: a total of sixteen aircraft. With full fuel, a bomb and gun ammunition, the Skua was slightly unstable in yaw making formation a bit difficult until some fuel was burnt off but all the pilots were experienced on type and knew the aircraft and its idiosyncrasies well. The route to and from the target was worked out meticulously with the assistance of Hatston's Operations Officer, Lieutenant Commander A St J Edwards RN, and after a stream take-off on the west-facing runway the aircraft turned to fly over St Magnus Cathedral in the darkness to Auskerry Light, from which they tracked 074 degrees for a landfall on the Norwegian coast at Marsten. This was carefully chosen so that a turn onto north along the coastal islands would lead directly to Bergen. A landfall in error to the south would still lead to Bergen but a turn onto north from landfall in error to the north would lead to the open sea. In fact all aircraft calculated their en-route wind with accuracy and made a perfect landfall. White Leader in the second group lost contact with the remainder but still made a perfect landfall and attacked some ten minutes after the remainder. As they approached Bergen, the two groups' leaders positioned themselves at about 12,000 feet for an attack out of the sun which was rising behind the mountains to the east. The target ships had all moved from the positions in which Hare had seen them but *Königsberg*, identified as a *Köln*-class cruiser, was seen alongside the Skoltegrund Mole where repairs were being carried out, starboard side to, bow pointing east.

Bill Lucy wrote the post-action report on the strike but left no first-hand account of his feelings. Fortunately his friend Dick Partridge did and some years later he wrote extensively about his recollections in *Operation Skua*.[12]

> I didn't have a very happy evening, making a poor effort at eating some tea and supper. I went to bed at 2100 and dozed fitfully until called with a cup of tea and sandwiches at 0330; and what a ghastly hour that is for a show of calmness, determination and leadership. However, as soon as I had something to do I felt better, and back at the airfield briefing my aircrews I didn't really have time for all those craven thoughts that plagued me at the hotel; just that nagging queasy feeling in the tummy remained, and an indecision as to whether one final visit to the loo would be advisable.

I watched my aircrews' faces when I told them what we were going to do. If their reactions were the same as mine originally were they didn't show it; they took it calmly and magnificently. There were a few questions and answers and then I warned the pilots about the take-off and forming up in the dark. The Skua with full armament and fuel was not very nice or easy to fly; it tended to be unstable fore and aft and would remain so until some of the fuel had been used up. I can only liken it to driving a car which tends to wander and needs constant steering even on a straight road. The last thing we wanted was a prang or two before we had even started.

Just before 0500 there was the muffled report of a Coffman starter. One engine sprang into life, closely followed by another, and another until all other sounds were drowned by the shattering noise of 16 Bristol Perseus engines running up. No time for nerves now; pilots were too busy checking their instruments and watching for their turn to taxi out for take-off. At 0500 Bill Lucy roared down the runway and got airborne, to be followed at intervals by the rest of his squadron. Then it was my turn. Followed by my pilots we gingerly flew round above the airfield in the dark as we gradually joined up in formation at 3,000 feet. Then Bill swung round on a course for Bergen, climbing slowly to reach 10,000 feet. We levelled out at that height and settled down to our most economical speed of 140 knots. It was important that the leaders should keep a constant speed and that followers should not drop astern; excessive use of throttle to catch up or slow down meant more fuel used and we didn't have any of that to spare!

I settled down 200 feet above and a few hundred yards on Bill Lucy's starboard quarter. For some reason I always preferred flying on the right when in formation, I don't know why. It was a dark night but there were stars which helped, and I had no difficulty in keeping the other squadron in view, unless we ran into cloud. More time, of course, to think now and I felt sorry for the back seat crews who had even less to do than the pilots; at least we had our instruments to check, our formation to keep and could curse at the aircraft which refused to stay trimmed fore and aft.

My observer called me up on the intercom and told me that he reckoned we had just passed the halfway mark and were well set to arrive on time. He also pointed out the whispy clouds that were beginning to form and said that he thought they might increase. I had already noticed them and told him that if I lost contact with the other squadron I would climb to 12,000 feet and he would have to navigate me to the target. He seemed very calm and happy about this.

The Bristol Perseus engine we were flying behind was the first of the sleeve-valve ones, and as such was as smooth as a sewing machine. Cruising along behind it had almost a soporific effect and, had the occasion not been so important, one's attention could easily have wandered after an hour or so at steady height and speed. The cloud was increasing; it was now almost three-tenths and occasionally I would lose sight of Bill Lucy's squadron. But on we went as smoothly as ever, both squadrons in fairly open formation. I was beginning to lose sight of them more often now and began to climb to 11,000 feet so that there would be a vertical separation between us. Suddenly I knew I had lost them and in the dark it was most unlikely I would pick them up again. I told Lieutenant Commander Hare, my observer, that I was out of contact with 803 NAS, that I was climbing to 12,000 feet and would be carrying out an attack independent of the other squadron. This separation of the squadrons would mean that instead of the continuous surprise attack of 16 diving Skuas, one squadron or the other was probably going to attack after an interval, thus minimizing the effect of surprise and certainly alerting the defences. There was nothing to be done about it and we had discussed and recognized this possibility.

Faint signs of the approaching dawn were now showing and I could already make out details of my nearest aircraft. I looked at my watch; it was 0640 and we had already been airborne for 1 hour and 40 minutes. Ten minutes later and my observer asked me to increase speed to 150 knots as he reckoned we had fallen a little behind schedule when climbing to 12,000 feet and he also asked me to keep a lookout ahead for the Norwegian coastline. Fear, excitement, apprehension, anticipation, call it what you will, was beginning to rise now, with that familiar feeling in the pit of the stomach. Suddenly I saw it, the coast of Norway; Geoffrey Hare saw it too and said 'I think we are bang on, maintain this course and keep an eye open for our rendezvous island and lighthouse'. It was daylight now and shortly before 0655 we both spotted the island just off the Bergen Fjord fine on our port bow. I glanced around and below for the other squadron, hoping that I could rejoin, but although the cloud had cleared away as we approached the coast there was no sign of them. The sun was just beginning to rise in a bright golden ball above the mountains which we knew cradled Bergen down to the water-line.

Calm, precise instructions were now coming from the rear cockpit over the intercom; 'start losing height at 300 feet per minute, speed 200 knots and follow the fjord'. I eased forward the stick, closed my following aircraft in a little, felt the speed building up, 170 knots, 190 knots, 200 knots and held it at that. No time for any feelings now other than intense concentration that was making me sweat a little. Suddenly ahead of us was Bergen, looking quiet and peaceful in the sparkling early morning sunlight. To port were three large fuel storage tanks and ahead and to starboard ships, but merchant ships only – no cruiser. There was no sign of activity of any sort, no enemy fighters and no anti-aircraft fire.

We were almost down to 8,000 feet when we spotted her, a long, thin, grey shape lying alongside a jetty. I pulled away to port in order to make a great sweep up to the mountains and over the town of Bergen itself and so attack out of the rising sun. Now I was heading back towards the German cruiser and concentrating hard to get my Skua and those following me into the correct position for starting our dive. This position was, in my opinion, of the utmost importance. Dive-bombing is a most accurate, perhaps THE most accurate method of delivering a bomb onto a selected target and the angle of dive determines the accuracy of the attack; too steep and the dive tends to get even steeper and out of control; too shallow and the target tends to disappear under one and accuracy is lost. But start the dive in just the right position so that you are going down at 65 degrees, then in a good dive-bomber like the Skua with its large flaps accurate bombing becomes almost easy.

Having reached a suitable position, I did a 90 degree turn to port, eased back on the stick, flaps down, further back on the stick, a half stall turn to starboard and then I was in a well-controlled dive with the cruiser held steady in my sight. I was losing height and down to 6,000 feet with the target still held steady in my sight when to my astonishment ahead of me I saw a Skua release its bomb and go racing away at water level. I later found that this was the last aircraft of 803 NAS so, quite fortuitously, we were going to carry out our planned continuous raid with all 16 aircraft!

I was attacking the ship from bow to stern and the only resistance being offered was coming from a light Bofors type anti-aircraft gun on the forecastle which kept firing throughout the engagement; tracer bullets were gliding past on either side. My dive was still firm and controlled with the ship held steady in my sight and I could see water and oil gushing out of her below the waterline and guessed that she had already been damaged. Down to 3,500 feet now and beginning to watch my height; mustn't lose accuracy by releasing too high and mustn't release too low and risk blowing myself up. 3,000 feet, 2,500, 2,000 and at 1,800 I pressed the release button on the stick and let my bombs[13] go, turning violently away to starboard and then down to water level when well clear.

As we raced low down the fjord at full throttle Lieutenant Commander Hare was telling me that he reckoned we had had a near miss on the ship's starboard bow when he suddenly said 'MTB travelling fast ahead of us', and there was a motor torpedo boat at full speed with decks crowded with servicemen. I turned towards her and as we got near gave a long burst with my front-guns and saw men jumping off and into the water. We were being fired on now by anti-aircraft batteries in the woods on the steep side of the fjord and in this mad dash we were making I was tempted to have a go at them too. Sensibly, I resisted this rash impulse and continued to climb to 5,000 feet over our rendezvous. There I saw the glad sight of Bill Lucy with all his squadron but one and I was soon joined by mine. Circling, waiting for Bill's straggler, was bad for my nerves as the excitement of the attack and getaway began to wear off. As I sat there jittery in my cockpit imagining hordes of Bf 110s arriving at any moment I was vastly relieved to see a single-engined monoplane approaching; Bill's missing Skua. We learnt later that this aircraft had dived with 803 NAS but had a hang-up and could not release his bombs. The pilot, determined not to jettison them, had laboriously climbed back up to 8,000 feet, circled over Bergen again and carried out a lone attack after we had all gone. This time the anti-aircraft gun on the forecastle was no longer firing.

Sixteen aircraft into the attack and 16 out! It seemed too good to be true and we had certainly damaged that ship, perhaps we had even sunk her. We were now on course for home and had been airborne for some two and a half hours with the best part of another two hours flying ahead of us. It would be touch and go, and should a head wind get up it seemed extremely likely that some of us at least would get very wet feet. After 10 minutes on our homeward course – disaster! The outer aircraft on my starboard side suddenly went into a vertical dive and hit the sea under full power; all that remained was a large circle of disturbed water and a few pieces of wreckage. There was nothing that could possibly be done save to continue on our long flight home. It was never possible to discover what happened but it seemed fairly likely that either the aircraft had been hit and succumbed to elevator control failure or the pilot had been wounded, held out so far, and then suddenly collapsed.

There was seven-tenths cloud now and moderate visibility as we steadily flew on at our most economical speed. By 0900 I had been airborne for 3 hours and 45 minutes which meant 35 minutes of our official endurance left, but still no sight of ship or land. I was now frequently looking at my watch and anxiously watching my fuel gauges, and I am sure everybody else was doing the same. It would be ironic if we all ended up in the drink after such a successful attack. The time was now 0935 and I had been airborne for our official endurance of 4 hours and 20 minutes when to my utmost relief my observer said quietly over the intercom 'Stronsay fine on our starboard bow'. Stronsay was the most easterly of the Orkney Islands and we were almost home.

I landed at 0945 having been in the air for four and a half hours. Some of the aircraft clocked up 5 minutes longer, depending on the order in which they had taken off and landed. Some marvellous stories ran round the squadron for days afterwards among the ground crews – 'he didn't have enough petrol in his tanks to cover a penny [on its side]'; 'as he taxied in towards me his engine cut dead, his tanks were completely dry'; 'his engine cut out as he touched down' – a certain amount of exaggeration no doubt, but it was assuredly true that we had mighty little to spare.

There was great excitement, congratulations and euphoria whilst we were being debriefed before going off to breakfast. General opinion among the naval pilots and observers was that our target had been a *Köln* class cruiser and we were all certain that she had been badly damaged, perhaps even sunk. This was confirmed later by a report from RAF reconnaissance flights and photographs which showed that the ship was sunk alongside the jetty. Later, intelligence from Norway established that she was in fact the cruiser *Königsberg*. Bill Lucy's rash, mad plan had worked for the loss of only one aircraft.

It was learnt later from Norwegian intelligence sources that German lookouts on the coast had been briefed that no British single-engined aircraft had the range to reach Bergen. They had assumed, therefore, that the two formations of aircraft were friendly and no warning had been given of their approach. Bill Lucy's after-action report adds more detail to Dick Partridge's account quoted above. The aircraft

SECRET

OWN AIR ATTACKS - REPORT.
(N.A.D. 729/39 - 23.11.39).

C.A.F.O. 3572/39.

No. 803 Squadron. Blue Leader.

Pilot - Lieutenant William Paulet Lucy, Royal Navy.
Observer- Lieutenant Michael Charles Edward Hanson, Royal Navy.

(1). Date. 10th April, 1940.

(2). Weather, sea and cloud conditions, visibility.

Extreme visibility. No cloud over target.

(3). Brief account of the circumstances, including composition and disposition, course and speed of enemy forces, particulars of attacking force, and tactics of approach.

Approach from 12,000 ft. down sun. No. target immediately visible. Target identified at 9,000 ft. (still up sun of target). Attack down sun. Bow to stern.

(4) Not applicable.

(5) (Bomb attack only).
(i) Nature of attack (high level or dive) and number and size of bombs dropped.

Dive Bombing. One 500 lb. bomb.
(ii) A diagram showing the fall of bombs relative to the target and, if possible, indicating the bombs dropped by each aircraft or formation and the approximate time interval between individual aircraft or formations.

See Appendix I attached.

(iii) Mean height of release. Angle of dive (dive-bombing only).

2000 feet. 60°.

(iv) Avoiding action taken by target.

Nil.
(v) Estimated effect of A.A. fire on accuracy.
Nil.

6. Estimate of damage caused to target.

Not known.

7. Particulars of enemy gunfire.

One H.A. gun at 8000 feet. Considerable pom pom fire observed.

8. Casualties and/or damage to own aircraft and how caused.

Nil.

9. Any other points of interest.

The combat report written by Bill Lucy and Michael Hanson after the *Königsberg* strike. (Author's collection)

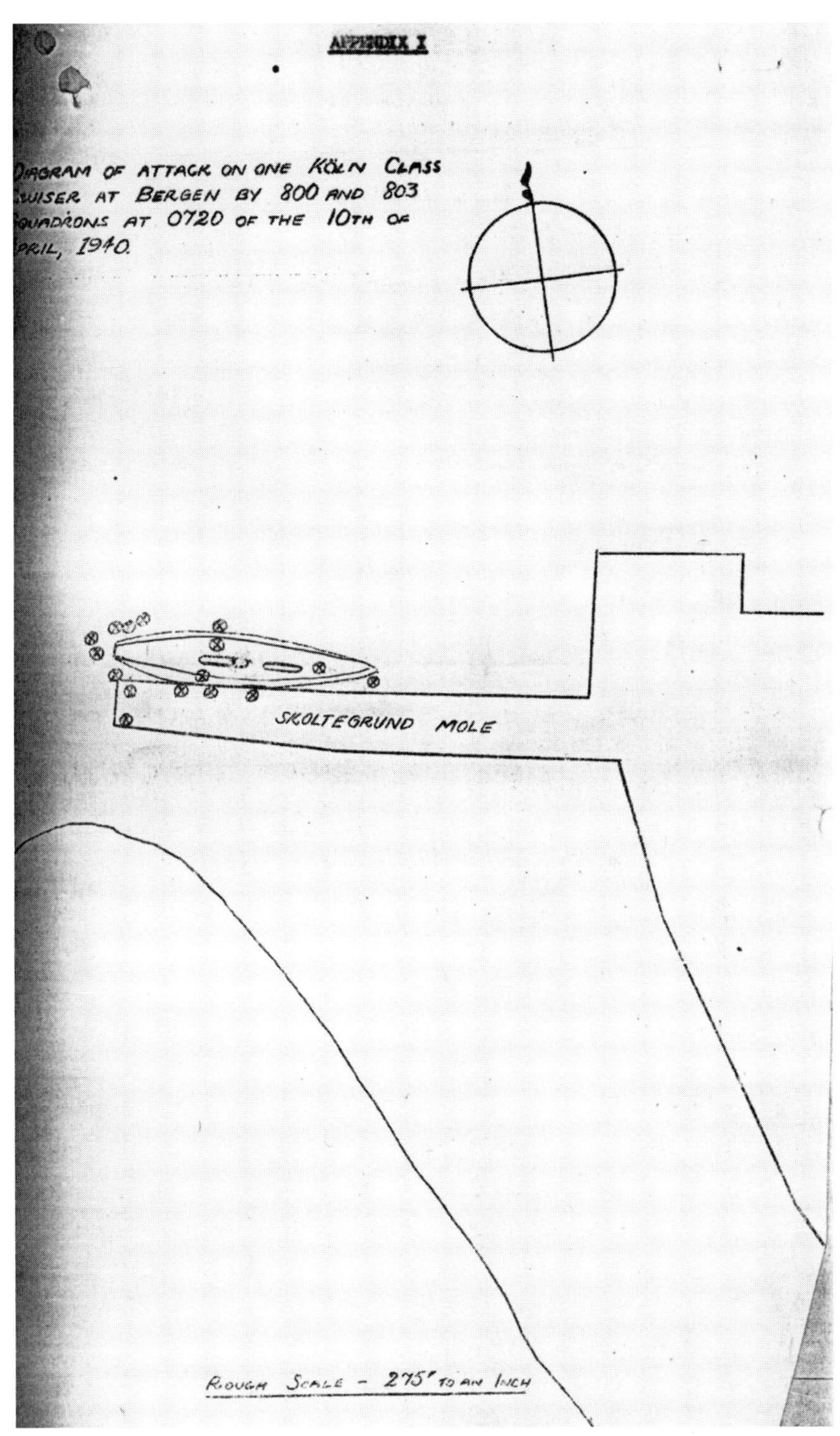

Bill Lucy's bomb plot attached to his after-action report showing where 800 and 803 NAS's bombs were seen to hit. Even the near misses caused extensive damage. (Author's collection)

that suffered a hang-up and went round for a second attack was White Leader, Lieutenant Taylour with Petty Officer Cunningham, actually one of Dick Partridge's 800 NAS aircraft. In addition to the single anti-aircraft gun on *Königsberg* that fired on them, several 'pom-pom type' weapons were seen to open fire from the shore; not only had the Germans been quick to deploy the Luftwaffe into Norway, they had lost no time in setting up anti-aircraft artillery in support of their landings. On examination after landing at Hatston, two aircraft were found to have been hit in the wing by small-calibre shells which had not affected their performance. The aircrew observed three direct hits on the enemy cruiser and at least one near miss which would also have caused damage. The mean error in bombing was calculated to be 50 yards, which compared most favourably with the pre-war average mean error of 70 yards by Skuas practising dive-bombing attacks. Considering that neither squadron had any recent dive-bombing practice and they were under fire, in some cases for the first time, this was a most creditable achievement, the more so as later aircraft reported finding their ability to aim accurately made more difficult by the smoke and dust thrown up by near misses that exploded on the jetty. The briefed rendezvous position was over the island of Lyso, 10nm due west of Bergen where the leaders were to wait ten minutes before setting heading for home. Any aircraft with less than 50 gallons of fuel at this point had been authorised to land in Norway well clear of Bergen. If the aircraft was serviceable, the aircrew were to attempt to obtain fuel from the Norwegian authorities and fly back to the UK on 11 April. If it was not serviceable, they were to destroy the aircraft and do what they could to get home. All sixteen aircraft had reached the rendezvous with over 50 gallons and re-formed into their sections but the post-action report differs slightly from Dick partridge's account, stating that Red Leader, Lieutenant B J Smeeton with Midshipman (A) F Watkinson as his observer, 'subsequently led his flight into a cloud, within which his wing men lost touch with him. He was not seen again, although one aircraft reported seeing a splash in the sea at about this time.' This account, written within hours of the strike, is probably the more accurate and it is likely that the aircraft had sustained damage that was not seen by the wing-men or that the pilot had been injured and lost control of the aircraft whilst attempting to fly on instruments. The exact cause was never determined and both aircrew were deemed to be missing, presumed dead. The remaining fifteen aircraft made good a track of 260 degrees for Sumburgh in the Shetland Islands, where aircraft with less than 30 gallons of fuel remaining were to land, and one did so. The remainder carried on to land at Hatston.

Bill Lucy and his strike force made history on 10 April 1940; for the first time a major warship had been sunk by air attack alone.[14] It was also of particular significance that although his aircraft had flown from a naval air station ashore, they were naval aircraft manned by pilots and observers trained specifically to locate, identify and attack warships at long range using the best attack tactics and techniques. In comparison, RAF bombers had failed to achieve any success against naval targets on a number of occasions in what it regarded as a secondary role for which its aircrew had not been trained. Naval aviation had also shown its potential to strike at the enemy where other, more conventional naval forces were unable to do so. Clearly, this ability would be enhanced when squadrons were embarked in their aircraft carriers, enabling them to move closer to the target, sustain them in operation and potentially avoid inclement weather. The facts that other forms of attack had been considered by the C-in-C Home Fleet and that Bomber Command had failed to achieve the aim of destroying the German cruisers emphasise the measure of achievement attained by 800 and 803 NAS under Bill Lucy's leadership on that day.

He ended his summary of the operation by writing that he believed the strike had been carried out under exceptionally favourable conditions and that the lack of serious opposition indicated that surprise had been achieved. Certainly strong winds would have prevented it and German awareness of the possibility that RN dive-bombing aircraft could reach Bergen, either from a carrier or a shore base in the Orkney Islands, might have led to precautions that might have caused greater casualties among the strike force. However, I believe that he was being unduly modest. Given that the weather was indeed suitable, the other favourable conditions were of the naval aircrew's own making. The carefully chosen route, accurately flown with the minimum fuel consumption, led to a perfect landfall which allowed them to make the best use of their remaining fuel and, despite their recent lack of dive-bombing practice, the attack itself had been well executed.

The German invasion plan, whilst in itself audacious, had been sufficiently rigid in its application to prevent the assault forces from taking steps to allow for a surprise strike of this nature by the Royal Navy. Whilst it might have been possible to provide air cover for the damaged warships left in Bergen, this would probably have had to consist of standing patrols which the Luftwaffe could ill afford at this time. The misguided briefing that no British single-engined aircraft could approach Bergen had proved to be a key factor that robbed the Germans of the warning time that might have allowed them to get fighters into the air. Whilst the Luftwaffe had shown itself on 9 April to be capable of carrying out predictive operations against British warships in the Norwegian littoral, it was not yet capable of reactive, defensive operations against naval air strikes from the sea, even this far south. It soon would be, however, as its strength in southern Norway grew.

Rear Admiral Bell Davies, RANAS, was touring the northern air stations in April 1940 and was in Edinburgh when news reached him of the German invasion of Norway. He travelled at once to RNAS Donibristle in Fife and flew from there to Hatston, arriving just as the Skua squadrons received orders to attack German warships located at Bergen.[15] He provided a tangible link with the RNAS which had done so much to develop strike warfare in the Great War and watched the aircraft take off. Only too well aware that they were operating to the extreme limit of their range and that the slightest miscalculation would cause them to run out of fuel over the sea, he 'awaited their return with deep anxiety'. He attended the debrief and learnt that they had certainly hit a cruiser but did not learn until some hours later when he had resumed his tour 'the splendid news that the cruiser had been sent to the bottom'.

In the Admiralty, the Director of the Air Division minuted[16] that the Director considered this to have been a model attack in every way which reaped the reward it deserved. 'DNAD considers that the principal lesson to be learnt from this operation is that if Fleet Aircraft are employed for the type of function for which they were designed, under careful planning and skilful leadership, they can achieve the results which have not been achieved by other aircraft'. The 5th Sea Lord (5SL), Admiralty Board Member for naval aviation, added a handwritten minute that this was 'a very carefully planned and well executed attack with successful results'. Admiral Sir Dudley Pound, 1SL, added his own handwritten comment: 'I entirely agree with 5SL and consider that a letter of appreciation should be sent … would 5SL draft letter and … also 'phone [to] confirm that awards to Fleet Air Arm are got out as quickly as those to RAF.' A letter was, therefore, sent to the Vice Admiral Commanding Orkney and Shetland Islands with copies to the C-in-C Home Fleet and Rear Admiral Naval Air Stations which stated:

> With reference to your submission number 448/O.S.327 of 15 April 1940, Their Lordships have read with much satisfaction the report by the Commanding Officer, RN Air Station Hatston, on the very successful attack by 800 and 803 Squadrons on enemy ships at Bergen on 10 April 1940 which resulted in the destruction of a German cruiser which has recently been confirmed to have been the *Königsberg*.
>
> They entirely concur in your remarks on this very carefully planned and well executed operation and request that you will convey their appreciation and congratulations to the Commanding Officer RN Air Station Hatston and officers and men concerned.

This letter must have given Bill Lucy and his colleagues keen pleasure but more was to follow. 1SL's instruction that awards were to be announced quickly was carried out and the *London Gazette* for 9 May 1940 announced awards for the *Königsberg* strike:

> Admiralty, Whitehall
> 9 May 1940
>
> The KING has been graciously pleased to give orders for the Following appointments to the Distinguished Service Order for daring and resource in the conduct of hazardous and successful operations by the Fleet Air Arm against the enemy, especially on the coast of Norway:–

To be Companions of the Distinguished Service Order
Captain Richard Thomas Partridge, Royal Marines
Lieutenant William Paulet Lucy, Royal Navy

His Majesty has also been graciously pleased to approve the following awards for similar services:–

The Distinguished Service Cross
Lieutenant Commander Geoffrey Hare, Royal Navy
Lieutenant Harry Ernest Richard Torin, Royal Navy
Lieutenant Michael Charles Edward Hanson, Royal Navy
Acting Lieutenant Edward Winchester Tollemache Taylour, Royal Navy
Midshipman (A) Thomas Anthony McKee, Royal Navy

The Distinguished Service Cross (Bar)
Acting Lieutenant Edward Winchester Tollemache Taylour, Royal Navy

The Distinguished Service Medal
Petty Officer Airman Harold Arthur Monk, FX76290
Acting Petty Officer Airman Howard Gresley Cunningham, FX76292

Mentions in Despatches
Lieutenant Commander Aubrey St John Edwards, Royal Navy
Lieutenant William Paulet Lucy, Royal Navy
Lieutenant Michael Charles Edward Hanson, Royal Navy
Lieutenant Robin Southey Bostock, Royal Navy
Lieutenant Cecil Howard Filmer, Royal Navy
Lieutenant Kenneth Vyvyan Vincent Spurway, Royal Navy
Acting Lieutenant Edward Winchester Tollemache Taylour, Royal Navy
Acting Petty Officer Airman Howard Gresley Cunningham, FX76292
Petty Officer Airman Christopher James Edwin Cotterill, F55040
Naval Airman 1st Class Frederick Percival Dooley, FX79189
Leading Airman Maurice Hall, FX76325

The awards were made for a number of different actions at this period and several people, including Bill Lucy, received more than one award in this *Gazette*.

Praise for the operation also appeared in the *Daily Telegraph* on 4 May 1940 when its New York correspondent interviewed Captain Wollaston of the US merchant ship *Flying Fish*. His ship had been in Bergen on 9 April when German forces seized the port. They had put armed guards in his wireless room and given him orders that she was not to sail until allowed to do so. He and his crew had watched, enthralled, in the early morning of 10 April as the Skuas scored hit after hit on the

German cruiser alongside the Skoltegrund Mole. They saw flames over 100 feet high and dense clouds of smoke issuing from the hull before the ship capsized and sank a few minutes after 0900.

Further Strike Operations against Bergen

There was a clear need to limit the flow of German material into Norway through Bergen and, after Admiral Forbes' decision not to risk the Home Fleet that far south, the Hatston Skua force represented the best option for doing so. A second strike, therefore, took place on 12 April led by Dick Partridge. 801 NAS had arrived from Evanton that morning and contributed two flights of three Skuas to the total force of nineteen Skuas that carried out the strike. Lieutenant Commander H P Bramwell RN, CO of 801 NAS took part but Bill Lucy did not. All Skuas were again armed with 500lb SAP bombs and full gun ammunition and the weather over the North Sea was forecast as a cloud base at 5,000 feet with visibility of 6 miles below it and a 10 knot wind from the north, veering southerly at up to 20 knots as the aircraft passed through a frontal system. The squadrons began to take off at 1405 in the order 803, 800 and 801 NAS with fifteen minutes between them and navigation followed the same route as on 10 April. The first aircraft arrived over the target at about 1630 just below the cloud base; there were no interceptions by enemy fighters and anti-aircraft fire was late in developing. The aircraft attacked in 60-degree dives with an average height of bomb release at 2,000 feet although two aircraft were forced to release higher because of concentrations of enemy fire. Dick Partridge selected a large oiler as his target and used both cloud and hills to mask his approach; his number 3, Petty Officer Hadley, detached to attack a stores ship and Lieutenant Finch-Noyes attacked a floating dock. Lieutenant Commander Bramwell was unable to identify a suitable target on his first pass and went around for a second pass during which he attacked a merchant ship alongside the floating dock. His wing-men attacked ships alongside a pier in Vaagen and other Skuas attacked merchant ships with military deck cargoes, warehouses and troop ships anchored in the roadstead. After releasing their bombs, most pilots strafed targets of opportunity with their front guns; these included a small U-boat seen leaving Kors Fjord, what were identified as gunnery training ships with seaplanes on their quarterdecks and a warehouse.

The American ss *Flying Fish* was still in Bergen. Captain Wollaston and his crew watched the whole attack and subsequently described it to the New York correspondent of the *Daily Telegraph*. They saw Skuas attack the German *Barenfels*, anchored next to them, with guns, and a number of rounds hit oil drums on the American ship's deck. None of the crew was hurt and the Chief Engineer, Chester Shimp, said that he saw the aircraft that fired these rounds as it flew low over the anchorage and noted bullet holes and damage near the cockpit from which he deduced that the pilot was not in full control of the aircraft. A few minutes later it made a forced landing 10 miles west of Bergen about 200 yards offshore between Foeroy and Asko Islands. This was Red 2 of 803 NAS, Petty Officer Gardner with his TAG Naval Airman Todd in Skua L3037. Both got out of the wrecked aircraft safely and were able to make their way back to the UK. The last aircraft to leave noted a huge explosion from the warehouse that had been attacked, probably indicating its use to store ammunition. Enemy fire had been seen to come from guns mounted on or near white oil storage tanks to the west of the anchorage and these were strafed as the remaining aircraft withdrew. They all got back to Hatston safely and at the aircrew debrief it was agreed that the number of close-range anti-aircraft guns had increased but the state of German preparedness was not good. The element of surprise had not yet been lost, aircrew felt that they were getting to know the harbour. There was much enthusiasm to carry out another strike despite the increasing risk of interception by the Luftwaffe.

A third strike, to be led by Bill Lucy, was therefore planned for 14 April by fifteen aircraft of 800 and 803 NAS, six from the former and nine from the latter. Their briefed intention was to reduce the number of alongside berths available to the Germans from which they could unload equipment and so the strike was to concentrate on the Skoltegrund Mole and other jetties. Weather was to play a more significant part in this strike, with extensive cloud cover over the North Sea at 5,000 feet decreasing to full cover at 700 feet with visibility of 2 to 4 miles beneath it at the Norwegian coast. Conditions over the target were forecast to be worse. Armament was the standard load of 500lb SAP bombs and gun ammunition, and Hatston Operation Order Number 3 called for the squadrons to take off fifty minutes apart so that smoke from bomb hits would not obscure targets for later aircraft and to avoid confusion with too many aircraft attacking under the low cloud in restricted visibility. The six aircraft of 800 NAS took off from Hatston at 0500 followed at 0550 by the nine aircraft of 803 NAS. Both followed the familiar track towards Marsten and the first group arrived over the Norwegian coast at 0700 and made their way under the lowering cloud to Bergen. The low cloud forced them to dive at a 45-degree angle and release at 1,000 feet but despite this the attacks were accurate and Dick Partridge's flight obtained hits on a stores ship alongside Dokskier Jetty, causing considerable damage. As they withdrew, pilots strafed two U-boats on the surface south-west of Korsnes Fjord and observed hits on their conning towers although it is doubtful that their rifle-calibre bullets caused much damage. Two motor launches were also strafed and left on fire with men seen abandoning them. The remaining aircraft of 800 NAS bombed ships alongside Dokskier and Skoltegrund with one bomb seen to detonate between a ship and the jetty, where it would have done considerable damage.

803 NAS arrived over Bergen at 0745 but by then the weather had deteriorated and only Bill Lucy's Blue Section got through; Red and Green Sections lost touch and found it impossible to get through. They jettisoned their bombs and

returned to Hatston. Despite the appalling weather, however, Lucy and Hanson led Lieutenant Fraser-Harris with Leading Airman Russell and Captain McIver RM with Leading Airman Barnard in line astern towards their target. They identified a transport ship alongside the Skoltegrund Mole and attacked it with a shallow, 40-degree dive technique, releasing their bombs below 350 feet. Lucy's bomb was seen to hit and caused a fire alongside the inboard side of the ship that spilled onto the jetty. Considerable small arms fire and light anti-aircraft fire were encountered which did not deter his attack but did cause a bullet hole in the port wing which had no effect on the aircraft's performance. After his attack Bill Lucy flew past a warship with a seaplane on deck but, by the time he had set his front guns to 'fire' he had insufficient time to fire an aimed burst at it. Almost immediately, however, he saw a large multi-engined flying boat on the water and he gave it a long, well-aimed burst of fire and saw it catch fire as he did so. A second front-gun attack was carried out on three single-engined floatplanes on the water. Here the bursts were more scattered and the effects were not seen.

Fraser-Harris, Blue 2, had little time to transfer his attention from his leader to the target and released his bomb at only 200 feet in a 50-degree dive but it also hit the target which he estimated to be an 8,000-ton motor vessel alongside the Skoltegrund Mole. He saw black smoke coming from its port quarter and fire emanating from the side of the ship closest to the mole. A warehouse was also seen to be on fire. After weapon release Fraser-Harris turned hard to follow his leader at low level out of the harbour; he saw the burning flying boat and saw, but did not attack, the seaplane-carrying warship.

McIver, Blue 3, having followed Bill Lucy so gallantly through the appalling weather, was shot down whilst making his attack, the result of which was not seen although it was thought that he had released his bomb. His aircraft was seen to be on fire as it crashed into the harbour from about 300 feet. Both McIver and Barnard were posted as killed in action.

Against the odds, complete surprise had been achieved for the third time and nine accurate bombs had been dropped on ships alongside the two jetties. Two ships alongside the Skoltegrund Mole were estimated to have been sunk which, added to the sunken *Königsberg*, had achieved the aim of limiting the number of berths available to the Germans for landing stores and equipment. The two ships alongside the Dokskier Jetty were estimated as damaged, together with the jetty itself. One flying boat had been destroyed, hits obtained on two U-boats and the two motor launches were believed to have taken heavy casualties. In his report of proceedings (ROP) to the Vice Admiral Commanding Orkney and Shetland Islands, Commander Howe, CO of RNAS Hatston wrote:

> The fact that Lieutenant William Paulet Lucy RN, who led 803 NAS, was able to get through and attack reflects the greatest credit on this officer whose bravery and determination I have already submitted to your notice. He was most ably assisted

> by Lieutenant Michael Charles Edward Hanson RN, his observer, who navigated him in making full use of his knowledge of the country gained in earlier attacks.

Fraser-Harris and McIver were also commended in the same report for following their leader in to attack under such adverse conditions.

After these three attacks on Bergen it was clear that the increasing strength of the German defences would make further set-piece strikes too costly and so it was decided, instead, to carry out more limited reconnaissance sorties with the object of attacking any German warship or supply ship found in Bergen or its approaches. The first was flown on 16 April by two aircraft of 803 NAS. The first was flown by Bill Lucy with Hanson and the second by Lieutenant Torin with Midshipman McKee. Their briefing was contained in Hatston Operation Order Number 4 with navigation following what was, by then, the usual route to Marsten for the very good reason that they had insufficient fuel to depart from it to any significant extent. On landfall, they were to split, with one aircraft heading north through the fjords to 60 50N and the other searching fjords to the south as far as 60 10N. They were then to return separately using Sumburgh as a diversion if short of fuel. The weather was good with a layer of cloud giving full cover at 1,500 feet and a second layer giving half cover at 7,000 feet. Both would be useful if the Skuas had to evade intercepting enemy fighters. Visibility was 20nm over the target but worse, with lower cloud, over the Shetland Islands. Armament for this sortie was one 250lb SAP bomb, eight 20lb HE bombs and full gun ammunition. Both aircraft took off at 0500 and they flew in section at 4,000 feet across the North Sea to Marsten, where they split as briefed at 0650. Bill Lucy let down to 1,000 feet and headed north, examining Hjelte Fjord, Mangers Fjord and Rado Fjord. A small grey vessel flying the German ensign was seen in position 60 31.9N 05 16E and Bill immediately climbed to set himself up for a shallow diving attack. He dived along the length of the vessel in order to maximise the chance of hitting it and released his bombs at 1,000 feet. The target tried to evade by altering course to starboard with the result that the stick of bombs fell in a line from its starboard quarter to the port bow as Lucy adjusted his aim in the dive. The 250lb and four of the 20lb bombs hit, four 20lb bombs were near misses on the port side. The mean point of impact was just aft of amidships: a perfect attack. The vessel was seen to sink rapidly. Herpo Fjord and Hjeltge Fjord as far as Helliso at 60 45N were then searched before turning for home, landing at Hatston at 0926.

The second aircraft headed south after the split and encountered a small 'coastal-type' U-boat on the surface under way and heading for the open sea at 60 08N 05 02E at 0705 about 2nm east of Marsten. Torin attacked it immediately in a shallow dive and released his bombs in a single stick at 2,000 feet. The target was straddled with the mean point of impact on the conning tower; the 250lb bomb was seen to detonate about 15 feet off the target's starboard bow and the 20lb bombs fell as hits and near misses all around the boat. A cloud of smoke and steam was seen to

The ship sunk alongside the Skoltegrund Mole on 14 April 1940. Together with the wreck of the *Königsberg* on the other side of the mole, this sinking achieved the aim of limiting the number of berths at which German ships could unload. (Author's collection)

come from one direct hit aft and, significantly, the boat did not attempt to dive but turned back towards harbour. No further targets were seen and a search of Kors Fjord, Leroosen, Kobbelden, Byfjord and Bergen was completed before returning to Hatston, landing at 0920. In addition to the two targets attacked, this offensive reconnaissance had identified a small depot ship near the damaged U-boat and ten merchant ships in the anchorage at Puddefjord. One 5,000-ton ship alongside the south side of the Skoltegrund Mole, bows west had a heavy list to port. A further 3,000-ton ship lay 300 yards astern alongside the same mole which was still burning with dense clouds of smoke rising from it. Dokskier and the naval jetty were both empty. Six ships flying the Danish and Swedish flags were anchored in Bergen harbour. A general impression was gained that the coast defence guns were not manned and, despite the low level at which the two Skuas flew, there had been no anti-aircraft fire. There was less evidence of enemy activity ashore than during the previous strikes.

Further offensive reconnaissance sorties were flown a day later on 17 April by Dick Partridge with Robin Bostock and Lieutenant Finch-Noyes with Petty Officer

Cunningham. The weather was somewhat worse than on the day before with full cover at 3,000 feet and a layer giving half cover at 1,000 feet. Wind on the outbound leg was southerly but before their return it veered to westerly and increased in strength. Armament was the same as on the day before. Dick Partridge found no target of military value and jettisoned his bombs into the sea before starting his return leg. Fuel became critical and he elected to land at the diversion airfield at Sumburgh. Unfortunately his aircraft, L3025, pitched onto its nose in the soft ground and was written off although neither he nor his observer was hurt. They flew back to Hatston in a Swordfish later that day. Finch-Noyes was more fortunate and he located the German gunnery training ship *Bremse* alongside the Dokskier Jetty in Bergen. He attacked it at 1150 but his bombs missed astern of the target and caused no obvious damage. There was light anti-aircraft fire from *Bremse* but none from the shore and nor was there any as he flew around the harbour taking photographs. The warehouse on the Skoltegrund Mole was seen to be burning still with a sunken merchant ship visible on the inland side of the mole. Having flown the southern reconnaissance, his fuel was less critical and he landed safely at Hatston.

The two offensive reconnaissance sorties brought to an end the strike operations mounted by disembarked Skua squadrons from RNAS Hatston against targets in the Bergen area during the early part of the Norwegian campaign. Apart from their significant contribution to that campaign, they had also retained responsibility for coastal convoy defence in Scottish waters since the RAF was unable to provide it, and for the air defence of Scapa Flow. Sorties for both these tasks had to be interspersed with the long-range strikes, and the skill with which the variety and number of missions were undertaken speaks volumes about the devotion of the aircrew and maintenance personnel who all found themselves at the forefront of a new kind of warfare.

Having taken part in some of the opening moves of the Norwegian campaign as an integral part of Home Fleet operations, Hatston also contributed to one of the last. On 21 June 1940 the battlecruiser *Scharnhorst* was reported to be at sea returning to Germany from Trondheim.[17] On learning of this the Operations Officer at Hatston managed to arrange and brief a daylight torpedo attack on her by six disembarked Swordfish of 821 and 823 NAS, neither of which had recent training in this highly specialised form of attack.[18] They intercepted *Scharnhorst* after a flight of 240nm, in itself no mean achievement, and attacked immediately in the face of heavy anti-aircraft fire which shot down two of their number. Unfortunately their inexperience showed and they dived straight into the attack without manoeuvring for co-ordinated approaches from different directions and all their torpedoes missed. It had been the first attack of its kind by torpedo aircraft against a capital ship at sea ever carried out and at 265nm from Hatston as the survivors turned for home, they were at the limit of their radius of action. In his subsequent report, RANAS described the attack as a gallant failure with inadequate force.[19]

Chapter 14

HMS Furious: *The First Strike Carrier in Action*

In retrospect, it seems remarkable that in early April 1940 the Home Fleet had been left without an aircraft carrier but the need to train aircrew for the rapid expansion of the Fleet Air Arm had been given priority and both *Ark Royal* and *Glorious* were in the Eastern Mediterranean where they could do so in relative safety. As mentioned above, *Furious* had only recently completed a refit, was only partially combat ready and had not operated very much with the rest of the Home Fleet.[1] In *Air Power and the Royal Navy*, Geoffrey Till considers that this was the reason why Admiral Forbes had not ordered her to sea. Indeed, his later despatch showed that on Sunday 7 April 1940 he did not even think the carrier was a part of the Home Fleet. If that was the case it was a grave oversight by his staff: even if she was not fully operational she was the only carrier likely to be available and every effort should have been made to get her to sea with Forbes' heavy force. The Admiralty, too, should have been more aware of her potential value in any encounter with the enemy. Till describes her commanding officer, Captain T H Troubridge RN as 'chafing at this inactivity' and apparently he raised steam on his own initiative. At 1637 on Monday 8 April the Admiralty ordered him to fly on his aircraft and to sail north in company with the battleship *Warspite* to rendezvous with Forbes two days later.

Furious lay off Greenock in early April preparing to rejoin the Home Fleet.[2] Her allocated air group comprised 816 and 818 NAS with Fairey Swordfish and 801 NAS with Blackburn Skuas. The former were disembarked at RNAS Campbeltown waiting to re-embark but 801 NAS was at RAF Evanton on the western shore of Cromarty Firth,[3] roughly 100 miles away. In fact it had not embarked in *Furious* since it had re-formed with Skuas at RNAS Donibristle on 15 January 1940. This may explain why Captain Troubridge did not take urgent steps on 7 April to move it closer to his ship so that it could embark at short notice. To complicate matters it had been at Evanton since 2 February and, whilst there, came under the operational control of RAF Fighter Command. *Furious* had not embarked a fighter squadron at all since the outbreak of war and would thus probably not have had Skua spares or suitable squadron mobile equipment (SME) on board – an oversight that was to cost the Home Fleet dearly. *Furious*' log for April[4] shows that despite having raised steam, Sunday 7 April was a relatively quiet day that provided a break from storing, ammunitioning and painting the ship and removing the dirt and grime left by the refit. Church parties were landed at 0905 and returned on board at 1105. On 8 April hands were turned to painting ship at 0600 and an ammunition lighter was secured alongside at 1120. Close-range weapons' crews carried out anti-aircraft drills from 1010 but two days in which 801 NAS could have been released by Fighter Command and moved to Campbeltown had been wasted. At 1637, when the Admiralty signal to sail was received, this routine changed abruptly but in his subsequent ROP Captain Troubridge described his allocated fighter squadron as being 'too far off to comply with what was obviously an urgent order'.[5] He felt unable to question the timing of the order and the Home Fleet was, therefore, committed to sailing into its encounter with the land-based air power of Fliegerkorps X without any embarked fighters. One can only imagine that, like the Admiralty War Room, Captain Troubridge was thinking only of a fleet-to-fleet action in which Skuas would have been of marginally less importance than the Swordfish. A drifter was immediately sent ashore to collect libertymen, and urgent preparations to secure the ship for sea began at 1700. At 1830 an oiler was brought alongside to top up the ship's fuel tanks with 350 tons of FFO and it was cast off at 2150 and special sea dutymen went to their stations at 2350.

At twenty minutes past midnight on Tuesday 9 April, *Furious* weighed anchor and passed through the Clyde boom defence gate at 20 knots about an hour later, heading around the Mull of Kintyre for an anchorage off Campbeltown which she reached at 0405. The two Swordfish squadrons had been warned immediately to make preparations for embarkation and arrangements had been made with the Flag Officer in Charge, Greenock, for personnel and stores to be embarked in the patrol vessel *Gleaner* and the rescue tug *Englishman*. Both met the carrier as ordered off Campbeltown harbour at 0500 and the transfer of men and equipment was complete by 0730. Measures to embark 801 NAS would have taken a few more hours and delayed *Furious*' arrival at the rendezvous with *Warspite* but would have deployed fighters off the Norwegian coast a fortnight earlier than subsequently proved possible. Surely this would have been worth it but, clearly, the type and scale of enemy air attack on the fleet later in that day and subsequently against the Allied expeditionary force in Norway was underestimated and a valuable opportunity was missed. At 0740 she weighed anchor again and proceeded to a position where she could land on her aircraft, escorted by the destroyers *Maori*, *Ashanti* and *Fortune*. Despite the storms over the North Sea, winds were light and variable and the sea calm at first, allowing 816 NAS to embark from 0955. The weather worsened as the forenoon progressed, however, delaying the recovery of 818 NAS until 1030. *Furious* then headed north at her best speed for the rendezvous north of the Shetland Islands. After passing through the Minches she took advantage of the good weather and maintained 27.4 knots for fifteen hours, effectively her maximum speed and a creditable performance for such an old warship. She met the other warships off Muckle Flugga and proceeded with them to join the Home Fleet off Bergen at 0745 on 10 April.

Her Swordfish were ordered to prepare for a torpedo attack on ships in Bergen but when Admiral Forbes decided that conditions were too dangerous to operate in waters over which the Luftwaffe was already dominating, she moved north with three battleships and other units of the Home Fleet towards Trondheim in order to attack a force of enemy cruisers reported there. At 0350 on 11 April 1940 *Furious* detached from the main fleet to carry out the first strike operations in history to be launched from an aircraft carrier. (Twenty-two years earlier, seven RNAS Sopwith 2.F1 Camels had been launched to attack the German airship base at Tondern from the same ship before her conversion into a flush-deck carrier;[6] they could not land back on board and those that returned had to ditch near the fleet. Her aircraft were not, therefore, capable of sustained carrier strike operations like the Swordfish in 1940). The whole air group was flown off starting with the nine Swordfish of 816 NAS from 0409 and followed by all nine Swordfish of 818 NAS at 0448. All were armed with torpedoes and their aim, made clear in *Furious* Operation Order Number 1, was to attack an enemy cruiser of the *Blucher* class reported to be at anchor in Trondheim Roads. This was the first large-scale torpedo attack ever carried out in operational circumstances. The weather was given at the aircrew briefing as scattered strato-cumulus clouds at 2,000 feet in the fjords and valleys but clear to seaward.

Strike Against Trondheim Fjord, 11 April 1940

Aircraft	Pilot	Observer	TAG
816 NAS			
U4A	Capt. A R Burch RM	Lt Cdr H Gardner	LA L A Webber
U4B	S/Lt (A) N Ball	–	NA R Pike
U4C	Mid (A) C D Livingstone	NA J Bristow	
U4F	Lt A T Darley	Lt D Sanderson	NA T P Dwyer
U4G	Lt (A) K G Sharp	–	NA S M Oliver
U4H	Lt (A) J Reid	–	NA G M Thompson
U4K	Lt (A) F Whittingham	Lt O M Cheeke	LA F White
U4L	Lt (A) M D Donati	–	NA A Purchase
U4M	S/Lt (A) P J Broughton	–	LA A J Atkin
818 NAS			
U3A	Lt Cdr P Sydney-Turner	Lt W Kellet	PO W Dillnut
U3B	Lt P Whitfield	Lt D J Godden	–
U3C	S/Lt (A) K Appleton	–	LA T G Cutler
U3F	Lt (A) G Smith	Lt R Dyer	LA D Milliner
U3G	S/Lt (A) P C Roberts	–	LA J Skeats
U3H	S/Lt (A) G R Hampden	–	LA H Simpson

U3K	Lt (A) S Keane	Lt D Langmore	LA L O Clarke
U3L	S/Lt (A) J Appleby	–	LA E Tapping
U3M	Mid (A) D H Dammers	–	LA A J Sturgess

Note that torpedo bomber reconnaissance (TBR) squadrons usually flew in the sub-flights of three in which they would attack ships from differing directions and only the leading aircraft of sub-flights flew with an observer on strike missions. The others flew with only a TAG in the rear cockpit. Note also the greater number of short-service (A) officers in these TBR squadrons compared with the Skua squadrons.

816 NAS was formed up over the ship by 0418 and departed on a track of 130 degrees at a speed over the sea of 88 knots whilst climbing through broken cloud to 7,000 feet. U4M lost touch with the formation during the climb and at 0512 a small warship identified as possibly either a light cruiser or large destroyer was seen to be under way in Skorjen Fjord but it was not attacked. Trondheim Fjord was reached at 0514 and the leader manoeuvred to get up sun of the anchorage, which was largely obscured by cloud. At 0519 Captain Burch led his squadron in a dive towards the centre of the anchorage from about 8,000 feet. At 3,000 feet they broke clear below the cloud base but saw only four medium-sized merchant ships. The aircraft levelled off and searched toward Rodberget Light where a *Köln*-class cruiser had been reported; they saw a German destroyer steering south down the north arm of Trondheim Fjord but, hoping for a better target, the leader turned onto south and headed down the eastern side of the fjord. U4M rejoined the formation at this stage.

No targets considered suitable having been found, Captain Burch led 816 NAS back up through the cloud and headed toward Skorjen Fjord to investigate the first enemy vessel they had seen. They could not locate it but what appeared to be a small cruiser was seen at anchor in an inlet 3 miles south of Agdenes Light. By now it was

Furious in wartime camouflage. Note the small island added in 1938 and the pole mast with its Type 72 aircraft homing beacon. (Author's collection)

A torpedo-armed Swordfish of 816 NAS photographed from another as the squadron crossed the Norwegian coast for the strike against enemy ships reported to be in Trondheim Fjord on 11 April 1940. (Author's collection)

0549 and the enemy was probably fully alerted to the presence of strike aircraft in the Trondheim area and so it was decided to attack this target of opportunity. The enemy ship was subsequently identified as a destroyer during the attack and it opened fire as the Swordfish dived from about 8,000 feet, 3 miles to the north of it. This meant that the aircraft had to pass around the stern of the enemy ship whilst in the dive in order to gain a torpedo-dropping position to seaward on the beam. The leader released his torpedo 1,200 yards from the stationary target at a height of 60 feet, speed 110 knots. The parameters were ideal and it appeared to run true but detonated after only 400 yards. At least one other torpedo detonated prematurely and all tracks appeared to stop 500 to 600 yards short of the target. On their return to *Furious*, examination of a large-scale chart revealed that the torpedoes would probably have grounded on shoals at the mouth of the inlet. Because they had been briefed to attack ships in Trondheim Fjord, the chart had not been shown to aircrew at their briefing. Anti-aircraft fire from the destroyer consisted mainly of close-range weapons in which a considerable amount of red tracer was used. An ineffective barrage burst at about 4,000 feet, badly directed, which might have come from either the target or a shore battery immediately behind it. The squadron joined up again and, after a brief reconnaissance of the upper reaches of Skorjen Fjord, took departure from Halten Light for the carrier at 0604 and landed on from 0630. The results were disappointing and it was immediately clear that too much reliance had been placed on reports by RAF reconnaissance aircraft which were clearly out of date by the time they were received in the Home Fleet and passed on to *Furious* by the C-in-C in his signal 1410/10.

The main lesson drawn from this was that recent reconnaissance information was vital if strikes against time-sensitive targets such as enemy warships involved in a complicated invasion plan were to be effective. Carriers had the obvious advantage of short transit times in comparison with bombers that had to fly all the way from the UK but they still needed accurate information about the enemy. It was also realised that the choice of weapon in coastal water or other specialised conditions needed careful considerations and that bombs might have been a better choice in narrow fjords where shoals and lack of manoeuvring space made torpedo attack difficult. Admiralty policy regarded torpedoes as better ship-killing weapons than bombs but their tactical use would have to be considered against local conditions. The difficulties of littoral warfare had not been studied in depth before the war and viable tactics and weapons had to be evolved as experience was gained.

818 NAS's briefed objective was to attack a cruiser of the *Hipper* class reported to be in Trondheim Fjord by the same out-dated intelligence contained in the C-in-C's signal 1410/10. They took off immediately after 816 NAS and proceeded towards their objective at 500 feet on a heading of 144 degrees. Each of the three-aircraft flights flew in 'V' formation and followed astern of the CO's flight. Their intention was to avoid enemy units reported to be at Rodberget anchorage but landfall was made further north than intended and the anchorage was over-flown on the way to Trondheim Fjord. No opposition was encountered but in their open cockpits the aircrew detected a strong smell of cordite. A destroyer was seen at anchor in Strommen Fjord and then a U-boat which dived rapidly 15 cables south-west of Rodberget Point. No cruisers were seen but a destroyer of the *Leberecht Maass* class was seen proceeding at 12 knots up the fjord toward Trondheim. Lieutenant Commander Sydney-Turner ordered his flights into echelon port so that they could set up a torpedo attack on the enemy vessel from a relative bearing of Green 120. Two torpedoes were reported as exploding under the target's stern and it was assessed to be badly damaged. It was seen to stop in the water but, as the aircraft made their getaway, they lost sight of it up sun.

The low-flying approach and attack had been successful in achieving surprise as the aircraft were not seen against the background of wooded, snow-covered hills until the last moment. The launch position on the target's starboard quarter was accepted so that time and surprise were not squandered trying to gain a more advantageous position on the north side of the fjord opposite the defences ashore in Trondheim. The torpedoes had initially been set to run at 20 feet but two were altered in flight to run at 12 feet when the target was identified as a destroyer and not the cruiser for which they had been briefed. All used the high-speed setting and duplex pistols set to detonate on contact or magnetic influence. Two warheads were seen to explode prematurely, possibly due to bad drops, and one failed to drop since only one of its strops had released. This torpedo was successfully jettisoned on the way back to the carrier. All Swordfish returned safely to *Furious* and landed on from 0630. Lessons were assimilated quickly and the C-in-C ordered a thorough reconnaissance of the whole Trondheim area and 2 aircraft were flown off for this task at 1040.

816 NAS Reconnaissance of Trondheim Area, 11 April 1940

Aircraft	*Pilot*	*Observer*	*TAG*
U4B	S/Lt (A) J N Ball	Lt A S Marshall	NA R Pike
U4H	Lt (A) J Reid	S/Lt (A) K H Gibney	NA G B Thompson

U4B was armed with four 250lb bombs and U4H with two 250lb and eight 20lb bombs and by the time they launched the weather was good, briefed as fine with no cloud, wind south-westerly Force 3, sea calm with 20nm visibility: ideal conditions for the reconnaissance. They were briefed to search Trondheim and the adjacent fjords and, once this was complete, to attack targets of opportunity.

The aircraft arrived over Trondheim at 1200, searched the area and took photographs. A number of seaplanes were observed moored in Trondheim roadstead and another was secured astern of a large merchant ship, one of four seen in the harbour. This element of the briefed mission was completed at 1220 and they flew on to Skjoren Fjord where the small destroyer attacked earlier with torpedoes still lay at anchor. The Swordfish went into line astern with U4B leading and set themselves up for a dive-bombing attack from 4,000 feet. The destroyer was bows-on to the head of the fjord and the Swordfish attacked in 60-degree dives on the target's port beam, an approach angle less likely to be successful than attacking along the line of the ship. All six bombs were dropped in a single pass but none of them hit and the destroyer was seen to be getting under way hastily as the attack had developed. As earlier, anti-aircraft fire from the ship was ineffective. U4H was chased by an enemy seaplane as it withdrew but evaded it by flying low through the mountains before rejoining U4B near the coast. The presence of the seaplane showed how vulnerable the fleet was to shadowers of even modest performance without fighters embarked. The two Swordfish landed on at 1345 after which *Furious*, which had been operating independently for flying, rejoined the main body of the fleet which steamed north for operations off Narvik, where Captain Warburton-Lee's destroyer flotilla had been action the day before. Warburton-Lee had died on the bridge of *Hardy* and was posthumously awarded the Victoria Cross.

At 1500 *Valiant* gained radar contact on enemy aircraft approaching the fleet from astern and they were seen at 1540. At 1543 *Furious* opened fire on them with other ships and the enemy carried out a series of ineffective, level bombing attacks from high level. One stick of bombs fell astern of *Furious* but the only damage she suffered was caused by her own gunners, who shot away her starboard W/T aerials. The sea/air battle continued until about 1645 by which time *Furious* had expended about 500 rounds of 4-inch ammunition and a considerable quantity of close-range ammunition without, as far as was known, hitting anything. For most of the ship's company it would have been their first experience of action. After noon the weather gradually deteriorated again and by midnight there was a Force 9 gale which continued into the following forenoon with visibility no more than 3 or 4nm.

The Home Fleet's heavy units, including *Furious,* arrived off Vestfjord at 0500 on Friday 12 April and at 0700 Admiral Whitworth's Battlecruiser Squadron joined them. Two aircraft were flown off for reconnaissance at 0730 while aircraft of 816 and 818 NAS were ranged and armed ready for a strike by both squadrons against enemy warships that were expected to be in the Narvik area. Enemy aircraft were sighted to the east and at 1532 action stations were sounded in response to a threatened enemy air attack and *Furious* was ordered to join the Battlecruiser Squadron to be covered by their anti-aircraft fire power. At 1610, as soon as the air raid was over, *Furious* began to launch Swordfish for a strike. As by now normal, they took off in two groups, the first comprising eight aircraft of 818 NAS, followed forty minutes later by nine aircraft of 816 NAS.

Strike against Warships in Narvik, 12 April 1940

Aircraft	*Pilot*	*Observer*	*TAG*
818 NAS			
U3A	Lt Cdr P G O Sydney-Turner	Lt W B Kellet	PO W Dillnut
U3B	Lt P Whitfield	Lt D J Godden	-
U3C	S/Lt (A) K Appleton	–	LA T G Cutler
U3F	Lt (A) G Smith	Lt R Dyer	LA D Milliner
U3G	S/Lt (A) P C Roberts	–	LA G J Skeats
U3H	S/Lt (A) G R Hampden	–	LA H Simpson
U3K	Lt (A) S Keane	Lt D E Langmore	NA L O Clarke
U3L	S/Lt (A) S G J Appleby	–	LA E Tapping

816 NAS

U4A	Capt. A R Burch RM	Lt Cdr H Gardner	LA L A Webber
U4B	S/Lt (A) N Ball	Lt A S Marshall	NA R Pike
U4C	Mid (A) C D Livingstone	Lt W Keppel	NA J Bristow
U4F	Lt A T Darley	Lt D Sanderson	NA T P Dwyer
U4G	Lt (A) K G Sharp	–	NA S M Oliver
U4H	Lt (A) J Reid	–	NA G Thompson
U4K	Lt (A) F Whittingham	Lt O M Cheeke	LA F White
U4L	Lt (A) M D Donati	–	LA A J Smith
U4M	S/Lt (A) P J Broughton	–	LA A J Atkin

The aim of this strike, detailed in *Furious* Operation Order Number 2, was to attack with bombs enemy destroyers that had survived the encounter with Captain Warburton-Lee's flotilla on 10 April. All Swordfish were armed with four 250lb SAP bombs and six 20lb bombs but the weather continued to be bad with full cloud cover down to 300 feet in the fjords although the base rose to 2,800 feet over Narvik itself. The sea was rough with visibility between 5 cables and 2nm. Lieutenant Commander Sydney-Turner briefed his crews to carry out a low-flying attack because of the extensive cloud, and 818 NAS found the hilltops on both sides of Ofot Fjord and behind Narvik itself obscured but managed to get themselves into an attacking position. Just as the aircraft spread out to do so and the third flight was detached to be able to attack at right angles to the others, the cloud base lifted significantly, leaving the aircraft exposed and removing their element of surprise but it was too late to alter the plan and the attack was pressed home. Enemy fire from destroyers and light guns set up on the ore quay began as the first Swordfish tipped into its shallow dive. A total of twenty-eight 250lb bombs and forty-seven 20lb bombs was dropped, aircraft U3H suffering blown fuses which prevented it from dropping the heavier weapons. Considering the conditions, the short time for target tracking allowed by the shallow 30- to 45-degree dives and extensive enemy fire, the attacks were well executed and at least three hits were claimed on destroyers with more on the ore quay. The whole strike had been carried out under conditions in which the aircrew had no previous experience or training.

Enemy fire was effective and six Swordfish were hit, two of which were shot down. Lieutenant Commander Sydney-Turner's U3A, airframe number P4212, was hit in the petrol pipe and force landed near Skjelfjord in Lofoten after he had led his squadron away from the target area. He and his crew were unhurt and were rescued by the destroyer *Grenade*. U3L was shot down and crashed into Ofot Fjord on fire. Sub Lieutenant Appleby and Leading Airman Tapping also survived and were rescued by *Grenade*. Sub Lieutenant Roberts and Leading Airman Skeats were injured in the legs but managed to recover to *Furious* successfully in U3G.

Furious in rough weather. (Author's collection)

Lieutenant Keane in U3K had his undercarriage damaged and so, rather than block the flight deck by crashing, he gallantly remained airborne in the vicinity of the carrier until after the 816 NAS recovery.

816 NAS had launched after 818 but with the same aim. It departed *Furious* after forming up at 1712 with a ground speed of 104 knots and landfall was made on Lofotodden Point at 1730, after which Captain Burch led his squadron towards the narrows near Baroy Island. Low clouds obscured the clifftops and shore features could not be identified; strong and variable winds were encountered in the fjords and, with only photographic reproductions of Admiralty charts and no land maps showing contours, littoral navigation proved difficult. Four British destroyers were sighted during breaks in the snow between 1750 and 1805 and the correct challenges and replies were made. At 1808 they saw aircraft of 818 NAS returning to the carrier from Narvik but from 1810 the weather deteriorated still further with the cloud base at 100 feet and visibility reduced to about 200 yards in a heavy snow storm. With the impossibility of releasing bombs accurately under such conditions and the imminent risk of flying into the steep cliffs, Captain Burch decided to turn back. By then the squadron found itself in a ravine 500 yards wide with the flights in line astern. The difficult operation of turning through 180 degrees was managed successfully by each flight in turn.

A Heinkel He 111 bomber showing its defensive gun armament in nose, dorsal and ventral positions. Just visible at the extreme tail is a fixed, remotely controlled 7.9mm machine gun specifically intended to engage fighters drawn into a chasing position astern. (Author's collection)

At 1915 the squadron passed Little Molla where the wind was estimated to be from 240 degrees at 50 knots although the visibility improved somewhat. The destroyer *Grenade* was sighted on an opposite course and, when challenged, she passed the heartening news that Appleby and Tapping were safe. It took 816 until 2010 to reach its last navigational way point at Lofotodden Point, from which a heading of 303 degrees was set for the carrier at a ground speed of 88 knots. By then, it was already twenty-two minutes after sunset and since his pilots had no recent night deck landing practice, Captain Burch was concerned for their safety. He asked *Furious* for a DF bearing in order to reduce the time it would take to find her to the minimum but Captain Troubridge was also worried about his valuable aircrew and, despite the risk, he ordered searchlights to be shone in the direction from which he expected the aircraft to return. These were seen at 2016 and the request for the bearing was cancelled as it would have compromised the carrier's position over a much wider area. *Furious* itself was sighted at 2025 and the recovery commenced at 2030, much to the relief of Lieutenant Keane and his crew, who were still orbiting the ship. *Furious* was pitching badly in the heavy seas and Lieutenant Donati hit the deck with his port wing tip on landing and, although he had caught an arrester wire, his aircraft slewed over the port side and parted the wire in the process. Pilot and TAG were both rescued by *Hero*, the plane-guard destroyer. Only then did Lieutenant Keane land on and, despite having one wheel missing, he made a near-perfect landing after dark with only a few gallons of avgas remaining. With the aircraft losses and damage sustained on 12 April, the air group was reduced from eighteen to thirteen serviceable Swordfish.

At 2250 the battlecruisers and *Furious* rejoined the heavy squadron of the Home Fleet and preparations were made for the attack on enemy destroyers in the vicinity of Narvik to be carried out the next day, Saturday 13 April 1940, by surface ships under Admiral Whitworth, who was now to fly his flag in *Warspite* and enter the fjords in her with a force of nine destroyers. Subsequently known as the Second Battle of Narvik, carrier aircraft were briefed to play a significant part in this action, specifically:

An anti-submarine patrol searching ahead of *Warspite* as she entered Vestfjord;
A patrol over Baroy Island;
A patrol over Ramnes at the entrance to Ofot Fjord;
A striking force over Narvik.

The arrival of the aircraft at their several destinations was timed to coincide with the arrival of *Warspite* at those places in order to give the capital ship the maximum protection against unexpected developments as she made her way into the 40nm-long Ofot Fjord. *Warspite*'s own Swordfish was catapulted off, piloted by Petty Officer Airman F C Rice and commanded by Lieutenant Commander W L M Brown RN[7] before the battle commenced and it was to play a decisive part. It flew up and down along the long, narrow fjord locating German ships and warning of the approach of their torpedoes. Brown reported the German destroyer *Erich Kollner* waiting in ambush in Herjangsfjord ready to fire its torpedoes as the British ships passed. Forewarned, however, the British destroyers approached the danger point at speed with their guns and torpedo tubes already trained to starboard and smothered the German ship in fire. Later, flying at 1,000 feet, Rice and Brown saw a U-boat on the surface at the head of Herjangsfjord and promptly attacked it with the two 100lb anti-submarine bombs the Swordfish was carrying. One of them was seen to pass through the U-boat's open forward hatch before detonating and as Rice climbed away, Brown saw the hull of U-64 cocked up in the air as it sank with members of its crew swimming for the shore. In his subsequent ROP, Admiral Whitworth wrote that he doubted 'if a ship-borne aircraft had ever been used to such good purpose'. Brown was subsequently awarded the DSC and Rice the DSM for their actions on this day.

Two Swordfish were flown off for the anti-submarine patrol at 0630 and a single aircraft at 1050 for Baroy, after which the first two landed back on. Ten aircraft were flown off at 1215, one of which was for the Ramnes patrol and the remainder forming the Narvik strike force. While they were away another enemy air attack on the fleet developed which lasted until 1357. All the strike aircraft were armed with four 250lb bombs and eight 20lb bombs. The former were connected to the bomb distributor, the latter to the pilot's selector panel. One attacking dive was to be made by each aircraft, the bomb distributor being operated first and then the 20lb bombs were released.

816 and 818 NAS, Narvik Strike, 13 April 1940

Aircraft	*Pilot*	*Observer*	*TAG*
816 NAS			
U4A	Capt. A R Burch RM	Lt D Sanderson	LA L A Webber
U4C	Mid (A) C D Livingstone	–	NA J Bristow
U4G	Lt (A) K G Sharp	–	NA S M Oliver
U4K	Lt (A) F Whittingham	Lt O M Cheeke	LA F White
U4H	Lt (A) J Reid	–	NA G Thompson
U4M	S/Lt (A) P J Broughton	–	LA A J Atkin
818 NAS			
U3F	Lt (A) S Keane	Lt D E Langmore	NA L O Clarke
U3B	Lt P Whitfield	Lt R Dyer	LA J Blain
U3M	Mid (A) D H Dammers	–	LA A J Sturgess
U3C	S/Lt (A) G R Hampden	–	NA R Dale

Weather conditions remained bad with a cloud base at 500 feet, heavy rain and occasional snow showers. Visibility was 500 yards, increasing in places to 3nm. In the vicinity of Narvik it deteriorated still further. Despite this, the Baroy Island patrol got through and confirmed that the island was still unoccupied by the Germans. The aircraft exchanged identities with *Warspite* and then returned to *Furious*, its mission completed. The Ramnes patrol aircraft found the weather to be so bad that it was unable to get through and, therefore, the pilot searched adjacent fjords for U-boats and then returned.

The Narvik strike force launched from 1220 and proceeded to make a landfall at Lofotodden; the aircraft then proceeded along Vestfjord with the flights in line astern. At 1323 they neared Baroy Island and the weather improved dramatically to give a cloud base at 1500 feet with 5nm visibility. Five minutes later *Warspite* and her accompanying destroyers were seen proceeding along Ofot Fjord engaging the enemy with gunfire, the thunderous concussion of the 15-inch guns causing avalanches in the snow on the surrounding mountains. Gun flashes were seen from shore batteries at Narvik and from enemy destroyers manoeuvring in Herjangsfjord. Captain Burch led the strike force as high as he could below cloud at 1345; the force was timed to arrive at the moment the surface ships opened fire and it had succeeded in doing so. Individual aircraft then picked targets and attacked them in 60-degree dives from about 2,000 feet at which height the enemy destroyers could just be made out. The conditions were not ideal for accurate bombing but two hits were claimed and the effect of the air strike combined with the fire from the battleship and destroyers must have had a profound effect on enemy morale. In the confusion of evading enemy fire after attacks, damage caused by the bombs was difficult to assess but two straddles with 20lb bombs were claimed.

After attacking, aircrews had been briefed to make their way individually at low level to Baroy Island where the leader was to circle for twenty-five minutes waiting for others to join him. Two Swordfish of 818 NAS failed to arrive at the rendezvous. U3C was shot down and both Sub Lieutenant Hampden and Naval Airman Dale were subsequently reported missing. U3M was badly damaged by enemy fire but managed a successful forced landing ashore. Midshipman Dammers was wounded in the left hand but Leading Airman Sturgess was unhurt. U4G was badly damaged in the starboard upper mainplane, probably by a 37mm shell, but succeeded in making it back to *Furious*; its TAG, Naval Airman Oliver was slightly wounded by splinters. The remainder were undamaged and rejoined the leader for the return flight. Conditions in the narrows were as bad as before but the departure point was found and the aircraft flew the 60nm over the stormy sea with their usual accurate navigation. *Furious* sighted her returning aircraft at 1557 and turned into the gale force wind to recover them. The aircraft began landing-on at 1610 and completed the evolution in record time despite winds gusting to over 50 knots and a badly pitching deck. Considering that the visibility during this operation seldom exceeded 3 miles, the accuracy of Lieutenant Sanderson's navigation had played a key part in this successful naval operation and the signal 'BZ – manoeuvre well executed', received from the C-in-C Home Fleet as the last aircraft landed on, was largely due to him. Flying stations were secured at 1720. On 25 June Burch, Keane and Sanderson were awarded the DSC for their actions on this day; Skeats was awarded a DSM and Appleby, Roberts, Sydney-Turner and Tapping were mentioned in despatches.

Overnight the fleet steamed north to be in the vicinity of Andenes Light by 0600 on Sunday 14 April. No major flying operations were attempted but three reconnaissance sorties were flown off at 0600 to search Vaags and adjacent fjords and to photograph targets listed by the staff. The weather had, by then, moderated, and the sun shone. The objectives were accomplished without incident and the aircraft returned between 0930 and 1000. At 1220, two further Swordfish were flown off to investigate Tromso, where the enemy had been reported landing but no sign of hostile forces was seen. They returned and landed on at 1530 and at 2050 *Furious* was detached with orders to proceed to Tromso, refuel and then to operate under the orders of the Flag Officer (FO) Narvik. However, it transpired that the oiler *War Pindari* was not due for another two days and *Furious*' fuel reserves, although low, were sufficient for another day's flying and it was decided that she should continue the reconnaissance of Vaags Fjord and the Narvik area from a position inside the islands, roughly 70N 20E. A new escort comprising the destroyers *Isis*, *Ilex* and *Imogen* joined *Furious* off Fugloy Island at 0600 on 15 April and the group entered a lonely fjord which, having no name on the Admiralty chart, was named as '*Furious* Fjord'. Three aircraft were launched at

1050, one briefed to photograph the Narvik area and two to carry out an anti-submarine patrol in Vaags Fjord. Regrettably, despite the excellent weather conditions, the camera in the reconnaissance aircraft malfunctioned but the observer carried out a visual search and reported eleven enemy aircraft parked on the frozen Lake Hartvig, near Bjerkvik north of Narvik. It was decided to attack them immediately. The two anti-submarine aircraft had seen British troops being landed at Harstad but had not located any U-boats despite one being reported near Andenes Light. A single aircraft was launched to prosecute this potential threat at 1514 and returned at 1830 having seen no sign of it.

816 and 818 NAS, Lake Hartvig Strike, 15 April 1940

Aircraft	*Pilot*	*Observer*	*TAG*
816 NAS			
U4H	Capt. A R Burch RM	Lt Cdr H Gardner	NA G Thompson
U4B	S/Lt (A) J Ball	Lt A S Marshall	NA R Pike
U4C	Mid (A) C Livingstone	Lt W Keppel	NA J Bristow
U4F	Lt A T Darley	Lt D Sanderson	NA T Dwyer
U4K	Lt (A) K G Sharp	S/Lt (A) M Cardwell	LA F White
U4M	S/Lt (A) P Broughton	Mid (A) W Bland RNVR	LA A J Atkin
818 NAS			
U3B	S/Lt (A) P C Roberts	S/Lt (A) C Simpson	LA J Blain
U3F	Lt (A) G Smith	Lt R Dyer	LA D Milliner
U3K	Lt (A) S Keane	Lt D Langmore	NA L O Clark

The weather for the strike was good with visibility in excess of 10nm and cloud limited to light strato-cumulus near the mountain tops. All aircraft were armed with eight 20lb bombs which, it was thought, would have a greater impact spread than 250lb bombs whilst still causing damage or destruction to aircraft in the open with blast or fragments. Additionally, one aircraft carried two 250lb SAP bombs to see what effect these would have on the frozen lake surface. The launch commenced at 1726 after which the aircraft formed up quickly and headed for Rolla Island where they made landfall before navigating accurately to Lake Hartvig. The attacking run was made from an initial point 5 miles to the west of the lake and each Swordfish pilot was briefed to select one enemy aircraft as his target and release all his bombs in a single pass in a 40-degree dive at 700 feet. All bombs released from their aircraft correctly with no hang-ups. At least two direct hits were observed and most other bombs dropped sufficiently close to have caused damaged. Four Swordfish used their front guns to strafe aircraft and reported a number of hits; the flattened ice that constituted the runway was rendered unserviceable by a number of bomb hits and the 250lb bombs actually caused large holes in the ice.

A Swordfish floatplane, identical to the one embarked in *Warspite,* being hoisted inboard from the water by the ship's crane. (Author's collection)

There was a great deal of enemy anti-aircraft fire from close-range weapons situated around the edges of the lake and U4B, airframe number P4167, was hit in the petrol tank and a small explosion followed which caused a fire on the port side of the engine. Sub Lieutenant Ball managed to extinguish the fire by diving towards Herjangsfjord but had insufficient fuel to fly back to the carrier so he ditched in Ofot Fjord alongside the destroyer *Zulu* which used its whaler to rescue the crew. The observer, Lieutenant Marshall, jettisoned the Syko encrypting machine before ditching but managed to retain the Naval Aircraft Code Book (copy Number 34) and Observers' Confidential Note Book. Midshipman Bland in U4M was slightly wounded in the left leg by a bullet. *Furious*, having recovered the anti-submarine patrol, proceeded into the open sea from 'her' fjord and prepared to recover the strike force after sunset. The aircraft did not return until 2200, well after dark, and *Furious* had to switch on all her deck lights to help the pilots. The full extent of enemy opposition was revealed after the aircraft had landed when it was discovered that four aircraft were damaged. Both U4H and U4K had spars holed and broken in their starboard mainplanes and were lucky to have made it back to the ship, both examples of how sturdy and reliable Swordfish were. The other two had numerous bullet holes, including some in U4M's dinghy.

Furious remained at sea overnight before anchoring off Tromso at 0600 on 16 April with only 27 per cent fuel remaining. Contact was made with the British

Consul and the local Norwegian naval authorities. The latter proved most helpful and provided maps and charts of the Narvik area besides revealing that 12,000 tons of FFO were available in the port. A lighter containing 1,000 tons was organised immediately and arrived at 1500. There was, however, the problem of how to pump the fuel from the lighter into the carrier. Several expedients were tried but the eventual ingenious solution came from the Tromso Fire Brigade who offered two fire engines which proved to be able to pump the oil at an acceptable rate. The process was slow, however and took the whole of 17 April.

Operational plans for the next period at sea needed to be made but, since being placed under the orders of the Flag Officer Narvik, Admiral of the Fleet Lord Cork and Orrery, *Furious* had not heard from him and nor was it known for certain where he was. Captain Troubridge decided, therefore, that in the absence of any new instructions his aircraft would continue to fly reconnaissance flights in the Vaags Fjord/Narvik area. An officer was sent to Narvik in a Norwegian flying boat to try to establish contact with the Flag Officer; meanwhile *Furious* completed refuelling, cast off the lighter at 0545 and sailed from Tromso at 1200 on 18 April. Two of the ship's motor boats were lowered, armed with depth charges and instructed to patrol Langsund to prevent U-boats gaining access to the fjord. Once in open water, three aircraft were flown off, one to photograph the Narvik area, one to reconnoitre Vaags Fjord and, whilst doing so to try to locate Flag Officer Narvik, and a third to reconnoitre to seaward of *Furious* Fjord.

At 1350 while *Furious* was passing through Gros Sundet, an enemy aircraft was sighted to the north at about 7,000 feet. It was engaged by gunfire but carried out two slow and deliberate level bombing attacks from the starboard beam without being deterred. On the first pass six small bombs were dropped as sighters, which missed by a considerable margin. On the second pass two large bombs were dropped which narrowly missed the flight deck and detonated in the water about 15 yards off *Furious*' port side. The shock from the explosions was felt throughout the ship and, shortly afterwards, it was noticed that the starboard inner high-pressure turbine was vibrating badly and making unusual noises. This turbine had given trouble before but there had been insufficient time to repair it in the recent refit. After its attack, the enemy aircraft remained overhead for some minutes watching for results before flying away to the south. The lack of embarked fighters to deal with such a threat needs no further mention.

At 1515 two of the reconnaissance aircraft were landed on. The Vaags Fjord patrol had exchanged signals with the cruiser *Enterprise* in which Flag Officer Narvik was embarked and had informed him that *Furious* was awaiting his instructions. This aircraft also reported that the weather to the south had deteriorated with extensive snow storms which looked bad for the Narvik patrol aircraft, which needed to climb to over 7,000 feet for a direct return to the carrier over mountains. It would have barely enough fuel for a low-level return around the coast. *Furious* waited for the aircraft near the briefed recovery position until it must certainly have reached

Map of the North Sea and Norwegian littoral, the battle-space in April/May 1940.

the limit of its endurance and then proceeded to Tromso. Shortly afterwards it was learnt that the aircraft had hit a power cable strung across a fjord near Tromso and had crashed at Kvalsund, killing Lieutenant Whittingham the pilot and seriously injuring his observer Lieutenant Cheeke. The TAG, Leading Airman White, was slightly injured and both Cheeke and White had been rescued by a Norwegian ship.

Now that the Luftwaffe had located the carrier she could not continue to operate near Tromso without fighter cover but before she could move far it was necessary to take on fuel from *War Pindari*. *Furious* anchored off Tromso at 2100 on 18 April, taking the opportunity to open the damaged turbine casing. Several blades were found to be broken and so it was decided to disconnect the starboard inner shaft and to run on the remaining three shafts, so as not to cause further damage but retain sufficient speed to operate aircraft. On 19 April *War Pindari* came alongside at 0200 and fuel oil was transferred. At 0730 enemy aircraft were reported to be approaching Tromso by Norwegian intelligence and the cruisers *Devonshire* and *Berwick* cleared the harbour at 0800, Admiral Cunningham in the former instructing *Furious* to do the same as soon as she had embarked enough fuel to satisfy her immediate need. Another air raid warning was received at 0830, fuelling was stopped and *War Pindari* cast off at 0900. *Furious* then cleared the harbour at 20 knots, her best speed, with air raid sirens wailing ashore but, fortuitously, Tromso was then obscured by a snow storm.

She made for the open sea intending to be in a position 30nm west of Andenes Light at dawn on 20 April from where sorties ordered by Flag Officer Narvik could be flown. However, at 0804 on 19 April a signal was received from the C-in-C Home Fleet warning that five enemy destroyers were heading north with the possible destination of Narvik and, prudently, a reconnaissance aircraft was flown off to search ahead of *Furious*. Unfortunately, when this aircraft, U3K, returned at 2000 the ship was enveloped in a blinding snow storm and, despite its close proximity, Lieutenant Keane was unable to locate it. After waiting and hoping for a clearance until his fuel became critically low, he was ordered to divert ashore. He made a forced landing on the frozen shore of Skogsfjord near Ringvassoy at 2030 and while he and his crew, Lieutenant Marshall and Naval Airman Clark, were subsequently rescued unhurt, the aircraft was a write-off. This reduced *Furious*' air group to only nine Swordfish and she was nearing the end of what she could practically achieve.

Furious arrived at her pre-arranged launch position at 0230 on 20 April. There was already enough light to fly but the weather was atrocious with violent snow storms that reduced visibility to zero. Some aircraft might have reached Narvik but the prospect of recovering them afterwards was negligible and, since so few remained Captain Troubridge took the decision to postpone flying operations and FO Narvik was so advised. Troubridge added, however, that should the Admiral consider missions to be vital, aircraft would be launched at all costs. *Furious* then turned out to sea, planning to return at 1500 in case the weather had shown signs

Captain T H Troubridge RN photographed later in the Second World War when he commanded the aircraft carrier *Indomitable*. (Author's collection)

of improvement but in fact it continued to deteriorate and by 2200 gusts of wind measured 60 knots in continuing snow fall. She returned to the launch position at 0230 on 21 April, by when the weather had moderated slightly. Six aircraft were flown off, three for a reconnaissance of Narvik and three for a reconnaissance of Vestfjord, both tasks having been ordered by FO Narvik. The Narvik aircraft returned in less than an hour having encountered low clouds inshore which prevented them from flying over land or in the fjords. The Vestfjord aircraft were recalled and all landed on safely. If his aircraft were to make any meaningful contribution to military operations ashore at Narvik, Captain Troubridge realised that the carrier would have to move to a position where its aircraft would not have to climb over 7,000-foot mountains to reach their objectives. A major assault was planned for 22 April and F O Narvik considered it highly desirable that as many aircraft as possible should support it. Accordingly, it was decided to shift the operating area to a position west of the southern Lofoten Islands from which aircraft could fly low over the sea, even in snow storms, to reach their objectives. The disadvantage, of course, was the 150nm transit to Narvik which allowed the Swordfish only an hour on task if they were to return with enough fuel to locate the carrier and land on safely.

Bomb-armed Swordfish U4B of 816 NAS taking part in the attack on shipping in Narvik on 12 April 1940. (Author's collection)

The new area was reached at 0300 on 22 April in a heavy blizzard under solid cloud cover. By 0800, however, patches of blue sky were visible with snow showers reduced to fifteen to twenty minutes' duration. A 'ripple' flying programme was begun which aimed to keep one or two aircraft over Narvik constantly in order to discourage the Luftwaffe from dropping supplies to the beleaguered German garrison by parachute. Each Swordfish was armed with four 250lb bombs and the crews were given pre-briefed targets on which to drop them if, at the end of their time on task, no target of opportunity had been attacked. The first aircraft, U3B, launched at 0810 followed by U3G an hour later. U3B reached Narvik at 0945, approaching from the south-west and circled the town looking for suitable targets. Rombaks Fjord was searched next and it was noticed that the railway line was in use as far as the tunnel at Straumaness but not beyond. The aircraft's briefed route then followed the road from Oyord to Lake Haln, which appeared to have snowdrifts on it, over a stranded German destroyer near Troldviken, which appeared to have sunk, and past Lake Hartvig which was found to have no aircraft on it. U3B then returned to Rombaks Fjord in order to bomb the railway at Forsneest, east of the tunnel. All four bombs dropped correctly and two hits were observed. No movement was seen in Narvik but railway trucks appeared to have been shunted and roads used recently.

U3B landed on at 1200 and minutes later the cruiser *Aurora* reported that U3G, airframe number P4163, had been shot down over Narvik by German anti-aircraft fire and crashed north of the town. The observer, Lieutenant Messenger, and TAG, Leading Airman Cutler, died of their wounds but the pilot, Lieutenant Roberts, was only slightly injured and was rescued by a boat from *Aurora*. A third aircraft, U4F, had been launched at 1010 and flew through heavy snow up Vestfjord into Ofot Fjord. A break allowed it to climb to 2,000 feet over Bogen where no sign of German activity was seen. Lakes in the vicinity were checked and found to be unused by enemy aircraft. It then flew to Rombaks Fjord where *Aurora* warned the crew by flashing light about the effective German anti-aircraft fire from positions in Narvik. At 1210 U4F bombed the railway at Sletts, all four 250lb bombs being released as a stick by the distributor using a shallow dive technique from 2,000 feet. No hits were seen, however, and the aircraft then made its way to the west, flying down the fjords at 50 feet in heavy snow that reduced visibility to 2 cables or less. The crew, which comprised Lieutenants Darley and Sanderson with Naval Airman Dwyer, described this sortie as their worst; Darley was so exhausted that he had to be helped from the cockpit after landing on safely.

U3H took off at 1104 and found blizzards with cloud on the deck when it reached the coast. The crew attempted to get into Vestfjord by passing Baroy Island on both sides but neither was successful and they turned back, joining U4F as they did so. U4G and U4C were launched at 1215 but they too encountered appalling weather conditions at Baroy Island and returned. They were fortunate to land on just before a snow storm reduced visibility around the ship to zero. Continued attempts to fly were clearly not worth the risk and so, since the escorting destroyers were short of fuel, it was decided to head for Vaags Fjord for the double purpose of obtaining fuel and attempting to communicate with FO Narvik. During the passage, a signal was received from FO Narvik which gave instructions for the support the army would need for its attack on Narvik, which had been postponed until 24 April, a change that had not been communicated to *Furious*. Andenes Light was identified at 0300 on 23 April and *Furious* had aircraft ready to fly if necessary but the weather remained bad, making the entry into Topsundet Fjord an anxious affair in low visibility. FO Narvik was just sailing in the cruiser *Effingham* but ordered *Furious* to anchor in Bygden Fjord to refuel from a tanker that was due in the afternoon. The opportunity was taken to make contact with the military headquarters ashore and with the cruiser *Southampton* which was acting as anti-aircraft guard ship to try to gather intelligence about the forthcoming attack so that aircrew could be adequately briefed about how best they could provide support for it.

The engine room staff had begun to notice peculiar noises coming from the port outer high-pressure turbine and after anchoring the casing was opened so that it could be examined and several blades were found to be missing. The C-in-C was informed and his staff ordered that shaft to be disconnected, leaving the ship with only two serviceable shafts out of four. *Furious* remained in Bygden Fjord awaiting the tanker, which did not arrive until 2030 on 24 April. Weather conditions remained atrocious with visibility seldom exceeding a cable in heavy snow. During that afternoon the carrier was ordered to return to the UK forthwith in order to carry out urgent repairs and replace the aircraft lost by her depleted squadrons. Both the ship and her naval air squadrons were exhausted and there was little more that they could have done. She sailed at 0900 on 25 April escorted by the destroyers *Isis*, *Ilex* and *Imogen*, passing the Andenes Light at 1600 and at 2300 the destroyers *Delight*, *Diana* and *Imperial* joined her screen. On 26 April aircraft were flown off for anti-submarine patrols with others to be air-tested after repair work. Constant searches were carried out in the areas ahead of the force and despite deteriorating weather *Imogen* gained an Asdic contact on 27 April at 1010 and attacked with three patterns of depth charges. Quantities of bubbles were subsequently seen on the surface and responsible lookouts claimed to have seen a periscope break surface briefly but there was no hard evidence that a U-boat had been sunk. *Delight*, *Diana* and *Imperial* detached to enter Scapa Flow at 1800 on 27 April but *Furious* and her escort continued to the Clyde where the repairs were to be carried out. She continued to fly anti-submarine patrols until 1000 on 29 April when fog put a stop to them as she passed west of the Hebrides. The Clyde gate was passed at 0728 on 29 April and *Furious* anchored in P4 berth at 0803. Work to clean the ship after weeks spent in action began immediately and lower deck was cleared to pay the men. Divisions, with virtually the whole ship's company fallen in on the flight deck, were held at 1500 on 30 April.

Thus ended a deployment that had seen an aircraft carrier in prolonged action for the first time in history and it was appropriate that this historic ship, on which Squadron Commander Dunning RNAS had carried out the first landing on a warship under way[8] in 1917 and which had so many other links with the Navy's early carrier experiments, was the one to do it. Massed torpedo attacks had been carried out on enemy warships, shore targets had been bombed effectively and military forces ashore had been supported against superior enemy forces on land and in the air. All these had been new forms of warfare and there were some who thought that these were not 'proper' tasks for naval aviation but, thankfully, there were many more senior officers who realised that pre-war dogma had been wrong and that aircraft carriers and their aircraft, taken together as what would now be described as a weapons system, represented the most effective way of deploying tactical aircraft in such unforeseen circumstances. As it developed, the Second World War would abound with operations that followed the example set by *Furious* and her handful of Swordfish aircraft. Though her sorties were limited in size, the scope and purpose of her operations rapidly became normal in both the RN and USN. Captain Troubridge's subsequent report of proceedings gives insight into the changes that converted the theory of peacetime operation into the harsh reality of war during the first combat deployment by any aircraft carrier. Significantly, he observed that Admiral Forbes' order to fly in bad weather on 12 April was the catalyst for further successful operations in adverse weather since it had given the aircrew confidence. The ability of *Furious*' navigating officer to put the ship in the pre-briefed recovery position on every occasion also did much to improve aircrew morale and set a standard of professionalism that many later generations of navigators would do well to study. He was subsequently decorated for his important part in the campaign.

The self-imposed limitations caused by the absence of 801 NAS were keenly felt. Troubridge noted that the Luftwaffe attack on the fleet on 11 April and the attack on *Furious* by a lone bomber on 18 April – the latter having time to drop sighting bombs undisturbed by anti-aircraft fire – might have turned out very differently had Skuas been able to intercept the enemy. With her own fighter protection he felt that *Furious* could have operated much nearer Narvik in the later stages of the deployment, thus maximising the use of TBR aircraft over the land. From the material point of view, he saw the Swordfish as too slow to carry out attacks in daylight when the element of surprise was absent; seventeen of the eighteen aircraft embarked were hit at some time by enemy fire and it was fortunate that more had not been lost. *Furious*' aircraft had operated in roles that had never been foreseen for naval aviation before the reality of war made them imperative. This led Troubridge to make a number of detailed recommendations to improve future carrier capabilities. These included embarking general purpose, as well as semi-armour piercing bombs and comprehensive map coverage of land areas in which ships were likely to operate. A second cypher book should be carried in aircraft carriers as the amount of signal traffic needed to brief and operate aircraft had overloaded the decoding team on his ship with their single volume. This had led to delays of over four hours in clearing signal traffic, which was quite unacceptable. Another point, quickly grasped, was the vital need for a debriefing team. Before the war, returning aircrew had told the captain and Commander 'Air' about the success or failure of their mission. Off Norway in April 1940 the captain and his flying staff were far too busy operating the ship and generating new sorties to give sufficient attention to this task and, in any case, the wealth of material produced by returning aircrew was so varied (Troubridge used the word 'amazing') that it would 'require the analysing powers of a King's Counsel' to gather a coherent picture from it. Pilots were trained to concentrate on their getaway after a torpedo attack and it was considered important that an observer should be specifically briefed to watch for the results of attacks in the minutes between weapon release and potential impact.

The last paragraph of Captain Troubridge's report,[9] written while the ship was on passage to the Clyde, cannot leave the reader unmoved:

> It is difficult to speak without emotion of the pluck and endurance of the young officers and men, some of them Midshipmen, who flew their aircraft to such good effect. Once their baptism of fire had been successfully undergone their morale and spirit rose as each obstacle was in turn successfully surmounted. All were firing their first shot, whether torpedo, bomb or machine-gun in action, many made their first night landing on 11 April and, undeterred by the loss of several of their shipmates, their honour and courage remained throughout as dazzling as the snow covered mountains over which they so triumphantly flew.

Statistics

Distance flown by *Furious*' aircraft:	23,870nm
Bombs dropped:	250lb SAP: 116 20lb HE: 293 total weight: 15.25 tons
Torpedoes dropped:	18
Aircraft lost:	9
Aircraft damaged:	17, but no aircraft was damaged beyond the capacity of the ship's air engineering team to repair it.
Photographs taken:	295
Casualties:	3 killed 2 missing 5 wounded 2 injured

Chapter 15

HM Ships Ark Royal *and* Glorious *in Action off Norway*

The scale of attack the Luftwaffe could generate against the Home Fleet and Allied forces committed to operations in central Norway had come as an unpleasant shock. By early in the afternoon of 9 April Admiral Forbes had already realised that his choice of sea operating area depended more on the Luftwaffe's radius of action than the potential presence of enemy surface ships and the lack of aircraft carriers within his force immediately became a limiting factor. Considering the months of planning at the insistence of the First Lord that had preceded British plans to precipitate activity in the Norwegian littoral by laying mines inside territorial waters and the potential German sensitivity over its iron ore supplies through Narvik, this lack of air cover is surprising. What is even more surprising in retrospect is that the Admiralty War Staff thought that the Home Fleet could cope with whatever action followed activities off the Norwegian coast without an aircraft carrier forming part of the Home Fleet. *Furious* was just out of refit and was ordered to sail as an afterthought without previously concentrating her naval air squadrons where they could be ready to embark at short notice. *Ark Royal* and *Glorious* were absent in the Mediterranean for what was described as 'essential training for new pilots as the Fleet Air Arm expanded'.[1] Both were recalled to the UK after 9 April and plans formulated to use them to cover the landing of military forces in central Norway: Operation DX.

In the opening stages of the Norwegian campaign, for which *Furious* had sailed so hastily, the Admiralty had anticipated a fleet-on-fleet action at sea. When British and French troops were landed at Namsos and Åndalsnes on 14 April 1940 a new phase began in which the Allies found themselves committed to operations ashore for which they were unprepared and largely defenceless against overwhelming air attack by the Luftwaffe. Their original aim had been to surround Trondheim and then drive the enemy out of it to recover the port and its nearby airfields which were regarded as the key location from which central Norway would be controlled, but German tactical air power appeared to make this difficult if not impossible. Within hours of the first major clash between Allied and German forces the argument put forward by the bomber lobby in the Air Ministry and accepted by successive British governments – that air attacks on enemy factories and cities would be the principal means of waging any future war – was exposed for the fallacy that it was. The effective defeat of the Allied Expeditionary Force in Norway can be blamed

Ark Royal turning into wind to launch aircraft. (Author's collection)

squarely on those who had dismantled the Army's tactical air force after 1919 and refused to allow the RN to procure the aircraft it needed to create a fast, mobile strike force capable of taking the fight inland from the sea. However, while the Army had no tactical air arm of its own, the RN did have its own carrier force and even though its aircraft might not be the best of their kind, they were still able to put up a gallant fight in support of the men ashore, as we shall see.

The Home Fleet did what it could to support the Army from the outset. Warships were anchored close inshore to provide high-angle anti-aircraft fire over the harbours where troops and their supplies were landed. Far from providing the necessary air cover as proponents of joint operations had requested before the war, the RAF now declared itself unable to do anything unless the Navy provided ships to move its aircraft to Norway and to transport the fuel, ammunition, maintenance personnel and aircraft spares that would be needed to sustain them in action. They also required engineers ashore to construct temporary airfields for them to use and troops to protect them. The obvious advantages of aircraft carriers that were not only mobile airfields but which provided their own technical and logistic support had been rejected over the previous two decades by politicians with their own agendas and the Air Ministry which had wanted to follow its own concept of warfare with little sympathy for the needs of its sister service ministries. Unfortunately for the troops on the ground in Norway, there was no time to put matters right before Norway fell.

Ark Royal and *Glorious* were recalled to join the Home Fleet as soon as possible. They arrived in Scapa Flow and refuelled before embarking their Skua squadrons and sailed later on the same day. Vice Admiral Wells, Vice Admiral Aircraft Carriers (VAA), flew his flag in *Ark Royal* and he was given specific operational orders by Admiral Forbes which were contained Home Fleet Memorandum HF01325/629 dated 22 April 1940. He was instructed to deploy the Aircraft Carrier Squadron into a position in the Norwegian littoral where it could provide fighter protection for the Allied expeditionary forces in Namsos and Åndalsnes and Allied shipping in the area. In doing so it was accepted that his ships would be within range of the Luftwaffe bomber force by then stationed in southern Norway. He was also to use both his Skuas and Swordfish to attack enemy aircraft, airfields and shipping in the Trondheim area and to disembark an RAF Gladiator squadron to operate from the frozen Lake Lesjaskogvann inland from Åndalsnes. Admiral Wells was also instructed by the Admiralty to carry out a detailed reconnaissance of Lake Jonsvatnet which, it was thought, might be used as an airfield by the enemy. The radar-equipped cruiser *Curlew* was included in the carrier task force specifically to provide fighter direction that would enable enemy aircraft to be intercepted as far as possible from the fleet. This was the first use of planned defence in depth by any navy in which fighters formed an outer layer under radar control, medium guns fired a barrage through which the enemy must fly to attack and close-range weapons engaged individual targets. Other ships in Admiral Wells' Operation DX task force included the cruiser *Berwick* and the destroyers *Hyperion*, *Hereward*, *Hasty*, *Fearless*, *Fury* and *Juno*.

Admiral Wells had to select an area for flying operations that was sufficiently near the coast to allow three Skuas to be maintained on CAP over both Namsos and Åndalsnes throughout the lengthening hours of daylight and from which the flexibility of the Skua could be used to strike targets in Trondheim on their way to the CAP station. It was not known when the airfield on the frozen lake would be ready to receive the RAF Gladiators of 263 Squadron which were to be flown off *Glorious* as soon as readiness ashore was signalled.[2] The RAF pilots had said that they would be unable to navigate from the sea to their new airfield and so two Skuas were held in readiness to lead them ashore in two groups and locate Lake Lesjaskogvann for them. The C-in-C Home Fleet's orders called for flying operations to begin on 24 April as soon as the carriers arrived within range of their objectives but, somewhat optimistically, they instructed Operation DX to cease as soon as the RAF Gladiator squadron was established ashore. Unfortunately, there was no direct communication between the Army ashore and the carriers but the means of doing so was investigated urgently.

In carrying out his orders Admiral Wells was conscious that, for the first time in history, carrier-borne aircraft were to operate in prolonged operations off a hostile coast in the face of a better-equipped land-based air force. The carrier task force sailed from Scapa Flow at 1315 on 23 April and passed west of the Orkney and Shetland Islands before turning east to reach a position at 64 34N 07 00E, approximately equidistant at 120nm from Namsos, Trondheim and Åndalsnes, the maximum distance at which it was thought possible to operate fighter CAPs over the forces ashore.

Embarked Aircraft of Operation DX, 23 April 1940

Ark Royal

800 NAS:	9 Skuas and 2 Rocs
801 NAS:	9 Skuas and 3 Rocs
810 NAS:	12 Swordfish
820 NAS:	9 Swordfish
Ship's flight:	1 Walrus (intended for SAR duties)

Glorious

802 NAS:	9 Sea Gladiators
803 NAS:	11 Skuas
804 NAS:	9 Sea Gladiators
263 RAF Squadron:	18 Gladiators

The planned flying programme on 24 April was ambitious. 800 NAS was to fly off three Skuas, 6K, 6L and 6M, led by Lieutenant K V V Spurway RN to CAP over Åndalsnes followed by three 801 NAS Skuas, 7K, 7L and 7C, led by Lieutenant C P Campbell-Horsfall RN to CAP over Kyam. Simultaneously Swordfish and Skuas from *Ark Royal* were to be launched for strikes against targets in the Trondheim area. From 1000 in the last stages of the approach to the combat area, *Glorious* had maintained three Sea Gladiators on CAP over the task force and *Ark Royal* maintained two Swordfish on anti-submarine patrol. Both patrols were of two hours' duration with aircraft landing on when they saw their reliefs take off. The CAP fighters were briefed to remain in the vicinity of the carriers and not to chase off after enemy aircraft which withdrew after they made an interception and to keep a sharp lookout for shadowing aircraft, especially flying boats, at low level that might have approached under the radar coverage.

Instructions for the strikes were contained in VAA's memorandum AC 0565 dated 23 April 1940 which called for nine Swordfish to attack enemy aircraft reported on the frozen Lake Jonsvatnet by a reconnaissance aircraft a day earlier. In addition to the CAPs, five Skuas were to attack seaplanes reported at anchor in

Trondheim and cover the Swordfish strike. Six further Swordfish were to strike Vaernes airfield, six Skuas were to strike shipping in Trondheim harbour and a further six were to search fjords in the vicinity of Trondheim for enemy warships, which were to be attacked immediately if found. After all these attacks, aircraft were to search for enemy landing grounds and seaplane bases out to 10nm from Trondheim.

In the event heavy snow showers disrupted the flying programme from 1330 onwards but the CAP flights got airborne from *Ark Royal* at 1635 and made a landfall at Bud where they found the weather to be better with extreme visibility. They saw little activity beneath them and decided not to strafe what they thought were German troops at one point because it was found difficult to distinguish friend from foe, or even the lines being held, in the deep snow. Their return was helped by Leading Airman Clayton of 801 NAS in 7L who showed considerable initiative by improvising changes to his R 1110 W/T set which enabled him to obtain beacon bearings from *Ark Royal* at this extreme range. They returned to the coast at Bud in deteriorating weather and both 6M and 6K suffered engine failures and ditched near their carrier. Both crews were rescued by destroyers and the remaining four landed on at 2045.

803 NAS Army Support over Åndalsnes, 24 April 1940

Section	*Pilot*	*Observer/TAG*	*Aircraft*
Blue Leader	Lt W P Lucy	Lt M C E Hanson	7F
2	Lt A B Fraser-Harris	LA G S Russell	7G
3	Lt J M Christian	NA S G Wright	7H
Red Leader	Lt L A Harris RM	PO K G Baldwin	7P
2	Lt C H Filmer	NA H Pickering	7Q
3	Sub Lt A T Easton	NA A J Hayman	7C

803 NAS's strike was led by Bill Lucy and comprised two flights, Blue and Red, each of three Skuas. They took off from *Glorious* at 1639 and crossed the coast in company at 6,000 feet over Bjornsund, climbing to 8,000 feet over Åndalsnes. A British cruiser and two escort vessels were seen in Romsdals Fjord as the aircraft headed up Romsdalen Valley. At 1755 a Heinkel He 111 was seen flying in the opposite direction along the valley, bombing the railway line between Kors and Lymbas. Both sections attacked it with front guns and it was seen to crash. At 1810 a second He 111 was seen flying up the valley in the vicinity of Lake Lesjaskogvann and was attacked by individual aircraft, the flights having become split up during the first attack. Hits were seen on this aircraft which dived away and jettisoned its bombs. At 1820 a Dornier Do 17 was seen and attacked by Bill Lucy and Christian

but the latter had expended all his front-gun ammunition and his attack was carried out with the TAG's rear gun. An RAF officer, Squadron Leader Straight, on the ice at Lesjaskogvann subsequently confirmed seeing the two Heinkels crash and the Dornier was recorded as damaged.

By 1825 all six Skuas had fired out all their ammunition and they reformed as two sections in 'vic' formation. At 1900 Lucy led them over Åndalsnes to show the troops on the ground that, at last, they had fighter cover. The Luftwaffe, on the other hand, had been over-confident in operating bombers singly without their own fighter protection. The Skuas took departure from Skalmen Light at 1928 and sighted *Glorious* at 1955. All six aircraft landed on safely by 2030 but despite its success, this had been a hazardous sortie with the aircraft operating at up to 200nm from the carriers. Bill Lucy's 7F was found to have been hit five times by return fire from the bombers and 7P had been hit three times but neither aircraft was damaged seriously.

Minutes before 803 NAS's aircraft had got airborne, Admiralty signal 1530/24 had been received in *Glorious* directing that the RAF Gladiators should be flown ashore to Lesjaskogvann at 1700. They were ranged as soon as the last Skua left the deck and flown off in two groups, the first at 1725 and the second at 1805. Each was led by a Skua to give navigational assistance and both groups reached the makeshift airfield safely without enemy opposition, those enemy aircraft that were in the vicinity having been taken out by the Skuas. By the time 803 NAS had landed on there was little daylight left and it was decided to postpone offensive sorties against Trondheim until the next day, a decision reinforced by Admiralty signal 1947/24 received at 2300 which gave instructions that even if the Gladiators were able to operate on the next day, 25 April, the carriers were to continue to provide a CAP over Namsos and to attack objectives in the Trondheim area. During the night the carrier task force moved north to be further away from German bomber bases.

From midnight the force steered towards an operating area approximately 120nm from Trondheim and Namsos, close enough to provide adequate CAP over the Army ashore but sufficiently far out to sea to make the Luftwaffe's task of finding the ships difficult. The aim of the striking forces was to carry out attacks on the targets that had been postponed the day before because of bad weather plus an enemy cruiser reported in Admiralty signal 1616/24 to be alongside Bratora Wharf. The first range on *Ark Royal* comprising eight Swordfish of 810 NAS led by Captain N R M Skene RM was flown off at 0300 followed by a second range comprising six Swordfish of 820 NAS led by Captain A C Newsom RM. They were all armed with four 250lb SAP bombs and eight 20lb HE bombs and the weather was good with light wind, excellent visibility and a cloud base of 5,000 feet over the target area. 810 NAS was to attack enemy aircraft believed to be operating from the frozen Lake Jonsvatnet and a direction-finding station reported to be at the north-east corner of the lake. Lieutenant N R Corbet-Milward RN in 2K suffered an engine failure on take-off and ditched, slightly delaying the remainder, but he and his TAG, Leading Airman J Black, were unhurt and rescued by a destroyer. The remaining seven Swordfish of 810 NAS entered Gulosen Fjord at 0436 to avoid the heavy anti-aircraft guns now known to be concentrated around Trondheim itself and Jonsvatnet was reached at 0455. It was empty. Despite the reports that had reached the Admiralty from RAF reconnaissance flights, no trace of aircraft, buildings or, indeed, any sign of enemy activity was seen despite a twenty-five-minute search around the area. The lake appeared to be melting around its edges and it was thought that this might explain its lack of use. This appeared to be yet another instance of too much reliance being place on out-of-date information by a remote headquarters, and the need for carriers to generate their own pre-strike reconnaissance was emphasised.

After this setback Captain Skene led his aircraft to the briefed alternate target at Vaernes airfield and at 0520 a column of black smoke was seen rising from it which came from a hangar destroyed by 820 NAS's attack. After forming into line astern 810 NAS pilots carried out a dive-bombing attack from 5,000 feet on aircraft and installations from 0525. They encountered intense close-range fire from points around the airfield but none of the Swordfish was hit. Hits were achieved on another hangar next to the one destroyed by 820 NAS which caused an intense fire. A large transport aircraft was destroyed and several buildings and gun positions were hit. At 0535 the Swordfish left Vaernes and headed for the rendezvous at Halten Light but they did not all manage to join up. Two aircraft, 2R and 2G, failed to find *Ark Royal*. The crew of 2R ditched and were subsequently found in their dinghy by the destroyer *Maori* which had been sent to search for them along their likely line of approach. 2G had asked for a course to steer and been given a heading by Captain Skene's observer, Lieutenant J E Smallwood RN. Bearings of 2G's transmissions taken in *Ark Royal* showed that it had been approaching the fleet on the correct course and at 0745 *Maori* was sent to search along the bearing but neither it nor a subsequent search by two aircraft found any trace of 2G or its crew.

820 NAS had been briefed to attack aircraft and hangars at Vaernes and all six aircraft had the same bomb load as 810 NAS. They crossed the coast 10nm south of Kya Light at 5,000 feet just below the overcast, intending to pull up into it if intercepted. Trondheim Fjord was reached at 0441 and the target was approached from the north-west across the eastern end of Aasen Fjord. The CO, Captain A C Newson RM, ordered his aircraft into line astern by sub-flights at 0448 and his own flight into echelon port at 0450, his intention being that each aircraft would attack targets in pre-briefed strips across the airfield, attacking from west to east with about thirty seconds between sub-flights. 4F and 4G scored direct hits on the westernmost hangars, causing the column of smoke seen later by 810 NAS. Further hits were made on paved runways and huts on the northern side of the airfield and a number of photographs were taken of the airfield, Aasen Fjord and merchant shipping in Trondheim harbour by Lieutenant A W Dayrell RN, the observer in 4F. All six Swordfish made it safely back to the task force but Captain Newson's 4A

ditched before it could land on; the cause of his engine failure was thought to be fuel starvation due to the connection from his long-range tank breaking adrift during the flight, and this failure was reported to the Admiralty by signal. Newson, his observer Lieutenant Commander G B Hodgkinson RN and TAG Leading Airman R McColl, were picked up unharmed by a destroyer and the remainder landed on safely undamaged by enemy fire over the target. 800 and 801 NAS were launched at about 0420 to ensure that fighters were airborne to give cover throughout the time that the Swordfish were airborne but no close escort was provided.

Five aircraft of 803 NAS had been launched from *Glorious* at 0315, again led by Bill Lucy.

803 NAS Attack on Seaplanes in Trondheim Harbour, 25 April 1940

Section	*Pilot*	*Observer/TAG*	*Aircraft*
Blue Leader	Lt W P Lucy	Lt M C E Hanson	7F
2	Lt A B Fraser-Harris	LA G S Russell	7G
3	Lt J M Christian	NA S G Wright	7H
Red Leader	Lt L A Harris RM	PO K G Baldwin	7P
2	Lt C H Filmer	NA Culleford	7Q

All five Skuas were armed with one 250lb and eight 20lb bombs and they were briefed to attack seaplanes reported to be moored in Trondheim harbour. If none was found they were to attack shipping as alternate targets and on completion they were to provide cover for the Swordfish before returning to *Glorious*. They arrived over the harbour at 0440 and began dive-bombing attacks on nine twin-engined floatplanes that were seen to be moored in the south-west corner of Trondheim Roads; this time the intelligence was not stale. Once down at low level they strafed the seaplanes with front guns before reforming. Michael Hanson saw that there were no warships in the harbour but counted six merchant vessels and he took a number of photographs. Heavy anti-aircraft fire by guns of about 3-inch calibre was seen coming from several locations. He too saw the large pall of smoke rising from Vaernes and used it to help close with the Swordfish which were then escorted to Lake Selbus, after which they made use of cloud cover to return to the task force independently. Surprisingly, in view of the lack of results from the search carried out by 810 NAS, Hanson saw three enemy aircraft on Lake Jonsvatnet. At 0520 Bill Lucy led his aircraft back to Trondheim at very low level where they carried out a second strafing on the surviving floatplanes which they saw being hauled out of the water onto a beach. One Skua which had not yet dropped its bombs attacked a large supply ship alongside the south mole but the result was not observed. As they headed for the coast, Lieutenant Fraser-Harris in 7G made a forced landing in the shallow partially frozen water of Sujorn Fjord near a village. Both aircrew were seen to climb out of the aircraft uninjured. The remainder sighted *Glorious* at 0650 and recovery was completed by 0715.

Another flight of 803 NAS comprised 3 Skuas led by Sub Lieutenant (A) G W Brokensha RN launched at 0415 with the same bomb load briefed to search fjords south of Trondheim for enemy warships and shipping. If none were found they were to attack shipping in Trondheim harbour. Two oilers were seen at pipeline terminals at Thamshaven, near the southern end of Orkedale Fjord but they flew on looking for warships. When they reached Trondheim they saw merchant ships

Photograph taken from a Swordfish of 820 NAS while it was attacking Vaernes airfield on 25 April 1940. Note the column of black smoke from a burning hangar visible just beyond the lower wing-tip. (Author's collection)

The burning hangar at Vaernes on 25 April with Swordfish still in action overhead. (Author's collection)

being attacked by Skuas and decided to return to the oilers and attack them at 0700. They dive-bombed and set them on fire with several hits and then joined up with a group of 5 Skuas and 4 Swordfish from *Ark Royal* for mutual protection. They landed on from 0735.

Ark Royal had flown off nine Skuas of 801 and 800 NAS led by Lieutenant Commander H P Bramwell RN, the CO of 801 NAS, at 0420. They were armed with the standard mix of 250lb and 20lb bombs with front guns and were briefed to use the larger bombs on shipping and smaller weapons on floatplanes. The cloud base over the coast remained at about 5,000 feet but unlike the earlier strikes, this one encountered snow showers. The approach was made over a thin layer of broken cloud in line astern formation ready to attack as soon as a target was seen. When no warships were seen, Bramwell decided to attack two large merchant vessels at anchor off Trondheim. A classic dive-bombing attack was carried out with weapon release at 2,000 feet. All nine Skua dropped their 250lb bombs and four 20lb bombs on the targets, which were seen to have been straddled. One direct hit, probably from a light bomb, was seen on the stern of one of the vessels before the aircraft split up to attack individual targets, including four smaller vessels with their remaining bombs. No direct hits were observed but a warehouse, next to one of the ships alongside, was set on fire. All these ships were strafed in front-gun attacks. Two aircraft searched further away and found a Junkers Ju 88 and a damaged Heinkel He 111 on a frozen lake; both were strafed, the Ju 88 seen to be hit and its gunner, who had opened fire in return, was silenced. A considerable amount of anti-aircraft fire was aimed at the Skuas and several were damaged but none of them seriously. All nine landed-on by 0730.

These strikes had all caused damage to enemy aircraft, shipping and installations. Lieutenant Fraser-Harris who had force-landed in 7G met a Norwegian officer while he was ashore who had escaped from Trondheim shortly after the attacks. From him he learnt that at least six German floatplanes had been destroyed, a fuel dump at Vaernes set on fire and at least five German aircraft destroyed there on the ground. More damage had been inflicted but these were the only details of which he was absolutely certain. The loss of the floatplanes severely restricted the Luftwaffe's ability to carry out long-range reconnaissance flights over the sea and made the task of locating the carrier task force that much more difficult.

Once all the strike aircraft had departed the force, three Skuas of 800 NAS were launched at 0455 for CAP over Namsos led by Lieutenant E G D Finch-Noyes RN. They were briefed to make contact with the radar-equipped cruiser *Calcutta* once airborne since she maintained an air plot and could direct them towards enemy aircraft as they were located. They were also briefed to patrol the railway line between Namsos and Grong, looking for movement. They maintained contact with *Bittern*, the sloop providing anti-aircraft fire for troops close inshore. Before long *Calcutta* directed them onto an aircraft which, when intercepted, was seen to be an enemy Heinkel He 115 twin-engined floatplane. All three aircraft made two firing passes at the aircraft, which took violent evasive action and climbed into the overcast at about 4,000 feet. It was assessed as damaged. Visibility decreased as the Skuas reached Foling but they could see that the road bridge had been destroyed although the road and railway appeared intact. No troops or transport were seen but the road seemed to have been well used. Namsos itself had been badly bombed and looked to have been evacuated. On the return flight the flight saw a Junkers Ju 88 and gave chase but it accelerated away from them with ease and they had no height advantage.

Ark Royal launched a further three Skuas of 800 NAS led by Dick Partridge to replace them on CAP at 0610 which was also briefed to contact *Calcutta* for fighter direction. No enemy aircraft were encountered by this flight and the patrol passed uneventfully. All three Skuas landed on safely at 1015 and on completion of this recovery the task force altered course to the north-west at 18 knots to move away from the Norwegian coast. Subsequent alterations of course were made to close the

Heinkel He 115 floatplanes photographed by Michael Hanson as 803 NAS Skuas attacked them in Trondheim harbour on 25 April 1940. (Author's collection)

Shetland Islands and at 1930 a signal was made to the C-in-C Home Fleet to say that Operation DX had been completed and that the task force was returning to Scapa Flow due to the shortage of fuel in the screening destroyers. However, Admiral Forbes responded with his signal 2252/25 saying that DX was not over, that a fresh destroyer screen was being provided and that the present screen, when relieved, was to refuel at Sullom Voe. *Grenade*, with other destroyers in company, had been ordered to rendezvous with the carrier task force at 0700 on 26 April in position 65 00N 05 15E and overnight the carriers altered course to the south-east in order to make that position. The Allied intervention in central Norway clearly lacked overall cohesion and there was insufficient communication between VA Aircraft Carriers, the C-in-C Home Fleet and the military command ashore for the carrier task force to gain a full picture of what was required from it. The serviceability, or otherwise, of the RAF Gladiators at Lake Lesjaskogvann was an unknown quantity but it now appeared that they had made little difference as far as the Army in contact with the enemy was concerned. It should be noted, of course, that the Gladiators had no means of carrying out controlled interceptions, no practical command and control facilities and, probably, no very clear idea of the air picture or the situation on the ground away from their improvised airfield on a frozen lake.

As Admiral Wells' carrier task force approached the rendezvous at 0700 on 26 April there was no sign of the replacement destroyers and so three Swordfish that had been briefed for an anti-submarine patrol were re-briefed to search for them. They were not, in fact, far away: the aircraft located them at 0710 and at 0725 *Grenade*, *Beagle*, *Fortune*, *Volunteer*, *Encounter* and *Escort* took over screening duty, releasing the other destroyers to refuel at Sullom Voe. Several urgent calls for air cover had been received overnight from Åndalsnes and so, since there were too few Skuas to cover Namsos as well, the carriers began flying operations 120nm off Åndalsnes, a decision subsequently endorsed by signals from Admiral Forbes. No strikes were planned but *Ark Royal* and *Glorious* were to fly off CAP Skuas to support the Army ashore at two-hourly intervals throughout the day while Sea Gladiators from *Glorious* were to CAP over the fleet. The first Åndalsnes CAP launched at 1000 comprising 6 Skuas of 801 NAS led by its CO Lieutenant Commander Bramwell. They coasted in at 10,000 feet in perfect visibility and established communications with the radar-equipped cruiser *Curacoa* which provided fighter direction; it was close to the coast in order to provide such anti-aircraft gunfire as it could for the forces ashore. The Skuas flew over Lake Lesjaskogvann, now referred to as 'Gladiator Lake' and saw two Gladiators take off; the swept runway was still conspicuous and bomb craters were seen all over the lake surface. At 1145 three Heinkel He 111 bombers were seen closing Åndalsnes and all six Skuas attacked them in turn. Bramwell saw his front guns hit the starboard engine of one enemy bomber which caught fire, and his wing-man scored hits on the port engine. The aircraft was seen to crash into a snowdrift. A second Heinkel was last seen losing height with smoke and oil pouring from it and the third evaded attack and fled. None of the Skuas was damaged and all landed on by 1330.

The second CAP was provided by three Skuas of 803 NAS from *Glorious* led by Bill Lucy with Michael Hanson as his observer leading Blue Section in 7F. They took off at 1158 with full gun ammunition but no bombs and established the CAP station over Aalesund at 11,000 feet at 1231. At 1308 a formation of Heinkel He 111s was seen at 12,000 feet and Blue 2, Lieutenant Filmer, broke away to carry out an individual attack, after which he was seen to be diving away leaving a trail of smoke. Bill Lucy with Lieutenant Christian on his wing got into position on the bombers' starboard beam and engaged but they lacked the speed advantage that height would have given them and the enemy turned onto south-east and used their superior speed to draw away after the opening rounds had been fired at them. One was seen to drop out of formation, though, before they disappeared from sight at 1335. Filmer's Skua came down near Aalesund; he was subsequently rescued but his TAG, Petty Officer Baldwin, had been killed by return fire from the bombers.

By 1350 Bill Lucy's depleted section was over Åndalsnes at 12,500 feet and they saw a British warship under way just off the harbour. Events then moved quickly, Bill Lucy saw a Dornier Do 17 flying west at about 12,000 feet, then Michael Hanson saw an enemy aircraft at low level attacking the ship but its bombs were missing astern. They turned to intercept the Dornier but as they did so a third enemy aircraft was seen, a Heinkel He 111 several thousand feet below them, setting itself up to attack the ship. This was a better target and Bill Lucy gathered momentum by diving onto its port quarter, followed by his wing-man, and opened fire at short range seeing his bullets strike the enemy aircraft, which began to emit smoke and descend with its undercarriage down. He carried out one further firing pass and saw the Heinkel crash into the fjord at 1412; it floated for about three minutes and some members of its crew were seen to get out and swim over to a small boat that put out from the shore. Both aircraft had fired out their ammunition and so they returned to *Glorious*, landing on at 1540. This had been Bill Lucy's fourth fighter 'kill' but after their debrief it became clear that the Skua was vulnerable to return fire from enemy bombers, especially when attacks could be pressed home to close range. 7F was found to have been hit six times and one bullet had damaged the hydraulic system, a second had penetrated the front engine casing and a third had punctured the port main-wheel tyre. Taken with the fact that 7Q had been shot down by return fire, this was cause for concern but in no way limited the way Bill Lucy and his contemporaries went after enemy aircraft at every chance. A faster fighter would have given pilots more attacking options.

The next CAP was flown by three Skuas of 800 NAS from *Ark Royal* led by Dick Partridge. They launched at 1410 and made landfall at Bud at 1500 flying at 9,000 feet. They immediately saw two Heinkel He 111s over Åndalsnes, one level with them and another at 10,000 feet. Dick Partridge went for the lower one and fired out all his ammunition to no visible effect. Sub Lieutenant B H Hurle-Hobbs RN[3] engaged the higher aircraft but failed to score hits. The third Skua, flown by Petty Officer J Hadley, also attacked the lower Heinkel but was seen to break away violently and lose height. His TAG, Petty Officer W Crawford, informed Dick Partridge that his pilot had been wounded in the face but had elected to rejoin the leader rather than force-land. Having fired out their ammunition the three aircraft returned to *Ark Royal* and landed on at 1615. The Skua lacked both armour for the pilot and an armoured windscreen as the extra weight would have slowed it still further; Hadley's windscreen had been smashed by return fire from the Heinkel he had attacked and his wounds were caused by the splintered glass.

A further CAP of three Skuas from 803 NAS led by Sub Lieutenant Brokensha was launched at 1632 and established an orbit over Åndalsnes at 14,000 feet from 1718. They saw no sign of enemy air activity but the town beneath them appeared to be burning extensively. At 1840 they saw more Skuas arriving on CAP and decided to return to the fleet. The next CAP had not been due to launch until 1830 but two urgent signals[4] were relayed by *Flamingo* from the military commander ashore

Skuas from 803 NAS at low level attacking Trondheim harbour on 25 April. (Author's collection)

which said that unless something could be done to limit the incessant Luftwaffe attacks, the military position ashore would be untenable. In view of this, it was decided to launch a double CAP of six Skuas as soon as possible and these were provided by both 800 and 801 NAS; they flew off at 1700 led by Lieutenant Finch-Noyes. The weather remained fine for this last sortie of the day but no enemy aircraft were encountered until 1905 when a single Heinkel He 115 floatplane was seen flying south along the coast at 4,000 feet. Three Skuas attacked it in turn and saw the enemy rear gunner cease firing and fuel pouring from the port float after their bullets hit. The Heinkel was chased down to sea level and Finch-Noyes fired a long burst which caused fuel to stream from the starboard float. When all three Skuas ran out of front-gun ammunition they positioned themselves to give the TAGs a shot at the damaged aircraft. Long bursts were fired at the engines which were seen to hit by their tracer content but the Skua's lack of a 'killing' weapon was never more emphatically demonstrated and the badly damaged enemy aircraft was last seen flying towards Trondheim. All six Skuas landed on from 2110 after which the carrier task force moved away to the north-west for the night.

Reports now began to arrive which showed that the situation ashore was grave. The RAF's 263 Squadron on 'Gladiator Lake' had already been virtually wiped out and Admiralty signal 1941/26 instructed VAA to continue flying the

A Heinkel He 111 photographed from the Skua that was chasing it near Åndalsnes on 26 April 1940. Closing to within firing range from this far astern was almost impossible without a considerable height advantage. (Author's collection)

maximum scale of CAP over Åndalsnes on the next day, Saturday 27 April. The C-in-C Home Fleet signalled in his 1244/26 that the Army planned to construct three further airfields ashore for RAF fighters but he instructed VAA to maintain the CAP with *Ark Royal* while *Glorious*, which had less endurance, was to return to Scapa Flow after another day's flying to refuel and embark replacement aircraft before returning as quickly as possible. Again, the lack of cohesion between the Admiralty War Room and the C-in-C Home Fleet is clear. VAA responded with his signal 2300/26 in which he expressed concerns. A quarter of his Skua force had already been lost in action, others required battle-damage repair and he doubted that a single carrier was adequate to provide CAP over the Army ashore as well as her own defensive fighter and anti-submarine patrols. However, in order to concentrate the remaining Skua assets where they could be used to best effect, 803 NAS was instructed to re-embarked in *Ark Royal* at the first opportunity on 27 April to operate its aircraft within a 'pool' of Skuas, moving its maintenance personnel across to the 'pool' as soon as circumstances allowed.[5] Given the serious overall situation, the C-in-C's reply, contained in his 1003/27 received in *Ark Royal* at 1145, was inevitable. VAA was to continue to provide the maximum possible fighter protection over Norway and, in addition, to carry out further bombing raids on enemy installations in the Trondheim area. The signal ended by saying that the cruiser *Sheffield* was to join the carrier task force as a permanent radar guard ship. The Royal Navy's small air arm now found itself the only means of providing fighter cover for an expeditionary force on foreign soil that was facing a tactical air force designed and equipped to support its own military operations. Inadequately equipped and without the personnel reserves the Air Ministry had always argued that it would never need, the Fleet Air Arm now had no choice but to fight on to the finish, doing the best it could.

Apart from the ever-present air threat, the danger of U-boat attacks steadily increased and on several occasions screening destroyers prosecuted Asdic contacts with depth charge attacks from 0345 on 27 April. Three Skuas of 801 NAS were launched at 0800 led by Lieutenant R L Strange RN to CAP over Åndalsnes. They flew over 'Gladiator Lake' shortly after 1010 at 10,000 feet and almost at once Number 2, Sub Lieutenant P E Marsh RN, saw two Heinkel He 111s at about 2,000 feet in a valley below them. Strange ordered him to lead the attack and he dived to engage one of the Heinkels head-on while the others positioned themselves for a quarter attack. Marsh saw his bullets hit and the enemy aircraft was seen to crash into a wood. The other Heinkel took violent evasive action and, despite having obviously been hit, it got away but had ceased to be a threat, the fighters' main aim. After this success the section coasted out and landed on at 1155.

At 0930 a lookout in *Ark Royal* spotted an enemy aircraft low on the horizon shadowing the force. A radar report from the cruiser *Curlew* confirmed the presence of enemy aircraft and Blue Section, comprising three Sea Gladiators of 804 NAS led by Lieutenant R M Smeeton RN were flown off *Glorious* to intercept them, quickly joined by a single aircraft of 802 NAS that had been on fleet CAP. Directed onto the shadower by radar, they identified it as a Heinkel He 111 which dived to sea level at full throttle. It was attacked in turn by all four Sea Gladiators but only Sub Lieutenant (A) R R Lamb RN got into a position close enough to see his bullets hit 350 yards astern of the enemy. After a long burst it pulled up and then dived back to sea level, trailing brown smoke from the starboard engine. After another long burst smoke came from the port engine but there was no reduction in its speed. Further bursts caused the aircraft to fly erratically and it actually hit the surface of the sea but still flew on at high speed. It was not seen to crash but it was subsequently learnt from Norwegian intelligence that it had crashed on landing at Stavanger.

A second Åndalsnes CAP was flown by the only four serviceable Skuas left in 803 NAS, led by Bill Lucy, launched from *Glorious* at 1035. They split into Blue and Yellow sections at 1125 but Bill Lucy's Blue saw no enemy aircraft and returned to the fleet at 1430. On arrival overhead they were ordered to land on *Ark Royal*. Yellow section led by Sub Lieutenant Brokensha was more fortunate and they saw a single Heinkel He 111 bombing Åndalsnes from 11,000 feet at 1240. They attacked it immediately and the Heinkel was seen to jettison its remaining bombs and evade to the south-east. With the added speed of his dive, however, Brokensha saw his bullets strike the fuselage and starboard engine. His wing-man, Lieutenant L A Harris RM, hit the port engine and they both saw the aircraft crash into a mountainside. CAP was resumed at 1300 and they departed for the fleet at 1315. They too were instructed to land on *Ark Royal* so that all the Skuas were now concentrated in the carrier that was to remain.

Three Skuas of 800 NAS led by Dick Partridge were flown off at 1230 and went 'feet dry' near Bud at 1327. Almost at once they saw a single Heinkel He 111 at 13,000 feet bombing a British warship close to the coast. Sub Lieutenant Hurle-Hobbs carried out a well-calculated, full-deflection beam attack while Partridge and Taylour gained height for an attack. The bomber turned away to the south but the three Skuas gave chase and continued to make firing opportunities in a running engagement. The Heinkel was eventually seen to crash near Grotli, 20nm south of Åndalsnes. Unfortunately, Dick Partridge's engine was hit by return fire and he was forced to carry out a dead-stick landing on a frozen lake, also near Grotli and not far from where the Heinkel came down. Both he and Robin Bostock were unhurt[6] and, after many adventures, managed to get back to the fleet. The remaining two Skuas landed on safely at 1540.

At 1340 a single Swordfish was launched to carry a message to *Black Swan* in accordance with instructions contained in Admiralty signal 1158/27. The printed message was contained in a weighted bag and informed the ship that her code cyphers were probably compromised and instructed her to recode the indicator group in order to provide a safe means of communication between Åndalsnes and the Admiralty. This was an illustration, if one were needed, of just how difficult communications between the expeditionary force and the outside world trying to help it were at this stage. The bag was successfully dropped onto a beach near *Black Swan*'s sea boat and was immediately taken back to the ship. The Swordfish had arrived while the ship was being bombed and the whole mission was completed successfully under the most hazardous conditions.

At 1515 *Ark Royal* launched five Skuas for what proved to be the largest air combat involving carrier-borne aircraft to date. The aircraft were drawn from both 800 and 801 NAS with one flight led by Lieutenant Finch-Noyes and a second by Lieutenant Commander Bramwell. As they made their way up the fjord to Åndalsnes they saw a convoy of British ships heading for the town and at 1615, just as it was at its most vulnerable, it was attacked by two Junkers Ju 88s diving on it from 9,000 feet. The Skuas attacked without hesitation and followed the bombers into their dives. Bramwell and his wing-man concentrated their fire on one of the enemy and saw both its engines on fire but they broke off when 'numerous Heinkels' were seen, and all five Skuas climbed independently to gain attacking positions. A number of individual combats ensued as targets were engaged, the Skua crews using both front and rear guns. None of these bombers succeeded in attacking the convoy but bursts of anti-aircraft fire from it indicated yet more Heinkels approaching from the north. These were also engaged individually and a further series of 'dog fights' ensued. Both enemy formations were completely broken up, none pressed home its attacks with any determination and only two enemy bombers managed to release weapons anywhere near the convoy.

800 and 801 NAS Fighter Combat over Åndalsnes, 27 April 1940

Pilot	*Observer/TAG*	*Aircraft*
Lt E G D Finch-Noyes	PO H G Cunningham	6F
PO H A Monk	LA W J Tremeer	6G
Mid L H Gallagher	LA L C Eccleshall	6H
Lt Cdr H P Bramwell	Lt J W Collett	7A
S/Lt (A) B F Wigginton	NA E J Adlam	7C

Surviving records do not single out individuals but they do make it clear that the performance of these Skua crews was magnificent. As pilots ran out of ammunition they continued to make dummy attacks on the enemy to deter them from attacking the convoy. This combat lasted for only about fifteen minutes, during which four enemy bombers were shot down; about thirty had been engaged and decisively defeated. After what amounted to the Fleet Air Arm's largest and most successful air combat so far, the five Skuas left the retreating Heinkels and set heading for the fleet. All had landed on safely by 1820 but as they did so Captain D4 signalled[7] that a German airman had been rescued from the water who admitted that five Heinkels had been shot down.

A further CAP of three Skuas from 801 NAS led by Lieutenant W C A Church RN was flown off at 1645 and saw a single Heinkel He 111 as it approached Åndalsnes at 1735. It was attacked immediately but dived away at full throttle and, with no speed advantage, the Skuas were drawn into a stern chase. Church's aircraft, 7L, airframe number L2931, was hit by return fire and seen to burst into flames; within seconds the engine detached from the fuselage and the aircraft crashed vertically into the sea. The remaining two Skuas, flown by Lieutenant R C Hay RM[8] and Petty Officer H Kimber, continued to engage the enemy bomber and shot it down into the sea, after which they returned to the spot where 7L had come down but saw nothing on the surface but a partially inflated life raft and a petrol slick. Lieutenant Church and his observer Sub Lieutenant (A) D G Willis RN were presumed to have been killed in action and no trace of them was ever

A Skua pilot's eye view of Åndalsnes on fire on 26 April 1940. (Author's collection)

found. No other enemy aircraft were encountered and the flight returned to *Ark Royal*, landing on at 1855.

At 1700 the original destroyer screen returned from Sullom Voe and resumed their duty. The last aircraft were recovered at 1930 and VAA ordered the task force to move to a position from which strikes could be launched against Trondheim at dawn on the following day, Sunday 28 April, as directed by the C-in-C Home Fleet. At 2100 *Glorious* detached as intended to return to Scapa Flow screened by *Hasty*, *Fury*, *Grenade*, *Escort*, *Encounter*, *Volunteer*, *Beagle* and *Fortune* with the intention that they should also refuel. *Hyperion*, *Hereward*, *Fearless* and *Juno* remained with *Ark Royal* and her task force.

Early in the morning of 28 April *Ark Royal* arrived at the designated launch position 64 58N 08 08E and ranged a strike force of Swordfish, six each from

820 and 810 NAS, the former led by Lieutenant R N Everett RN in 4K and the latter by Captain N R M Skene RM in 2A. The weather was clear with no cloud, extreme visibility and no wind. There was, thus, no chance of using cloud cover to achieve surprise or to evade enemy fighters if they were intercepted but at least the targets would stand out clearly and accurate weapons delivery was possible. All the Swordfish were armed with four 250lb GP bombs, six 20lb HE bombs, two 25lb incendiary bombs and full gun ammunition; they began to take-off at 0305. As the last aircraft cleared the deck, a second strike was ranged comprising seven Skuas of 800 and 801 NAS, each of which was armed with a single 250lb SAP bomb and eight 20lb HE bombs with full gun ammunition.

820 NAS made landfall at Kya Lighthouse at 0405 and headed for Vaernes airfield at 6,000 feet. They approached from the north in the grey light before the sun rose and fire was opened on them by anti-aircraft guns on the western side of the airfield when they were about 3nm from it. As they got closer a considerable amount of short-range fire was aimed at them from positions all round the airfield; 4C was hit in a lower main plane but continued its attack. The first bombs were dropped from diving attacks on barrack blocks north of the airfield at 0532 and hits were observed with all types of bombs. The squadron then withdrew and, despite several being damaged, all six landed on safely by 0615. 810 NAS made its landfall 10nm further south at 9,000 feet and came under fire at 1440. The enemy gunnery appeared to be good for height but in error for line, no doubt due to the German predictors being unable to cope with the low speed of the Swordfish, a recurring theme in the months and years to come. From 0443 a dive-bombing attack was made on the same barracks that 820 had attacked but Lieutenant D F Godfrey-Fausset RN broke away to make a determined attack on a hangar which he destroyed, adding it to the hangar he had destroyed in the previous attack on the airfield. Three aircraft received minor damage but all six landed on safely by 0610.

A single Swordfish was flown off with the second range, briefed to carry out a photographic reconnaissance of the forts at the entrance to Trondheim Fjord and the seven Skuas were briefed to attack shipping in Trondheim harbour with warships as first priority and merchant ships as alternatives if none was seen. Their lighter bombs were to be used on floatplanes, many of which still seemed to be operational from the harbour. The Skuas flew in two loose sections within sight of each other and made their landfall at Halten Light at 0430 flying at 13,000 feet. They achieved tactical surprise over the harbour with no anti-aircraft fire until the first two Skuas had completed their attacks. No warships were observed so they attacked four merchant ships and about eighteen large floatplanes found moored in the harbour. The Skuas increased speed in a shallow dive to 8,000 feet and then tipped into steeper dives to line up with individual targets. The 250lb and two 20lb bombs were dropped on the ships with at least one direct hit being observed. The dive angle was then reduced to allow pilots to aim at the floatplanes, which were moored close together, and drop their remaining small bombs. Again hits were observed and near misses would have caused damage with blast and splinters. Anti-aircraft fire developed at this stage but no aircraft was hit. Six Skuas returned to *Ark Royal* and landed on safely by 0635 but one, 6M flown by Midshipman (A) L H Gallagher RN with NA G W Halifax as his TAG, became detached, failed to find the carrier and returned to land on a frozen lake near Åndalsnes. He found a damaged RAF Gladiator nearby and used his initiative to transfer avgas from it to fill his own tanks.[9] Next he obtained a Norwegian school atlas, took off and used the atlas to navigate across 350 miles of sea to Sullom Voe in the Shetland Islands where he refuelled again before flying on to RNAS Hatston to await developments.

Other survivors at this time included Dick Partridge and his observer. After burning their aircraft they had made for a small house nearby which they found to be empty. However, a few minutes later three German survivors from the Heinkel they had shot down arrived and the survivors spent a strained night together. Next morning a Norwegian ski patrol arrived which spoke neither English nor German and Dick had a difficult time convincing them who was who. Eventually the correct interpretation was reached, the Germans were arrested and Partridge and Bostock were given skis, which they had never used before, which enabled them to reach the coast and rescue 50nm away.

Sheffield joined the task force at 1135 on 28 April and took over fighter direction duty from *Curlew*, which returned to Sullom Voe to refuel. Throughout the forenoon urgent calls for air support were received from Molde, Åndalsnes and convoy TM1. The three Skuas of Blue Section of 803 NAS led by Bill Lucy which had been on standby were, therefore, launched at 1105 to provide cover in Skuas 6H, 6K and 6L. They crossed the coast over Bud at 1214 flying at 11,500 feet and at 1218 saw a Junkers Ju 88 about 7,000 feet below them bombing a British escort vessel leaving Molde harbour. Bill Lucy dived on it but the enemy saw him and made off at high speed. He tried a beam attack but the bomber's speed was too great and after a short, inconclusive, burst of fire he broke off. Sub Lieutenant Brokensha failed to get into a firing position but Petty Officer A G Johnson managed to carry out a quarter attack off a 'perch' position which soon became a stern attack because of the enemy's speed but he managed to hold a good, if brief, firing position astern of it at 270 knots and fired a series of short bursts which he saw hit. The Junkers jettisoned its bombs and dived away but then appeared to lose control and it was seen to crash on the west side of an island.

At 1245 three Heinkel He 111s were seen above the section but Johnson, who was detached from the others, had sufficient momentum to pull up and carry out an immediate attack, firing out his front-gun ammunition at one of the bombers which jettisoned its bombs and escaped to the south. Bill Lucy with Brokensha on his wing climbed for position above the other two Heinkels and carried out successive attacks from astern on one of them. Its starboard engine stopped, its undercarriage came down and it was seen to tip over and crash into a valley. At 1310 Lucy and Brokensha returned to Åndalsnes, where the saw a Junkers Ju 88 but

Ark Royal being missed by high-level bombers. (Author's collection)

its high speed prevented them from engaging it. Petty Officer Johnson remained on patrol over Molde. At 1320 Bill Lucy saw eight Heinkel He 111s in formation level with his flight at 9,000 feet and he immediately attacked the starboard wing aircraft, which was slightly out of position and, therefore, not as well protected by cross-fire as the others. Successive attacks were made until it was seen to catch fire and crash into the sea. The engagement had developed into the second large-scale dog fight by Skuas against the Luftwaffe and the remaining Heinkels held formation and headed north-west towards the carrier task force.

While Michael Hanson sent a warning message to the fleet, Bill Lucy managed to get into a position at 1345 which was 1,500 feet above and slightly ahead of the enemy formation's leader. He then dived into a slashing attack, only ceasing fire and breaking away at the very last moment to pull up into an 'Immelman' wing-over manoeuvre to maintain his height advantage. The effect was dramatic. The enemy formation broke up completely, jettisoned their bombs and turned away to the south-east. Brokensha picked an individual target from the melee and fired out his front-gun ammunition into it; he saw it disappear into cloud with its starboard engine stopped. Bill Lucy attacked the one Heinkel that was still heading in the general direction of the fleet and saw it, too, turn away to the south-east and jettison its bombs before it flew into cloud as he ran out of ammunition. Johnson, still over Molde, saw the retreating Heinkels coming at him from the sea and, with no front-gun ammunition, he positioned his aircraft so that his TAG, Leading Airman F Coston, could engage one with his rear gun. A long burst at one was seen by both of them to hit and set the port engine on fire and it dived steeply into cloud but was not seen to crash. All three Skuas returned safely to *Ark Royal*, Johnson individually homing by beacon despite the carrier being 90nm off the coast and the aircraft having a defective component in its receiver which Coston repaired in flight – an achievement for which he was commended in Bill Lucy's subsequent report. After this particularly successful sortie the aircraft landed on at 1500.

Bill Lucy's two 'kills' were his fifth and sixth. Both were credited to him by the Admiralty but at the time it was reluctant to seek publicity for individual acts of gallantry and the achievement was not announced to the public. In any other air arm, including the US Navy, it had been the convention since the First World War that a pilot who achieved five or more 'kills' in air combat was described as an 'ace'. Bill Lucy had achieved that number and was not only the first pilot in the Royal Navy to do so in the Second World War, he was the first pilot in any of the air arms of the British Empire and its Commonwealth to do so. Taken with his leadership of the strike that sank the first major warship in history to be sunk by air attack, we can look back and see that Bill Lucy was the outstanding pilot of the early war period. He deserves far greater recognition for his achievements.

The day, 28 April, was far from over, however, and at 1140 reports were received in *Ark Royal* that German bombers were attacking convoy TM1 escorted by the cruiser *Calcutta*. Three Skuas were flown off at 1140 led by Lieutenant Finch-Noyes to go to its aid. When they arrived over the cruiser they found that attacks had ceased forty minutes earlier but a lone Heinkel He 111 was seen approaching and it was attacked by all three fighters. Clearly badly damaged, it was assessed as having crashed into the sea. After this a number of enemy aircraft appeared and the Skuas split up to attack individual targets. Lieutenant Taylour followed a Junkers Ju 88 into its dive-bombing run and harassed it to the extent that its bombs were seen to fall over 200 yards wide of its target. Petty Officer Monk attacked four enemy aircraft with his front guns, leaving one of them with an engine on fire. When out of ammunition he carried out five dummy attacks on enemy bombers to prevent them from bombing the convoy accurately. Finch-Noyes attacked three enemy aircraft, one of them in a head-on pass in which he saw many rounds hitting home; the aircraft, a Junkers Ju 88, pulled up sharply into cloud and was lost to view. On completion of this short but sharp engagement the Skuas flew back to *Ark Royal* and landed on safely by 1540.

The Luftwaffe was noticeably growing in strength daily and by now knew the approximate position in which the carrier task force was operating. Shortly after Bill Lucy's Skuas had broken up one bomber formation heading for the task force, *Curlew* gained radar contact on more enemy aircraft closing it from the south-east at 6,000 feet. Minutes later three Junkers Ju 88s were seen bearing 140 degrees at 12nm. Only two of them pressed home their attack through the anti-aircraft barrage, choosing *Ark Royal* and the cruiser *Berwick* astern of her as targets. One stick of bombs fell close the carrier but the aircraft that dropped them was shot

The sloop *Flamingo* under air attack in the confined waters of a fjord whilst supporting the troops ashore on 26 April 1940. (Author's collection)

down, crashing into the sea near the destroyer *Hyperion*. No ships were damaged. Fleet CAP had been carried out by Sea Gladiators from *Glorious* but in her absence *Ark Royal*'s Rocs were reserved for the task. Statements in some earlier accounts that they were never embarked in a carrier or that they were never used in combat from a carrier are not factually correct: they were but they were certainly not successful in their intended role. A section of three was held at alert on deck and scrambled at 1215.

801 NAS Roc Fleet CAP, 28 April 1940

Pilot	*Observer/TAG*	*Aircraft*
Lt R C Hay RM	NA S Bass	7P
Sub/Lt (A) J E Myers	NA D Bolton	7Q
Mid (A) G C Baldwin	LA S Smailes	7R

No enemy bombers remained in the vicinity of the force once the Rocs got airborne but they sighted a Heinkel He 115 floatplane which was clearly shadowing and guiding the bombers onto their targets. They succeeded in driving it off but lacked the speed to destroy it or even chase it and landed on to refuel and re-arm at 1330. The same aircrew and aircraft were launched again at 1430 against another shadower, this time a Heinkel He 111. Again they drove it off but could not get the turret gunners into positions from which they could open fire and it escaped.

By noon on 28 April VAA was becoming concerned at the scale of operations to which his fighter pilots were committed and his signal 1206/28 to Admiral Forbes pointed out that his fighter personnel had now been in action for five successive days and were showing definite signs of strain. This was much more than Operation DX had originally been intended to contribute to the campaign in central Norway and he proposed that *Ark Royal* should withdraw to the north-west for forty-eight hours before recommencing operations which, as far as he knew, might have no end in sight. The C-in-C Home Fleet's response, contained in his signal 1453/28, indicated that he intended to approve this proposal and after the last aircraft were landed on at 1615 the task force altered course to the north-west, away from the German bomber threat. At 2049 a further signal from the C-in-C, 1848/28, instructed *Ark Royal* to be in position 62 00N 04 00W at 1100 on 30 April in order to fly on replacement fighters from RNAS Hatston, and VAA agreed in his 2253/28 that he would do so.

During 29 April the carrier task force shaped a course to be at the rendezvous where it would join *Glorious* and the battleship *Valiant* which was to replace *Sheffield* as radar guard ship. The rendezvous was made at 1100 on 30 April as planned but by then the C-in-C had changed the earlier plan and ordered *Glorious* to embark

Glorious photographed from *Furious* with a range of Sea Gladiators aft. The destroyer in the foreground is *Diana*. (Author's collection)

the replacement fighters 'to reduce the potential chances of mishap' – whatever they were supposed to be. Unfortunately, weather delayed their embarkation and the C-in-C ordered *Glorious* in his signal 2224/29 to delay sailing until she had embarked them and only then to rejoin the carrier task force. At 1120 *Ark Royal* flew off the single Walrus and three Swordfish to Hatston to clear hangar space for the expected fighters and the opportunity was taken to land copies of the reports of proceeding covering Operation DX thus far and target photographs for onward transmission to the Admiralty and C-in-C Home Fleet. On this day, however, the military authorities ashore finally decided that their position was untenable and plans to evacuate Åndalsnes and Namsos were being hastily prepared. At first these required the evacuation of both to begin on the night of 1/2 May 1940 but the situation at Åndalsnes became so grave that the withdrawal was brought forward to the night of 30 April. Fighter cover during the daylight hours of 1 May was, therefore, of critical importance and the carrier task force shaped a course to an operating area off the coast in order to provide it.

At 0400 on the morning of 1 May 1940 three Skuas of 801 NAS launched from *Ark Royal* to cover Åndalsnes and any convoys immediately to seaward of it.[10] No enemy aircraft were seen in the vicinity of Åndalsnes but as the CAP returned to the carriers they saw a single Junkers Ju 88 attack *Ark Royal* but miss. They chased it away but failed to get into firing range. At 0445 in response to repeated calls for help from the Army ashore, three more Skuas of 801 NAS were launched to CAP over the town but they, too, failed to find any enemy aircraft. At 0700 a series of radar reports from *Valiant* indicated that the task force was being shadowed by enemy aircraft. Three Rocs were flown off at 0715 to intercept them, one of them chased an enemy aircraft thought to be a Junkers Ju 87 but failed to catch it. The other two saw nothing, but lookouts in the fleet saw Heinkel He 115 floatplanes at long range for the remainder of the day. At 0751 a Junkers Ju 88 dived out of the sun and dropped a bomb that missed *Ark Royal*'s port quarter, it was not seen until the last moment and not engaged by anti-aircraft fire until it was flying away. At 0755 another Junkers Ju 88 carried out a dive-bombing attack on *Ark Royal* and dropped a bomb which fell only 50 yards astern; further attacks followed at 1523, 1544, 1605, 1823 and 1849.

Glorious joined the force at 1005 screened by *Acheron*, *Antelope* and *Beagle*. She had embarked the eighteen Sea Gladiators of 802 and 804 NAS, twelve Swordfish, three Skuas and a Roc. Continued bad weather had prevented her from embarking all the intended fighter reinforcements but at least her Sea Gladiators were now available for fleet air defence. A signal from the C-in-C Rosyth who acted as the interface between the RN and RAF communication systems now informed VAA that long-range RAF Blenheim fighters would assume responsibility for CAP over Åndalsnes from 0600 on 2 May. Since the first two Skua CAPs had seen no enemy air activity it was decided to move the carrier task force further north in order to provide cover for the evacuation of Namsos, due to start that night, which was

Sea Gladiator landing on. (Author's collection)

beyond the radius of action of RAF Blenheims. Repeated attacks were made on the carriers by enemy bombers and the Sea Gladiator CAP was doubled. Anti-submarine patrols by Swordfish were maintained, making progress to the north slow as the carriers had to turn into the light southerly wind at high speed to fly them off. Between 1100 and 2130 *Glorious* maintained six Sea Gladiators in the air with three more at immediate alert on deck. Yellow Section comprising three Sea Gladiators of 804 NAS led by the CO Lieutenant Commander J C Cockburn RN was airborne for two hours between 1215 and 1415, during which time they maintained radio silence and saw no enemy activity. Blue Section, which took off at 1430 led by Lieutenant R M Smeeton RN, did see action, however. They intercepted and damaged one Heinkel He 111 at 1520 and drove off a second at 1600. In both cases the Sea Gladiator proved to be too slow to keep enemy bombers in range and achieve kills.

From 1523 to 1610 high-level attacks were carried out on the fleet by enemy bombers estimated to be at 17,000 feet. The carrier task force was in line astern formation in the order *Ark Royal*, *Valiant*, *Glorious* and *Berwick* with seven destroyers screening them and was carrying out Zig-Zag Pattern 10 but the first attacks were carried out while the sun was astern of them and the enemy aircraft were not seen until they dropped their bombs, all of which missed. One of these attacks was the one intercepted by Smeeton's section and in his subsequent combat report he commented that he believed that the heavy ships were operating too closely together, thus giving better target opportunities for the enemy's level bombers. He also commented that the zig-zag in use was too short in period to give sufficient displacement from the mean line of advance to disturb the bombers' aim. The ability of enemy aircraft to achieve near misses after dropping bombs almost at will would seem to endorse this view and the optimum fleet disposition in the face of enemy air attack was another of the many tactical lessons learnt by the RN during this first series of sea/air battles. It is also interesting to note how Smeeton was 'thinking as a sailor', viewing the overall picture.

At 1630 804 NAS Red Section took off led by Lieutenant R M P Carver RN with Lieutenant D C E F Gibson and Sub Lieutenant M F Fell RN as his wing-men.[11] A series of abortive chases under radar direction ended at 1800 when they intercepted and damaged a Heinkel He 115 shadower. Their ammunition was expended in a series of attacks but the enemy eventually made off. At 1800 Blue Section from 802 NAS led by Lieutenant J P Marmont were scrambled from deck alert and 804 NAS' Yellow Section led by Lieutenant Commander Cockburn were launched early at 1815 to give nine fighters airborne to oppose a large number of hostile aircraft seen on radar. Unfortunately, during their recovery to land on *Glorious* at 1830 Lieutenant Carver's section was fired on by all ships' close-range anti-aircraft weapons and by 4-inch guns from *Berwick*. Poor aircraft recognition by ships' gunners was to be a recurring theme and the problem had still not been solved in the British Pacific Fleet during 1945. Cockburn's section saw six Junkers Ju 87 dive-bombers 3nm away on an opposite course closing the carriers at 12,000 in open 'V' formation and the Sea Gladiators each half rolled onto the tails of the enemy aircraft and fired at them in short bursts until they commenced their dives. At this point Cockburn ordered his section to break off as he assumed – wrongly, as it transpired – that the fleet's anti-aircraft guns would engage the enemy. They did not and from 1823 to 1855 the Luftwaffe sought to synchronise dive-bombing attacks by Junkers 87s with high-level bombing attacks. Radar gave good warning of their approach at 30 to 40nm but despite this the fleet's guns did not open fire because the single-engined Junkers were misidentified as friendly. One Junkers was shot down by Lieutenant Marmont and its crew of two were rescued by *Encounter* at 1858. A melee now ensued during which the ships' gunners fired at every aircraft in sight, including the Sea Gladiators. After their dives, several Junkers 87s strafed *Fury* and others attacked the Swordfish on anti-submarine patrol, damaging it slightly. Several Sea Gladiators were damaged by return fire but no ships were hit.

In addition to their single 'kill' the fighters did valuable work breaking up enemy bomber formations and putting pilots off their aim but on this occasion radar direction did not work. *Valiant* passed a stream of bearings and distances, many of which were actually the CAP fighters, and their sheer numbers confused the plot. *Glorious* subsequently debriefed VAA that it was difficult to know what information to pass to fighters on R/T and what to pass to lookouts and gun directors. Fighter section leaders reported that they were constantly fired on by the fleet and this did little to help them in their task. The embryo fighter direction organisation was clearly swamped by the scale of the action on this day. There can be little doubt that this was the most testing day for the fleet's air defence organisation and it clearly still had much to learn, both doctrinally and tactically, but lessons were learnt that would have application throughout the war. With so much pre-war theory shown to be wide of the mark these lessons were invaluable. The Luftwaffe also discovered its own shortcomings. Reconnaissance aircraft had found the fleet but bomber crews lacked the skill to hit individual ships and in most cases were employing techniques that were unlikely to enable them to do so.

In his combat report dated 2 May 1940, Lieutenant Commander Cockburn showed his evident frustration after the events the previous day. He stressed the fact that, having been embarrassed by the lack of anti-aircraft fire when gunners had misidentified the Junkers Ju 87s as friendly, subsequent fire from both *Glorious* and *Valiant* had appeared to concentrate on the fleet's own fighters. Fortunately, he noted, it was grossly inaccurate! He also commented that all his fighters were heavily handicapped by having to fly at low rpm with the weakest petrol mixture in order to eke out their fuel to stay airborne for the two hours ordered for CAP sorties, a time that was thirty minutes in excess of the manufacturer's recommended safe endurance in the Sea Gladiator's Release to Service. He believed that operations on 1 May had brought out three points very clearly:

1 The Sea Gladiator had insufficient performance to chase and hold in gun-firing range the aircraft in service with the Luftwaffe.
2 A high concentration of fire was needed to ensure a 'kill' in the short time between an enemy aircraft being seen and dropping its weapons on the fleet. Naval fighters needed heavier armament to achieve success within that time.
3 Naval fighters needed much greater endurance than the Sea Gladiator, about five hours, to prevent the CAP carrier from having to turn constantly into wind to operate them.

He concluded his report by noting that points 1 and 2 above could be overcome by equipping RN fighter squadrons with Spitfires[12] and all three points by equipping them with any US Naval fighter.

At 1805 four Skuas of 803 NAS, two of Blue Section led by Bill Lucy and two of Yellow Section led by Sub Lieutenant Brokensha, were launched to CAP over the cruiser *Devonshire* which had reported enemy aircraft in its vicinity. They encountered extensive fog but Brokensha's section found a clear patch over a British convoy and its escort. Unfortunately, the convoy opened fire on them and, despite their use of the correct recognition signals and flashing the correct reply letters with an Aldis lamp, Brokensha was shot down into the sea. Luckily he and his

An RAF Gladiator photographed close to the trees on Lake Lesjaskogvann by an 803 NAS Skua. (Author's collection)

TAG, Petty Officer S E Andrews, were unhurt and rescued by *Nubian*. Bill Lucy's section patrolled over Namsos and took photographs but saw no enemy aircraft. The three surviving Skuas subsequently landed safely on *Glorious*. At 1805 *Ark Royal* launched a further three Skuas of 803 NAS, Green Section, led by Lieutenant J M Christian RN to CAP over Namsos, and then a further two of 800 NAS to intercept a Heinkel He 115 that was shadowing the force. The Namsos CAP saw no enemy activity but the interceptors engaged the Heinkel and scored hits before it made off.

The scale of air attack on this day had caused VAA concern and in his signal 1922/01 he informed Admiral Forbes that he no longer considered it possible to maintain a position from which his aircraft could give support to the forces. He stated that it was his intention to withdraw to the north-west, out of range of German air attack. This signal crossed with the C-in-C's 1853/01 which ordered VAA

The burning oil tanker at Thamshaven photographed from Sub Lieutenant Brokensha's aircraft of 803 NAS, shortly after he dive-bombed it. (Author's collection)

to move northwards to provide fighter protection for Namsos whilst continuing to carry out bombing attacks on Trondheim. After some discussion with his staff, VAA made a further signal to Admiral Forbes reporting the day's shadowing and bombing during the move to the north and stating that the air operations ordered in 1853/01 were 'no longer practicable by a carrier force in this area'. Subsequently a further signal, 2052/01, was received from the C-in-C directing the carrier task force to return to Scapa Flow. The first period of intensive operations by a strike carrier task force in the history of warfare was over.

Some redistribution of aircraft was carried out on the passage to Scapa, ordered in the C-in-C's signal 1951/02. The Roc had proved to be a failure and all of them were to be disembarked for other, less demanding, duties ashore. The Skua squadrons were to be concentrated in *Ark Royal* once more and at 0805 on 3 May, therefore, five Rocs from *Ark Royal* and one from *Glorious* were flown off to RNAS Donibristle in Fife. The type was to see no further embarked service. All of 803 NAS's Skuas returned to *Ark Royal*. *Ark Royal* and *Glorious* together with other ships of the task force and their screening destroyers returned to Scapa Flow at 1100 on 3 May.

In Appendix 34 to his Report of Proceedings dated 23 May 1940, Admiral Wells summarised the aircraft carriers' contribution to Operation DX. He listed twenty enemy aircraft destroyed by the fleet's fighters, although post-war analysis of German records was to show that of the five Heinkel He 111s claimed on 27 April only one had in fact been shot down and the other four probably damaged, albeit some of them severely. Notwithstanding this, the fact was that a number of enemy bomber formations had been broken up and none of the ships had been hit or damaged. Ships' gunfire, on the other hand, had only shot down one enemy aircraft and it was now realised that anti-aircraft gunnery had been over-valued in the inter-war years; fighters offered by far the best air defence option for the fleet, especially if US Naval types could be procured and brought into service quickly. During Operation DX the RN had lost a number of its own aircraft and VAA noted that *Ark Royal* had sailed with twenty-one Swordfish and eighteen Skuas and of these four of each had been lost. *Glorious* had lost five Skuas. No Sea Gladiators or Rocs had been lost. By later standards in both the RN and USN, these losses were not heavy but in April/May 1940 they represented a significant percentage of the aircraft embarked and were a new experience.

Admiral Forbes summed up the reports from Admiral Wells and his carrier captains in a letter to the Admiralty.[13] His summary read:

> The conduct of these operations, which were maintained to the limit of endurance of the personnel, reflects the greatest credit on all concerned.
>
> The skill and determination displayed by the flying crews is worthy of a better vehicle. It is understood that there is a possibility of obtaining modern American carrier-borne fighter aircraft.[14] If this is so, and the aircraft are suitable, it is hoped the opportunity will not be missed.

For this first battle involving a carrier task force the RN had deployed a balanced force of two carriers supported by a radar-equipped direction ship with cruisers and destroyers to provide defence against air and surface attack.[15] It committed all five of its existing fighter squadrons to Operation DX and the replacement aircraft flown onto *Ark Royal* on 30 April had come from a sixth squadron originally due to have formed on 1 May. The total commitment of the RN to the campaign was evidenced by its attempt to provide a substitute for the RAF's absence for days on end, always within range of enemy bombers and in waters threatened by U-boats. The success achieved by the Skuas was significant. Although faster than enemy reconnaissance floatplanes and flying boats, they were out-performed by bombers with the sole exception of a fully loaded Heinkel He 111, but once it jettisoned its bombs it too could outrun a Skua at the same height. At first the Skua pilots had achieved few 'kills' but as they gained experience they learnt to use high diving speed to catch the bombers, and their shooting improved so that the first pass usually inflicted sufficient damage to slow the enemy to a speed within the Skua's reach. The first sure sign that the fighter pilots were gaining the ascendancy came on 27 April when a number of bombers were shot down and all the others driven off. It was ironic that the Army commander ashore chose this day to write that 'our own air was conspicuous by its absence'.

Ark Royal and *Glorious* could never hope to provide complete cover in the face of overwhelming enemy air superiority. Later experience with carriers operating fifteen times as many aircraft was to show that a really determined enemy could nearly always break through at times. However, their aircraft undoubtedly reduced the weight of bombs dropped on the ill-fated expeditionary forces in central Norway and the Germans learnt a new respect for aircraft carriers and their fighters

Namsos photographed from a Skua of 803 NAS on 1 May 1940. (Author's collection)

that was to influence all their future actions. The Luftwaffe's lack of experience in locating and attacking ships at sea led to a fresh emphasis being put on the training of Fliegerkorps X as a specialised anti-shipping force.

The Report of Operations by Lieutenant General H R S Massy DSO MC,[16] Commander-in-Chief North Western Expeditionary Force in Norway makes several revealing comments. In it he said:

> As in Poland the Germans have used their Air Force in the closest co-operation with their military forces.[17] … I have no hesitation in saying that a degree of co-operation between the Army and the Air Force, comparable to that which is now the case with the Germans, is essential if we are not to remain at a dangerous disadvantage.

This was a damning indictment of government defence policy between the wars with regard to the Army and its potential to deploy expeditionary forces. With regard to the RN he reported:

> co-operation between the Navy, including the Fleet Air Arm, and the Army has been of the highest standard possible. The whole of the forces operating in Norway fully realise the debt of gratitude they owe to their sister-service both for the support the latter gave them ashore and for the efficiency with which they were withdrawn at the end. The arrival of the carriers of the Fleet Air Arm off the coast, and the operation of the Skuas and Rocs, gave a respite from bombing to the ports, especially Namsos, which was invaluable. The Germans would not face our Fleet Air Arm fighters which were handled with a boldness that was an inspiration to the troops who watched their manoeuvres from the ground.

Chapter 16

Killed in Action

OPERATION DX HAD SEEN the 'dawn' of carrier strike, the first time in history that an aircraft carrier task force had carried out sustained operations against enemy ships, U-boats and aircraft off a hostile shore, but it was not quite the end of RN carrier operations in the ill-fated Norwegian campaign. German forces in Narvik had been isolated since the losses suffered by the Kreigsmarine in the two battles fought in early April but were supplied by Luftwaffe Junkers Ju 52 transport aircraft and continued to hold out against the encircling Allied forces. British attempts to assault and capture the port were eventually successful on 28 May but by then the situation on the Western Front was deteriorating fast[1] and the rapid progress of German armoured columns through Belgium and France posed such a threat that the Allied governments decided to abandon Narvik from 4 June 1940. Three carriers were involved in operations off Narvik, two of which had ferried into the area of operations RAF fighters which managed to operate with some success from a new airfield at Bardufoss.

Carrier Operations off Narvik in brief

On 4 May *Ark Royal* sailed again with 800, 801 and 803 NAS's Skuas forming part of her air group for operations in support of the British assault on Narvik and she operated aircraft every day until 19 May when she moved north to refuel at Tromso. On 3 May *Glorious* arrived off Greenock in the Clyde where she embarked eighteen RAF Hurricanes of 46 Squadron and the Walrus amphibians of 701 NAS; both types being craned on board from lighters. She sailed on 14 May in company with *Furious*, which was ferrying RAF Gladiators to Norway, and arrived off Narvik on 18 May, where 701 NAS was disembarked to Harstad. Bad weather prevented the Hurricanes from being flown off,[2] however, and *Glorious* had to return to Scapa Flow to refuel on 22 May with the Hurricanes still on board. On 24 May she sailed for Norway again and flew the Hurricanes off to Skaanland on 26 May. *Ark Royal*'s Skuas escorted and covered them until they were able to move on to Bardufoss. *Glorious*' air group had been reduced to make room for the aircraft she ferried but 802 NAS had been retained and a section of their Sea Gladiators shot down a Heinkel He 115 shadower on 28 May. She lacked the fuel to carry out sustained operations this far north and had less enduration than *Ark Royal*. For this reason she returned to Scapa Flow on 30 May, for what was to be the last time, to refuel.

Once the RAF fighters became operational, *Ark Royal* also returned to Scapa Flow to refuel, returning in early June to cover the evacuation of Allied forces from Narvik.

It was sad that Allied success in Narvik was so short-lived; the RAF had learnt valuable lessons about deployed fighter operations and had more success over Narvik than it had further south. In its short period of operations, the Bardufoss fighter wing flew 638 sorties and engaged in ninety-five air combats, shooting down twenty-seven enemy aircraft for the loss of seven of its own.[3] They showed, in fact, what could have been achieved by a properly constituted expeditionary force with its own tactical air force as the Royal Flying Corps had once been. *Ark Royal*'s Skuas also had success during this period, shooting down six enemy aircraft,[4] damaging a further eight and driving off at least eighteen bombers which were prevented from completing their attacks. Five Skuas were shot down but only one crew was killed in action: Bill Lucy and his observer Michael Hanson.

The Loss of Bill Lucy

Bill Lucy was obviously moved deeply by Norway, the land his carrier task force had been committed to defend, and on 30 April he wrote a poem about it which he forwarded to his parents. Fortunately they treasured and kept it along with many other documents from this period. They allowed me to have a copy of it and it is reproduced below:

Reflections of an Aviator at Sea
April 30th 1940

A glorious day, sun shining on the mountains;
In the villages the snow is melting;
At sea the waves, half asleep, are resting
After a wild and stormy winter.

The birds are welcoming another spring;
The flowers spring up bright and gay;
Small fish in the hillside streams leap in the air;
Milch cows browse quietly in the fields.

Why is the sea so empty, where are the ships?
Why do men lurk in the woods, idle?
Why do men curse the sun, and pray
That fogs and rain and gale and night may come?

Far up above this world our God has made,
A man-made speck appears, its noisy drone
Is heard, and down below, men shudder, children scream.

Hurtling towards the earth it comes:
Death and destruction follow fast:
Towns rock and churches fall; fires spring up;
Will no one put them out? It can't be done.

Swiftly another speck appears,
Another drone, and yet another vast explosion
Rocks and shatters all that man holds dear.

Far higher still a smaller speck is seen
And yet another, two at least, or three.
Police of the air; for one short spell
The air is cleared of harbingers of death.

Vengeance is swift; hurtling to earth in flames
A bomber twists and turns; its agony of death
Is fearful. By its side the swift pursuer, too,
Comes crashing down and shares the grave.

Why should this be? Who is the monster
Who turns day to night, and cheerfulness to tears?
Will no one stem this tide, will no one say
Peace, goodwill towards men, all men?

Some day these wild destructive forces will be spent:
Behind will remain bitterness sadness and grief.
Pray God a wiser generation rise,
When we can praise, not curse, the heavenly skies.

The tempo of *Ark Royal*'s flying operations was increased on 14 May 1940 and she moved nearer the coast in order to provide continuous fighter cover for the Army as it advanced on Narvik. The CAP was carried out by a section of three Skuas of 801 NAS led by Lieutenant Commander Bramwell.[5] After strafing what were described as 'derelict' German transport aircraft at Lake Harvig, known to the aircrew as *Furious*' Lake, they saw no sign of enemy air activity and recovered safely to the carrier. The second CAP comprised three Skuas of 803 NAS led by Bill Lucy in L2925, 8F. As usual he flew with Michael Hanson in his rear seat and his wing-men were Lieutenant T E Gray RN with Leading Airman A G Clayton

Glorious turning into wind to launch RAF Hurricanes of 46 Squadron for their flight to Skaanland on 26 May 1940. (Author's collection)

in 8G and Petty Officer A H Glover with Naval Airman S G Wright in 8H. They took off at 1330 and went 'feet dry' over the coast at 1405. All three aircraft carried 100lb bombs which were dropped on *Furious*' Lake at 1450 to break up the ice and Gray observed that Bill Lucy scored a direct hit on his designated target. Next they orbited over Narvik for an hour until a report was received that the battleship *Resolution* was being attacked by a single Heinkel He 111. Bill Lucy led his section towards it and climbed to 17,000 feet to give a probable height advantage. After seeing the enemy aircraft they chased it away to the south for about ten minutes without getting into a firing position and at this stage Petty Officer Glover became detached. A further report was received from *Resolution* that it was firing at another bomber that was seen to drop bombs which missed a destroyer 'by two lengths'.[6] This machine then climbed steadily out of the fighters' range but then things began to happen quickly.

Five enemy aircraft were seen approaching from the east, two pairs and a single, at 18,000 feet. Bill Lucy and Gray split and immediately attacked the leading pair head-on to break up the formation, after which they turned to attack the enemy from astern. Bill Lucy's attack set one Heinkel's port engine on fire and then he dived on the second pair, which had descended to sea level. Gray saw Bill carry

Glorious launching 46 Squadron Hurricanes on 26 May 1940. (Author's collection)

out a further attack on one of these, closing to almost point-blank range to ensure that his bullets hit but then he appeared to swing away and the Skua seemed to flash as he passed it, only 50 feet above the water. Gray fired a 'good burst and observed port engine smoking in one machine' but then broke off his own attacks and searched for his leader. He saw wreckage including a Skua tail unit and dinghy off Tranoy. There was no sign of either Lucy or Hanson in the water but Gray flew across the fjord and communicated with the destroyer *Whirlwind* off Ransundet which he then led back to the crash site where debris was still floating. *Whirlwind* managed to recover Bill Lucy's body but found no sign of Michael Hanson. As was normal practice, Bill Lucy was given a naval burial at sea some hours later. Both naval officers, therefore, have no known grave but the sea. Lieutenant William Paulet Lucy DSO RN is commemorated on the Fleet Air Arm War Memorial at Lee-on-Solent, Hampshire, on Bay 1 Panel 2. Lieutenant Michael Charles Edward Hanson is commemorated on the same panel.

Gray spent so long trying to direct the destroyer to the crash site in case there was a chance of saving his CO that he was left with insufficient fuel to fly back to *Ark Royal*. At 1800, therefore, he carried out a forced landing near Ankenes. The destroyer *Encounter* was close by and embarked the crew by boat. Their aircraft, L2918, could not be recovered and so it was set on fire after the beacon set, Very pistols, parachutes, W/T coils, transmitter/receiver unit, generator, Lewis gun and pans of ammunition had been salvaged from it.

The Lucy family learnt of Bill's death from an Admiralty telegram handed in at 1222 on 15 May 1940 and received at Sutton Valence Post Office at 1248. Addressed to Mr F W Lucy of Langley Lodge, Sutton Valence, Kent, it read: 'From Admiralty deeply regret to inform you that your son Lieutenant W P Lucy has been killed on active service.' A letter, written by the Admiralty Secretariat was written and posted on that same afternoon, 15 May, which read:

Admiralty
15th May 1940

Sir,
In confirmation of the Admiralty's telegram despatched this morning, I am commanded by My Lords Commissioners of the Admiralty to state that they have learnt that your son, Lieutenant William Paulet Lucy DSO Royal Navy, lost his life yesterday, 14th May, during aerial operations over the North Sea.

My Lords desire me to express to you their very deep regret at receiving this intelligence which follows so hard upon the recognition of his services by His Majesty the King, and their profound sympathy in the great loss which you have sustained.

I am, Sir,
Your obedient Servant,
R H A Martin

It is usual for commanding officers to write to the next of kin when one of their men is killed in action but the letters subsequently written to Bill Lucy's father were far from routine.[7] They were as follows:

Buckingham Palace

The Queen and I offer you our heartfelt sympathy in your great sorrow.
We pray that your country's gratitude for a life so nobly given in its service may bring you some measure of consolation.

George RI

F W Lucy Esq JP

Admiral Wells, Vice Admiral Aircraft Carriers, sent Mr Lucy a handwritten letter dated 22 May which read:

HMS ARK ROYAL
At sea
22 May 1940

Dear Mr Lucy,
May I offer you my deepest sympathy on the loss of your gallant son. He flew on board this ship from *Glorious* on 27th April having already done magnificent work from that ship. On one occasion his patrol of 3 Skuas shot down 3 enemy bombers in the course of which they attacked 8 Heinkel 111s in formation, forced them to drop their bombs in the sea, broke them up and shot one down in flames. I was much impressed with your son the moment I saw him. A fine leader who set a wonderful

example to his Squadron. On my return to London on 3rd May I recommended him for an Immediate decoration, this would have meant a bar to his DSO which he had already earned.[8] We sailed the next day and he continued his great work until he was shot down on 14th May, if it had to be – an end I know he would have chosen for himself. He and Lt Hanson his observer were indeed a wonderful pair. Your boy was without doubt one of the outstanding fighter pilots of the Fleet Air Arm, with the heart of a lion.

Yours sincerely,
L V Wells
Vice Admiral

Captain C S Holland had only taken over command of *Ark Royal* on 10 April 1940 but he, too, felt compelled to write to Mr Lucy in praise of his son.

HMS ARK ROYAL
At Sea
29.5.40

Dear Mr Lucy,
I have been meaning to write to you but have not had the chance of doing so as I have been unable to post a letter.

Your son died in a very gallant fight against the enemy. He was, as he always did, attacking hard and pressing home his attack in the way which had already earned him three mentions in dispatches.

Suddenly his aircraft was seen to burst into flames and dive into the sea. His body was recovered by a destroyer, but I am sorry to say I cannot say whether he was buried at sea or on land.[9]

I have only been in command of this ship a short time, but from my own experience I know we have lost a very gallant and brave leader who never hesitated to attack the enemy with all his might and prowess.

Please accept from myself, my officers and ship's company our deepest sympathy and regrets at your loss, which is also ours.

I am so very sorry to be unable to tell you more or to write further and believe me I would have done so if I could have.

Yours very sincerely,
Cedric Holland

Mr Lucy received many other letters from which I have selected four that illustrate the admiration in which Bill Lucy was held across the naval service. The first of these was from Captain C Moody RN who was Director of the Naval Air Division at the Admiralty. He wrote:

Naval Air Division
Admiralty

May 20th 1940

Dear Mr Lucy
I am taking the liberty of writing to offer you my deepest sympathy in the loss of your very gallant son – I never met him but as Director of the Naval Air Division I have seen all the reports on Fleet Air Arm actions. His name constantly came up directly the war started and has done so with increasing emphasis ever since.

Apart from reports by Senior Naval Officers I have now seen a report from the Commander-in-Chief RAF Fighter Command under whose orders your son's squadron operated in the winter. He (Air Marshal Dowding) was much impressed by Lieutenant Lucy.

I feel that the knowledge that he had so rightly been awarded the DSO and that he had been remarked on so often by Senior Officers of both Services may be some slight but poor consolation to you. You have lost a very gallant son and a very fine gentleman. I make it a rule in my position not to attempt to write letters such as this one except to the relations of officers I knew: but I hope you will forgive my breaking this rule in this case as I feel so deeply what a loss you and the Fleet Air Arm have suffered.

Yours sincerely,
Clement Moody
Captain RN

Next came a letter from an officer on the staff of RANAS at Lee-on-Solent who knew Bill Lucy and clearly felt his loss very deeply:

Office of the
RANAS
Lee-on-Solent
Hants

My dear Mr Lucy,
You do not know me, and I must apologise also for writing this on my typewriter. It is a hot afternoon and I am 'staff-tired' too and never being much good at handwriting, I will tell you what I want to tell you much better if you will forgive it being typed.

Your son was in the *Hermes* with me when we were in China, and later I knew him both at Eastleigh and Hatston. So I developed for him that affection and admiration which all of us in the Fleet Air Arm had for him, and which made us all feel 'he would' when it became known that he was the very embodiment of the spirit of the Fleet Air Arm which came into its own in the Norwegian Campaign.

Having to operate from ships, our aircraft are never the latest and fastest. The Air Force experts in our own as in other Air Forces are apt to laugh at the performance of the FAA aircraft and at what would happen to them if they came up against modern fighters and bombers.

With such aircraft and against such a feeling, Lucy led the Fleet Air Arm against Heinkels and Dorniers and Messerschmitts – against well defended gun areas, in every kind of weather: and somehow or other the Heinkels and Dorniers and Messerschmitts didn't ever seem to want to stay to see just how bad the Fleet Air Arm aircraft were. I was told that Lucy always had to chase them and overtake them from above to bring them to action at all. It was a case of 'he who laughs last, laughs best' and Lucy laughed best of all and put the Fleet Air Arm aircraft on the map.

Before the Norwegian Campaign, the Fleet Air Arm had barely been heard of by the public. Then the Fleet Air Arm suddenly did for the Army at Åndalsnes what the Air Force did for the Army at Dunkirk; and they did it with Swordfish and Skuas not with Spitfires and Hurricanes and Defiants.

Everyone was amazed, the Germans most of all. It was the spirit of the Fleet Air Arm which made that evacuation possible and of that spirit, Lucy was the embodiment and the leader.

Knowing him even as well as I did, I know what his loss must mean to you; so I wanted to write and tell you that we who are left in the Fleet Air Arm to continue, and to try and follow his example, know that Lucy neither lived nor died in vain.

Yours very sincerely,
John Harvey
Cdr RN

Although clearly written in some haste, this letter reveals its author's assumption, fed by years of operation under Air Ministry control, that carrier-borne aircraft must necessarily be inferior to those operated exclusively ashore. As the US Navy was soon to prove and we now know from years of operational experience, this is not the case. I have included it, however, because it shows the widespread admiration for Bill Lucy across the service.

Two further letters, one from Lieutenant Harry Torin of 803 NAS and another from his wife show the regard in which Bill Lucy was held by his squadron:

The Albany Hotel
Hastings
Sussex

Dear Mr Lucy
As a member of your son's squadron may I offer you my deepest sympathy in the loss of such a brave man.

I have been the First Lieutenant of the squadron under him since he commanded and have been on all the Bergen raids with him and for a short time on the *Glorious*.

Apart from being a wonderful squadron leader he was one of the bravest and most daring men one could ever find.

Though I am at the moment on sick leave, I know that his loss is felt most terribly by all members of the squadron.

I don't know if you have heard the story of the 7 Heinkels which is just one of his numerous achievements. On his way back to the *Glorious* from a bombing raid he and another machine in company with him came upon 7 Heinkels coming out to bomb the *Glorious*. Without any thought he immediately set on them. They brought down some of them and the remaining three dropped their bombs into the sea and fled. I have talked to the other officer who was with him and he cannot get over the marvellous way in which Bill set about them.

Once again may I offer you my deepest sympathy. I loathe the thought of going back to that squadron without Bill in command.

If there is anything further I can tell you about Bill, or if I wasn't there, find out for you, I should be happy to do so.

Yours sincerely
Harry E R Torin
Lieut. RN

The Albany Hotel
Hastings
Sussex
May 18th

Dear Mrs Lucy,
I want to join my husband in deepest sympathy in your great loss. Bill was a great friend of ours and we admired him so much, everybody in Kirkwall talked of the wonderful way he led his squadron in the raids on Bergen – he always chose the most dangerous job to do himself.

The night before he embarked we dined with him and had such a happy evening. Bill talked so beautifully of his family for the first time to us. He had been to Church in the morning as well. I am proud to have known him and his memory will live with us. I pray God to comfort you dear Mrs Lucy.

Sincerely,
Mercia Torin

The Fleet Air Arm Memorial at Lee-on-Solent is next to the former RN Air Station which was the wartime headquarters and drafting barracks of the Fleet Air Arm. (Philip Yetman collection)

The central column of the Memorial at Lee-on-Solent reads: 'THESE OFFICERS AND MEN OF THE FLEET AIR ARM DIED IN THE SERVICE OF THEIR COUNTRY AND HAVE NO GRAVE BUT THE SEA 1939–1945'. (Philip Yetman collection)

The names of Lieutenant W P Lucy DSO RN and Lieutenant M C E Hanson DSC RN are close to each other on the Fleet Air Arm Memorial at Lee-on- Solent, Bay 1 Panel 2. (Philip Yetman collection)

FRYER W.A.F.
HALLEWELL J.L.
HANSON M.C.E., D.S.C.
HEBBLETHWAITE S.F.V
HOSKIN M.C.
KENNAWAY C.S.H.
LUCY W.P., D.S.O.

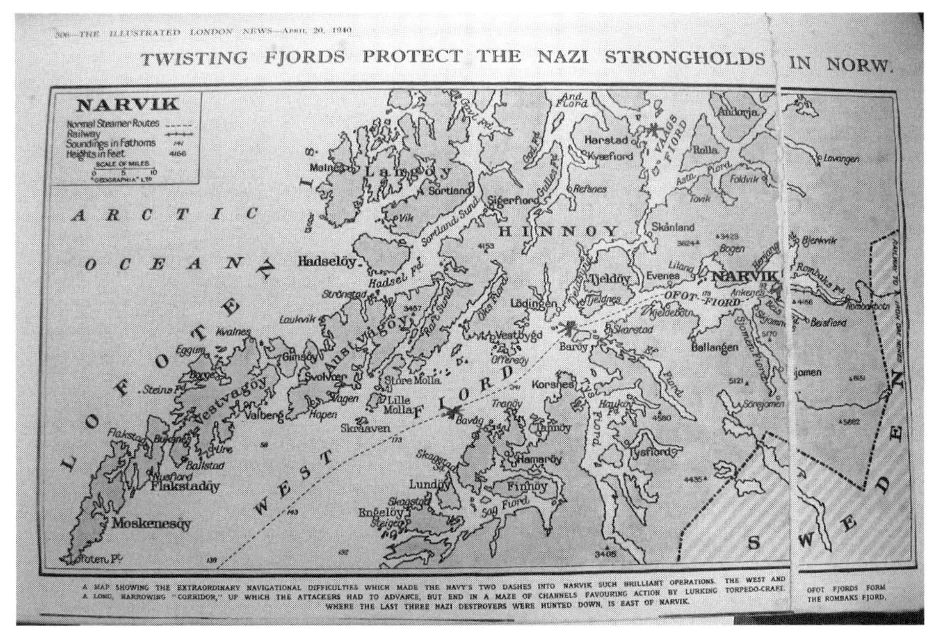

306—THE ILLUSTRATED LONDON NEWS—APRIL 20, 1940

TWISTING FJORDS PROTECT THE NAZI STRONGHOLDS IN NORW.

A MAP SHOWING THE EXTRAORDINARY NAVIGATIONAL DIFFICULTIES WHICH MADE THE NAVY'S TWO DASHES INTO NARVIK SUCH BRILLIANT OPERATIONS. THE WEST AND A LONG, NARROWING "CORRIDOR," UP WHICH THE ATTACKERS HAD TO ADVANCE, BUT END IN A MAZE OF CHANNELS FAVOURING ACTION BY LURKING TORPEDO-CRAFT. WHERE THE LAST THREE NAZI DESTROYERS WERE HUNTED DOWN, IS EAST OF NARVIK.

OFOT FJORDS FORM THE ROMBAKS FJORD,

The map from the *Illustrated London News* with which Lieutenant Commander Rogers showed Bill Lucy's parents where his Skua, L2925, crashed and where he was buried at sea with naval honours from the destroyer *Whirlwind*. The lower pencilled cross by Bavag shows where the aircraft came down. The upper cross near Baroy Island shows where Bill Lucy was buried at sea. (John de Lucy collection)

Part of the Lucy family photographed at home before setting out to see the Coronation Review in the summer of 1937. Bill Lucy's caption to this photograph read, 'My Hillman AKO 374 – From left to right Sister Joyce, self, Father Francis, Mother Violet and Sylvia – Still at home, Langley Lodge'. (John de Lucy collection)

On reading through the Lucy family papers I was delighted to find that Mr and Mrs Lucy continued to correspond with those who had written to them and did indeed seek to find out more about what had happened. They organised a memorial tablet in their local church and on 26 July Admiral Wells wrote to accompany 'one of *Ark Royal*'s small ensigns to place with your son's memorial tablet'. He added, 'we have lost many fine officers since, but I will never forget your boy. He would be proud to know what fine work his squadron has done since.'

On 22 August 1940 Mr and Mrs Lucy were given more detail of their son's burial at sea by Lieutenant Commander John Rogers RN who had commanded the destroyer *Whirlwind* off Norway on 14 May. Unfortunately she had subsequently been torpedoed and sunk on 5 July 1940 by U-34, 120nm west of Land's End, Cornwall, with the loss of fifty-seven lives. Commander Rogers was able to explain that they had seen the Skua crash and were already accelerating towards the spot when Lieutenant Gray's TAG, Leading Airman Clayton, signalled them by flashing light asking for help. On arrival between 1700 and 1800 they were able to pick up Bill Lucy's body and saw aircraft wreckage but, unfortunately, it sank before it could be examined. As *Whirlwind* could not make harbour the next day, he explained that Bill was given a naval burial off Baroy Island at 1100 on 15 May 1940 and marked the position for them on a map of the approaches to Narvik that had appeared in the *Illustrated London News* of 20 April 1940. He also marked the position where Bill's Skua, L2925, had come down. Lieutenant Commander Rogers had read the service himself and three rounds were fired by a guard as the body was committed to the deep; just the ending Mr and Mrs Lucy believed Bill would have wished.

Throughout this book I have used Bill Lucy's career to show how naval officers learnt to fly and operated in the Fleet Air Arm through the difficult years of divided control and also how they seized the opportunity to achieve everything they could when full control was restored after the Inskip Award. I hope that this chapter will have demonstrated that Bill Lucy was not just a good example; he was the outstanding strike fighter leader of his generation. He led the first aircraft strike ever to sink a major warship; he was the first British fighter 'ace' of the Second World War and he was admired by a range of people from the King, through admirals, directors in the Admiralty Staff, contemporaries and those whom he led in action. He richly deserves his place in history.

Chapter 17

Heavy Losses after the Withdrawal from Narvik

By late evening on 28 May 1940 Allied forces had captured the town of Narvik and were advancing along the railway line that carried iron ore from Sweden during the winter months. Demolition work was carried out on the ore quays, the electric power supplies and the railway line itself and then immediate preparations were made for withdrawal.[1] Air cover for the expeditionary force, when flying operations from Bardufoss were not limited by fog, was provided at this stage by the RAF Hurricanes and Gladiators but Lord Cork, C-in-C Northern Norway, asked for the Home Fleet to cover the final stages of the withdrawal. Accordingly *Ark Royal* and *Glorious* arrived off the Norwegian coast with their screening destroyers on 2 June. *Ark Royal* was intended to provide fighter cover but *Glorious*, with her more limited endurance, had been deployed with a reduced air group specifically to recover as many Gladiators and Hurricanes as possible. None of the RAF pilots had ever landed on a carrier before but they had asked to be allowed to try rather than destroy their aircraft and there was a general consensus that soon every available fighter would be needed to defend UK airspace. Whether the handful of fighters was worth endangering a valuable aircraft carrier deployed without its full air group is a moot point and not a risk that should have been taken as lightly as it was.

In the absence of the carrier task force during late May, naval aviation had been represented in the area by the six Walrus amphibians of 701 NAS which had operated from Harstad after being delivered by *Glorious*. They had conducted a spirited, if short, campaign carrying out a number of missions that even the aircraft's staunchest advocates would hardly have considered possible a month earlier. These included reconnaissance, bombing, VIP transport and Army support. On 6 June they had dive-bombed an enemy-held harbour and both dive-bombed and strafed German troops and vehicles.[2]

The withdrawal from Narvik proved to be better planned and executed than many other aspects of the ill-fated campaign in Norway. Store-ships and fifteen troop transports were sent to Harstad, arriving on 2 June, where they loaded with minimal interference from the enemy; perhaps because it did not occur to the German High Command that the British would withdraw so soon after capturing Narvik, perhaps because its attention was focused on events in Belgium and France. They sailed on 7 June with 10,000 Allied troops embarked and considerably more equipment than the Army had thought it could save. 15,000 troops had sailed before that in six large troopships on 4, 5 and 6 June without interference from the enemy and on 7 June fighters from *Ark Royal* took on the air defence task as the RAF fighters flew out to *Glorious* to land on. In the event, ten Gladiators of 264 Squadron and seven Hurricanes of 46 Squadron were all that had survived at Bardufoss and all of them landed on successfully.[3] None had arrester hooks but the Hurricane pilots put sandbags in the rear of their aircraft to move the centre of gravity aft and help them achieve the slow, nose-high attitude they needed for landing. Their gallant demonstration that landing modern high-performance monoplane fighters on the deck of an aircraft carrier was perfectly feasible was timely and showed the way ahead for the re-equipment of the RN fighter squadrons. It was, of course, something the US Navy already knew but the Air Ministry had argued that it would not be a realistic proposition. It is ironic that a handful of gallant RAF pilots should be the ones to prove the Air Ministry wrong; tragically the majority died soon afterwards. The last men were evacuated on 8 June and joined a convoy escorted by the battleship *Valiant* and destroyers from the Home Fleet. *Ark Royal* landed on five of the 701 NAS Walrus on 7 June and then joined the convoy and reached home waters safely.

Unfortunately on 7 June *Glorious* had asked permission to leave the Narvik area with a screen of only two destroyers, far fewer than on her previous transits of the North Sea, in order to return to the UK independently, and this was granted by VAA. To put this into context, no troopships or store-ships had been lost or damaged on their passages to and from Vestfjord and only one in central Norway. It seemed, therefore, that control of the open sea had been effectively secured but this was not, in fact, the case. A German force under Admiral Marschall comprising the battlecruisers *Scharnhorst* and *Gneisenau* with the heavy cruiser *Hipper* and 4 destroyers had sailed from Kiel on 4 June with the intention of attacking British shipping off Harstad on the night of 8/9 June. Evidently the Germans had no idea that Narvik was already being evacuated, nor were they aware of the vulnerable convoy movements stretching across the North Sea from northern Norway to the UK, but on 7 June Marschall received air reports of two groups of ships and decided to intercept the most southerly. When found on the morning of 8 June this was discovered to consist of the tanker *Oil Pioneer* and its escorting trawler *Jupiter* in company with the empty troopship *Orama* and the hospital ship *Atlantis*. The status of the hospital ship was respected but the other three were all sunk. However, after reporting this action to Group Command West, Marschall was ordered to carry on with the planned attack on Harstad and leave convoys to *Hipper* and the destroyers. Marschall had by then deduced that an evacuation was in progress, though, and ordered *Hipper* and the destroyers to Trondheim on 8 June to refuel while he continued to search the open sea for further targets. Their movements went undetected by any reconnaissance aircraft of RAF Coastal Command and so no warning was given to Admiral Forbes or Lord Cork that they were at sea.

Loss of Glorious

At about 1600 on the afternoon of 8 June a lookout in *Scharnhorst* saw smoke on the starboard bow and the German force altered course towards it. As the masthead appeared above the horizon it was identified as the aircraft carrier *Glorious* with only the destroyers *Acasta*, Commander C E Glasfurd RN, and *Ardent*, Lieutenant Commander J F Barker RN, in company. Admiral Marschall ordered action stations and astutely manoeuvred to windward so that the carrier would have to turn towards him in order to fly off her aircraft.[4] Surprisingly, however, *Glorious* had no reconnaissance aircraft airborne and no strike force ranged ready for immediate launch. The subsequent Board of Inquiry into her loss by the C-in-C Rosyth found that no aircraft had been operated from *Glorious* for the previous twelve hours, no lookout had been posted in the crow's nest despite the conditions of extreme visibility and no ammunition or fuses suitable for surface action were available at the guns until after the action commenced. As soon as the German ships were seen, *Glorious* turned away and increased speed while the two destroyers laid a smoke screen, but she had been caught completely unawares and vulnerable.

Scharnhorst opened fire at 1630 at a range of 28,000 yards and as soon as the two battlecruisers found the range with their 11-inch guns the result was inevitable. Desperate efforts were made in *Glorious* to arm and range a small strike of three Swordfish but space was congested by the presence of the Gladiators and Hurricanes which could not be folded. One of the first German shells hit the bridge, killing everyone on it. Subsequent shells smashed into the flight deck and hangar with the result that it was soon over. At about 1720 *Glorious* was stopped and on fire when the order was given to abandon ship. At 1728 the destroyer *Ardent*, having fired all its torpedoes at the enemy, was overwhelmed by gunfire and sunk. At 1740 *Glorious* rolled to starboard and sank with eventual loss of over 1,500 men, leaving *Acasta* alone. She managed to fire a salvo of torpedoes at the enemy before she, too, was overwhelmed and sunk at 1806, although one of her torpedoes hit *Scharnhorst* abreast her after gun turret and caused severe damage. The Germans made no attempt to pick up survivors from the cold, northern sea and made for Trondheim, thus leaving the convoys further north untouched. The few who survived spent some fifty-seven to sixty hours in the sea before help arrived and were not helped by the fact that *Glorious*' Carley floats did not have provisions and water supplies attached to them as they should have done.[5] The Board also found that an enemy sighting report appeared to have been transmitted by *Glorious* on low power and so it is doubtful whether any other warships picked it up. Also there had been reports of enemy activity on the Narvik wavelength but, on leaving, *Glorious* had chopped to the Home Fleet wavelength and would not have received them. In his remarks, the C-in-C Rosyth concluded, '*Glorious* appears to have been caught unprepared for action and to have been unsuspecting of enemy forces in her vicinity and no evidence has been obtained as to why this state of affairs existed.' The full reasons probably died with her captain and will never be fully clarified.

By the time Grand Admiral Raeder heard of the action he was also aware that the British had evacuated Narvik and the troop convoys had returned to the UK unscathed. He referred to the sinking of *Glorious* as 'mere target practice and so hardly to be termed a momentous victory'.[6] Whatever his view, it was a disaster for the RN's embryonic Air Branch with the loss of a valuable aircraft carrier and a number of pilots and observers who were desperately needed for the creation of new squadrons and training the first wartime generation of RNVR aircrew for service in the front line. In the short term the impact of their loss could hardly have been worse but more losses would follow in less than a week. On 11 June three officers and thirty-five men of *Glorious*' ship's company and one man from *Acasta* were picked up by a small Norwegian fishing vessel and landed in the Faeroe Islands. Another rescued five men from *Glorious* who, with two men from *Ardent* picked up by a German seaplane, became prisoners of war.

In his analytical masterpiece *Air Power and the Royal Navy*, Geoffrey Till noted that, 'in retrospect, it is easy to see that serious mistakes were made in this encounter. The *Glorious* should not have been authorised to proceed to base independently in such dangerous waters.' He believed that various factors had played a part in this tragedy and noted that her captain, Captain G. D'Oyly Hughes DSO DSC RN, although acquainted with naval flying, was not an aviator and had a personal preference for independent action. He was in dispute with his Commander (Air), whom he had placed under arrest and left at Scapa Flow. D'Oyly Hughes was evidently anxious to return to base in order to end as soon as possible what must have been a highly uncomfortable situation. It would seem that for this reason the *Glorious* signalled VAA in the early hours of 8 June and requested permission to proceed ahead to Scapa Flow 'for the purpose of making preparations for impending courts martial'.[7] Accordingly *Glorious* left the carrier task force at 0350 with an inadequate screen of only two destroyers. In retrospect it is clear that this detachment should neither have been requested nor granted but it is significant to note that by this point passage across the northern North Sea between the UK and Norway had become almost routine. No one in the Admiralty War Room or the Home Fleet Staff expected to find enemy surface ships in the area and the flag officers off Narvik, with no advice to the contrary, assumed that the British had sea control in the area. To make matters worse, several operations were being conducted at once and *Glorious*' secondary ferrying role had placed her at the periphery of events. She should either not have been there in the first place or committed fully to air superiority operations within the carrier task force with a full air group embarked. Geoffrey Till also noted that the variety of operations being undertaken had led to 'such a state of disarray that RAF Coastal Command was not even informed that an evacuation was in progress and that special vigilance was necessary'.[8] Given the

The running range of 800 and 803 NAS Skuas about to launch from *Ark Royal* on 13 June 1940 to attack *Scharnhorst* in Trondheim. (Author's collection)

momentous events further south at this time, including the Dunkirk evacuation, the collapse of French resistance and Churchill's recent move from First Lord of the Admiralty to Prime Minister, this could well have been the case.

Heavy Casualties in the Skua Squadrons

The Norwegian campaign effectively ended with a further attempt to use naval aircraft to attack enemy warships located in a Norwegian harbour which could not otherwise be brought to action by the Home Fleet. *Scharnhorst* had put into Trondheim to effect temporary repairs after the damage inflicted by *Acasta*. She had been located there by RAF reconnaissance together with two enemy cruisers, and Bomber Command had attacked them on 11 June claiming three hits, one on an 8-inch cruiser and two on a smaller vessel. The Admiralty then proposed using Skuas from *Ark Royal* to attack *Scharnhorst*[9] in its signal 1706/11. A launch position 170nm from Trondheim was proposed and agreement was reached between the Admiralty and RAF Coastal Command that four Beaufort bombers of 18 Group would carry out a synchronised attack on Vaernes airfield, where German fighters were known to be based. Six Blenheim long-range fighters, also from 18 Group, would support the Skuas,[10] the whole strike to commence at 0200. Despite the fact that torpedoes were regarded as better 'ship-killing' weapons than the 500lb bomb, it was decided to use Skuas, rather than Swordfish for the strike because the anchorage at Trondheim was well inland from the sea and there might be insufficient room for the aircraft to manoeuvre to carry out a torpedo attack. There were other problems which were highlighted by the Naval Air Department at the Admiralty; these included the almost continual daylight this far north in June and the long overland transit after crossing the coast which would give the enemy time to alert the defences. Without the crucial element of surprise, even with the support of the diversionary RAF strike and the long-range fighters, the Skuas would be hard pressed to achieve their object. The synchronisation of different air striking forces controlled by different headquarters with land-based aircraft flying from distant bases with only a sketchy idea of what was going on would be difficult to achieve.

Attack by Skuas from *Ark Royal* on *Scharnhorst* in Trondheim, 13 June 1940

Pilot	*Observer/TAG*	*Aircraft*
803 NAS		
Lt Cdr J Casson	Lt P E Fanshawe	7A
Sub Lt G W Brokensha	LA F Coston	7B
PO T F Riddler	NA H T Chatterley	7C
Lt C H Filmer	Mid (A) T A McKee	7F
Mid (A) A S Griffiths	NA F P Dooley	7G
Sub Lt J A Harris	NA G R Stevenson	7L
Lt D C E F Gibson	Sub Lt M P Gordon-Smith	7P
Sub Lt R E Bartlett	NA L C Richards	7Q
PO H Gardiner	NA H Pickering	7R
800 NAS		
Capt. R T Partridge RM	Lt R S Bostock	6A
Lt K V V Spurway	PO R F Hart	6K
PO H A Monk	PO R S Rolph	6C
Lt E D G Finch-Noyes	PO H G Cunningham	6F
Mid L H Gallagher	PO W Crawford	6G
Mid D T R Martin	LA W J Tremeer	6H

The fifteen Skuas from *Ark Royal* were led by Lieutenant Commander J Casson RN who had replaced Bill Lucy in command of 803 NAS.[11] The launch began shortly after midnight and, as usual, they flew in three-aircraft sections and had climbed to

11,000 feet by the time they reached the coast north-west of Trondheim at 0123. All except the last flight worked their way around *Scharnhorst* in order to attack her from bow to stern, the best angle to attain hits, but they were heavily engaged by anti-aircraft fire as they did so. They carried out a standard dive-bombing attack, releasing their 500lb SAP bombs at about 3,000 feet and headed down the fjord towards the sea but as they did so they were attacked by enemy fighters including Messerschmitt Bf 109s and 110s. Only seven aircraft returned to *Ark Royal* and all but one of these flew at low level close to the cliffs at the side of the fjord to limit the attacking fighters' options and give the TAGs the best chance of engaging them accurately with their rear guns.[12]

In his initial report on the strike, dated 15 June 1940,[13] VAA informed the C-in-C Home Fleet and the Secretary of the Admiralty that Lieutenant Spurway in 6K had:

> observed the splash of a near miss when diving to attack behind his leader, 6A. This was before 6A released. It is confirmed from other pilots that the visibility did not prevent splashes of misses being seen, in fact three other near misses were observed. After 6A released, 6K observed a more vivid flash than anti-aircraft guns on the ship appeared to be making, at a point aft of the funnel on the port side … photographs taken from 6K immediately after the attack show a column of smoke emanating approximately from this position.

Lieutenant Gibson was sure there was no smoke over the ship during his attack but Petty Officer Hart, the observer of 6K, saw a flash on the port side abaft the funnel which was noticeably more vivid than the fire from the anti-aircraft guns. This flash was seen about five to six seconds after release.

In his full report,[14] Admiral Wells brought out further points about the strike. He believed that the task force reached the flying-off position undetected but to drive off possible shadowers and to engage enemy bombers if they appeared, a section of three Skuas had been maintained over the force from 2230 on 12 June to 0550 on 13 June when *Ark Royal* was ordered to return to Scapa Flow by the C-in-C Home Fleet. The launch position was 65 00N 04 50E and each of the strike aircraft had been armed with a single 500lb SAP bomb. The decision to send fifteen Skuas had been based on several considerations. These were:

(a) Only 15 of the pilots available had previous experience of dive-bombing with the Skua, a reflection on the losses already suffered in the campaign.
(b) Other Skuas had to be retained to maintain CAP stations for several hours.
(c) With the prevailing light wind, fifteen was the maximum number of aircraft that could be flown off with a full load. There had to be space forward of the range for the first aircraft to take off and the round-down aft of the range could not be used because of its curvature.

Scharnhorst was briefed as the primary target if it was located and the importance of gaining surprise was stressed, the aircrew were informed that Blenheims would give them fighter support during the attack and that Beauforts would attack Vaernes airfield not earlier than 0200. At 0305 the carrier task force altered course onto 170 degrees, into wind, in readiness to land on the returning Skuas. By 0345 only seven had returned and landed on; Because of the light wind *Ark Royal* had left her position in the force and from 0345 she slowed to resume her ordered station. Course was maintained on 170 degrees in case there were any stragglers but by 0425 it was clear that there were none and course was altered to 270 degrees. Shortly before this a bank of fog was seen to be approaching rapidly from windward and the force had only just steadied on its new course when it entered the fog bank. Fortunately one of the Skua CAP in the overhead waiting to recover was able to report a clear area bearing 030 degrees and the force headed for it. At 0512 the fog cleared and *Ark Royal*, screened by *Kelvin* and *Escort*, went ahead at 28 knots to gain sufficient sea room to turn into wind and recover the last Skua CAP. They were recovered by 0550 when course was altered again to 270 degrees , speed 22 knots to return to Scapa Flow in accordance with the C-in-C's signal 0518/13.

VAA made the following remarks on the strike:

> Owing to the conditions of light and sky which was clear except for some very light cloud, and to the 50nm which lay between the coast and the anchorage, surprise was not achieved and the Skuas were met with fighter opposition and intense anti-aircraft fire.
>
> It is difficult to judge whether the Beauforts' attack on Vaernes aerodrome carried out just before the Skuas' arrived served to distract the attention of the defence from the approach of the Skuas, or whether it had an adverse effect against surprise. Many enemy fighters were certainly over the anchorage at the time the Skuas dived to attack but this may have resulted from their being reported during their passage from the coast.
>
> It is not considered that failure to find the ship owing to the fog was the cause of the loss of any of the striking force. The time interval between the first Skua to return and running into the fog was one hour and five minutes and no signals from any of the missing aircraft were heard.
>
> There is no doubt that the attack was most courageously pressed home by the striking force in the face of intense anti-aircraft fire both from warships and the ground, and of enemy fighter opposition.
>
> I consider that at least one and possibly 2 hits were obtained on the battlecruiser *Scharnhorst*.
>
> Recommendations for awards have been forwarded under separate cover'.
>
> L V Wells
> Vice Admiral

Glorious at sea off the coast of Norway. The aircraft right aft is a Hurricane, the aircraft forward of it is a Swordfish. (Author's collection)

Ark Royal's Combat Report Number 11, rendered in accordance with Confidential Admiralty Fleet Order 3572/39, was attached to VAA's report[15] and added more detail. All the strike aircraft had committed to 60-degree dive attacks, releasing their bombs at 3,000 feet. Some aircraft were seen to become separated from their leaders when taking avoiding action but the anti-aircraft fire appears to have been disregarded by the majority. Long-range anti-aircraft fire was assessed as inaccurate. Ships and shore batteries' close-range weapons were more accurate up to 8,000 feet and each ship used a different colour tracer. Casualties included four Skuas each from 800 and 803 NAS including both commanding officers. Lieutenant D C E F Gibson RN[16] was the senior surviving officer of 803 NAS and he reported:

> After having flown inshore for about 10 minutes, we turned to the south and approached the target at about 10,000 feet, still proceeding at slow speed. Shortly before reaching Trondheim, 803 NAS formed into line astern and 800 NAS broke away to carry out a separate attack. We carried out a shallow dive to 8,000 feet and made our approach. While still north of the target, which was one battlecruiser and one heavy cruiser, heavy anti-aircraft fire developed. By the time I was in a position to attack from north to south along the deck of the battlecruiser the anti-aircraft fire was exceedingly fierce.
>
> Lieutenant Commander Casson was leading the squadron round to attack from south to north (from bow to stern). As I was the last section to attack, I considered

it not worthwhile to expose my aircraft to an extra 5 minutes of anti-aircraft fire. We attacked from stern to bow of the enemy, being in a perfect position to do so. There appears to be only two survivors from the south to north (bow to stern) attack.

Although we have no record of having hit the target, our bombs seem to have fallen close around it, one being estimated at fifteen feet from its stern.

With one exception, all the survivors escaped at low level by low-flying in the ground mist. The exception was Sub Lieutenant (A) Brokensha who circled the area twice to see if he could help anyone.

Many Me 109 [sic] fighters were seen to attack Skuas and four Me 110 [sic] fighters were present, though they held off. I, myself, was subjected to a poor-spirited attack by the Me 109s when in my dive. One Me 110 was driven off by the Skua it attacked.

From what we saw, those who were attacked by fighters were those who climbed after attacking and did not take advantage of the ground mist. As we had no height and negligible performance, it would have been suicidal to have gone to their assistance.

We gained the impression that the diversion created by the Beaufort bombers was a mistake. It appeared to take place a little too soon and destroyed any possibility of surprise. There are contrary opinions on this matter.

We did not see the Blenheim fighters until after we had left the coast. Four of our aircraft failed to return.

Lieutenant K V V Spurway RN was the senior surviving officer of 800 NAS and he reported:

On approaching Trondheim at about 11,500 feet, several warships were sighted at anchor off the town and these were photographed.

These included a battlecruiser, *Hipper* class cruiser, another cruiser, a destroyer and some smaller unidentified ships.

On approaching the ships, intense anti-aircraft fire of every type was encountered, both from ships and the shore. The fire from the battlecruiser and cruisers was very heavy and they appeared to be using many Bofors or Oerlikons, firing tracer up to 8,000 feet and above. Each ship used a different colour of tracer and seemed to be firing by the 'hosepipe' method.

The Skuas of 803 and 800 were forced to take violent evasive action and the attack was, therefore, somewhat confused. 6K followed 6A (Captain Partridge) down on the battlecruiser. The splash from a near miss was observed close to the latter's quarter, and a vivid flash was observed by the pilot of 6K as he dived. It appeared to come from abaft the funnel on the starboard side. 6K's bomb was released at 3,000 feet and on pulling away, the observer reported that he had seen a flash, possibly caused by 6K's bomb on the port side abaft the funnel. The photograph taken directly after 6K's bomb had fallen shows considerable smoke over the battlecruiser.

6K pulled up to 5,000 feet until clear of the gun area and then dived low over the land to the northward as an Me 110 was observed on the starboard beam. An Me 109 was observed some distance away. The fighters apparently failed to observe 6K against the dark ground. 6K subsequently returned in company with 6G which joined up on leaving the coast. 6K landed on at 0330.

Photographs were taken by Petty Officer Hart, the observer in 6K, under extremely difficult conditions as the pilot was taking violent evasive action at the time.[17]

Other aircraft were observed to attack the *Hipper* class cruiser on the right, but no hits were observed by 6K. The weather was hazy with a clear sky and the movements of aircraft were hard to follow against the ground or water.

Two large fires were observed ashore. One in the vicinity of Vaernes aerodrome and the other further west.

No Blenheims or Beauforts were sighted. A large number of He 115s were observed in the water off the town and 2 were seen in the air in the vicinity.

A large ball of flame was seen in the air over the ships by Petty Officer Hart. It is possible that this was an aircraft shot down in flames.

The combat report by aircraft 6C flown by Petty Officer H Monk DSM with Petty Officer R S Rolph as his observer was not forwarded to VAA but is of interest because this was the aircraft that drove off a Messerschmitt Bf 110. The incident took place at 4,000 feet as 6C was carrying out a dive-bombing attack on *Scharnhorst*. The Bf 110 attacked the Skua and Rolph immediately opened fire on it; Monk jettisoned his bomb, put down full flap and turned hard towards the enemy fighter, forcing it to overshoot. Monk then reversed his turn and fired a five-second burst into the enemy at 100 yards. As the enemy aircraft climbed away, Monk was able to pull up and get in another short burst from underneath. Overall the Skua fired 250 rounds from its front guns and 100 from the rear gun. The Bf 110 then fired a few short, inaccurate bursts from about 1,000 yards and then made off.

In his own covering remarks[18] on the reports forwarded to him, Admiral Forbes observed:

> a surprise attack on Trondheim is very difficult to achieve and I think it reasonable to assume that the Skuas were reported by coast watchers at least 20 minutes before they arrived over the target. In that time there could have been several fighters at 10,000 feet over the enemy ships … it is interesting to note that all but one of the survivors got away by low-flying tactics. The attacks were courageously pressed home.

From the eight Skuas that failed to return, ten aircrew became prisoners of war and six were killed in action. Those who became prisoners included both squadron commanding officers, Lieutenant Commander J Casson RN and Captain R T

Glorious on fire and sinking on 8 June 1940. (Author's collection)

Partridge DSO RM. The others were Lieutenant P E Fanshawe RN, Lieutenant C H Filmer RN, Midshipman (A) T A McKee RN, Naval Airman G R Stevenson, Sub Lieutenant R E Bartlett RN, Naval Airman L C Richards, Petty Officer H G Cunningham and Midshipman (A) D T R Martin RN.

Those killed in action included Dick Partridge's observer, Robin Bostock, who had been mentioned in despatches twice; the gallant Midshipman Gallagher who had refuelled his Skua from a crashed Gladiator and been awarded both a DSC and a mention in despatches, and Lieutenant G E D Finch-Noyes who had been awarded a DSC and two mentions. The list included:[19]

Lieutenant R S Bostock RN	mid*	800 NAS
Petty Officer W Crawford		800 NAS
Lieutenant E D G Finch-Noyes RN	DSC mid*	800 NAS
Midshipman (A) L H Gallagher RN	DSC mid	800 NAS
Sub Lieutenant (A) J A Harris RN		803 NAS
Leading Airman W J Tremeer		800 NAS

Fortunately, we do have two 'voices' from those who took part in the strike, from Donald Gibson of 803, who made it back to *Ark Royal*, and from Dick Partridge who was shot down and taken prisoner. Both give very clear pictures of the aircrews' feelings on that fateful day from their different perspectives. In *Haul Taut and Belay*,[20] Donald Gibson gave a unique description of events which adds colour to his necessarily brief combat report quoted above:

Admiral 'Nutty' Wells, Vice Admiral Aircraft in *Ark Royal*, was invited by the Admiralty to attack the Germans when we were in range; this he decided to do and I am sure that there is much to be said for his decision as we certainly would have looked cowardly if we had not gone in. He and others were influenced by Major Partridge's brilliantly successful raid, in very different circumstances at Bergen. Had we been at a stage in the war when the Admiral, or any one of his staff, knew anything about planning offensive sorties, the raid would never have been sent in daylight against fighter defences, making a landfall sixty miles[21] from the target, with an arrangement for the hornets' nest – the German fighter airfield – to be stirred up five minutes before the arrival of our slow unmanoeuvrable strike aircraft.

The raid was planned to take off at midnight and strike at two am, all in daylight. A few minutes before the Skuas struck, RAF Beauforts were to strike Vaernes airfield, where the German fighters were stationed. During the time that the Skuas were on the target 6 RAF Blenheims were to provide us with fighter cover. As I write this I hear retired German Air Force officers laughing.

Nine aircraft of 803 and 6 of 800 took part, the squadrons were commanded by Lieutenant Commander Casson 803 and Major Partridge DSO, 800. Lieutenant Commander Casson had been with us a very short time, having replaced the heroic Lieutenant Bill Lucy DSO, a brilliant fighter pilot, recently killed in Norway. Lieutenant Commander Casson was the son of Sybil Thorndike, the actress, he was an amateur conjurer and reputed to be a member of the Magic Circle. Major Partridge was a very experienced dive-bomber pilot. The sinking of the *Königsberg* had not gone un-noticed by the Germans, the Japanese and the American Navies. Unfortunately for members of our two squadrons, it had also been noticed by our own people who, being ignorant of the principles of air warfare, imagined that the dive-bomber was the answer to all problems, regardless of the prevailing circumstances.

Squadrons were briefed twice for the operation, just before tea and again before take-off. Both squadron commanders disliked the plan but it had been ordered by the Admiral and that was that. The distance from the ship to our landfall called for about an hour's flying, followed by fifty or sixty miles through the fjords to our target. One thing that could be said in its favour was that it was one of the sorties ordered for Skua squadrons in which it was fairly certain that aircraft would have enough fuel as it was not unknown in *Ark Royal* at that time to see one or two Skuas in the water in the wake of the ship, having just failed to make it. In fact, one gallant officer, the late Freddie Charlton, normally carried a screwdriver so that he could unscrew the clock from the dashboard while his observer launched the dinghy.

At the briefing we realised that we were in for a nasty job. We were, by this time, used to danger and were not unnecessarily apprehensive but it was not an easy time for us between tea time and midnight. We were exceptionally intelligent young men with imagination and one or two wrote letters for others to post in case of dire events. I believe that John Casson did some conjuring tricks in the wardroom ante room, but he did not come back, being captured and made a prisoner of war. I often wondered whether it would have been a good thing if he produced an egg from the ear of the German officer in charge of his captives; perhaps he did.

We took off at midnight. Some stayed up to see us off and a stout lieutenant commander did not improve our morale by shaking hands with all of us. We staggered off with our 500 pound semi armour piercing bombs and flew for an hour to our landfall, which was an island called Froya. There were lighthouses in this area and I am sure someone rang up Trondheim to warn them of air attacks.

We approached Trondheim harbour in a shallow dive. Our Beaufort friends had been there, as planned, a little before, thus ensuring that all the German fighters were in the air ready for us. Every ship in the harbour and the shore batteries fired on us with all they had. A feature was their extensive use of tracer ammunition so that we could really see it and we flew through a heavy storm of projectiles.

The target was the German battlecruiser *Scharnhorst* and we had been briefed to attack the vessel independently if the situation made it necessary. John Casson put the squadron into line astern formation and started to work round the target to attack it from bow to stern, but this would involve more flying while exposed to attack, not only from flak but also from the many Messerschmitt 109s and 110s now keeping company with us. Pat Gordon-Smith, my observer, in his matter of fact voice, told me that four Messerschmitt 109s were astern of our section and I could see four Messerschmitt 110s on my starboard beam. I could also see Skuas going down in flames; being in a perfect position, I therefore led my lot down, attacking from stern to bow.

This bombing attack could be compared to the charge of the Light Brigade, had they been attacked by cavalry on their flanks during their approach to the guns, because as well as diving straight at the guns we were being picked off by fighters on the way down. At that sort of moment in life, one is really too busy to be scared.

My section followed me in the dive and I believe we got one near miss and there may have been one hit. There was a considerable ground mist and on releasing our bomb I went straight on down into the streets. I always say that I left Trondheim by road at about two hundred and fifty miles an hour. I do remember that on the outskirts I saw a horse above us – it was grazing on a bank – but by then we were alone and found the small island from which we were briefed to take departure and this we did. Some ten minutes later, chatting with Pat, I was alarmed to see a formation of twin-engined aircraft ahead, however this turned out to be our Blenheim fighter escort, somewhat late, and Pat called them up on his Aldis lamp and advised them to go home; had they continued they would have been shot down.

We were the last of the survivors to land on. The fleet then sailed into a small but dense fog, where it remained for some time. I believe they were shepherded out by Sub Lieutenant Hurle Hobbs, who was leading the Skua patrol which was protecting the fleet; he could see the tips of their masts.

Lieutenant Spurway on *Ark Royal* after the *Scharnhorst* strike on 13 June 1940. His Skua's wings have been folded and he is being marshalled into Fly 1. He was the senior surviving officer of 800 NAS after Dick Partridge was shot down. (Author's collection)

> After refreshment in the wardroom we turned in. I had learned some important lessons about air warfare and perhaps the most important one is that ideally all future admirals should be shot at in an aeroplane while they are still young. Despite these events I maintained a great admiration for Admiral Wells who was full of fighting spirit and a staunch friend of us young aviators.

Dick Partridge, one of those shot down and taken prisoner, gives us a very clear idea of what it was like to be there in *Operation Skua*.[22] After describing how he had been told by Commander (Air) to work out a plan for the attack with John Casson he mentions the long and demoralising wait until the final aircrew briefing at 2300 on 12 June. During the day they had been told that if for any reason the Beauforts were not available, VAA would cancel the strike. At the briefing, however, they were told that the diversionary bombing by RAF Coastal Command had been confirmed, 'so we would just have to do the best we could and get on with it'. He continued:

> We had been airborne now for well over an hour and ahead of us I could see the first land which Robin told me was the northern end of the island of Froya. All aircraft

were nicely in position and so far we had seen nothing, neither ship nor plane. As we passed over the island, in this very clear visibility, I could see a lighthouse and thought it highly probable that the Germans would have an observation post there to give good warning of any attack by sea or air. Now we were crossing over the mainland coast proper and there, confound it, was another lighthouse or coastguard station. I couldn't help but believe that the wires back to Trondheim were humming with the news that an enemy bombing force was approaching and I could imagine the alarm being sounded at the aerodrome with Me 109s [sic] and 110s being scrambled one after another.

John Casson now started to go into a shallow dive, our speed building up to about 200 knots, and I asked Robin how far there was to go. He said he reckoned we were about 25 miles from Trondheim and that we should arrive there in about 10 minutes almost exactly at 0200. So far, so good. I was looking anxiously ahead for anti-aircraft bursts in the air which would mean that the Beauforts were there and, I hoped, creating havoc with the Messerschmitts at Vaernes airfield. But as yet the air was clear and still as ever. Speed was now building up to 240 knots, height 9,000 feet as John Casson manoeuvred to arrive over target on time and at precisely the pre-arranged height.

I looked at my watch – it was 3 minutes to our deadline. There ahead of us I could see quite clearly the town of Trondheim and lying in the fjord the German fleet. I call it a fleet because it appeared to me that there were dozens of ships, including 2 larger ones that I assumed to be *Scharnhorst* and *Gneisenau*, which were obviously to be our targets if we could reach them. There was still no sign of the Beauforts and I think that it was at that moment that John Casson and I knew we would have to go it alone, as we had always suspected.

Then the German anti-aircraft fire opened up. I think only those who have experienced it can appreciate the volume of fire that a concentration of warships, supported by a considerable number of shore batteries, can put up, and can understand when I describe this barrage as intense with tracer bullets floating upwards and past us in thick showers. John Casson swung away to port putting his aircraft in open line astern and I did the same to starboard. As I did so I saw a twin-engined Me 110 flash past us heading for the other squadron and shortly afterwards a Skua spiralling downwards in flames. We were going to be sitting ducks for these Messerschmitts and I wondered how many of us were ever going to be able to get into a proper dive-bombing position to drop an accurate bomb. Robin suddenly said 'Me 109 port quarter', and I took violent evasive action so that he shot past and under us. As I pulled round in a very tight turn I could see that all the Skuas of both squadrons were scattered and acting independently and that there were 109s and 110s all over the place. I saw one Skua carrying out what appeared to be a beautifully controlled dive-bombing attack on the further large ship but also had a fleeting glance of his dive getting lower and lower until he hit the water at full power with a horrible crash.

I asked Robin if there was anything on our tail and he replied 'no'. I decided that it was now or never and that if I was going to get into position to attack I must sacrifice some height in order to build up my speed on the run in. I put the nose down into a medium dive and headed at 260 knots towards the nearest pocket battleship [sic]. At just under 6,000 feet I was in position to attack, pulled up to lose speed and came off a stall turn with flaps down into a dive. This dive was started lower than I would have liked and the AA fire coming from the ship was indescribable. At 1700 feet I released my bomb and, veering violently to port, flaps now raised, continued on down to sea level and headed away across the fjord. Poor old Robin, who must have been having kittens[23] in the rear cockpit whilst all this was going on, now reported that we had had a near miss ahead of the enemy ship and also that at the moment there was nobody on our tail though he had seen two more Skuas crash into the water. After five minutes of flying at zero feet we were well clear of the target area but by no means out of danger. Robin and I had often discussed what to do in this sort of situation. Flying at water or ground level offered the best chance of concealment but little chance of survival if we were attacked by superior forces and the aircraft was hit. Flying at any height from 1000 feet upwards offered less chance of concealment but an obvious chance of baling out. We had both agreed to opt for the chance of baling out and so I was now beginning to climb to gain height. We had reached 3,000 feet when Robin said 'aircraft slightly above – port bow', and a quick glance showed a single-engined seaplane of all things about to cross in front of and slightly above us. I eased back gently on the stick to raise my nose and as he passed in front of me I got in a quick burst with my front-guns. This may have been a big mistake on my part; either he hadn't seen me or he had mistaken me for an Me 109. At any rate his reaction to my burst of fire was a violent diving turn back towards Trondheim and that was a direction in which I was not going to chase him although even a Skua could have overtaken such an aircraft without too much trouble. But not only did he turn towards Trondheim, he also fired a four-star white Very light similar to the one fired by the submarine we had caught on the surface at Larvik. This could either have been a German recognition signal of the day or it could equally well have been a signal indicating the presence of hostile aircraft.

After this little incident we were at 4,000 feet, about 20 minutes away from Trondheim and not all that far from the coast. I was just beginning to think that we had got away with it when over the intercom Robin said quietly 'two 109s coming up fast astern'. This was the dreaded situation we had often anticipated and had been frightened even to imagine, it scared us so much. We both knew that, barring some sort of miracle, we had really had it this time. Inexplicably, as far as I was concerned, I felt no fear or panic, merely my usual fatalistic calm and a determination to give them a run for their money. Had it been only one Messerschmitt we were dealing with it is just possible we might have got away with it, but two gave us no chance at all. The Me 109 was at least 80 mph faster than we were, was more manoeuvrable and was armed with cannon. In spite of this I had a trick or two up my sleeve and felt that if we could survive long enough and at the same time work our way out to sea we could possibly get rid of them; for I knew that shore-based fighter pilots never relished too much flying over water out of sight of land. If we could somehow remain in one piece till we were 50 miles off shore I felt there was a chance that they might give up the chase.

I felt terribly exposed sitting high up in the Skua's cockpit, with a large expanse of windscreen in front of me which was not bullet-proof, Neither was there any armour under my seat or at my back and the large petrol tanks were not even self-sealing if hit. Robin of course, was equally unprotected and had the unnerving view of every attack as it came with only a single Vickers K-type machine gun to defend us from stern attacks. The odds were surely stacked against us!

I have spoken before of the Skua's great, big, strong flaps that helped to make it such a good dive-bomber. I now planned to use these flaps to help avoid the approaching attacks at the same time working my way towards the sea. As soon as Robin shouted they were about to attack in line astern 'Now!' I went into a 45 degree dive and when they opened fire as my speed built up to 250 knots I suddenly put my flaps down. The result was instant, dramatic and very uncomfortable! We decelerated violently and at the same time shot straight up 500 feet or so and the attacking 109s passed underneath us. It speaks a lot for the ruggedness and strength of the Skua that it could stand this sort of treatment, while I continued to work my way towards the coast. Three times the 109s repeated this type of attack unsuccessfully and I was wondering how long it was going to be before they realised that they would have to change their tactics. Unfortunately not for very long … .

Robin suddenly said 'one attacking from astern and one on starboard beam'. This was decidedly awkward and meant that my 'flap' tactic would make me an easy target if the aircraft on the beam waited until I had avoided the stern attack. So this time I did a really tight turn to starboard and managed to get a quick head-on burst at my beam attacker. Of course this left me more vulnerable to the stern attack and I could see his tracers going past me. I was still working my way towards the coast but our enemies' performance was so superior that they could attack, climb away, circle round and attack again. It couldn't last.

Robin had just said again 'attack astern and abeam' when I felt a thud that shook the aircraft and a large piece about the size of a soup plate came away from my starboard wing. It was probably a cannon shell but as it was outboard of the ailerons I had still had control of my aircraft. They were circling and climbing ready for another attack – but this time there was no warning of firing from Robin. Suddenly the petrol tank behind my instrument panel, only a foot or two from my lap, went up in a roar of flames. From then on my actions were essentially reflex and must have been carried out at lightning speed.

I can remember slamming back my cockpit hood and the resulting slipstream drawing a great sheet of flame up between my legs, across my face and out of the cockpit; I can remember hitting the quick-release of my fighting harness, and then the next thing I was aware of was a violent and painful yank at my crotch. Inconsequentially I thought 'that will teach you to have your parachute harness properly and tightly adjusted!' and there I was at 3500 feet floating down with an Me 109 heading straight for me. As I was bracing myself for him to open fire he swerved to one side and was away. I looked around for another parachute – there was none. What had happened to Robin? Had he been killed in that last attack on us? Had he been unable to get out? Or was he still in the Skua now spiralling downwards and thinking it was brilliant evasive action I was taking? The Skua hit the fjord below and disappeared in a cloud of spray and wreckage. Robin, my observer, friend and good companion in many good and bad times was dead, but exactly how and when he died we shall never know.[24]

I was now at 2,000 feet and floating down gently in complete silence. I looked down and saw that I was heading for the centre of a fjord. It wasn't the main Trondheim Fjord but an offshoot: even so it appeared to be a mile or two wide. I know the theory of being able to guide a parachute by pulling on the shroud lines, but I tried this with no effect at all other than nearly to collapse the canopy. Gently I drifted down; at 500 feet I was still heading slap for the middle of the fjord. I removed my flying boots and let them drop into the water then, in order to avoid getting tangled up in the parachute, at about 15 to 20 feet I turned and hit the quick-release buckle and dropped into the water. As I went under I felt a great searing pain as the salt water came into contact with my burnt face. With my Mae West[25] flotation waistcoat on I soon popped spluttering to the surface and surveyed my situation. From eye level a few inches above the water's surface either shore of the fjord appeared to be miles away and I knew I'd never make it swimming. I also knew that with my flotation waistcoat on I wasn't going to drown. God knows why or how, I was still alive but apparently destined to die of exposure in the icy waters of this remote and isolated Norwegian fjord.

I had been swimming for about 20 minutes, getting very weak and the shore I was aiming for appeared as far away as ever. Self-preservation is a great spur and I guess I was going to go on swimming until I could swim no more. Suddenly I heard noises that sounded very like those made by oars in rowlocks and looking over my shoulder saw the bows of a small rowing boat bearing down on me. I was too far gone to feel any of the things I ought to have felt, like the joy and relief at being rescued at last. I was mentally and physically drained and exhausted and I suspect in a state of deep shock as well. The boat was quickly alongside me and I was seized by the arms and seat of my trousers by two men, hauled on board, thrust into the bottom of the boat and covered quickly and completely with a tarpaulin. As I lay there, gasping and shivering in the dark, I was conscious of the boat being rowed rapidly back to shore. The boat grounded, I was uncovered, helped out and half carried, half dragged to a farmhouse nestling close to the fjord shore. I had been rescued by two Norwegian fishermen from the farm who had rowed out to me, well

> knowing that anything moving on land or water was inviting machine gun attack from the air. To these two gallant men I undoubtedly owe my life.
>
> My memories of the next forty-eight hours are vague and hazy. I can remember being stripped and rubbed down in the farm kitchen and being dressed in borrowed clothing which included a fine knitted traditional Norwegian cardigan. I can remember being examined in a Norwegian doctor's surgery for broken bones or other injuries but can't remember how I got there. It was he who dressed and bandaged my burnt face and gave me a warm drink from a cup with a spout as my lips were too painful for normal drinking, and I think it must have been this doctor who decided that my presence must be reported to the Germans so that I could get proper medical treatment. Fortunately, when my cockpit went up in flames I had had my goggles down and this protected my eyes and saved me from certain blinding. So, save for a burnt face I was still in remarkably good physical condition and had a long and restful night in the farmhouse.
>
> The next day a car pulled up at the farm with three German NCOs and I was handed over to them and driven away. This was the start of five years, all but one month, as a prisoner of war.

It was also probably the last act of the strike by Skuas against the *Scharnhorst* anchored off Trondheim and the end of the period I have described as 'the dawn of carrier strike'.

Chapter 18

Retrospection

Despite opposition from the Air Ministry and politicians who thought of air operations after 1919 as independent entities that would be completely unrelated to operations on sea or on land, the Admiralty succeeded in creating an aircraft carrier task force under its own administrative and operational control by 1940 that was effective enough to take on the unexpected and disparate tasks encountered by the Home Fleet. This was an enormous achievement and both the Navy and the nation should take enormous pride in it. It is certainly true that its aircraft, for a variety of reasons, were not the best that could have been procured but the new Air Branch personnel were proud of their sea service and determined to show what naval aviation could achieve, even against heavy odds. They had expected to take part in open sea operations against the German Kreigsmarine but were not deterred in April 1940 when they found themselves in action against the Luftwaffe, the world's most powerful air force, in the Norwegian littoral. The Air Ministry had, quite simply, got it wrong when it stated that naval aircraft would never need to face high-powered, land-based fighters on equal terms. Also wrong was the same Ministry's oft-stated view that minimal reserves of naval pilots, observers and aircraft to replace likely losses in action would suffice.

The Air Ministry had concentrated on its own, independent war plans but in the harsh test of reality in the Norwegian littoral it found that it relied on the Navy to get its aircraft into action effectively. Joint operations had counted for little in its pre-war plans and both the British Army and the RN had suffered in consequence. Despite all these negatives the Admiralty had been sufficiently air-minded throughout the period described in these pages to press for full control of the air arm it knew would need if there was to be another war. Thank goodness for the men of vision, especially Admiral Chatfield, who achieved a force with equipment that proved to be just adequate for the task of fighting a well-equipped, brutal enemy that had spread destruction across Europe in the preceding months.

If the equipment was not of the best, the aircrew certainly were, epitomised by Bill Lucy and his contemporaries, and it was they who made the difference. They were trained to strike from the sea by day or night even in the worst weather and to get the best from their mediocre aircraft. RAF aircrew had no less courage but were let down by a system that had not trained them adequately to use their aircraft or equipment to best advantage over an unfamiliar environment, the sea. Hank Rotherham's comments on bombsights give us important insight about this. Better training for RAF aircrew came later when its necessity became clear even to the Air

Fairey Albacores ranged on *Indomitable*. (Author's collection)

Ministry. The effectiveness of missions by RAF aircraft, including reconnaissance, was limited at first by the Air Ministry's determination to be completely independent of the other services' communications, command and control systems. This failing made RAF aircrew unaware of the full picture and introduced unnecessary delays to the dissemination of time-sensitive information. It should also be noted that the RAF relied on the mis-employment of aircraft carriers as ferries to deploy its fighters and their support structure to Norway and also had to request Fleet Air Arm observers to fly in Coastal and Bomber Command aircraft to help with safe navigation over the sea and identify enemy warships when they were encountered.

Well-handled Skuas and Swordfish were just adequate for the task in Norway, but as high-performance German fighters moved to bases further north and the Luftwaffe gained experience of warfare at sea they could not have remained so for much longer. The campaign emphasised the need for the Fleet Air Arm to be re-equipped with better fighters as a matter of urgency and the Admiralty procured them in several different ways. Deliveries of the Fairey Fulmar had already begun and squadrons began to re-equip with them from the summer of 1940 but it was accepted that the RN needed single-seat fighters with a higher top speed. The Skua remained a good dive-bomber but there was no room on carrier decks for them as the new fighters came into service. The last front-line Skuas were withdrawn in mid-1941 and the remaining aircraft were relegated to second-line duties.

Grumman G-36 naval fighters were procured from America, paid for with US dollars from the British government's rapidly dwindling reserves, and the first of an initial batch of eighty-five was delivered in the autumn of 1940. 804 NAS re-equipped with them in October, superseding Sea Gladiators. Named Martlet in RN service, these aircraft were the equivalent of the USN F4F-3 with 1,200hp Wright Cyclone engines and non-folding wings. Compared with the Skua's 198 knots they were capable of 272 knots at medium level and had the robust undercarriage required for successful deck operation. Later versions had Pratt and Whitney Twin Wasp engines and folding wings like the USN F4F-4. The USN adopted the name Wildcat in 1941 and the RN adopted the same name to achieve Allied commonality.

The second single-seat fighter was the Hawker Sea Hurricane, an obvious choice after the RAF Hurricanes landed on *Glorious* in June 1940. Sea Hurricanes were conversions of RAF aircraft and, therefore, lacked folding wings but they were fitted with arrester hooks, with local strengthening around the attachment point, and strengthened airframes to allow catapult launches. The Sea Hurricane was capable of 300 knots at 22,000 feet and was the fastest fighter in RN service until the introduction of the Seafire, a navalised version of the RAF Spitfire, in 1942. The first Sea Hurricane unit was 880 NAS which formed at RNAS Arbroath in January 1941. By then the RNVR pilots were becoming available in growing numbers and

A Fairey Barracuda armed with a practice torpedo. The square light area under the wing was a 'bow window' which gave the observer a 180-degree view from right forward to right aft. There was a similar one on the starboard side to give complete 360-degree observation. (Author's collection)

Sea Hurricanes of 880 NAS, the first unit to be equipped with the type, ranged on *Indomitable* in 1942. (Author's collection)

the RN was, at last, able to expand the number of embarked squadrons to match the growing number of aircraft carriers coming into service.

Re-equipment of the torpedo bomber squadrons with more advanced aircraft proved to be more difficult and revealed that although the Admiralty had regained administrative control of its air arm, its attempts to procure new aircraft were still given lower priority than even the most pedestrian new types for the RAF. The intended replacement for the Swordfish was the Fairey Albacore which began to re-equip squadrons from March 1940 but it was still a biplane and offered little improvement in performance over the aircraft it replaced. It was actually withdrawn from service before the Swordfish.

The next step was to be the Fairey Barracuda, a large monoplane which was to carry a Mark XIIB torpedo over a greater radius of action than its predecessors. It was also to have the world's first analogue computer-controlled torpedo sight so that the weapon could be aimed accurately at its target. It was to have been powered by the remarkable Rolls-Royce Exe,[1] conceived in 1936 as a very advanced, twenty-four-cylinder, 90-degree, X-shaped engine similar in concept to the Vulture that was developed for the Avro Manchester bomber. It was a pressure-air-cooled sleeve-valve engine that was both lighter than the more conventional Merlin engine and had no need for its coolant fluid, radiators and the 'plumbing' that connected them. It had a significantly lower drag factor and the early production versions would have delivered 1,200hp. A development Exe was fitted in a Fairey Battle test aircraft and proved so trouble-free that it remained in use until 1943 when the lack of spare parts eventually grounded it. It was significantly faster than all Merlin-powered Battles. Unfortunately for the RN, Rolls-Royce terminated work on the Exe in 1939 in line with government policy to concentrate on Merlin production and development. Of interest, the less-advanced but equally high-technology Vulture was retained in development because the RAF wanted it: a further demonstration of the priorities laid down at this time by the new Ministry of Aircraft Production (MAP). The Barracuda had to be redesigned to take the Merlin 30, which was significantly heavier than the Exe and had a greater drag factor, both factors which limited the aircraft's eventual performance.

A second blow came in the summer of 1940 after the fall of France when the MAP gave absolute priority to fighter production and work on the Barracuda prototype was halted. By the time the first Barracuda eventually flew in August 1942 the number and variety of equipment that needed to be incorporated into naval aircraft had grown and it had to be fitted with radar, improved communications, an array of new weapons and a strengthened airframe to carry them. The designed maximum weight grew from 10,500lb to 14,250lb with no increase in engine power to compensate for it and this both decreased performance still further and increased the stresses on the airframe. By then the magnificent Grumman TBF Avenger, designed to a later USN specification, was already coming into service.

A USN F4F-3 photographed in 1940. The RN had already ordered the type by April 1940 and allocated it the name Martlet but, unfortunately, none were delivered until after the Norwegian Campaign. (Author's collection)

In summary, the Barracuda had been a radical aircraft when the Admiralty asked for it in 1937 but it missed its generation because the British government failed to understand the RN's critical and legitimate need for a new carrier-borne strike aircraft. In fact, the MAP which had been intended to streamline aircraft production had exactly the opposite effect and delayed the service entry of the Navy's Barracuda by a considerable margin. Had it come into service as the Admiralty wanted in 1940 it would have been a 'game changer', the right aircraft in the right place at the right time. When it did arrive three years later it was not the aircraft the Fleet Air arm required and its time of opportunity had been missed.[2]

Returning to events in 1940, it has to be said that no matter how successful the carrier task force was in the Norwegian campaign up to the first days of June, it could never have hoped to defeat the Luftwaffe in a prolonged campaign. It had, however, demonstrated the potential of carrier strike and the new Air Branch took considerable pride in its ability to do so, despite having lost a significant number of aircraft and aircrew. It had done well in a type of conflict that few had predicted and showed itself well able to deploy with surprise and flexibility into situations where it would provide the only form of air power available to the British armed forces – something today's joint command organisation would do well to study in depth and understand fully. Carrier-borne aircraft also showed themselves to be adept at supporting the Army in joint and amphibious expeditionary operations.

Of interest, despite adopting the new title of Air Branch after the Inskip Award, the term Fleet Air Arm continued to be used, both officially and unofficially; you will have seen it in Chapter 16 and others. The term Fleet Air Arm was eventually re-adopted officially in 1953 to mark the Coronation of Her Majesty Queen Elizabeth II and remains in use today both in Great Britain and Australia.

Carrier strike became a fundamental part of the Royal Navy's operations from 1940 until HMS *Ark Royal* IV paid off in 1978. After that the three light carriers of the *Invincible* class with their embarked Sea Harrier STOVL strike fighters had a strike capability after 1981, demonstrated with distinction in the South Atlantic War of 1982, but the capability was effectively lost when the Sea Harrier was prematurely withdrawn from service in 2006 and the Harriers of Joint Force Harrier spent the majority of their time ashore, including deployments to land-locked Afghanistan. The 2010 Defence Review removed HMS *Ark Royal* V unexpectedly from service with immediate effect and in the British government's words, ended carrier strike capability 'temporarily'. In late 2018 HMS *Queen Elizabeth* is carrying out sea trials and is due to deploy with an air group including F-35 lightning strike fighters in 2021. She will be followed by her sister ship *Prince of Wales* after 2020 and Great Britain will once more have a carrier strike capability. Whatever form it takes and whatever advanced technologies change the way in which things will be done, the whole concept had its 'dawn' in the waters off Norway in the spring of 1940 and we should remember with pride the men who achieved so much with so little.

Notes

Chapter 1: RAF Contingents in His Majesty's Ships

1 Ray Sturtivant, *British Naval Aviation: The Fleet Air Arm, 1917–1990* (London, Arms & Armour Press, 1990), p. 10 et seq.
2 David Hobbs, *British Aircraft Carriers: Design, Development and Service Histories* (Barnsley, Seaforth Publishing, 2013) p. 47 et seq.
3 Ibid., p. 51 et seq.
4 Hugh Popham, *Into Wind: A History of British Naval Flying* (London, Hamish Hamilton, 1969), p. 88.
5 David Hobbs, *The Royal Navy's Air Service in the Great War* (Barnsley, Seaforth Publishing, 2017), p. 472 et seq.
6 Ray Sturtivant with Dick Cronin, *Fleet Air Arm Aircraft, Units and Ships, 1920 to 1939* (Tunbridge Wells, Air Britain (Historians), 1998), p. 36 et seq.
7 I have to say that a study of the deeply specialised RAF of 2017, a century later, shows how fundamentally wrong the Air Ministry's early concept really was.
8 Geoffrey Till, *'Air Power and the Royal Navy, 1914–1945: A Historical Survey* (London, Macdonald and Jane's Publishing, 1979), p. 43 et seq.
9 Lieutenants C L Howe, D M Marshall, L M Robinson, M Farquhar, L D Mackintosh DSC and J A Garland RN.
10 G A (Hank) Rotherham, *It's Really Quite Safe!* (Belleville, Ontario, Hangar Books, 1985), pp. 55–6.
11 The present RN observers' badge was introduced in 1942 when it was finally accepted by the Admiralty that they formed a fundamental part of a naval air squadron and needed to be recognised as aircrew.
12 The first post-RNAS Naval Pilots' Course began at Netheravon on 16 June 1924 and was completed on 12 December 1924.
13 Patrick Abbott, *The British Airship at War, 1914-1918* (Lavenham, Terence Dalton, 1989), p. 116.
14 Sixteen of the forty-nine were American.
15 Ces Mowthorpe, *Battlebags: British Airships of the First World War* (Stroud, Alan Sutton Publishing, 1995), p. 138.
16 Patrick Abbott and Nick Walmsley, *British Airships in Pictures* (Isle of Colonsay, House of Lochar, 1998), p. 76.

Chapter 2: Politics and the Trenchard/Keyes Agreement

1 Contained in GT.6478 in the National Archive at Kew and quoted in Stephen Roskill, *Naval Policy between the Wars. 1: The Period of Anglo-American Antagonism, 1919–1929* (Barnsley, Seaforth Publishing, 2016), p. 251 et seq.

2 Admiralty Board Minute 627 forwarded to the Air Ministry by letter on 20 February 1919 and contained in ADM 167/56 at the National Archives, Kew.
3 Minutes of this meeting are contained in ADM 1/8563 at the National Archives, Kew.
4 Copied in the Admiralty Weekly Order issued on 27 May 1919.
5 The correspondence over this vexed question is contained in ADM 1/8574 at the National Archives, Kew.
6 The original is held in the Air Historical Branch, file 1D2/100.
7 Roskill, *Naval Policy Between the Wars 1*, p. 255 et seq., quoting Andrew Boyle, *Trenchard: Man of Vision* (London, Collins, 1962).
8 The original is in Command 467 at the National Archives, Kew.
9 Boyle, *Trenchard: Man of Vision*, p. 351.
10 Beatty's flag captain throughout the war in HMS *Lion* and HMS *Queen Elizabeth* and, himself, a future 1SL.
11 Admiralty Office Memo 80 contained in ADM 116/2683 at the National Archives, Kew.
12 Air Ministry letter of 5 July 1920 contained within ADM 1/8589 at the National Archives, Kew.
13 Air Ministry letter of 11 March 1921 contained within ADM 1/8602 at the National Archives, Kew.
14 Paper CID 135C in the National Archives, Kew.
15 David Hobbs, *The Royal Navy's Air Service in the Great War* (Barnsley, Seaforth Publishing, 2017), pp. 364–77.
16 Paper CID 149C in the National Archives, Kew.
17 Richard Bell Davies, *Sailor in the Air: The Memoirs of the World's First Carrier Pilot* (Barnsley, Seaforth Publishing, 2008), p. 209 et seq.
18 CID 150C of 16 September 1921 and minute by Beatty of 7 October 1921 circulated as CID 153C, both in the National Archives, Kew.
19 Roskill, *Naval Policy between the Wars 1*, p. 230 et seq.
20 Bell Davies, *Sailor in the Air*, p. 211 et seq.
21 Chatfield letter to Keyes from RMS *Olympic* dated 25 or 28 October 1921 quoted in Roskill, *Naval Policy between the Wars 1*, p. 267.
22 Hobbs, *The Royal Navy's Air Service in the Great War*, Smuts and his deliberations are covered from p. 364 onwards.
23 An undated copy of the Admiralty memorandum with other relevant papers is contained in ADM 1/8618 at the National Archives, Kew.
24 Who, as a captain, had been Churchill's naval adviser from 1911 to 1913 while the latter was First Lord.
25 The original is contained in Air Historical Branch file ID.2/100 at Bentley Priory.
26 *The Oxford English Dictionary* defines this as 'wholeness'.
27 His arguments can be found in CID 113A dated 21 July 1922 at the National Archives, Kew.
28 Command 2029 in the National Archives, Kew.
29 Ibid., p. 277 et seq.

30 On 22 March 1937 during the debates that led to the Inskip Award. Hansard, *Parliamentary Debates, House of Commons*, vol. 321, col. 2592, quoted in Roskill, *Naval Policy between the Wars 1*, p. 376.
31 The correspondence between the First Lord and the Air Secretary throughout this period is containing in AHB IDI/97 at the Air Historical Branch, Bentley Priory.
32 Ibid.
33 CID 503B in the National Archives, Kew.

Chapter 3: Joining the Royal Navy as an Officer and Training to be a Pilot

1 Data taken from Lucy's service history document held in the MOD Archive, a copy of which is in my own archive.
2 Who had qualified as a Gunnery Officer in 1905 but, like many other RN officers, taken a keen interest in naval aviation as it developed.
3 Naval pilot training had shifted from RAF Netheravon to RAF Leuchars in 1927.
4 Theo Ballance, Lee Howard and Ray Sturtivant, *The Squadrons of the Fleet Air Arm* (Stapleford, Air Britain Publishing, 2016), p. 113.
5 Ray Sturtivant with Dick Cronin, *Fleet Air Arm Aircraft, Units and Ships 1920 to 1939* (Tunbridge Wells, Air Britain (Historians), 1998), p. 40.
6 Ibid., p. 392.
7 Ibid., p. 187.
8 Later to earn his place in history after becoming a Captain RN as the instigator of the angled flight deck.

Chapter 4: Technology: Ships, Aircraft, Weapons and Tactics

1 R A Burt, *British Battleships of World War One* (new revised edition) (Barnsley, Seaforth Publishing, 2012), p. 216.
2 Norman Friedman, *British Cruisers: Two World Wars and After* (Barnsley, Seaforth Publishing, 2010), p. 63.
3 Douglas Morris, *Cruisers of the Royal and Commonwealth Navies* (Liskeard, Maritime Books, 1987), p. 166.
4 Richard Perkins, *British Warship Recognition. Volume III: Cruisers, 1865–1939, Part 1* (Barnsley, Seaforth Publishing, 2017), p. 170.
5 David Hobbs, *The Royal Navy's Air Service in the Great War* (Barnsley, Seaforth Publishing, 2017), p. 76 et seq.
6 J David Brown, *Warship Losses of World War Two* (London, Arms and Armour Press, 1990), p. 58.
7 Owen Thetford, *British Naval Aircraft since 1912* (London, Putnam, 1962), p. 214.
8 Francis K Mason, *Hawker Aircraft since 1920* (London, Putnam, 1991), p. 225 et seq.
9 Ray Sturtivant with Dick Cronin, *Fleet Air Arm Aircraft, Units and Ships 1920 to 1939* (Tunbridge Wells, Air Britain (Historians), 1998), p. 225 et seq.

10 David Hobbs, *British Aircraft Carriers: Design, Development and Service Histories* (Barnsley, Seaforth Publishing, 2013), p. 68 et seq.
11 The Atlantic Fleet was renamed the Home Fleet in March 1932.
12 Hobbs, *British Aircraft Carriers*, p. 70.
13 David Hobbs, *A Century of Carrier Aviation* (Barnsley, Seaforth Publishing, 2009), p. 153 et seq.
14 David Brown, *Supermarine Walrus I and Seagull V Variants*, Profile 224 (Windsor, Profile Publications, 1971), p. 48.
15 Morris, *Cruisers of the Royal and Commonwealth Navies*, p. 177.

Chapter 5: Doctrine, Operations and Exercises

1 Thomas C Hone, Norman Friedman and Mark D Mandeles, *American and British Aircraft Carrier Development, 1919–1941* (Annapolis, Naval Institute Press, 1999), p. 85.
2 Ibid., p. 107 et seq.
3 Based on the experience some officers had gained flying in RNAS flying boats over the North Sea during the Great War.
4 Francis K Mason, *The Hawker Hurricane* (London, Macdonald, 1962), p. 115.
5 Hone, Friedman and Mandeles, *American and British Aircraft Carrier Development*, p. 111.
6 Geoffrey Till, *Air Power and the Royal Navy, 1914–1945: A Historical Survey* (London, Macdonald and Jane's Publishing, 1979), p. 143.
7 Hone, Friedman and Mandeles, *American and British Aircraft Carrier Development*, p. 125.
8 Till, *Air Power and the Royal Navy*, p. 137 et seq.
9 The steam-powered submarines of the K class were specifically designed to have the surface speed to operate with the battle fleet, diving when ordered to attack the enemy, to act effectively as submersible destroyers. Despite its enthusiasm for the project the RN never entirely worked out how to command and control such a flotilla.
10 Exercise ZP Serial V Part II of 10 March 1938, a report contained in ADM/3873 at the National Archives, Kew.
11 Stephen Roskill, *Naval Policy between the Wars. 1: The Period of Anglo-American Antagonism, 1919–1929* (Barnsley, Seaforth Publishing, 2016), p. 131 et seq.
12 Servicemen who took part in operations on Russian soil between 1918 and 1920 were awarded the British Great War Medal which, therefore, was in continuous issue from 1914 to 1920.
13 Details of RN involvement in this crisis are contained in ADM 137/1768 at the National Archives, Kew, and are quoted in Roskill, *Naval Policy between the Wars 1*, p. 181 et seq.
14 David Hobbs, *British Aircraft Carriers: Design, Development and Service Histories* (Barnsley, Seaforth Publishing, 2013), p. 43.

15 Neil McCart. *HMS Hermes, 1923 and 1959* (Cheltenham, Fan Publications, 2001), p. 28.
16 Stephen Roskill, *Naval Policy between the Wars. 2: The Period of Reluctant Rearmament, 1930–1939* (Barnsley, Seaforth Publishing, 2016), p. 264.

Chapter 6: Observers

1 G A (Hank) Rotherham, *It's Really Quite Safe* (Belleville, Ontario, Hangar Books, 1985), p. 55 onwards.
2 E Keble Chatterton, *English Seamen and the Colonization of America* (London, Arrowsmith, 1930).
3 Rotherham, *It's Really Quite Safe*, p. 61.
4 The observer in a Fairey IIIF sat behind the pilot and his only means of communication was a Gosport tube, a voice pipe down which he could shout instructions. There was no need for the observer to communicate in the carrier circuit and, therefore, his silence would not have been unusual.
5 Dual ranked as a Squadron Leader RAF.
6 Transferred to the RAN in 1938 and renamed HMAS *Hobart.*
7 This was actually another of the Osprey's roles when no other fleet requirements aircraft where available.
8 Voice radio did not come into widespread use in naval aircraft for another two years.

Chapter 7: Progress in the United States Navy

1 David Hobbs, *The Royal Navy's Air Service in the Great War* (Barnsley, Seaforth Publishing, 2017), p. 482.
2 Later Sir Stanley Goodall KCB RCNC, Director of Naval Construction 1936–44.
3 Norman Friedman, *US Aircraft Carriers: An Illustrated Design History* (Annapolis, United States Naval Institute, 1983), p. 31 et seq.
4 David Hobbs, *A Century of Carrier Aviation: The Evolution of Ships and Shipborne Aircraft* (Barnsley, Seaforth Publishing, 2009), p. 99 et seq.
5 David Hobbs, 'The Aircraft Carrier: The Experience of its Conception, Procurement and Operation', in John Reeve and David Stevens (eds), *The Face of Naval Battle* (Crows Nest, New South Wales, Allen & Unwin, 2003), p. 131 et seq.
6 Thomas Wildenberg, *Billy Mitchell's War with the Navy: The Interwar Rivalry Over Air Power* (Annapolis, Naval Institute Press, 2013), p. 148 et seq.
7 Adolphus Andrews Jr, Admiral with Wings: The Career of Joseph M Reeves', BA Thesis, Princeton University, 1943.
8 This was what the retaining wires had been intended to do. There can be no doubt that Busteed's retaining wires represented a blind alley.
9 Friedman, *US Aircraft Carriers*, p. 105.

10 Standing with arms outstretched during a prolonged recovery was a demanding task and batsmen had to be physically fit.
11 Thomas C Hone, Norman Friedman and Mark D Mandeles, *American and British Aircraft Carrier Development, 1919–1941* (Annapolis, Naval Institute Press, 1999), p. 48 et seq.
12 Admiral of the Fleet Lord Chatfield, *It Might Happen Again* (London: William Heinemann, 1947), p. 105.

Chapter 8: The Inskip Award

1 Later Admiral of the Fleet Lord Chatfield GCB OM KCMG CVO PC.
2 Admiral of the Fleet Lord Chatfield, *It Might Happen Again* (London: William Heinemann, 1947), p. 102 et seq.
3 Inskip was an interesting personality with a highly regarded legal background. He was appointed as a KC in 1914 and, after the outbreak of war, served in the Naval Intelligence Department within the Admiralty. From 1918 to 1919 he was Head of the Naval Law Branch despite having entered politics as the MP for Bristol (Central) after the 1918 general election. He was appointed Attorney General in 1928 and a member of the Privy Council in 1932. Admiral Chatfield replaced him as the Minister for Defence Co-ordination in 1939 when Inskip became Secretary of State for the Dominions. He later became First Viscount Caldecote.
4 The failure, prior to 1942, of Bomber Command to achieve any meaningful victories would seem to illustrate that the RAF had actually made little contribution to the practice of independent air warfare either.
5 Later Admiral of the Fleet Sir John Cunningham GCB, himself 1SL from May 1946 to September 1948.
6 Contained within Air 8/223 at the National Archives, Kew. It was originally classified as Secret but was down-graded to an open document that could be viewed by the public in March 1966. A photocopy is in my own archive.
7 Inskip Report para 3.
8 Inskip Report para 4.
9 The Report's impact on the future of the Royal Navy was so important that I want readers to see exactly what Sir Thomas Inskip wrote rather than my interpretation of his words.
10 Unfortunately, this was the system that was to fail the BEF so completely in May 1940.
11 Contained within COS 552 dated 2 February 1937 in the National Archives, Kew.
12 If only they had known the area of the Atlantic that would also have to be covered after June 1940.

Chapter 9: The Air Branch of the Royal Navy in 1939

1 Admiralty, *Naval Staff History: The Development of British Naval Aviation, 1919–1945. Volume I* (London, Admiralty, 1954), p. 13 et seq.

2 Ibid., p. 3.
3 Hugh Popham, *Into Wind: A History of British Naval Flying* (London, Hamish Hamilton, 1969), p. 119.
4 The Admiralty Information Department produced a booklet on the achievements of naval aviation in 1943 which was entitled *Fleet Air Arm*; perhaps it considered 'The Air Branch of the Royal Navy' to be too much of a mouthful. The term Fleet Air Arm was officially re-introduced by the Admiralty in 1953 to mark the Coronation celebrations of Her Majesty Queen Elizabeth II and it has been used ever since.
5 The others were Portsmouth and Chatham. The system of port drafting continued until 1957 when, to economise on manpower, a centralised drafting system was established with its headquarters at Haslemere.
6 He and Bell Davies would have known each other well from their days in the RNAS.
7 Richard Bell Davies, *Sailor in the Air: The Memoirs of the World's First Carrier Pilot* (Barnsley, Seaforth Publishing, 2008), p. 230 et seq.
8 Geoffrey Till, *Air Power and the Royal Navy, 1914–1945: A Historical Survey* (London, Macdonald and Jane's Publishing, 1979), p. 55 et seq.
9 Ray Sturtivant with Dick Cronin, *Fleet Air Arm Aircraft, Units and Ships, 1920 to 1939* (Tunbridge Wells, Air Britain (Historians), 1998), p. 306.
10 John Wellham. *With Naval Wings* (Staplehurst, Spellmount, 1995), p. 25 et seq.
11 The RNZN was not formed until 1942 and prior to that it was the New Zealand Division of the RN. Thus the RN already owned recruiting depots in New Zealand and many of the thousands of volunteers who came forward were drawn into the Air Branch, which was most in need of numbers.
12 Brian Lavery, *Hostilities Only: Training the Wartime Navy* (Greenwich: National Maritime Museum, 2004), p. 182.
13 The former Butlin's holiday camp.
14 After the war the TAG Association was the only RN veterans' group that was only open to those who had qualified; no one other than a TAG could join.
15 Lavery, *Hostilities Only*, p. 116.
16 Details of artificer training during this period are contained within ADM 1/17685 at the National Archives, Kew.
17 Lavery, *Hostilities Only*, p. 116.
18 'OC' indicated an officers' rather than general service cook but these were not generally allocated to naval air squadrons.

Chapter 10: Royal Navy Aircraft in 1939

1 Thomas C. Hone, Norman Friedman and Mark D. Mandeles, *American and British Aircraft Carrier Development, 1919–1941* (Annapolis, Naval Institute Press, 1999), p. 97 et seq.
2 Ibid., p. 113 et seq.
3 Air Council summary EPM 139(38) dated 20 September 1938 from the archive of the late David Brown, Head of the Naval Historical Branch, a copy of which is now in the author's archive.

4 Who had extensive aviation knowledge, having served as captain of *Furious* and Rear Admiral Aircraft Carriers in succession to Henderson.
5 A former RNAS officer who had actually flown Fairey Campania seaplanes off the deck of HMS *Campania*. As one of the senior officers within the RAF who were expected to give advice on naval air matters, one would like to think that he retained some sympathy for the RN cause.
6 Owen Thetford, *British Naval Aircraft since 1912* (London, Putnam, 1962), p. 191.
7 William Green, *Famous Fighters of the Second World War, Second Series* (London, Macdonald, 1962), p. 25.
8 H F King, *Armament of British Aircraft, 1909–1939* (London, Putnam, 1971), p. 198.
9 Fairey construction number F.1754.
10 H A Taylor, *Fairey Aircraft since 1915* (London, Putnam, 1974), p. 231 et seq.
11 Fairey construction number F.2038.
12 Ray Sturtivant with Dick Cronin, *Fleet Air Arm Aircraft, Units and Ships, 1920 to 1939* (Tunbridge Wells, Air Britain (Historians), 1998), p. 205.
13 K5660, K5661 and K5662.
14 Ray Sturtivant with Mick Burrow, *Fleet Air Arm Aircraft, 1939 to 1945* (Tunbridge Wells, Air Britain (Historians), 1995), p. 71.
15 Later Rear Admiral Sir Matthew Slattery.
16 One in 1940, 415 in 1941, 271 in 1942, 592 in 1943 and 420 in 1944.
17 Terence Horsley, *Find, Fix and Strike* (London, Eyre and Spottiswoode, 1943), p. 19 et seq.
18 Tri-nitro toluene.
19 Official RN figures from the archive of the Naval Historical Branch.
20 A J Jackson, *Blackburn Aircraft since 1909* (London, Putnam, 1968), p. 399 et seq.
21 Peter C Smith, *Skua: The Royal Navy's Dive-Bomber* (Barnsley, Pen & Sword Aviation, 2006), p. 16 et seq.
22 Eric M Brown, *Wings of the Navy*, London, Macdonald and Jane's Publishing, 1980), p. 29 et seq.
23 Jackson, *Blackburn Aircraft since 1909*, p. 411 et seq.
24 Brown, *Wings of the Navy*, p. 36.
25 Compiled from statistics in the Admiralty Summary of Aircraft held in the Director General Aircraft (Naval) Department.
26 Described earlier, operated in battleship and cruiser flights although several were deployed to Narvik during the Norwegian campaign.
27 Operated in some light cruiser flights.
28 Now Heathrow International Airport.
29 Which still exists on display at the Fleet Air Arm element of the National Museum of the Royal Navy at RNAS Yeovilton.
30 Horsley, *Find, Fix and Strike*, p. 25.

Chapter 11: Squadron Command

1 Although there were several instances of senior officers taking civilian flying lessons during their leave periods to better understand how their aircrew operated. In one anecdotal instance, I found that an RN captain had actually joined the RAFVR to learn to fly during a spell ashore in the 1930s. He failed to turn up when mobilised as a Pilot Officer in September 1939 and was threatened with prosecution but when the Air Ministry learned that he was in command of one of HM Ships at sea the case was quietly dropped!

2 A Lieutenant would automatically be promoted to Lieutenant Commander eight years after his original appointment as a Lieutenant. The date of promotion from Sub Lieutenant to Lieutenant was decided by seniority gained from professional exams taken whilst under training. Promotion beyond Lieutenant Commander was by selection. Similar rules applied in the RM but promotion for short-service RN, RNR and RNVR pilots was by selection at all ranks.

3 This chapter has been structured around my knowledge and experience as a naval pilot although I must stress that I did not start flying until 1969. Few things had changed, however.

4 In a front-line unit they flew with all pilots and observers when disembarked to check their knowledge of the squadron's aircraft, its systems and all current flying procedures.

5 Pre-war long-serving sailors had often been allowed to keep small pets in their mess such as a parrot. The expression 'arrived with nothing but his bag, hammock and birdcage' is descriptive.

6 Some wartime diary officers took a personal pride and kept their work when the unit disbanded. Regrettably, many of these have been discarded by families who did not realise their historical value when the original owner died.

7 Lieutenant Lucy kept a handwritten journal at this time and a copy of it was made available to me by his nephew John de Lucy. I have used extracts from it extensively in the latter part of this chapter.

8 759 NAS had originally formed on 26 May 1939 and re-formed as a fighter school and pool unit for trained pilots, still at Eastleigh, on 1 November 1939.

9 Major R T Partridge, *Operation Skua* (Yeovilton, Fleet Air Arm Museum, 1983), p. 41.

10 He was promoted to Commander in 1942, Captain in 1948 becoming the first Captain of HMS *Ark Royal* IV in 1955. He was promoted to Rear Admiral in 1958, serving as Flag Officer Flying Training.

11 Naval officers were not encouraged to marry young. Pay was not that good, although food and accommodation were free. Marriage allowance was not paid to officers under the age of 25. Before the war it was unusual for career officers to marry before they had reached their early thirties and could afford to support a family. Of course flying pay did make a difference and some aviators did marry young.

12 RN air squadrons were still provided with shot guns, cartridges, throwers and clay pigeons into the 1970s in the well-founded belief that they enhanced pilots' hand/

eye co-ordination as well as maintaining their ability to aim a weapon against a moving target.

13 Every naval air station had an Admiralty-pattern squash court situated in the wardroom accommodation area, again with a view to encouraging hand/eye co-ordination in every way possible.

Chapter 12: Naval Aviation in the First Months of the Second World War

1 Admiralty, *Naval Staff History: The Development of British Naval Aviation, 1919–1945. Volume I* (London, Admiralty, 1954), p. 87 et seq.
2 Italy did not enter the war on the side of the Axis Powers until June 1940 and Japan did not enter until December 1941.
3 Stephen W Roskill, *The War at Sea, 1939–1945. Volume 1: The Defensive* (London, Her Majesty's Stationery Office, 1954), p. 103.
4 Winston Churchill, *The Second World War. Volume I: The Gathering Storm* (London, Penguin Books, 2005), p. 387.
5 Michael Apps, *The Four Ark Royals* (London, William Kimber, 1976), p. 108 et seq.
6 Ibid., p. 110 et seq.
7 Ibid., p. 71.
8 Roskill, *The War at Sea, Volume 1*, p. 105 et seq.
9 Ben Jones, *The Fleet Air Arm in the Second World War* (Farnham, Ashgate Publishing, 2012), p. 45 et seq.
10 J David Brown, *Warship Losses of World War Two* (London, Arms and Armour Press, 1990), p. 27.
11 Roskill, *The War at Sea, Volume 1*, p. 106.
12 David Hobbs, *British Aircraft Carriers: Design, Development and Service Histories* (Barnsley, Seaforth Publishing, 2013), p. 59.
13 Ibid., p. 34.
14 In 1939 the RAF had only twelve biplane flying boats based outside the UK: four in Gibraltar, four in Aden and four in Singapore. There were six modern Sunderland flying boats in Hong Kong. There were also twenty-four Wildebeeste biplane torpedo bombers in Singapore and four in Hong Kong.
15 Derek Howse, *Radar at Sea* (Basingstoke, Macmillan, 1993), pp. 25, 26.
16 Information about fighter combat sorties is gathered from combat record cards in the archive of the Naval Historical Branch, now in Portsmouth Naval Base, copies of which are in the author's own archive.
17 Howse, *Radar at Sea*, pp. 31, 32.
18 Individual account of Lieutenant McEwen's action contained in the 1960 *Fleet Air Arm Review*, published for the RN Air Stations of the Home Air Command, p. 67.
19 It was due to be fitted in the refit planned in the United States from December 1941. Unfortunately she was sunk before it took place.
20 *Flight Magazine*, 22 November 1957.
21 Roskill, *The War at Sea, Volume 1*, p. 69.
22 Ibid., p. 111 et seq.

23 Ray Sturtivant with Dick Cronin, *Fleet Air Arm Aircraft, Units and Ships, 1920 to 1939* (Tunbridge Wells, Air Britain (Historians), 1998), p. 350 et seq.
24 John Jordan and Stephen Dent (eds), *Warship* (Oxford, Osprey Publishing, 2018), p. 37 et seq.
25 Admiralty, *Naval Staff History: The Development of British Naval Aviation, 1919–1945. Volume II* (London, Admiralty, 1956), p. 341.
26 Major R T Partridge, *Operation Skua* (Yeovilton, Fleet Air Arm Museum, 1983) p. 45 et seq.
27 Ibid., p. 48.
28 'Memories of Bill Lucy', a document written by Major Partridge in 1988 in the possession of the Lucy family, a copy of which was made available to the author.
29 Approximate bearings from an aircraft were and are given in the clock code. It is a useful way of directing another pilot's eyes towards something.
30 Telegram A.434 21/3 from 18 Group to Hatston for 803 Squadron, a copy of which was made available to the author by John de Lucy.
31 Lucy family papers.

Chapter 13: The German Invasion of Norway and Strike Operations from RNAS Hatston

1 Winston Churchill, *The Second World War. Volume I: The Gathering Storm* (London, Penguin Books, 2005), p. 522 et seq.
2 Stephen W Roskill, *The War at Sea, 1939–1945. Volume 1: The Defensive* (London, Her Majesty's Stationery Office, 1954), p. 156 et seq.
3 The *Altmark* had been one of the *Graf Spee*'s support ships and had prisoners taken from British merchant ships sunk by the pocket battleship on board when she attempted to run the British blockade and return to Germany.
4 David Hobbs, *The Royal Navy's Air Service in the Great War* (Barnsley, Seaforth Publishing, 2017), p. 449 et seq.
5 Detail for the remainder of this chapter has been taken from the Home Fleet War Diary in the Naval Historical Branch, Portsmouth, a copy of which is in the author's possession. It has been amplified by individual ship and naval air squadron Reports of Proceeding (ROPs), from the same source, a copy of which is in the author's archive and by the individual Fleet Air Arm fighter combat record cards compiled by the late J David Brown, Head of the Naval Historical Branch, and left to me with the stricture that I 'get on and use them in a book'.
6 Report of the Commander-in-Chief Navy to the Fuhrer dated 9 March 1940.
7 Churchill, *The Gathering Storm*, p. 541.
8 Geoffrey Till, *Air Power and the Royal Navy, 1914–1945: A Historical Survey* (London, Macdonald and Jane's Publishers, 1979), p. 15.
9 Sir Philip Vian, *Action This Day* (London, Frederick Muller, 1960), p. 37.
10 Donald Macintyre, *Narvik* (London, Pan Books, 1962), pp. 60–1.
11 Major R T Partridge DSO RM, 'Memories of Bill Lucy', written in 1988 and made available to the author by John de Lucy.

12 Major R T Partridge, *Operation Skua* (Yeovilton, Fleet Air Arm Museum, 1983), p. 51 et seq.

13 In *Operation Skua*, Dick Partridge uses the phrase 'let my bombs go' but this must be a figure of speech since his combat report, rendered on his return to Hatston in accordance with CAFO 3572/39, clearly states that the aircraft was armed with a single 500lb SAP bomb Mark II.

14 In December 1937 the 450-ton USN gunboat *Panay* had been sunk 'in error' by Japanese dive-bombers and a few hours earlier the destroyer *Gurkha* had been sunk but neither of these could be defined as major warships.

15 Richard Bell Davies, *Sailor in the Air: The Memoirs of the World's First Carrier Pilot*, (Barnsley, Seaforth Publishing, 2008), pp. 233, 234.

16 M/08282/40, Register Number NAD 387/40 dated 15 April 1940, now in the National Archives, Kew, and a copy of which is in the author's archive.

17 Till, *Air Power and the Royal Navy*, pp. 27 and 28.

18 J. David Brown, *Carrier Operations in World War II* (Barnsley, Seaforth Publishing, 2009), pp. 15 and 16.

19 RANAS Report dated 1 December 1941 contained within ADM 116/4455 at the National Archives, Kew.

Chapter 14: HMS Furious*: The First Strike Carrier in Action*

1 Geoffrey Till, *Air Power and the Royal Navy, 1914–1945: A Historical Survey* (London, Macdonald and Jane's Publishers, 1979), pp. 13, 14.

2 As in Chapter 13, detail for this chapter was compiled using the Home Fleet War Diary in the Naval Historical Branch, Portsmouth, and I have copies of relevant sections in my own archive. It has been amplified by individual ship and naval air squadron Reports of Proceedings from the same source and ships' log book entries from the National Archives, Kew. I have also used individual aircraft combat reports and fighter records compiled by the late J David Brown when he was Head of the Naval Historical Branch.

3 Later transferred to the RN and commissioned as an RN Air Station, HMS *Fieldfare*, in June 1943.

4 In the National Archives, Kew.

5 HMS *Furious* Report of Proceedings dated 30 April 1940 contained in ADM 199/479 at the National Archives, Kew.

6 David Hobbs, *The Royal Navy's Air Service in the Great War* (Barnsley, Seaforth Publishing, 2017), chapter 17.

7 Unlike the RAF, where the pilot was always the aircraft captain, in the Fleet Air Arm the senior member of aircrew was the aircraft captain and frequently this would be the observer.

8 Hobbs, *The Royal Navy's Air Service*, chapter 11.

9 HMS *Furious* 4/320 dated 17 April 1940 in the Naval Historical Branch Archive, a copy of which is in the Author's archive.

Chapter 15: HM Ships Ark Royal *and* Glorious *in Action off Norway*

1 As in the previous two chapters, I have compiled the material for this part of the book from the Home Fleet War Diary in the Naval Historical Branch in Portsmouth and have retained photocopies of the relevant sections in my own archive. The research was amplified by reference to individual ship and naval air squadron Reports of Proceedings from the same source and ship's log book entries from the National Archives, Kew. Records of strike missions and individual fighter combat have been researched using data compiled by the late J David Brown when he was Head of the Naval Historical Branch and left to me in his will.
2 They had been loaded on the ship by lighter in Scapa Flow.
3 As far as I am aware, we are in no way related.
4 *Flamingo*'s 1515/26 and 1540/26.
5 Theo Ballance, Lee Howard and Ray Sturtivant, *The Squadrons of the Fleet Air Arm* (Stapleford, Air Britain Publishing, 2016), p. 115.
6 They set fire to the cockpit after landing and the aircraft, L2940, subsequently sank to the bottom of the lake but its remains were recovered in 1974 and are now on display at the National Museum of the Royal Navy, Fleet Air Arm Section at RNAS Yeovilton.
7 Captain, 4th Destroyer Flotilla signal 1601/27.
8 Later to become the strike co-ordinator for the British Pacific Fleet with a total of thirteen 'kills'. In American terms he was a fighter 'ace' and the top-scoring Royal Marines pilot to date.
9 Michael Apps, *The Four Ark Royals* (London, William Kimber, 1976), p. 131.
10 Regrettably the crew and duty lists of these early-morning sorties do not seem to have survived.
11 All three of whom went on to achieve high rank in the post-war Navy.
12 The RN eventually adopted the Seafire, a naval variant of the RAF Spitfire but Cockburn had no means of knowing the problems that would be caused by its weak undercarriage in operations from the deck of aircraft carriers.
13 C-in-C Home Fleet 810/HF 1325 dated 14 May 1940 sent from HMS *Rodney*, a copy of which is in the author's archive.
14 The Admiralty was already making arrangements to procure the Grumman F4F, which was initially known as the Martlet in the RN. Its USN name was the Wildcat and this was also adopted by the RN in 1944.
15 J David Brown, *Carrier Fighters* (London, Macdonald and Jane's Publishing, 1975), pp. 49, 50.
16 My wife Jandy's maternal grandfather.
17 Supplement to the *London Gazette* of Tuesday 28 May 1946, no. 37584, pp. 2607 and 2608.

Chapter 16: Killed in Action

1 Geoffrey Till, *Air Power and the Royal Navy, 1914–1945: A Historical Survey* (London, Macdonald and Jane's Publishing, 1979), p. 14 et seq.

2 David Hobbs *British Aircraft Carriers: Design, Development and Service Histories* (Barnsley, Seaforth Publishing, 2013), p. 73.
3 Till, *Air Power and the Royal Navy*, p. 24.
4 J David Brown, *Carrier Fighters* (London, Macdonald and Jane's Publishing, 1975), p. 47.
5 Peter C Smith, *Skua: The Royal Navy's Dive-Bomber* (Barnsley, Pen & Sword Aviation, 2006), p. 129.
6 The detail for this section is drawn from Lieutenant Gray's combat report, Appendix 7 to the Narrative of the Vice Admiral Aircraft Carriers, Operational Report of Blue Section for 14 May 1940. It is signed T E Gray, Lieutenant RN and a copy of it is in the author's archive.
7 Copies of all these letters were made available to me by John de Lucy, Bill Lucy's nephew and are in my archive.
8 In the event, this bar to his DSO could not be awarded since it cannot be given posthumously.
9 Captain Holland did not know at the time he wrote this letter that Bill Lucy had been buried at sea.

Chapter 17: Heavy Losses after the Withdrawal from Narvik

1 Stephen W Roskill, *The War at Sea, 1939–1945. Volume 1: The Defensive* (London, Her Majesty's Stationery Office, 1954), p. 193 et seq.
2 J David Brown, *Carrier Operations in World War II* (Barnsley, Seaforth Publishing, 2009), p. 15.
3 The Gladiators could, at best, be considered obsolescent and were no match for the German fighters that would operate over southern England in the weeks ahead. The number of Hurricanes was but a fraction of the number that were being abandoned in France as their RAF forward airfields were over-run. One can only admire the enthusiasm of the RAF pilots to save their aircraft but not the command decision to risk so many lives and valuable ships by allowing them to do so.
4 Geoffrey Till, *Air Power and the Royal Navy, 1914–1945: A Historical Survey* (London, Macdonald and Jane's Publishing, 1979), p. 25.
5 Board of Inquiry Report by the Commander-in-Chief Rosyth dated 3 July 1940, p. 5. A copy is in the author's archive.
6 Ibid., p. 25.
7 Note by Commander E G le Guyt RN dated 15 May 1968 and contained in ADM 199/478 at the National Archives, Kew.
8 Till, *Air Power and the Royal Navy*, p. 26.
9 ADM 199/480, Operational Reports, in the National Archives, Kew.
10 Admiralty, *Naval Staff History: The Development of British Naval Aviation, 1919–1945. Volume I* (London, Admiralty, 1954), p. 107.
11 Captain L A Harris RM had commanded 803 NAS temporarily after Bill Lucy's death until 23 May 1940 when Lieutenant Commander J Casson RN was appointed

in command. After he was taken prisoner on 13 June 1940 Lieutenant J M Bruen RN was appointed in command and the squadron's leadership achieved some stability.

12 Author's interview with Petty Officer R S Rolfe in 1998. He also believed that since both he and his pilot were petty officers, living in the same mess on board, they had a better rapport than many of the officer pilot/rating TAG crews and often discussed what they would do in certain situations.
13 A copy of which is in the author's archive.
14 A.C.0565 dated 18 June 1940, a copy of which is in the author's archive.
15 A copy of which is in the author's archive.
16 Another Skua pilot who achieved flag rank after the war, eventually leaving the service as Vice Admiral Sir Donald Gibson KCB DSC.
17 Unfortunately I have been unable to locate copies of these.
18 1118/K.F.1350 dated 27 June 1940, a copy of which is in the author's archive.
19 Taken from the Fleet Air Arm Roll of Honour prepared by Captain F Milner RN and Captain R F Shercliff RN in association with the Fleet Air Arm Museum, a copy of which is in the author's archive.
20 Vice Admiral Sir Donald Gibson, *Haul Taut and Belay* (Tunbridge Wells, Spellmount, 1992), p. 48 et seq.
21 Different reports and accounts give different distances from landfall on Froya Island to Trondheim. The distance between the North Sea side of Froya and the centre of Trondheim is 55nm.
22 Major R T Partridge, *Operation Skua* (Yeovilton, Fleet Air Arm Museum, 1983), p. 97 et seq.
23 An English expression for wild alarm.
24 He has no known grave but the sea and is commemorated on the Fleet Air Arm Memorial at Lee-on-Solent, Bay 1 Panel 2.
25 Slang term for the type of life jacket worn by British aircrew at this period.

Chapter 18: Retrospection

1 The first Rolls-Royce engine to be named after a river.
2 Interestingly the Barracuda was replaced in RN squadrons by USN-supplied Avengers twice. Lend/Lease Avengers replaced Barracudas in a number of squadrons in 1943 and Mutual Defence Aid Programme Avengers replaced the remaining Barracudas in 1953.

Bibliography

Primary Sources

Admiralty, *Naval Staff History: The Development of British Naval Aviation, 1919–1945. Volume I* (London, Admiralty, 1954).
Admiralty, *Naval Staff History: The Development of British Naval Aviation, 1919–1945. Volume II* (London, Admiralty, 1956).
Air Historical Branch, file ID.2/100 at Bentley Priory.
Relevant sections of the Home Fleet War Diaries held by the Naval Historical Branch, when it was situated in Empress State Building, London, copies of which are in the Author's archive.
Relevant Reports of Proceeding and individual combat reports held in the archive of the Naval Historical Branch (Empress State Building and New Scotland Yard) and the MOD archive when it was situated at Hayes.
Supplement to the London Gazette dated 28 May 1946, *Operations in Central Norway, 1940* (London, His Majesty's Stationery Office, 1946).
The National Archives

Published Secondary Sources

Abbott, Patrick, *The British Airship at War, 1914–1918* (Lavenham, Terence Dalton, 1989).
Abbott, Patrick and Walmsley, Nick, *British Airships in Pictures* (Isle of Colonsay, House of Lochar, 1998).
Admiralty, *Fleet Air Arm: The Admiralty Account of Naval Air Operations* (London, His Majesty's Stationery Office, 1943).
Allen, Wing Commander H R, *The Legacy of Lord Trenchard* (London, Cassell, 1972).
Andrews, C F and Morgan, E B, *Supermarine Aircraft since 1914* (London, Putnam, 1981).
Andrews Jr, Adolphus, 'Admiral with Wings: The Career of Joseph M Reeves', BA Thesis, Princeton University, 1943.
Apps, Lieutenant Commander Michael, RN, *The Four Ark Royals* (London, William Kimber, 1976).
Ballance, Theo, Howard, Lee and Sturtivant, Ray, *The Squadrons of the Fleet Air Arm* (Stapleford, Air Britain Publishing, 2016).
Bell Davies, Vice Admiral Sir Richard, VC CB DSO AFC, *Sailor in the Air: The Memoirs of the World's First Carrier Pilot* (Barnsley, Seaforth Publishing, 2008).
Bowyer, Chaz, *Eugene Esmonde VC DSO* (London, William Kimber, 1983).
Boyle, Andrew, *Trenchard: Man of Vision* (London, Collins, 1962).
Brown, D K, *Nelson to Vanguard: Warship Design and Development 1923–1945* (London, Chatham Publishing, 2000).

Brown, Captain Eric, CBE DSC AFC RN, *Wings of the Navy* (London, Macdonald & Jane's, 1980).

Brown, Captain Eric, CBE DSC AFC RN, *Wings of the Luftwaffe* (Manchester, Crecy Publications, 2010).

Brown, J David, *Supermarine Walrus I and Seagull V Variants*, Profile 224 (Windsor, Profile Publications, 1971).

Brown, J David, *Carrier Fighters* (London, Macdonald and Jane's Publishing, 1975).

Brown, J David, *Warship Losses of World War Two* (London, Arms and Armour Press, 1990).

Brown, J David, *Carrier Operations in World War II* (Barnsley, Seaforth Publishing, 2009).

Burt, R A, *British Battleships of World War One* (new revised edition) (Barnsley, Seaforth Publishing, 2012).

Chatfield, Admiral of the Fleet Lord, PC GCB OM etc, *The Navy and Defence* (London, William Heinemann, 1942).

Chatfield, Admiral of the Fleet Lord, PC GCB, OM etc, *It Might Happen Again* (London, William Heinemann, 1947).

Chatterton, E Keble, *English Seamen and the Colonization of America* (London, Arrowsmith, 1930).

Churchill, W S, *The Second World War. Volume I: The Gathering Storm* (London, Penguin Books, 2005).

Churchill, W S, *The Second World War. Volume II: Their Finest Hour* (London, Cassell, 1950).

Cumming, Anthony J, *The Royal Navy and the Battle of Britain* (Annapolis, Naval institute Press, 2010).

Cumming, Anthony J, *The Battle for Britain: Interservice Rivalry between the Royal Air Force and Royal Navy, 1909–40* (Annapolis, Naval Institute Press, 2015).

Dickens, Captain Peter, DSO MBE DSC RN, *Narvik: Battles in the Fjords* (Shepperton, Ian Allen, 1974).

Ellis, Paul, *Aircraft of the Royal Navy* (London, Jane's Publishing, 1982).

Friedman, Norman, *US Aircraft Carriers: An Illustrated Design History* (Annapolis, United States Naval Institute, 1983).

Friedman, Norman, *British Carrier Aviation* (London, Conway Maritime Press, 1988).

Friedman, Norman, *British Cruisers: Two World Wars and After* (Barnsley, Seaforth Publishing, 2010).

Green, William, *Famous Bombers of the Second World War* (London, Macdonald, 1959).

Green, William, *Warplanes of the Second World War: Fighters. Volume 1* (London, Macdonald, 1960).

Green, William, *Warplanes of the Second World War: Fighters. Volume 2* (London, Macdonald, 1961).

Green, William, *Famous Fighters of the Second World War, Second Series* (London, Macdonald, 1962).

Green, William, *Warplanes of the Second World War: Flying Boats. Volume 5* (London, Macdonald, 1962).

Green, William, *Warplanes of the Second World War: Floatplanes. Volume 6* (London, Macdonald, 1962).

Haarr, Geirr H, *The German Invasion of Norway* (Barnsley, Seaforth Publishing, 2009).

Haarr, Geirr H, *The Battle for Norway April–June* 1940 (Barnsley, Seaforth Publishing, 2010).

Harrison, W A, *Fairey Swordfish and Albacore* (Marlborough, Crowood Press, 2002).

Hobbs, David, *A Century of Carrier Aviation: The Evolution of Ships and Shipborne Aircraft* (Barnsley, Seaforth Publishing, 2009).

Hobbs, Commander David, MBE, *British Aircraft Carriers: Design, Development and Service Histories* (Barnsley, Seaforth Publishing, 2013).

Hobbs, Commander David, MBE, *The Royal Navy's Air Service in the Great War* (Barnsley, Seaforth Publishing, 2017).

Hone, Thomas C, Friedman, Norman, and Mandeles, Mark D., *American and British Aircraft Carrier Development, 1919–1941* (Annapolis, Naval Institute Press, 1999).

Horsley, Lieutenant Commander Terence, RNVR, *Find, Fix and Strike* (London, Eyre and Spottiswoode, 1943).

Howse, Derek, *Radar at Sea* (Basingstoke, Macmillan, 1993).

Jackson, A J, *Blackburn Aircraft since 1909* (London, Putnam, 1968).

Jarrett, Philip, *Fairey IIIF: Interwar Military Workhorse* (Ringshall, Ad Hoc Publications, 2009).

Jenkins, Commander C A , OBE RN, *HMS Furious. Part II: 1925–1948*, Warship Profile 24 (Windsor, Profile Publications, 1972).

Jones, Ben, *The Fleet Air Arm in the Second World War* (Farnham, Ashgate Publishing, 2012).

Jordan, John and Dent, Stephen (eds), *Warship* (Oxford, Osprey Publishing, 2018).

King, H F, *Armament of British Aircraft, 1909–1939* (London, Putnam, 1971).

Lamb, Gregor, *Sky Over Scapa, 1939–1945* (Orkney, Byrgisey, 1991).

Lavery, Brian, *Hostilities Only: Training the Wartime Navy* (Greenwich: National Maritime Museum, 2004).

Le Masson, Henri, *The French Navy. Volume 1: Navies of the Second World War* (London, Macdonald, 1969).

Lenton, H T, *German Surface Vessels. Volume 1L Navies of the Second World War* (London, Macdonald, 1966).

Lenton, H T, *British Battleships and Aircraft Carriers, Navies of the Second World War* (London, Macdonald, 1972).

Lenton, H T, *British Cruisers, Navies of the Second World War* (London, Macdonald, 1973).

Lloyd, Stuart, *Fleet Air Arm Camouflage and Markings: Atlantic and Mediterranean Theatres, 1937–1941* (Stamford, Dalrymple & Verdun Publishing, 2008).

Macintyre, Captain Donald, DSO** DSC RN, *Wings of Neptune - The Story of Naval Aviation* (London, Peter Davies, 1963).

Macintyre, Captain Donald, DSO** DSC RN, *Narvik* (London, Pan Books, 1971).

Mason, Francis K, *The Hawker Hurricane* (London, Macdonald, 1962).

Mason, Francis K, *Hawker Aircraft since 1920* (London, Putnam, 1991).

McCart, Neil, *HMS Hermes, 1923 and 1959* (Cheltenham, Fan Publications, 2001).

McCart, Neil, *Three Ark Royals, 1938–1999* (Cheltenham, Fan Publications, 1999).
McMurtrie, Francis E, AINA, *British, French and German Warships at a Glance* (London, Sampson Low, Marston, 1940).
Morris, Douglas, *Cruisers of the Royal and Commonwealth Navies* (Liskeard, Maritime Books, 1987).
Mowthorpe, Ces, *Battlebags: British Airships of the First World War* (Stroud, Alan Sutton Publishing, 1995).
Partridge, Major R T, DSO RM, *Operation Skua* (Yeovilton, Fleet Air Arm Museum, 1983).
Perkins, Richard, *British Warship Recognition. Volume III: Cruisers, 1865–1939, Part 1* (Barnsley, Seaforth Publishing, 2017).
Poolman, Kenneth, *Ark Royal* (London, William Kimber, 1956).
Popham, Hugh, *Into Wind: A History of British Naval Flying* (London, Hamish Hamilton, 1969).
Reece, Colonel Michael, OBE, *Flying Royal Marines* (Eastney, Royal Marines Historical Society, 2012).
Reeve, John and Stevens, David (eds), *The Face of Naval Battle* (Crows Nest, New South Wales, Allen & Unwin, 2003).
Reynolds, Clark G, *The Fast Carriers: The Forging of an Air Navy* (Annapolis, Naval Institute Press, 1992).
Roskill, Captain Stephen W, DSC RN, *The War at Sea, 1939–1945. Volume 1: The Defensive* (London, Her Majesty's Stationery Office, 1954).
Roskill, Captain Stephen W, DSC RN, *Naval Policy between the Wars. 1: The Period of Anglo-American Antagonism, 1919–1929* (Barnsley, Seaforth Publishing, 2016).
Roskill, Captain Stephen W, DSC RN, *Naval Policy between the Wars. 2: The Period of Reluctant Rearmament, 1930–1939* (Barnsley, Seaforth Publishing, 2016).
Rotherham, Captain G A (Hank), DSO OBE CM RN/RCN, *It's Really Quite Safe* (Belleville, Ontario, Hangar Books, undated).
Seedie, *Seedie's List of Fleet Air Arm Awards, 1939–1969* (Tisbury, Ripley Registers, 1990).
Smith, Peter C, *Skua: The Royal Navy's Dive-Bomber* (Barnsley, Pen & Sword Aviation, 2006).
Sturtivant, Ray, *British Naval Aviation: The Fleet Air Arm, 1917–1990* (London, Arms & Armour Press, 1990).
Sturtivant, Ray, with Burrow, Mick, *Fleet Air Arm Aircraft, 1939 to 1945* (Tunbridge Wells, Air Britain (Historians), 1995).
Sturtivant, Ray, with Cronin, Dick, *Fleet Air Arm Aircraft, Units and Ships, 1920 to 1939* (Tunbridge Wells, Air Britain (Historians), 1998).
Swanborough, Gordon and Bowers, Peter M, *United States Navy Aircraft* (London, Putnam, 1990).
Taylor, H A, *Fairey Aircraft since 1915* (London, Putnam, 1974).
Thetford, Owen, *British Naval Aircraft since 1912* (London: Putnam, 1962).
Thomas, Andrew, *Royal Navy Aces of World War 2* (Oxford, Osprey Publishing, 2007).
Till, Geoffrey, *Air Power and the Royal Navy, 1914–1945: A Historical Survey* (London, Macdonald and Jane's Publishing, 1979).
Vian, Sir Philip, *Action This Day* (London, Frederick Muller, 1960).

Warlow, Lieutenant Commander B, RN, *Shore Establishments of the Royal Navy* (Liskeard, Maritime Books, 2000).
Wellham, Lieutenant Commander J W G, DSC RN, *With Naval Wings* (Staplehurst, Spellmount, 1995).
Wildenberg, Thomas, *Destined for Glory* (Annapolis, Naval Institute Press, 1998).
Wildenberg, Thomas, *Billy Mitchell's War with the Navy: The Interwar Rivalry Over Air Power* (Annapolis, Naval Institute press, 2013).

Index